# STRANGERS ON THE WESTERN FRONT

# STRANGERS ON THE WESTERN FRONT

## Chinese Workers in the Great War

*Xu Guoqi*

*Harvard University Press*

*Cambridge, Massachusetts*

*London, England*

*2011*

*Library of Congress Cataloging-in-Publication Data*

Xu, Guoqi.
Strangers on the Western Front : Chinese workers in the Great War / Xu Guoqi.
p. cm.
Includes bibliographical references and index.
ISBN 978-0-674-04999-4 (alk. paper)
1. World War, 1914–1918—Conscript labor—Europe.    2. World War,
1914–1918—Participation, Chinese.    3. World War, 1914–1918—Great Britain.
4. World War, 1914–1918—France.    5. Foreign workers, Chinese—Europe—History—
20th century.    6. Working class—China—History—20th century.    7. China—Relations—
Great Britain.    8. China—Relations—France.    9. Great Britain—Relations—China.
10. France—Relations—China.    I. Title.
D639.L2X8    2011
940.3089'951044—dc22        2010019900

*To Ann*

*Whose love and sacrifice made this book possible*

# CONTENTS

# NOTE ON ROMANIZATION

This book employs the *pinyin* system for the transliteration of Chinese names, with the exception of names such as Confucius and Mencius, whose established spellings are familiar in the West. In citing Western-language sources that use older or different spelling systems, however, references to persons and places have been left unchanged.

# Strangers on the Western Front

# INTRODUCTION

*Strangers on the Western Front* is about the journey of 140,000 Chinese, most of them illiterate peasants, to Europe during World War I. These laborers were recruited by the governments of France and Britain to help both countries in their Great War against the Germans; later, when the United States joined the war, the Americans took advantage of their labor as well. South Africans, Indians, Vietnamese, and many other laborers went to France during the war to support the British and French. Many went because they came from colonial countries and had to answer the call from their imperial masters. But China, no country's colony, sent by far the largest number of men, and its laborers worked in Europe the longest.[1] The Chinese came voluntarily and their contributions were the most significant.

This book is the story of these laborers' personal experiences of the war, of Europe, of working, and of Western people. I also describe how race and class affected their treatment not just by various Westerners, but also by their own country and its elites. More importantly, I highlight the laborers' unrecognized contributions to the war and also to China's historic search for a new national identity, and their place in the first large-scale encounter of Eastern and Western civilizations in the early twentieth century.

By focusing on this rarely studied group of Chinese who became directly involved with the Great War, I address questions such as why China wanted to send laborers, what happened to them when they arrived in Europe, and (most importantly) what role they played in China's struggles to gain a fair foothold in the emerging international order. Rudyard Kipling's famous lines "East is East, and West is West, and never the twain shall meet, till Earth and Sky stand presently at God's great Judgment seat" might sound imperialistic, but most people miss his next telling lines:

1

But there is neither East nor West, Border, nor Breed, nor Birth,
When two strong men stand face to face, tho' they come from the ends of
the earth!

Here even the imperialist poet realized that the borders between East and West were perhaps not so clear-cut. For the Chinese laborers who journeyed to Europe, East and West did meet, and on a large scale. Most interestingly, this meeting occurred through largely illiterate men who had little understanding of international relations when they were chosen to make the trip. They were in some senses like pieces of blank paper. Even though they were frequently derided by Westerners as coolies, Chinks, or Chinamen, I will argue that these Chinese not only made a crucial contribution to the Allied war effort but also figured importantly as messengers between the Chinese and Western civilizations.

After all, the Great War was allegedly about civilizations. Inter-Allied victory medals were awarded to everyone who served in the fighting or worked as civilians contracted to the armed services in every allied country, apart from China and Montenegro.[2] The medal was inscribed on the back with the words "The Great War for Civilization, 1914–1919" and on the front with the names of allied or associated nations and their respective designs. As one scholar eloquently argued, the Great War was not only about loss or gain of military or economic powers: "For the British, this was a war to preserve the system of British order," which seemed under attack "by everything that Germany represented." Like Britain, the Germans considered the war "a spiritual conflict." This same author concluded, "For the Germans this was a war to change the world; for the British this was a war to preserve a world. The Germans were propelled by a vision, the British by a legacy."[3] Thus the "Guns of August" were really fighting for the "Ideas of August." Henry James, the influential American author, brooded on August 5, 1914, that the outbreak of the Great War might plunge "civilization into this abyss of blood and darkness" and "give away the whole long age during which we have supposed the world to be, with whatever abatement, gradually bettering."[4] An American officer wrote shortly after the conflict ended, "When the real story of the Great War is written and some dispassionate appraisal is made of the causes of victory, it will be found that the laurel of civilization's triumph will rest with no single nation."[5] Clearly, these discussions of clashes of civilizations lay within the boundaries of the West. By examining the work and experience of the Chinese laborers, we may gain a new perspective on the differences between Eastern and Western civilizations, and their fusions and new understandings about the war and subsequent developments in China and the rest of the world.

To a great extent, then, this book reconsiders the Great War via a group of marginalized and largely forgotten participants: the Chinese laborers. Did they understand the war? Did the military authorities of Great Britain, France, and the United States, or the Chinese government, provide them with any information about the war and its significance? What were their memories of the war and of their experiences in the West? For many years most scholarship on the Great War has been focused on questions of blame—which country bears most responsibility for starting the war and which must bear the blame for the collapse of the postwar world order that triggered World War II. This book, despite its criticism of the treatment of the laborers and racism against the Chinese, actually focuses on long overdue and delayed credit and recognition. It will consider just how the laborers contributed to the Allied victory and how they triggered new ways of thinking about China and the world among Chinese elites.

A key theme in modern Chinese history is China's search for a new national identity and its place in the world community. Few realize the important role the laborers played in that project. This book demonstrates that although most of the Chinese laborers were illiterate farmers with no clear ideas about China or the world when they were selected to go to Europe, they had a part in developing that new national identity and would play an important role in China's internationalization. As a result of their personal experiences in Europe and daily work with Americans, British, French, and fellow laborers from other countries, the Chinese developed a unique perception of China as a nation and as a member of the family of nations. Through their work with the Chinese laborers in Europe as YMCA secretaries or educators, future Chinese leaders—Yan Yangchu (James Yen), Jiang Tingfu, Lin Yutang, Cai Yuanpei, and Wang Jingwei, among many others—became convinced that China could one day emerge as a powerful nation. This book examines how the experience of working with the laborers gave the Chinese elites a new appreciation of the Chinese working class as well as new ideas about fixing China's problems. Their perceptions of China's future changed dramatically. This book further explores what the laborers learned from their personal experiences and from their interactions with YMCA secretaries and other Chinese elites. Besides offering an analysis of the laborers' physical journey—an interesting topic in itself—this book will chart China's journey to becoming a key player in a new international political system.

The Chinese government and social elites were deeply involved in the laborers' story. From the beginning, Chinese elites, whether government officials, independent thinkers, or educators, considered the idea of sending laborers to Europe from a broad perspective. First, the laborers were crucial and coherent parts of the grand plan to have China join the community of nations as an equal member. The thinking went that having Chinese laborers work side by side with Westerners in France would forge a crucial link between China and the West, and would be a daily reminder to the world of the strategic relevance of China's "laborers as soldiers" program. The key to understanding the intensity of Chinese interest in the European war is that it was seen as an effective vehicle by which the Chinese could push for internationalization at home and establish their nation anew abroad.

Besides China, many other countries played a part in the laborers' journey. Britain, France, Canada, and the United States were key. This book will examine their collective involvement and shared memories or forgetfulness of that involvement. I address many questions that have never been seriously raised: Why did the French and British governments turn to China for help in the first place? How did the Chinese seize on this opportunity and come out with a plan that effectively worked around repeated blockage to China's participation in the war effort—a key element in its drive for international acceptance and the recovery of territory unjustly lost to Japan and other countries? Who were the key players on the recruitment issue in Europe and China? How were the laborers recruited? Who were these laborers? How were they selected? What happened to them before and after they were chosen to go to Europe? And how many actually managed to go?

If historians know little about the interactions between the governments of China, Britain, and France regarding the laborers' journey, even fewer know of the American and Canadian connections. After the United States joined the war in 1917, the American Expeditionary Forces (AEF) contracted with the French government for about 10,000 of the French-recruited Chinese to aid in the American war effort. The story of how Americans and Chinese interacted in a foreign land and risked their lives together is a unique chapter in Sino-American relations. How did the Americans treat the Chinese helping them in Europe given the legal discrimination Chinese suffered in the United States? What did Chinese laborers think of the Americans? How did the Chinese laborers fit into President Woodrow Wilson's idealist new world order, and how did the Chinese respond to Wilsonianism?

Even today the Canadian story remains practically unknown. Between 1917 and 1920 most Chinese laborers went to France and returned to China from Europe through Canada. The Canadian government, at the request of the British authorities, managed the passage and provided all necessary arrangements for the Chinese between Vancouver and Halifax. The reason for our collective ignorance of the Chinese Canada passage is largely because the Canadian government succeeded so well in blacking out the news. Canadians were not alone in the cover-up. Few people in the world have ever known or fully understood the Canadian involvement. Drawing on materials from Canadian archives and private collections, I analyze what happened to the laborers in Canada, how they traveled from the Canadian West to the east coast, why the Canadian government allowed them no freedom en route, and the kind of life they led as they waited—often for several weeks—for passage to Europe.

Details of the Chinese experience in Europe allow interesting glimpses into the play of race, gender, and class in the early twentieth century. They suggest how national conceptions of race shaped the quite different treatment the Chinese received from the French, British, Canadians, and Americans—who were fighting for the same cause, after all. Cross-racial relations between Chinese men and French women during and especially after the war were both common and a cause for worry in French officialdom and society.

Interactions between the Chinese laborers and young Chinese elites had an immense impact on their self-perceptions and views of each other. Little has been related about how an internationally prominent mass education movement was influenced and later transformed by Yan Yangchu's work with his countrymen in France. It is well known that future communist leaders such as Deng Xiaoping and Zhou Enlai went to Europe after the war to see the center of the Western civilization. Following in the footsteps of the laborers also surely framed the development of their thinking and political commitment. To a great extent, the laborers played a crucial role in shaping or reshaping Chinese elites' perception of China and accordingly changed the course of Chinese history. This book examines the interactions between the laborers and the elites and what they learned from each other.

Shandong Province, the birthplace of Confucius and Mencius, plays its own role in this story. In the early 1920s Shandong had a population of 30 million,[6] almost twice that of France. Most of the laborers who went to Europe came from Shandong. The major motivation behind China joining the war was the hope of recovering Shandong Province, a crucial part of which had become a German concession since 1898. Japan, which declared war on Germany in the summer of 1914 and did all its actual fighting in the Great War on Shandong soil, unfortunately soon took over the province. Recovering Shandong and preventing further Japanese incursions were only the most pressing reasons for China's plan to send laborers to France. When the great powers decided at the postwar peace conference to allow Japan to keep Shandong, this triggered the May Fourth Movement, whose influence in Chinese history remains relevant even today. This "Shandong betrayal" provided a handy weapon by which the U.S. Congress was able to block U.S. participation in the League of Nations even though its designer, President Woodrow Wilson, was a key figure in the postwar world order. And because of the Shandong clauses, China fatefully refused to be a party to the peace treaty. How the Shandong issue influenced the laborers' mind-set and how these laborers contributed to the efforts to recover their native province is a fascinating story.

During the Great War Chinese laborers not only witnessed a civilizational battle, they took active part in it. Despite its importance, this story is all but unknown.[7] "The part played by the Chinese coolie in winning the war for civilization has never been properly appreciated by the world at large," declared one YMCA official in France.[8] To date, no book exists in any language that deals with this topic despite its critical significance.[9] The most recent book on the subject for both students and researchers, titled *Researching World War I* (2003), alludes only once to "Chinese labor" in an otherwise detailed work of almost 500 pages.[10] To be sure, writing such a book has been extremely challenging because of the elusiveness of the widely scattered evidence and long-standing neglect.

Given the challenges of making a thorough examination of the story of Chinese laborers in the Great War, our collective amnesia and ignorance are perhaps unavoidable. As one British newspaper noted in 1972, the story of the Chinese in Europe "is all but forgotten."[11] This lack of public information occurred because many of the nations involved tried to keep it secret from the very beginning. The British War Office had no wish to publicize the fact that it intended to seek Chinese help. As one scholar has pointed out, public references to the use of Chinese labor in France by Britain "were few, often quite inaccurate, and occasionally deliberately biased for the purposes of Allied propaganda. The War Office wittingly discouraged contemporary comment for fear that organized labor in Great Britain itself would raise its voice in protest." The fear was that the Chinese would later be brought to work in the UK itself. The British Foreign Office shared the War Office's concern and worried about embarrassing parallels some would draw with the inhumane treatment of Chinese laborers in South Africa in 1903 and 1904 by the government of J. Arthur Balfour.[12] Even the Chinese government played a part in the cover-up. China, a neutral nation until 1917, did not want Germany to know that it had cooperated in the "laborers as soldiers" strategy, and its officials always tried to downplay the importance of the laborers' recruitment. Moreover, because most of the men were illiterate, they were unable to leave detailed accounts of their experiences. Few war diaries or personal reflections written by or about the Chinese laborers have survived. The warring countries' strict censorship policies have also certainly contributed to our collective ignorance.

To make the situation worse, a constructed memory that developed especially after the war took hold and has continued to shape European attitudes toward the Chinese. As Belgian archivist and scholar Dominiek Dendooven has observed, "Of all coloured recruits, the Chinese loom largest of all in the collective memory of the Flanders Westhoek."[13] Dendooven correctly points out that few of the "many tens of stories" of armed raids, murders, and rapes by Chinese laborers that were (and still are) told by the Belgians were based on fact. In the nearly lawless situation of the former front right after the war, where the nearest police station was to be found tens of kilometers away and where the few already returned inhabitants lived in pillboxes or hastily built wooden huts, "the Chinese were ideal scapegoats to blame for unsolved crimes." In the absence of proper study, it is little wonder that the "stories about these supposed brutal armed raids, rapes etc. still live on in the region's collective memory today."[14]

The Belgian case is not unique. The general perception of the Chinese in Britain was negative as well. With first-person accounts, one book suggests that a group of British girls in France was "generally rather scared" of the Chinese laborers. According to these girls, "on the whole" the Chinese "were lazy and useless," and they added that a murder almost took place when a girl paid one Chinese worker more than another for a decorated bullet case. Another girl had the same memory: "I remembered one said he would knife me because I had ordered an engraved shell case from him, and he had spoiled it by making it black and I refused to have it. One was always hearing tales of them being found murdered." Although the Chinese may have committed serious crimes in France (just like American and British soldiers), they were not monsters, notwithstanding these perceptions. These negative perceptions likely arose through misunderstandings or miscommunication, which were plentiful throughout the war. The Chinese laborers in France were hardly "marauding." As English writer Kate Summerscale pointed out, "They had gained a reputation for great stoicism and industry. If the English women found them ugly and horrifying, it may be because they served as symbols, or repositories, of an ugly and horrifying war."[15]

In his book *Pantheon de la Guerre: Reconfiguring a Panorama of the Great War,* the historian Mark Levitch tells the fascinating story of "The Pantheon"—a cyclorama about 402 feet in circumference and 45 feet high, whose total area would nearly have covered an American football field. The work was constructed on government-allotted land in Paris and was celebrated as a grand monument to the war. Two French academic artists, Pierre Carrier-Belleuse and Auguste-François Gorguet, assisted by twenty other established French artists, worked on "The Pantheon" after the war started in 1914, and the completed structure was inaugurated in Paris just before the Armistice. It included about 5,000 full-sized portraits of wartime figures from France and its allies to convey the official propaganda line that so many nations had sided with France against the German barbarians. It was also meant to represent the Great War and artists' contributions to the war effort. Although a private undertaking, it received official support from the French government and military authorities. It was opened with great fanfare by French president Raymond Poincaré on October 19, 1918. In its earliest version the design included Chinese laborers, but after the United States entered the war, the artists realized that they needed space for the Americans and decided to paint over the Chinese to make room for the American section.[16] Thus, even in this commemorative work, the record of the Chinese laborers was erased; as Levitch correctly points out, "The Pantheon" is a particularly poignant instance of how the war "has been remembered—and forgotten."[17]

Of the Americans who died in the "war to end all the wars," General John J. Pershing said, "Time will not dim the glory of their deeds."[18] But in the Chinese laborers' case, time has consigned their story nearly to oblivion. It is time to restore the memory of these laborers and situate it in its rightful place in both Chinese and world history. It was only in the 1980s and 1990s that the French government erected a bronze plaque on the wall of a Paris railway station and installed a monument in a small park near Chinatown to commemorate Chinese contributions to winning the war. The monument has an inscription in Chinese and French that says, "In memory of Chinese workers and fighters who died for France in the Great War." Although both signs are tiny and symbolic, and are the only public reminders of the 140,000 Chinese who labored in France during the Great War, it is a positive beginning.

The Chinese government and general public have been both ignorant and indifferent to the laborers and their journey. Until recently these men had been all but forgotten by their own motherland.[19] The time has arrived for a book that shows a thorough international history of their experience. I am hoping this book will serve as a meeting ground between Western and Chinese history and will generate international dialogue about our shared history and civilizations. Drawing on personal letters, diaries, YMCA reports, and official documents from China, Canada, Britain, France, the United States, and elsewhere, this book tries to remedy lapses and provide a model for tackling similar historical problems. It will hopefully prompt other reconsiderations of "big history" by paying attention to little-noted linkages such as those provided by the Chinese laborers in the Great War. Of course, one book cannot adequately deal with all the issues in detail, but it can serve as a foundation from which future scholars can pursue the topic. As the prominent World War I historian Jay Winter argues, historical memory is a process.[20] I am hoping this book will initiate the process of remembering these Chinese laborers with respect. The following pages are their story, told for the first time from the perspective of international history.[21]

# 1

---

## GREAT WAR AND GREAT CRISIS

---

### *China, Britain, France, and the*
### *"Laborers as Soldiers" Strategy*

The "Guns of August" in 1914 declared that the existing world order was collapsing. Germany, the "rising power," had challenged the status quo by forcing major powers one by one into a confrontation. Great Britain and France got into the fight immediately, and by spring 1915 both countries realized that they were facing deadly challenges. Not only was their political power at stake; their fundamental value systems and even their very existence were in danger as well.

### China's Crisis

The Great War coincided with a period of tremendous changes in China, including the collapse of the Confucian civilization and lack of a strong central government. How did the changing or challenged civilizations in China and the West affect each other during this period of transformation and in the long run? While the major European powers had been preparing for a final showdown since the late nineteenth century, the traditional identity of the Chinese state had disintegrated after the Japanese victory in the Sino-Japanese War of 1894–1895. Between 1895 and 1919, the Chinese people suffered political chaos, economic weakness, and social misery, but this was also a period of excitement, hope, high expectations, optimism, and new dreams. The time period can be compared with the Warring States era in ancient Chinese history, in which different political and philosophical ideas flourished in a period of political decentralization or the revolutionary period in Europe described in Charles Dickens's famous novel, *A Tale of Two Cities:* "It was the best of times, it was the worst of times, it was the age of wisdom, it was the age of foolishness."[1]

In 1912 China became a republic. Freshly sprouted newspapers, magazines, publishing houses, and modern education found the Great War in Europe both fodder and impetus for new ideologies and new concepts of history. New political ideologies (nationalism rather than Confucianism; nation-state instead of culturalism), the return to China of Western-trained students, the activism of a new bourgeois class (rather than the old gentry and traditional mandarins), the emergence of a public sphere and modern print media, and, above all, the changing international system all pushed China toward painful but unavoidable self-renewal. For the first time, broad-based public opinion and its social and intellectual resources played a crucial role in shaping China's political, cultural, and social directions. Now Chinese of a wide social and geographical range became immersed in international affairs, and demanded and even initiated a new diplomacy aimed at renewing the state and preparing its entry onto the world stage as an equal member.[2] Chinese elites of all persuasions agreed that China must change or die.

As the international community moved toward the brink of World War I, China was in the throes of a great transformation that was closely linked to the dangerous situation the country faced after its defeat by the Japanese in 1895. Although China had suffered one defeat after another at Western hands since the Opium War in the 1840s, only the Sino-Japanese War of 1894–1895 really compelled the Chinese to think seriously about their destiny and the value of their civilization. More importantly, it caused them to question their traditional identity. This new realism marked a profound, even revolutionary change in Chinese attitudes toward world affairs at the turn of the twentieth century. Chinese elites, no matter what their attitudes toward Chinese tradition and civilization were, agreed that if China was to survive, it had to change.

The Chinese sense of frustration, humiliation, and impotence in the face of Western incursions and a Westernized Japan provided powerful motivations. Chinese political and intellectual culture from 1895 to 1914 was shaped by a dual process: intensive internalization and internationalization. Internalization, which was preparatory to internationalization, refers to the process and conditions whereby China renewed itself and prepared for internationalization. Internationalization is the process by which China adopted and modified external impulses and made them its own, including embracing and adapting Western education, selecting and transforming political theories, debating and choosing from among competing foreign political models, and developing new techniques and institutions to promote the interests of the new Chinese nation in the world arena. Internationalization, then, bridged China's domestic reforms and agendas and its foreign policy. Internationalization and internalization would eventually turn China upside down and transform it in unprecedented ways, in both its internal politics and foreign relations. Internationalization meant that China actively engaged in and was engaged by the international system, ideas, forces, and trends; it was a process that compelled China to associate with the international system. Internationalization was driven by shifts in the flow of social, intellectual, economic, ideological, and cultural resources between China and the wider world, as well as by new Chinese interest in foreign affairs and China's position in the world. Internationalization took two forms: a process of passive or perhaps emulative responses; and an active, creative, and progressive one. The passive or emulative internationalization responded to intensified foreign invasion and encroachment on Chinese territory; it also included strong foreign influence in Chinese port cities, the Chinese economy, finance, markets, and overall development. Progressive internationalization involved actions initiated by the Chinese; it included embracing Western education, political theories, and foreign political models, as well as actively promoting Chinese interests in the world arena.[3]

Reflecting on their country's status in the world after its defeat in the Sino-Japanese War, many Chinese elites began to seriously doubt the value of their traditional culture, history, language, and especially the attitudes and policies toward the outside world. The Chinese of this period largely lost the sense of sameness and historical continuity with pre-1895 China. This sense of lost identity is key to understanding the country after 1895, and especially its foreign relations. All politically conscious Chinese connected China's weakness and political chaos to the international system, providing the strongest motivation to enter and alter it. World War I became the first major global event to engage the imagination of Chinese social and political elites, among whom it generated great fascination and excitement.

Changes in Chinese worldviews and the destabilizing forces loosed by the war set the stage for China to play a role in world affairs, even if the war seemed to have no immediate impact on the country. Profound changes occurred in China between 1895 and 1914: The "new public" adopted nationalism and a new mentality toward world affairs.[4] The new Chinese approach, internationalism, was strongly undergirded by and predicated on a strong nationalism that actually transcended the usually polarized boundary between nationalism and internationalism. Furthermore, China's quest for a new national identity was promoted in this period by a curious mixture of political nationalism, cultural anti-traditionalism, and a strong desire for active engagement in world affairs. Although this combination necessarily riddled China's foreign policy with contradictions and ambiguities, it nonetheless set the stage for China's engagement with the new world order during World War I.

China's motivations to enter the war were clearly based in the sense of global and national *weiji* (crisis). As Europe's "generation of 1914" (too young, too innocent, and perhaps too utopian to suspect the bloody rites of passage that awaited them) went gladly to war in August 1914, the new generation in China experienced a sense of *weiji* at the challenge of dealing with new developments in the international system.[5] China recognized the dangers of becoming involved in the war involuntarily because the major belligerents all controlled spheres of interest in Chinese territory. Moreover, with the collapse of the old international system, China could easily be bullied by Japan. To discourage the war from spreading to China, the Chinese government on August 6 declared its neutrality. Regardless of Chinese intentions, German-controlled territory in Shandong Province would become a fighting ground.

Despite the dangers, some Chinese elites argued that the European war presented compelling opportunities. War could change the international system and allow China to join the community of nations. China might even inject its own ideas into shaping the new world order. Certain influential circles even suggested that China should declare war on Germany and then take back Shandong Province (or at least negotiate for its early return).[6]

Under the influence of such arguments, in August 1914 Chinese president Yuan Shikai told British minister to China John Jordan that the Chinese wanted to provide 50,000 troops to join the British military in an expedition to take back Qingdao, Chinese territory held under German control since 1898. Certainly China was not powerful enough to attack Germany by itself, and especially in light of Japan's ambition to take this territory, China needed the Allied support. Jordan rejected the idea outright, without even consulting his French or Russian colleagues, evidently assuming that Chinese cooperation was not needed.[7]

But the failure of this first attempt did not prevent the Chinese government from trying again, especially after it received the Twenty-one Demands from Japan in early 1915. On January 18, 1915, after it had already wrested control of Shandong Province from Germany, Japan, without regard for diplomatic norms, directly presented President Yuan with this ultimatum through its minister to China.[8] The demands consisted of five sections with total of twenty-one articles. These demands were so severe that presidential advisor George E. Morrison[9] called them "worse than many presented by a victor to his vanquished enemy."[10] Obviously, the Japanese intended to make China a vassal state while the other powers were preoccupied with European fighting. The French military attaché in Beijing, Captain de LaPomarede, pointed out immediately that this episode was a consequence of Japanese inclusion among the Allies.[11] Left with no effective options, both the government and the Chinese foreign policy public became determined to link China's fate to the postwar world order and international system, to cultivate the good will of the world community to win back what China had lost since the Opium War—dignity, sovereignty, and prestige.[12] By 1915, Chinese intellectuals and other social elites widely supported a new official goal of attending the peace conference. The challenge was how to win that seat.

Just as consideration of Qingdao compelled the Chinese to try to join the war in 1914, and the Japanese Twenty-one Demands made China determined in 1915 to win a place at the eventual peace conference, the prospect of joining the international system also provided important motivation for ongoing Chinese efforts to be an active party in the war. Japan, China's most threatening and determined enemy, had diplomatically aligned itself with the Allies: Britain and France. Why then did China choose to enter the war on the same side as Japan? The reason was strategic—China had to be part of the winning team to attend the peace conference on the best possible footing to represent its interests. Recognizing the obsession with its international status is key to understanding China's seemingly contradictory move. Once Yuan's government had linked its fate with the Allies, its foreign policy public demanded and supported determined and creative tactics.

Sending laborers as soldiers was an ingenious move in this direction. When Great Britain and France faced crises on the stagnant but murderous front lines, the maneuver would eventually succeed. As early as 1915, China worked out a laborers-as-soldiers scheme designed to link it with the Allied cause when its official entry into the war was uncertain. To establish a strong link with the Allied side and strengthen its case for claiming a role in the war, this new strategy was launched in 1915, and it was the Chinese rather than the Allies who initiated it. The idea of sending laborers to help the Allies was the brainchild of Liang Shiyi (1869–1933), who called it the *yigong daibing* (literally, "laborers in the place of soldiers") strategy.[13]

Liang Shiyi was brilliant for his financial ideas and his understanding of the big issues. He was an extremely influential politician during the Great War period and later became prime minister. Liang was born in Guangdong Province and served in many crucial posts in the government. As confidant of President Yuan Shikai, Liang was involved in all important policymaking discussions, especially in the area of foreign policy.[14] For a time during the World War I period, he actually controlled both China's finance and foreign policy.[15] Because of his wide influence and brilliant strategic thinking, he was dubbed the "Chinese Machiavelli" and the "copresident" *(er zong tong)*.[16] When the war broke out in Europe, he immediately sensed a great opportunity for China. He told Yuan Shikai that China should stop paying the Boxer Indemnity to all countries and should deposit salt and custom revenues in Chinese banks. He also argued that China should work with Britain to kick Germany out of Shandong Province and recover Qingdao before Japan could grab it. He even predicted that Germany would be defeated in the long run, so China should join the war sooner rather than later in order to have a voice in the postwar world. According to Liang Shiyi, joining the war would serve China's larger interests and its future.[17] But if China could not join the war militarily, other alternatives had to be devised quickly. Ye Gongchuo, a confidant of Liang Shiyi, wrote later that when war broke out in Europe, Liang Shiyi made several sweeping proposals *(da ji)* to the government concerning how China might take advantage of the European war to enhance its international status and rid itself of past national humiliations.

One of the so-called *da ji* was the labor plan. According to Ye, once Liang Shiyi got government authorization, he worked hard to turn the labor plan into a reality.[18] Liang's plan, although criticized by some as motivated by the prospect of personal profit, was a brilliant strategy. On his deathbed, Liang told family members that although he had made numerous mistakes in his life, his intention had always been to serve the interest of the nation and the people.[19] His labor plan seems to back up this claim.

Liang and his associate Ye Gongchuo worked out a detailed plan for using laborers as a crucial element of China's war policy.[20] The rationale behind the scheme in Liang's mind was this: The Chinese government wanted to link China to the international system and the Allies; sending laborers demonstrated Chinese sincerity and ability to help the Allies. Additionally, Germany could not charge China with violating its neutrality because these laborers would be hired through "private" companies.

China had come up with a workable plan to support the Allied side with labor, but how would France and Britain respond?

## The French Response

In 1915, as the Chinese reeled from the blow of Japan's Twenty-one Demands, the French faced the crisis of how to continue its deadly war without the manpower to fight on the battlefield while maintaining the home front. For France, the war started badly and had only gotten worse. As war got underway in Europe, Georges Clemenceau wrote an article for the *Saturday Evening Post,* claiming that "France is once again nothing more or less than a great battlefield."[21] Anyone who has ever visited the tiny village of Thiepval in northern France can appreciate the gravity of Clemenceau's point. Thiepval is the site of a towering triangular memorial to the Battle of the Somme; it commemorates the more than 73,000 British and Commonwealth soldiers who fell in the area, most of them during the Allied offensive between July 1916 and November 1916. During the Battle of the Somme, British forces suffered 131,000 dead and 288,654 wounded. Of those, 19,240 were killed in the first twenty-four hours. The French suffered an additional 204,253 casualties, while on the other side the Germans had between 450,000 and 600,000.[22] The French had to mobilize nearly 7.2 million of its population for the war effort, and nearly 1.5 million French soldiers were killed (Britain suffered some 1 million dead and millions more wounded).[23] The mobilization and casualties drastically contributed to a labor shortage. Finding new human resources had become important for winning or losing for France as it entered the summer of 1915, the second year of the war. The French government realized that it might soon go bankrupt in human resources because it simply did not have enough men to replace the dead and injured.

As early as March 17, 1915, the French Ministry of War discussed the idea of using Chinese laborers to do roadwork for the military. Not everyone in the ministry supported this notion. One senior general argued that the use of Chinese in the French military zones presented "serious disadvantages."[24] The idea was dropped. Several months later, however, the War Ministry reconsidered the value of Chinese labor, given that the war had become prolonged and it was necessary to mobilize all possible resources to defend France.[25] It is no surprise that when Liang Shiyi brought up his labor scheme with the French, they jumped at the opportunity. That June, the same month Liang made his proposal, French military authorities independently decided to seek China's help. They formally asked the French minister in Beijing, Alexandre R. Conty, to investigate the possibility of recruiting Chinese laborers, and France then commissioned the Truptil Mission to carry out recruitment. Liang's proposal was a godsend.

After discussions with Liang, Conty reported to his government on June 9, 1915, that the Chinese wanted to help, on one condition: Chinese laborers should be hired only by French "theoretically" private companies because China was still "officially" neutral. On November 4, 1915, Conty further informed his government that a very high Chinese official (presumably Liang Shiyi) confidentially told him that China could provide between 30,000 and 40,000 workers for France. On November 11, 1915, after some debate, the French War Ministry decided to go ahead with recruitment; on December 1, it selected a retired lieutenant colonel of the French army, Georges Truptil, to head a recruiting commission to China. Two weeks later, the Truptil Mission was on its way, and it arrived in Beijing on January 17, 1916.[26] One Chinese document clearly reports that it was French Minister Conty who introduced Triptil to the Chinese government to manage the recruitment business, and that Triptil had been sent by the French government.[27]

To avoid German charges of China's violating its neutrality, the Chinese side set up a private organization, the Huimin Company, to handle recruitment. The company was established in May 1916 by Liang Shiyi and the director of the Chinese Industrial Bank, Wang Keming. The Truptil Mission also pretended to be acting in a private capacity, with Truptil taking the cover of an agricultural engineer. The French contracted Huimin to recruit laborers in China, and that contract was signed on May 14, 1916, after a long negotiation. In the early days, the Huimin recruiting area mainly consisted of the northern Chinese provinces. Truptil also signed a contract with another Chinese company set up to hire skilled workers in Shanghai, and by January 23, 1917, he had assembled 600 of them. Although Truptil posted as a businessman from a private French agricultural company, and the French government promised that Chinese laborers were being recruited only for private purposes, the mission's military and official connections were obvious. From the outset, administration of the Chinese laborers in France fell to the direction of *troupes coloniales,* part of the French Ministry of War. But this arrangement clearly violated the agreement between China and France: China was not a French colony; the Chinese government was doing France a great favor by offering workers. Conty himself admitted that he was not comfortable and even felt ashamed by the word "colonial."[28] Moreover, the French government recognized that the Chinese workers would be assisting with French "national defense."[29] The Chinese government was fully aware of these issues, but chose not to contest them.

Germany was well aware of this point. According to G. Charles Hodges's report, "The Kaiser's henchmen in China's capital, the golden-handed Admiral Hintze [who was German minister to China], saw what those beginnings back in 1915–16 meant. . . . In Shanghai one day [in 1916] the consulate of the Teutons looked into the actions of a Chinese iron foundry with anxiety. The foundry seemed to have an insatiable demand for brass-smiths, ironsmiths and mechanics . . . One Chinaman would be seen talking most earnestly to another. It generally ended by Chinaman Number One taking Number Two to a consulate with which the Germans had held no traffic." Then "inside [the French consulate] a medical man and a mechanical engineer would look over Chinaman Number Two," and often "John Chinaman grinned and put his mark to a lengthy contract for service in France."[30] As soon as Germany learned of the French recruitment scheme, it protested repeatedly to the Chinese government, charging violation of neutrality because one Chinese worker counted as equal to one soldier for the Allied side. The Chinese government responded mildly by saying the workers went to Europe in a private capacity and had been recruited by private companies.[31] Of course, in its secret communications with local government, the Chinese Foreign Ministry admitted that in reality the recruitment was being conducted by the government, and it asked local governors to understand and support this carefully designed policy *(wei qu qiu quan zhi ku xin).*[32]

The Truptil Mission was not the only entity engaged in recruiting Chinese laborers for France. Other organizations with the same goal had also been set up. For example, on January 31, 1916, the French Ministry of Works agreed that the Société Franco-Chinoise d'Education, as its representative, would also begin to recruit Chinese laborers. In early 1917, with some connection to the recruitment plan of the Société, another recruiter, the so-called Louis Grillet Mission, arrived in China.[33] This mission also came under the French war machine's direct control and was officially subordinate to the Truptil Mission. But in fact it acted quite independently, mainly focusing its recruiting efforts in the southwest, especially Yunnan Province and Sichuan Province. When Truptil returned to France, Grillet took charge of both missions.[34] Although several French recruiting missions would be active in China over the course of the war, the Truptil Mission was the most effective and important among them.

The War Ministry's original plan was to recruit 40,000 Chinese workers, but by the time both sides entered final negotiations, French ambitions had expanded. The French decided to recruit at least 50,000 Chinese workers instead, and this was the figure recorded in the contract.[35] The first group of Chinese laborers arrived in France on August 24, 1916.[36] Prospects seemed bright with this boost to the French war effort, and the government congratulated itself on the idea that an additional 10,000 Chinese would become available each month. The French government calculated that by the end of 1917, there would be 100,000 Chinese laborers working for France. Officials had even decided how these laborers would be assigned. According to one document, the allotments were as follows: Armament would receive 20,000 laborers, the Ministry of War would receive 50,000, and transport would receive 30,000.[37] Unfortunately, things did not work out so well. The eventual recruitment figure was actually much smaller because of complications, one being the lack of cooperation between the French Foreign Ministry (Quai d'Orsay) and the War Ministry, specifically between its Beijing legation and the Truptil Mission. French minister A. R. Conty was not happy with a separate recruiting mission that operated beyond the jurisdiction of the legation. As early as December 3, 1915, two days after the Truptil Mission was selected, he charged that a recruitment mission under military jurisdiction would produce "a regrettable effect." Of course, this was only an excuse for Conty because he was not a man who honored commitments with the Chinese. The bottom line was that he had already engaged in negotiations with Chinese officials regarding recruitment and he felt that he should be in charge of the whole business. Conty was not fully cooperative with the Truptil Mission from the outset and took every opportunity to complain.[38] He grumbled openly that the mission did not handle contract disputes wisely, and "from the beginning" the French War Ministry had made decisions that were completely contrary to the opinion of the French legation in Beijing. This being the case, Conty could only "strive to repair or relieve to the extent possible the consequences of the errors committed in complete ignorance of the Chinese environment in which the recruitment operations take place."[39]

The French Foreign Ministry made blunders as well. Just as recruitment was getting started, it brought on the Laoxikai Incident, which occurred because of the arrogance of its legation in China and jeopardized the entire recruiting effort. The Laoxikai Incident took place on October 20, 1916, while Conty was in Paris, when the French chargé d'affaires Damien de Martel (1878–1940) issued orders to seize an area of Tianjin called Laoxikai by force. The point of this action was to extend the French concession, which had an original area of 250 acres. France had been eyeing the Laoxikai area for some time and in 1902 requested the extension of the Tianjin concession to this locality, which would triple its size. The Chinese refused. When the French proceeded to seize Laoxikai in 1916, the Chinese foreign policy public immediately responded by forming a "Society for the Preservation of National Rights in Tianjin," in which merchants and students were very active. At a general meeting held on October 23, the society decided to submit a demand urging the central government to break off commercial relations with France and prohibit further employment of Chinese workers in French enterprises, as well as demanding payment of wages in French currency. On November 2, a few days after a student demonstration, about 1,600 workers employed in French enterprises went on strike. A general boycott of French goods was also initiated in Tianjin. The boycott was actively supported by the Chinese Chamber Of Commerce and other local groups that were set up after the incident. They distributed funds and allocations of coal and rice to the strikers. Messages of solidarity came from many places, some as distant as Hankou, Chengdu, and Fujian.[40] A delegation of Tianjin businessmen visited the newly appointed foreign minister, Wu Tingfang, in Shanghai, where he resided in retirement (1912–1916), and told him of the "true state of affairs." They pressed him for a plan of action. Another group of Tianjin businessmen called upon him in Beijing shortly after he had opened talks with the French, to inquire about negotiations.[41]

The Laoxikai Incident would have in fact been resolved sooner had Britain not intervened. Britain was opposed to a French apology to China because of "the Allied humiliation involved." Furthermore, it worried that the agreement between France and China "formed a precedent for allowing the Chinese to restrict foreign trade and residence to areas of foreign concessions in treaty ports, the principle of which Britain had contested for seventy-five years."[42] However, under the strong pressure of Chinese public opinion and the Chinese government's use of that opinion as a bargaining chip, France did eventually retreat from the Laoxikai area.

Because of this background, the British minister to China, John Jordan, was puzzled by China's desire to enter the war on the Allied side. In December 1915, he wrote to Beilby Alston, the number two person at the British legation in Beijing, "It is sometimes a wonder to me that the Chinese have not gone into the German camp altogether and that they still profess so much friendship for the Allies."[43] In his letter to Lord Bryce, Jordan also indicated that "the Chinese attitude towards the Allies has been more than friendly. They have given substantial assistance in ways I cannot mention and have contributed very large sums to the various war funds."[44]

Still, the Laoxikai Incident had a very negative effect on the French recruitment of Chinese laborers. At one point, the supply of men was cut off entirely. After Laoxikai, public outrage made it impossible to recruit northern Chinese workers for a time, and the mission was forced to move south. However, public opinion in the south was not particularly friendly toward recruitment, either. In one telegram dated February 12, 1917, the governor of Guangdong Province suggested to the Chinese Foreign Ministry that because many people in his province opposed French recruitment, it should temporarily suspend activities in Guangdong. The Foreign Ministry agreed.[45]

Quarrels and the lack of close cooperation among the French hurt the recruitment business. Although in wartime the military had a louder voice and military control of recruitment continued, the Truptil Mission moved slowly and its work suffered from delays.[46] The lack of cooperation from Quai d'Orsay persisted even after the Truptil Mission ended. The French military authority made matters worse by terminating the recruitment of Chinese laborers in early 1918 without any advance consultation with the Chinese government. This unilateral and early termination violated the contract between China and France, and because the French legation in Beijing had guaranteed the contract in the name of the French government, Quai d'Orsay was left to clean up the mess. At first, the French chargé d'affaires in Beijing, de Martel, sent several telegrams to Quai d'Orsay, drawing its attention to the inappropriate action of the French military.[47] On February 9 and February 18, 1918, he warned of the cancellation's "inevitable consequences." He argued that because there remained a 15,000-man quota to meet, the unilateral termination of the contract by France legitimized the Huimin Company's demand for compensation of its loss. The French government had no justification for refusing to pay. De Martel also worried that the War Ministry's decision also set a risky precedent, which might hurt France in the future. For example, French business could be hurt should China follow suit and cancel its contracts unilaterally. Furthermore, French prestige was at stake because the contract had the French government's guarantee. With these considerations in mind, de Martel suggested that France should pay an indemnity to the Huimin Company as soon as possible in accordance with the terms of the contract.[48]

Based on arguments provided in de Martel's telegrams, the Quai d'Orsay sent several memoranda to the War Ministry drawing its attention to the serious consequences of breaking the contract. The War Ministry, however, did not agree. Its officials responded that many of the Chinese demands for compensation were unjustified. However, it did recognize the legal problems its action gave rise to and agreed to settle with the Chinese in "a spirit of conciliation." Even with this admission, a close reading of the War Ministry's reply shows a lack of sincerity and indifference to Chinese rights.[49] At one point, the War Ministry even argued that France could use the poor quality of Chinese laborers as grounds for refusing payment of the 2 million francs it owned to Huimin.[50] When the war was over, the Huimin had a deficit of 180,000 yuan.[51]

Bickering between Quai d'Orsay and the War Ministry concerning compensation of the Huimin Company indicates how poorly coordinated France's China policy had become. There was no consensus about how to recognize China's contribution to the war or how to accommodate other Chinese ambitions. It is also important to keep in mind that the French society was not enthusiastic about having Chinese laborers in France; its working class was appalled by the idea of Chinese taking away jobs. Leon Jouhaux, the head of the Confédération Générale du Travail (CGT), wrote in September 1916 to the French labor minister, "I must in the name of the C.G.T. . . . . protest against the introduction into our labor market of 20,000 new Chinese. . . . We judge it necessary that the use of Chinese coolies be limited once and for all to the circumstances that motivate it, and that everywhere upon demobilization French workers should be able to find, in the factories, the workshops, the stores and the yards the jobs they held before they left for military service."[52] In a major November 1916 editorial on Chinese laborers, Jouhaux reemphasized the theme of equality for French and foreign, arguing that

> No matter their color or their language, we cannot accept that the worker be brought among us as a slave, and be treated as a pariah ... this land must not become a cosmopolitan boulevard where all races may meet each other, with the sole exception of the French, because they have disappeared. It is imperative that all, in spite of the necessities of the present hour, concern themselves with the problem of the survival of the race. This will be the most important means to ensure that the French people do not lose the benefit of national prosperity, acquired at such cost.

Jouhaux's article drew on France's wartime peril to racialize the discussion of Chinese labor.[53] In January 1918, Chinese and French longshoremen in Rouen had a major clash. In commenting on the incident, the commander of the Chinese labor company noted that his charges had been provoked by "the shouts of civilians, mostly dockworkers, people of uncertain reputation whose opinions of Chinese workers are well known. They are convinced that the Chinese have come to take their jobs, thereby preventing them from earning a living."[54] To a certain extent, the opposition of the French working class discouraged the French government from taking full advantage of recruiting the Chinese laborers.

## Britain Finally Turns to China

When Liang Shiyi began thinking about his laborers-as-soldiers plan, his main target was Britain. According to the British military attaché in Beijing, Lieutenant Colonel David S. Robertson, Liang proposed the idea first to the British in early June 1915, suggesting that China supply Britain with 300,000 military laborers (along with 100,000 rifles) to serve under British officers wherever required.[55] Liang's original suggestion entailed use of military laborers, not hired workers. If Britain had accepted this proposal, China would have been fighting on the Allied side in 1915. Robertson was very supportive of using Chinese laborers in France and later played a key role when the British eventually adopted Liang's idea. Unfortunately, no one in the British government except

Robertson was interested. John Jordan termed the idea of using Chinese laborers for military functions "hardly practicable."[56] The British War Office agreed with Jordan, claiming that "the proposal to utilize Chinese either as fighting troops or for labour purposes" was "considered not to be feasible, as any such step would involve China taking her place on the side of the Allies against the central powers, and this had for political reasons been considered an impossibility."[57] Britain rejected the idea immediately and so Liang had turned to France.

The shortage of human resources became a serious problem for the British as well. As the *New York Times* reported, "The first problem [for Britain] was that of man power." In 1917, "all sources which could be tapped without trenching upon the essential supplies of the allied armies and the nation had been exhausted, and the question had narrowed itself down to that of finding substitutes for fit men of military age still engaged in industry."[58] Britain first tried to use help from its colonies and dominions. In early 1916, Britain decided to raise additional labor battalions from Canada "for service in France."[59] But help from Canada was limited because it had only a small population and had already contributed a large military force to Europe. The idea to use colonial forces also triggered unease and anger because it would undermine the image of Western civilization and the empire. To the colonists, using African or other colored people for war presented a great danger. The Boer newspaper in South Africa, *Ons Land,* noted shortly after the outbreak of the Great War: "The deployment of Arabian, Indian, and African troops on the European battlefields brings East and West, whites and blacks in close contact with one another. We cannot but wonder what the consequences of this will be. Senior citizens, women and children of the enemy will fall into the hands of these black and yellow auxiliary troops. . . . This can only be detrimental to the image of Western culture and of the whites." In May 1917, in a speech to the war cabinet in London, South African delegate General Jan C. Smuts spoke of dangers to the colonial system and to European civilization in general if black Africans were given arms on a large scale.[60] If using its own colonial laborers could present such problems, turning to China for help was even more humiliating.

Another major stumbling block to using Chinese labor, as in France, was the opposition of the British labor unions. The unions eventually reached a sort of agreement with the military authority that Chinese "would be used only as replacements for white personnel in France who were unfit for protracted heavy work and who would return to the home front either for immediate demobilization or to help with the war effort in some less demanding though unspecified category." The Chinese were definitely not to be introduced into Britain.[61] According to a London *Times* report in the summer of 1917, when the word got out that Chinese might be sent to work in Birmingham, the Birmingham trades council wrote to the Ministry of Munitions, stating that feelings were so strong that unless the Chinese were withdrawn, a firm stand would be taken against them.[62] Even during wartime, the government did not dare offend British labor. Labor obviously knew its influence: In one case, British laborers demanded to know whether the government was prepared for revolution if it refused to accept their demands for certain rights and conditions.[63]

A third reason for British hesitation was its uncertainty and misgivings about Chinese intentions. Even after Britain decided to turn to China for help, John Jordan was suspicious. In a report to the Foreign Office, he commented that the "new school of statesmen [in China] would not, in my opinion, view with favour the prospect of seeing their countrymen assisting European powers in a struggle on any terms which did not ensure them complete equality of standing and a voice in the subsequent settlement."[64] Jordan was right, of course. If Britain was not prepared to accommodate China's position, it was best not to accept Chinese assistance.

The preceding reasons explain why Britain refused the Chinese offer of help until it had no choice. In early 1916, the British War Office regarded the Chinese labor scheme with "the greatest apprehension." The War Office took the position that until "a definite assurance that the trades unions, tribunals, etc., at home would agree to release a corresponding number of men for active service at the front, no steps should be taken to replace them by Chinese and black labour."[65] Obviously, domestic and racial considerations were major factors, but everything had changed by the summer of 1916. Britain's very existence was at stake, and British arrogance had been replaced by desperation. Historian Paul Fussell has written that as early as the middle of November 1914, the huge casualties "had all but wiped out the original British army."[66] By 1916 the military situation was so bad that one Briton wrote that "we can turn to seek comfort only in the quiet confidence of our souls."[67] The Battle of the Somme had inflicted enormous British casualties, and manpower on the home front was in such a state that it was impossible to spare anyone without hurting the war effort. In July alone (the first month of fighting at the Somme), 187,000 British soldiers were killed, wounded, or went missing. By mid-August, total casualties had reached 223,000, and the British faced an acute manpower shortage. War secretary Lloyd George was heard to comment that "we are going to lose this war."[68] There was the clear impression in Britain that the war would be endless and drag on forever.[69] General Douglas Haig, commander-in-chief of British armies in France, wrote in a special order on August 4, 1916, "It is two years since the British army entered on the greatest struggle in the history of the world against the most formidable fighting machine that has ever been created—a machine fashioned by the unceasing effort of many generations for the deliberate purpose of imposing on all nations the will of one."[70] In the fall of 1916, one member of the House of Commons was so worried about the heavy casualties that he wrote to Lloyd George demanding that something be done. "Otherwise we should have no fighting Army next spring. At the present pace they will all be dead."[71] The London *Times* declared, "Every man who is fit for general service . . . is urgently needed by the fighting units. No one can be spared for the services of labor."[72]

The shortage of labor was so grave that under the Munitions of War Act, the British government would not allow anybody to strike or leave work, even for a single day. A member of Parliament cited a particularly striking example. A woman had missed a day's work. She was brought like a criminal before the munitions courts and was about to be fined, when a judicious question posed by the assessor revealed that the woman's baby had died, and she had taken one day off to bury the child. The employers had not taken the trouble to ascertain why the woman was away from her job.[73] Britain faced many challenges when the war broke out, but "the problem of labour is at the bottom of all these problems."[74] For Britain, labor was the key to winning. As one influential British politician argued on August 16, 1917, "It is not so much a question of the expenditure of money, it is not even a question of the ability with which those in the service of the State carry out its organization, it is not so much now a question of organization—it is a question of labour, and you want both an adequate supply of labour and a willing application of that labour by those who are responsible for its use."[75]

Clearly Britain needed outside help, even from a country like China. This extremity of the situation compelled the British authorities to reconsider their earlier position on the Chinese proposal. In an address to the House of Commons on July 24, 1916, Winston Churchill argued in terms of the search for labor resources: "I would not even shrink from the word Chinese for the purpose of carrying on the War. These are not times when people ought in the least to be afraid of prejudices. At any rate, there are great resources of labour in Africa and Asia which, under proper discipline, might be the means of saving thousands of British lives and of enormously facilitating the whole progress and conduct of the War. Remember that the Germans have what we have not got—that is, an enormous reserve of prisoners of war who have fallen into their hands in the early phases of the struggle."[76] By July 28, the Army Council decided to seek Chinese laborers to work in France.[77] On August 14, the British informed the French government that the British forces in France would soon also employ a considerable number of Chinese laborers.[78] H. R. Wakefield, a British officer, later wrote that the supply of white labor was then strictly limited, and the cold climate was unsuitable for black labor. This situation made the Chinese very valuable for the British. "The coolie is a splendid and versatile worker, inured to hardship and almost indifferent to the weather."[79]

David Lloyd George, in his capacity as head of the War Office, agreed in the summer of 1916 to the principle of employing Chinese labor for work "in France and in other theaters of war in order that the British labour now being employed in France etc may be released for work at home to mitigate the existing shortage of men in agriculture and industries."[80] Beginning that August, Great Britain put its own recruitment plan into action. Like the French, the War Office selected a representative, Thomas J. Bourne (1864–1947), who had been engineer-in-chief for the Beijing-Hankou Railway and had twenty-eight years' experience in China, to head the recruiting mission.[81] Bourne arrived in Beijing on October 28, 1916. Three days later, on October 31, 1916, he left for Weihaiwei, a British sphere of interest that would serve as his recruitment base, and started to work immediately. He had a valuable assistant in Theodore Roberts, a chartered accountant. The actual administration of the Labor Depot was assumed by G. S. Moss of the British Consular Service.[82] Moss actually replaced Bourne in summer 1918 to be the new War Office representative.

But from the very beginning, the British government had kept this recruitment secret—even from Parliament. On November 23, 1916, one MP asked Lloyd George whether Chinese were being employed in France by the British military and whether the government planned to use them in Britain as well. Lloyd George replied, "I am not prepared to give any information on this subject."[83] On November 28, 1916, the issue of using Chinese laborers was raised again, and Lloyd George was asked whether he could "inform the House where this [Chinese labor] corps is to be employed, when it was recruited, and what are the wages, hours, and conditions applicable to the men, and whether the corps is under military control." Once again, Lloyd George refused to address the issue.[84]

Weihaiwei was not the War Office's first choice for its recruitment operations, but its selection was the result of consultation and compromise between the War Office and the Foreign Office. When the War Office decided to use Chinese laborers, it initially proposed to enlist Cantonese at Hong Kong. This proposal was submitted to John Jordan, who was against the idea of recruiting workers in south China, believing that southerners were less suitable than northerners. Jordan's recommendations received crucial backing from the Hong Kong colonial authority. The governor of Hong Kong indicated that northern Chinese were more suitable for France on the following grounds: "1. They are inured to cold. 2. They eat farinaceous food. 3. They are more amenable to discipline. 4. They are not impregnated with malaria."[85] The scheme of using Hong Kong as a base was eventually dropped and the follow-up proposal was to recruit laborers at Weihaiwei.[86] Also deferring to John Jordan's suggestion, the recruitment for Britain was conducted under the name of the Weihaiwei government, and left the collection of laborers in Shandong Province under legation control. But the War Office would be in direct control of actual recruitment.[87]

The British mission, like the French one, was ineffective at first, but its efforts were complicated by different factors from those that had plagued the French. By late November 1916, it had recruited fewer than forty people for its first labor corps. Unlike France, Britain did not use Chinese contractors to do the recruiting; instead, its recruiting was carried out by agents of the British government. Without cooperation from the Chinese government, it was difficult for Britain to move ahead. Chinese cooperation, however, had conditions attached, as Jordan had pointed out earlier. The British chargé d'affaires in Beijing, Beilby Alston, described the situation in late 1916 to the British Foreign Office, "It seems quite clear that, if coolie recruitment is ever to materialize, more active steps must be taken at once. We are quite ready to give the necessary assurances to the Chinese government that they will be protected against aggressive action by enemy powers for supposed breach of neutrality."[88] Thus the Chinese government's involvement was crucial even for the British recruitment. As one contemporary observed, when Yio-Han Lee was approached for work as a laborer in France by a British recruiter, Lee suspected a trick. But a Chinese interpreter from his own province assured him that "the Chinese government itself would reach out the long arm of protection to him in France and would see the promises the foreign gentleman was making were kept."[89] With the assurance of government protection, he decided to go.

The Chinese were quite ready to respond. In December 1916 the British were still having trouble jump-starting their recruitment scheme, so the Chinese foreign minister told them that although his government could not openly assist their efforts it would help in any way it could *(zi dang an zhong jin li, bu bian ming zhu ye)*;[90] supplying labor for the Allies was deemed "very important" to Chinese international relations.[91] As the program began to move forward, the Chinese government provided a list of conditions to the British in exchange for Chinese manpower.[92] In a telegram from the Chinese minister to London on January 25, 1917, the Foreign Ministry officially and openly linked its labor scheme with larger plans. The dispatch asked Britain to agree to the following to obtain Chinese assistance in its recruiting effort:

1. Britain would allow China to delay payment of the Boxer Indemnity for fifty years with no increase in interest.
2. It would immediately allow China to raise taxes, an act of governance that had not been allowed by the great powers for some time.
3. Britain would help China secure a seat at the postwar peace conference.

Of these three goals, joining the peace conference was the most important, and the dispatch asked the Chinese minister to stress that point.[93] China also asked Great Britain to persuade the other powers to accommodate Chinese wishes. Although the Chinese did not achieve any of these above goals with this dispatch, the points did provide the basis for later successes.

One problem the British recruitment mission shared with the French effort was too strong a military orientation. Jordan pointed this out clearly: "Unless the situation clears there is even a possibility of our recruiting being stopped . . . I feel bound however from my knowledge of the Chinese to express my opinion that the scheme as now being developed by the War Office appears to me to be assuming too military a character and I fear this may further militate against it. If the project is to succeed at all, every effort must be made to keep the military nature of the organization in the background out here."[94] As with the French mission, China eventually chose not to make a fuss over this issue. But even the French presented a problem for Britain's initial recruitment: the disastrous Laoxikai Incident made recruiting in the north for *any* overseas service difficult. Alston reported that "the French incident at Tientsin [Tianjin] is primarily responsible for obstruction. It puts [a] stop to all recruiting for abroad in the province."[95]

Despite its many problems at the outset, the British recruitment effort soon paid off. According to one report from the French military attaché in London, General de La Panouse, by late April 1917 the British had sent 35,000 Chinese laborers to France to work for the British military, a number that greatly surpassed those working for the French.[96] The French naval attaché in London reported on June 1 that he had information that the British were even recruiting Tibetan workers to serve under the control of their War Office.[97]

How can we explain the success of the British recruiting mission? One obvious factor was the gradual removal of earlier obstacles. Most important was the close cooperation between the British Foreign Office and the War Office; the dialogue between the British legation in Beijing and the War Office representative was particularly productive.[98] First, the War Office kept legation head John Jordan closely informed about what was going on in its recruitment program. One of the War Office cables to Jordan stated that provisional terms it communicated to Bourne were subject to Jordan's concurrence. It also told Jordan that Bourne was instructed to consult with him closely. It even explained to Jordan why the War Office had to assign someone else to be in charge of the mission. "While leaving the collection of the men in Shantung under legation control, it is necessary, however, for the War Office to have an agent at Wei-hai-wei itself who will be responsible for receiving, approving, enrolling, clothing etc., the coolies after they have been collected, but subject to any advice to the contrary from you, he will remain throughout at Wei-hai-wei and leave all operations outside that territory to be carried out under your direction." In the same telegram, the War Office expressed its desire to "set the [recruiting] machinery going as soon as possible," and asked Jordan to "take the preliminary steps forthwith."[99] Of course, widespread British interests in China and the enormous experience of the British minister also played some role in the program's success.

For all the differences between the French and British recruitment efforts, there are obvious similarities as well. One aspect they shared was heavier recruiting in China's northern provinces, especially Shandong Province. Second, their main purposes were the same: for both countries, Chinese workers were to serve military needs and help them win the war. With the French and British military authorities doing the recruiting, Chinese workers came primarily under military management and were usually organized into military-type units commanded by officers.

It is interesting to note that during the war Britain was quite keen about propagandizing in China to boost its recruitment and prestige. From September 1917, when China had just declared war on Germany, twenty-six films from Britain were screened in China, together with thirty-five issues of official newsreels. These films were shown in fifty-one places on a total of 593 occasions.[100] The film, titled *Chinese Labour Contingent,* was released in January 1918, but it was not received well overseas; in fact it got the most negative comments of all the British films shown. Unfortunately, the source of this information did not explain what triggered the negative responses or from which locales they came.[101]

## A New China in a New World: The Visible Hand of the Chinese Government

France and Britain had every intention of keeping their recruitment efforts in China secret. This approach made perfect sense to them. To begin with, the appearance of depending on China in any sense was not good for their national image; second, the recruitment programs were military-related and therefore required secrecy. But why were the Chinese content to be complicit? There are many possible reasons why China was hesitant to showcase its labor plan. China remained a neutral country until 1917 and could not let Germany know with any certainty that its government was behind the recruitment programs. Moreover, because the plan was a vital part of China's grand strategy to become an equal member of the new world order, the Chinese did not want Japan and other imperialist powers to become alert and suspicious. As a weak nation that did not have a strong central government, China was in no position to offend powerful countries such as Germany and Japan. These considerations go a long way toward explaining China's careful discretion during the war. Later, when the plan did not bear important fruit, the Chinese lost any motivation to lay out the correct story. Yet, despite the official explanations that British and French recruitment of Chinese laborers was private business and had nothing to do with Chinese government, it is clear that the labor plan had been carefully designed and promoted by the Chinese government. This hidden Chinese official involvement was significant in many ways.

The Chinese decision to send laborers to Europe was unprecedented. Both the earlier Ming and Qing governments had strongly discouraged Chinese from going abroad, and even persecuted those who had.[102] In 1712, with considerable numbers of Chinese already residing abroad, an edict from the Qing court decreed, "Those who stay overseas permanently are liable to capital punishment and will be extradited from foreign countries by the provincial governors for prompt beheading." The Qianglong Emperor called overseas Chinese "deserters of the Celestial Empire," who would therefore receive no protection from China if they encountered trouble in other countries.[103] This remained official policy until 1893, when the Qing government finally abolished it.[104]

The anti-emigration policy was one manifestation of the Middle Kingdom syndrome and pointed to the isolationist mind-set of Chinese society at that time. The decline of this sort of thinking in the late nineteenth century coincided with a new desire to join the world system. No longer was the West dismissed as a land of demons; it was an example for China to follow, and going abroad had become a glorious privilege. As a result, the status of overseas Chinese was enhanced a great deal, and Republican China passed a series of laws in 1912, including the Provisional Constitution and Organization Act of Congress, which legalized the representation of overseas Chinese in domestic politics. In 1916, as Chinese laborers started to leave for France, the Ministry of Agriculture, Industry, and Commerce and the Chinese Foreign Ministry deliberated over new legislation to protect those workers overseas.[105] The new law soon passed; in 1917, with a huge number of Chinese laborers already in Europe, the State Council of the Beijing government set up a new office: the Bureau of Overseas Chinese Workers.[106] The 1915 laborers-as-soldiers program, therefore, should be seen as further evidence of the new Chinese thinking and the transformation of Chinese society in general, as well as an expression of China's eagerness to join the war.

Behind the scenes, the Chinese government worked very hard to protect its laborers and the nation's interest. According to an important document I discovered in the China Second National Historical Archives in Nanjing, the British government made an agreement with Chinese government about its recruitment of laborers. One item stated that the term of the contract was three years. If the British government, in extraordinary circumstances, wanted to change the terms, it had to get approval from the Chinese government and provide an extra six months' salary for the Chinese who were sent back (for no misconduct of their own) to China before the contract's termination date. The agreement also indicated that the Chinese should get a day off on Sundays and on Chinese National Day. The laborers should be treated the same as all other workers. The Chinese government had the right to send a person to take care of the laborers. The Chinese laborers were to work only in France; if the British wanted to use them somewhere else, it had to notify the Chinese government.[107]

In the French case, the Chinese government got involved as well. The Chinese Foreign Ministry reviewed the draft contract offered by the Truptil Mission and approved it before the contract could become official.[108] The Huimin contract was presented as a private one, but it was in every sense a governmental agreement. Both the French and Chinese governments were involved in its negotiation. When Beijing invited the Chinese legation in France to comment on the contract, the minister to France Hu Weide provided detailed suggestions. He argued it was extremely important that the Chinese should receive the same legal rights as French citizens and the same wages as French workers of the same category. He also suggested that the Chinese government should make sure the recruited laborers were of good character. He argued:

> Chinese workers in foreign countries today should be selected with their future place in China in mind. The best ones, who may be able to learn about the management of French factories can become excellent managers in China when they return. The rest, if we select well, at least can save enough money in France to open their own small businesses when they return. Therefore, it was crucial to make sure no hooligans, gamblers, and other bad types get selected.

Bad apples would not only make the good ones suffer and be a bad influence, they would also damage China's reputation. Unfortunately this actually played out because some bad characters did go, though in part because the French and British were more concerned with physical qualifications than with personal character. Minister Hu also suggested that the government should send along diplomats to protect the laborers' well-being. When the Foreign Ministry received this memo, it circulated it to the Chinese Ministry of Agriculture, Industry, and Commerce and asked the officials there to work together to implement the suggestions.[109]

To make sure the Chinese national interest and its laborers were protected, the Foreign Ministry demanded that the French government guarantee the Huimin contract. The Chinese government was especially determined that French government should promise that Chinese laborers would not be used for direct military action (article 1). It also demanded that the French government make sure that Chinese diplomats or consuls would be allowed to inspect the working conditions and well-being of Chinese working in French factories (article 14). The French government had to guarantee that the Chinese in France would be treated the same as French citizens and enjoy the same freedoms as the French. The French government and employers were to make sure that Chinese laborers were not abused by other workers (article 15).[110] Only after receiving written agreement on these points from the French government did the Chinese government finally approve the Huimin contract.[111]

The Chinese government's insistence that the French government provide written guarantee of the contract terms was a shrewd move. It rebutted German protests that China had violated its neutrality and at the same time protected the laborers' safety and interests. The German government made multiple protests against the Chinese labor plan for France, but each time the Chinese were able to deflect them with the argument that the British and French recruitments were organized by private agencies, not military agencies.[112] The French written promise that Chinese laborers would not be used for military action made it difficult for Germany to go further.[113] German protests correctly pointed out that Germany's enemies would be stronger with Chinese laborers' support. The Germans argued that one Chinese laborer arriving in France meant that the enemy had a new soldier.[114] German diplomats tried to stop the recruitment. In a dispatch to the Shandong Province local government, the German consul at Jinan wrote on February 2, 1917, that he had "received reliable information" that British missionaries were recruiting Chinese laborers in Shandong Province and asked local officials to "strictly prevent any such action."[115] But the Germans seemed to have been outmaneuvered. The Beijing government secretly informed its local officials how to handle the labor recruitment. In such communications,

Beijing made clear that the Chinese government actually stood behind the recruitment and that local government should support it because the laborers-as-soldiers plan was part of a larger national strategy.[116]

In a nice stroke of Machiavellian irony, while the Chinese government insisted to Germany that the French and British recruitment efforts were private in nature, Beijing actually tried to keep private local intermediaries out of the recruitment business. Some entrepreneurial Chinese got wind of the recruitment, quickly realized it might be profitable, and wanted to get involved. In early 1917, Chinese citizens Zhan Yougu and Zhou Laichang petitioned the government for permission to set up a company that would mediate between foreign recruiters and potential laborers, ostensibly in the name of better protecting the Chinese laborers' interests. Their application was rejected.[117]

The Chinese government was also quite serious when it suggested that it should send diplomats to oversee the interests of the laborers and monitor their treatment in France. One major initiative was the appointment of labor agents to negotiate with the British and French governments if problems arose. As early as 1916, China's Ministry of Agriculture, Industry, and Commerce, together with its Foreign Ministry, prepared a new law that would protect the laborers. It was soon approved.[118] The new law stipulated that, as necessary, the government should assign officials to protect the laborers' interests while they worked in France; these officials should be appointed jointly by the Foreign Ministry, the Interior Ministry, and the Ministry of Agriculture, Industry, and Commerce.[119] With more and more laborers shipping out to Europe, in September 1917 the State Council established the Bureau of Overseas Chinese Laborers under its direct supervision.[120] Zhang Hu was appointed its first director.[121]

In late November 1916, Li Jun was chosen to be the official in charge of the labor cohort recruited by the French. His official title initially was called *bao gong wei yuan,* or the official whose job was to protect laborers' interests. Li Jun had gone to school in Europe and was an effective and efficient person who was determined to fulfill his charge.[122] In his first announcement to the laborers, he declared that he would visit each and every Chinese camp sooner or later. He would try his best to help the laborers "enjoy all happiness, get rid of all misfortune." He encouraged the men to pay attention to the cultural differences between China and France and try to follow civilized behavior.[123] In his second announcement, he urged the laborers to use legal measures to settle labor disputes and asked them not to take matters into their own hands. They should follow the rules and laws, and not gamble or engage in other bad behavior.[124]

Li Jun was a most able agent, especially compared with his counterpart, Pan Lianru, assigned by the Chinese legation in London to be responsible for those men working under the British. Despite the fact that Britain recruited far more Chinese than France did, the Chinese legation in London could not assign a capable diplomat to look after the men working under the British Expeditionary Forces (BEF) in France. The legation claimed it was short of staff, so it was difficult to assign a seasoned diplomat to this duty. Pan, a Chinese student in Switzerland who was finishing his study, was selected for that service.[125] He resigned in November 1919, and the legation replaced him with a junior secretary. Pan does not seem to have done much; his reports, compared with Li Jun's, are sketchy at best.[126] Li Jun produced many detailed reports in which he discussed the conditions, food, and many other issues pertaining to the laborers. In one memo to the French authorities on October 1, 1917, he reported that the men were complaining about the horse meat provided to them. Li Jun informed the French that Chinese did not eat horse meat, and if they insisted that the laborers eat it, they would make trouble. The French immediately agreed not to do so.[127] The Chinese government was not blind to the fate of its laborers in Europe, and in many cases it strongly protested their mistreatment, demanding that the Allies respect the laborers' human rights and treat them the same as other people.[128]

Just as France, Britain, and the Chinese were realizing that the Great War precipitated a global crisis, the Chinese labor plan emerged, presenting advantages all around. Sometimes such expedients herald major changes. Mao Zedong's ping-pong diplomacy in the 1970s seemed insignificant—just a sports exchange—but in fact nudged Sino-American relations forward and transformed world politics. This laborers-as-soldiers plan involved hired workers, not ping-pong players, but it heralded a stage of the process that was similar to the ping-pong exchanges that led to Nixon's visit to Beijing, which sealed China's status as a world power. One YMCA document sums it up nicely: "Up to 1916 the Great War had so drained the man-power of Great Britain and France that these two countries began to recruit Chinese laborers for their respective military needs. At the time, the Chinese Government being unable to support the Allies with troops, readily gave its consent to the two said Governments which sent representatives to China for the purpose of recruiting laborers in large numbers. The success of this enterprise was in no small measure due to the efforts of the Chinese Government in greatly facilitating the recruiting processes as its contribution to the Allied Cause."[129] China had a long road to its present twenty-first century international status, but the initial steps had been taken.

# 2

## THE RECRUITMENT AND
## EUROPEAN ODYSSEY OF THE
## MEN FOR BRITAIN AND FRANCE

China, France, and Britain had one common interest in the Chinese laborers' recruitment: all three countries saw using their labor as critical to the fate of their nations. In the Chinese case, the laborers would link China with the Allied cause and promote China's entry into the world community as an equal member. For the British and French, the Chinese laborers meant vital help in winning the war.

For the laborers the perspective was quite different. Like Odysseus in Homer's epic, they sailed outward on a sea journey, saw a world-altering war, and then returned to a homeland transformed. Odysseus had a wise friend, Mentor, whose skill in giving advice meant that his name would be used as a verb meaning "to give wise advice," but Odysseus also faced perilous adventures with Harpies and other monsters. The Chinese laborers met both friends and monsters (fewer of the former than the latter).

This chapter considers the following questions: Who were these laborers? Where did they come from? How were they selected, and under what terms? What were the differences between their treatment at the hands of the French and British? And what were the conditions of their odyssey to France?

### Contracts: Responsibility and Evasion

Technically, the Chinese were hired laborers recruited on the basis of written contracts. The workers for France were governed by contracts signed between the Huimin Company and Colonel Truptil, the French official in charge of recruitment in China. The term of contract for common (nonskilled) laborers was five years, and laborers could be employed only for national defense, not for military operations. Their rights and independence would be protected by law on the same basis as French citizens, especially the right to practice their religion. They would enjoy the same holidays as French workers employed in equivalent jobs; moreover, they would have one day's leave on Chinese National Day.[1] In case of illness or accident, the employer, not the government, was to provide medical attention and medicine as long as they were not sent to the hospital. If it were necessary to send a laborer back to China, the French war authority would take charge.[2]

The French contract was so detailed that it even included rations of different types of food. For instance, the Chinese were entitled to a daily minimum of 100 grams of rice, although European food might be substituted if it were accepted as equivalent by the Chinese laborers. On the day they left China for France, they were to receive two blue cotton shirts, two pairs of blue cotton trousers, one pair of cloth shoes, one hat, two pairs of Chinese socks, one padded garment, one pair of padded trousers, one padded quilt for traveling, cooking utensils, one traveling bed, one pair of woolen lined trousers, and one straw mat.

The French were serious and conscientious about understanding the different tastes and customs of the visiting laborers, and the authorities prepared general guidelines about how to accommodate Chinese culture and customs.[3] The French government even set up an interministerial conference, which met frequently to coordinate foreign laborer issues.[4]

Differences between the French and British Chinese labor programs were notable. One big difference was in their method of recruitment. While France recruited mainly through Chinese contractors, Britain did it by itself. The British terms for the Chinese were less detailed, very brief, and intentionally misleading. Instead of a five-year contract, the Britain recruits were signed for a three-year term; moreover, the British military authority could terminate a contract after one year, giving six months' notice. Compared with the contract Chinese workers signed with the French, the British terms were not so favorable. As one British government report boasted, of all the contracts made with the Chinese, this one "was, from our point of view, the most satisfactory. It gave us power to hold them for a long period of time with the option of getting rid of them in a moderately short time."[5] Beilby Alston, a senior British diplomat in Beijing, claimed that the British deal meant "we are getting coolies free of cost as far as Chinese Government is concerned and also free of conditions as to their employment, while the French under their agreement with Chinese Government pay more than we and are subjected to many conditions."[6] Some have even wondered whether the British contract, so "cleverly contrived," was designed to leave "the Chinese in something of a legal hiatus, especially when one recalls that they were exposed to the full rigors of British military justice once in Europe."[7]

Another difference was that the British contracted directly with individual laborers, while the French worked through the Huimin Company or other recruitment companies. The pay was different. The Chinese laborer received 1 franc each working day under the British contract, far less than the pay under the French. But the British laborers' family in China received a monthly stipend of 10 Mexican dollars (the French-recruited laborers did not have this arrangement). British-recruited laborers received food, clothing, housing, health services, transportation, bedding, and other supplies free of charge. On the day they left for France, British-recruited laborers received a 20-dollar bonus. They were to work ten hours per day, seven days per week, but a shorter or longer period could be fixed by labor control on a daily average, based on ten hours per day, for seven days' work each week. Due consideration might be given to Chinese festivals, which the labor control officer would decide. To be fair, the British Expeditionary Forces (BEF) did sometimes allow the Chinese to take days off for holidays such as Chinese New Year and the Mid-autumn Festival. Leaders of gangs of sixty men got a 50 percent increase over the others (totaling 1.5 francs), and the monthly stipend for his family in China was 15 dollars. Skilled laborers got higher pay. Travel to and from France, board, clothing, lodging, medical attention, light, and heat were provided in all cases. According to British practice, daily wages were not paid during a laborer's illness, but food was provided. Monthly pay in China continued for up to six weeks of illness. After six weeks, the stipend in China was stopped. No daily pay was provided for time lost owing to worker misconduct. For offenses involving loss of pay for a stretch of twenty days or more, deductions would be made from the monthly stipend in China.

For the Chinese laborers under both Britain and France, they received (at most) moderate compensation considering their sacrifices and suffering in the course of the war. They earned no long-term pension, and in the British case, the attitude toward compensation for serious injury was niggardly at best. One man who lost sight in one eye from a shell splinter, and another who was blinded while working in a trench, received only 75 dollars each by the British in compensation.

Another man who lost an eye due to trachoma was paid only 30 dollars, although his condition was aggravated while he was in service. The British argued that it was not service related, but this person had been recruited as a healthy man and was blind when repatriated. The War Office's own representative agreed that this seemed "harshly inadequate if not inhumane."[8]

The Chinese government intervened several times, still negotiating as late as 1918 about the compensation for sick and deceased laborers. But the British kept dragging their feet, even though some British field officers acknowledged that existing compensation scales were not adequate, and senior British medical officers especially urged reconsideration of the scale of compensation, in particular for totally disabled laborers, on the grounds that the severe nature of some injuries had not been fully appreciated when the scale was created. They maintained that a "lump sum of $120 for a young man disabled for life with wife and dependents cannot be regarded as adequate and must mean penury and want for recipients. Although the scale was voluntarily accepted in contracts, coolies were not informed they would be exposed to shell fire and those injured by enemy action appear in any case to have claim to further compensation."[9] Even the British Army Council acknowledged that the British government had concealed something and not been entirely forthcoming when it signed the Chinese as laborers. The British had promised that laborers should not take part in military operations, yet many Chinese were severely injured or died from bombardment. The Chinese could rightly argue that the injury from bombs was extra-contractual, since they did not anticipate exposure to enemy action on the Western Front.[10]

Under pressure from Beijing, eventually the War Office agreed to adopt an amended compensation scale in late 1918: sick and wounded men were granted up to twelve months' allotment pay in cases of injuries or sickness certified as having been incurred through or aggravated by service conditions; those men who became totally blind, totally maimed, or incurably insane were granted compensation equivalent to eighteen months' allotment pay. In addition, a wound gratuity of one, three, or six months' allotment pay was granted to men certified wounded by enemy action. Next of kin to a man who had died "owing to service" would be paid compensation of eighteen months' allotment pay.[11] Even given the modest scale of such compensation, the British Army Council "felt unable to countenance certain proposals for a scale of continuing pensions in view of the obvious difficulty of administering such pensions in

China," and because the new scale was put forward by their representatives in China, they were not disposed to favor any all-around increase in the rates of gratuity already authorized.[12]

## Recruiting in China: Competition and Friction

France and Britain wanted the very best Chinese labor. Most of the British-recruited laborers came from northern China, in particular Shandong Province, which the British felt produced stronger men who were accustomed to weather such as that in France. The French also focused on northerners, although their recruitment base included Shanghai and southern China as well. According to one official YMCA communication, because of their "superior physique and greater endurance, all excepting two or three thousand of the Chinese laborers were selected from North China."[13] As the *New York Times* reported, only "the best selected stock" was going to France, a "large percentage" six feet tall.[14]

Not surprisingly, with both France and Britain recruiting in northern China, competition and conflicts over recruiting produced diplomatic friction. Because Britain could take advantage of its more widespread interests and breadth of experience in China, it usually had the upper hand. Even more discomfiting to the French, the British were recruiting Chinese to work on French soil. To put a stop to this practice, French authorities asked Britain in February 1917 to halt recruitment, arguing that if British military camps needed help, they could use Chinese laborers already recruited by France.[15] Britain responded that labor was a military problem, and both countries' military authorities had already solved it. Britain then counter-proposed the creation of different recruitment zones to avoid competition.[16]

But France remained determined to change the recruiting situation. On February 21, 1917, the French government sent another memorandum to Britain, proposing that the entire recruiting operation for both Britain and France be placed under the control of Colonel Truptil, who would hand over a certain portion of the Chinese workers to Britain. The British Foreign Office cynically noted in private, "Are we right in thinking that our recruiting scheme is now more successful than the French and that we are in a position to supply them with as many coolies as they can ship to France?"[17] In a handwritten comment on the French proposal, one official in the British Foreign Office angrily wrote that it was "very bad of the French to do this," and charged that they "want to nullify all our efforts."[18] In the end, the French proposal fell on deaf ears, and the British stuck to their idea of separate zones.[19]

Once the French realized that Britain would not compromise and would continue to recruit its own laborers, France had to reconsider the British suggestion of separate recruitment zones. On September 7, 1917, France told Britain that the idea of separate recruitment zones would be fine if Britain agreed that the French zone was in north China and the British would move to the south. This proposal was bound to fail, of course, since the British had given up the idea of recruiting southerners very early in their campaign. Britain had an extensive and highly developed recruiting organization in the Shandong area and, according to the British authorities, its recruitment in north China had "met with such success that coolies are now being dispatched to France at the rate of ten thousand per month." The British also argued that the French military authorities knew the Chinese laborers' importance to the British war effort, and the British government highly valued the Chinese contribution. Thus the British Army Council "would view with alarm any action which might prejudice the supply of recruits."[20] The negotiations went nowhere.

The finger pointing and competition continued to the last year of the war. When the French went to Qingdao, close to the British recruitment base, to woo Chinese laborers, the British senior diplomat, Alston, angrily declared, "All recruitment in China is for the same cause and it seems obvious that there should be no competition between Allies."[21] The British secretary of state for foreign affairs, Arthur Balfour, officially complained in his memorandum to the French government that it should "recognize that all recruitment in China is directed to a common end." He warned the French that "any action which is calculated to retard or impair the united efforts of the Allies is much to be depreciated." He further claimed that the Chinese Labor Corps raised for service with the British expeditionary force in France had "proved a great success." He asked the French government for "a free field in the zone which they have selected for their operations."[22]

Although French recruiting numbers remained low, British competition was not the only problem. Transportation proved another serious problem for France. Although the Allies tried to cooperate toward their common goal, each country made its own arrangements for transport from 1914 to the end of 1917. By late 1917, France was running into serious difficulties moving its recruits, and British assistance was not always forthcoming.[23] For example, in an agreement made between France and Great Britain on December 3, 1916, special provisions had to be inserted regarding a French request for assistance with transporting laborers from Asia.[24] To a great extent, the French recruiting program depended on Britain's help with transportation.

The importance of transport is reflected in the fact that after the war, Britain used its preeminence in this area to influence American policy. "The two-million-man American expeditionary force in France," wrote David Kennedy, author of *Over Here,* "constituted a kind of hostage that could be marooned in Europe if the British should decide to deny the use of their transport vessels to the United States."[25] The transportation issue often led to clashes between France and Britain despite the creation of the Allied Maritime Transport Council in late 1917. France's repeated requests for more tonnage continued to fall on deaf ears.[26] France even tried to enlist Japan's assistance to transport its Chinese workers; the Japanese government, however, was not interested. Germany's unrestrained submarine warfare, which began in 1917, further aggravated the French problem. When the United States joined the war, the issue became increasingly delicate because so much tonnage would be required to transport American soldiers. So, because of the transportation shortfall, the French military authorities decided to cancel the recruitment mission in China in the middle of January 1918.[27] On February 10, 1918, the French government officially halted the program.[28]

Britain also faced a transportation problem, but initially a less serious one. British shipping in June and July 1917 was down 10 percent compared with the previous year,[29] and the shortfall of tonnage would eventually compel Britain to stop its recruitment program.[30] Joseph Maclay, Britain's shipping controller, argued on January 17, 1918, that the question of stopping the entire import of coolies should be immediately considered. In addition to the great relief that would be afforded on the transatlantic run, where it was not possible to meet the American troops' requirements, there was the heavy transit across Canada. An estimated "10,000 additional American troops might be brought per month if the coolie traffic was entirely stopped."[31] Great Britain terminated its recruitment mission in China on April 14, 1918, about two months after France cancelled its own program.[32] The British War Office closed its Weihaiwei operation in August and moved the administration to Qingdao.[33]

The requirements for laborers were tough. French-recruited men had to be between twenty and thirty-five years old, and had to pass physical examinations both before they were selected and again before landing in France. British-recruited Chinese could be between twenty and forty years old, and they also had to pass stringent physical examinations. Sometimes up to 60 percent of the applicants were rejected for physical reasons. One well-informed British officer wrote in his diary, "Sixty of a hundred of these men had to be rejected as physically unfit." The rejected men were marked with a purple ink stamp to prevent them from applying again and then sent away.[34] Grounds for rejection included bad teeth or eye diseases. Considering that dental care did not exist for poor rural laborers, and eye problems went untreated, it is not surprising that so many failed the exam.

Trachoma was the principal reason men were rejected.[35] The British found that 10 to 15 percent of the early arrivals in France were still affected. As soon as the heavy incidence of trachoma was recognized, the War Office sent a telegram to the recruiting centers in China with instructions to require a stricter eye examination and to reject all men suffering from conjunctivitis. With the tougher examinations, the trachoma rate on arrival in France sank to 3 percent.[36]

Manico Gull, a British officer intimately involved in the Chinese labor business who later served as a paymaster for the laborers in China, provided a vivid picture of the process at the depot in Weihaiwei where recruits were "taken out of the reception shed in batches, they pass into a room in the center of the Depot where, stark naked, they are tested in exactly the same way as the British Tommy and may be rejected exactly on any one of the twenty-one grounds, from phthisis, bronchitis, or venereal disease to chronic inflammation of the eyes (trachoma), malaria, or bad teeth. Rejects get back into their old clothes and are given passages home and the cost of food on the return trip."[37]

One Chinese laborer described the examination experience this way:

When I arrived there I had to pass an examination. A foreign doctor felt of my body in different places. He held the flat of his hand over my chest, tapping the fingers with the fingers of his other hand. He examined the pulse of my left hand, but failed to examine the right one. He clamped an instrument into his ears and after shutting his eyes, applied the free end of the instrument to my chest here and there, front and back, while I had to count each time up to three. He opened my mouth to examine my tongue and teeth. He felt of my scalp. Even my eyelids he turned up. I confess I was glad when this gentleman moved on to the next fellow in the line for I had not the slightest idea what he might have in his head to try next. It was the strangest examination I ever saw. I was not asked to write a single character. However, I passed, and moved along inside the wire enclosure. There I found I was but one of several tens of thousands.[38]

After they passed the initial physical examination, Chinese recruits entered the so-called sausage machine, the process of turning a Chinese into a laborer for the British labor corps. The process included a haircut (getting rid of the queues), a thorough wash, the physical examination, being issued a brass bracelet with an identification number, and clean garments.[39] One prominent feature of the process was fingerprinting.[40] Each laborer was thumb-printed and assigned a number that was stamped on a brass identification bracelet in English and Chinese; the bracelet was then securely fastened around its wearer's wrist by a stud. The number was at once registered with its owner's name in English and Chinese upon what was called an identification paper. These became the laborer's only identification—his name was of no importance. By his number he was known in the Chinese recruitment camps and in Europe, by that number he was paid, and under that number each man's allotment was kept at the pay office. On arrival in Europe, the Chinese were fingerprinted several times again. One witness wrote, "When the coolies line up to be 'printed,' an impression of each digit is taken separately, then another impression of the whole five simultaneously, and the whole are taken in duplicate, making a total of twenty-four separate impressions for each coolie."[41]

British consul-general J. T. Pratt (later Sir John) was instrumental in designing and developing the recruitment procedure, including the idea of using numbers instead of names.[42] This system emerged from the chaos of the recruitment program's early days. Alwyne Ogden, a British diplomat in China who was actively involved in recruitment, later shared an inside story about the mess caused by the War Office's assumption that the process would be easy. "All you do," the British originally thought, "is get the man's name, his father's address, and send him a postal order once a month." However, as Ogden went on, "We found out after a bit that it wasn't so easy. To begin with, the man didn't know his own name. If you questioned him, he'd say 'well, I come from the Wong family village, so my name is probably Wong'. You'd say 'all right, well what is your personal name?' and he'd grin and say 'Wong.' We'd say 'well, what are you called at home' and he'd say 'well, I'm known as Number Five, or Little Dog or Big Nose.'" So to make it easier, they gave each laborer a number.[43]

The moment recruits left the sausage machine provided great amusement for a British officer. He described how the newly minted laborer "emerged from the nude anxiety of the doctor's chamber to be clothed in Depot garments, his old clothes remaining in a heap on the floor, and smilingly conscious at the symbolism of the change, he strutted into the next room as pleased as Punch." His bracelet securely fastened, the recruit turned next to a table where Chinese scribes filled in his papers to record his age, height, and the date of his appointment. The proud laborer then provided his address and that of his next of kin. Most important of all, he gave the name, address, and relation of the person to whom he wished his allotment or pay in China to be given. Next he passed into a waiting room where he was assigned to his laborers' section. The final stage was to put his fingerprints on both his identification paper and contract, the only reliable method of preventing substitution.[44]

One laborer remembered what happened to him after he had passed the physical examination and entered service with the British:

That day was a turning point in my life. For one thing, I was no longer my own master. I had nothing to say about the food I ate, the clothes I wore or how I wore them, the place where I slept or when I wished to sleep or get up, where I desired to go or the hour of my going and returning, what I desired to do or how I wanted to do it. Everything, it seemed, had been thought out for every one of us long before we arrived. My body seemed to be the important thing; for no one concerned himself over what might be going on in my head. It was assumed that I could see, hear, and talk. Of my own free will I was thinking constantly and comparing the old life with the new. . . . The last tie between the old and the new was broken when the clothes in which I arrived at the camp were taken from me and sent home. I hardly recognized myself in the strange uniform they gave me. My friends would not have known me either. Nor would they have believed it was their friend Li performing the most unusual tasks which I did daily without question. I was a changed man outwardly and I was conscious of an inner change already beginning. . . . Our officers devoted much attention to our bodily health. Whether we had been inoculated for smallpox as children or not, all of us received scratches in our arms according to the Western method. Food was good and plentiful. Windows were kept open at night. Hot baths with soap were provided. I recalled that never before had I felt so fine.[45]

The British-recruited Chinese stayed in camps in China for several months to train and drill in camps surrounded by barbed wire and security guards to prevent escape. Immediately after visiting a labor camp in Shandong Province, Daryl Klein, a second lieutenant in one of these camps, wrote that it was "for all the world like a prison camp" or "military camp."[46] Each day the laborers marched in columns, in uniformly tan leather-colored coats, with dark brown caps on their heads, drilling without arms. Although they were clumsy in the beginning, according to Klein, the Chinese "are quick to learn and of a willing temperament."[47]

## Numbers and Types

How many laborers eventually made the journey to France? All in all, about 140,000 Chinese laborers went to France to work for British expeditionary forces or French defense-related factories or companies. According to a detailed report, the Huimin Company organized twenty-five shipments of French-recruited laborers. Three sailed in one month from Tianjin. The first departure, on July 12, 1916, involved 1,698 laborers; the second, on July 17, 1916, had 1,365 men; the third, on July 25, 1916, numbered 1,984, making a total of 5,047 laborers. Following the Laoxikai disaster, Huimin had to move south to recruit through its branch in Hong Kong. Recruitment in south China started in December 1916 and lasted about five months. During those months, the Hong Kong Huimin Company managed to send laborers to France five times, with a total number of 3,221. Huimin also started to recruit laborers in east China at its Pukou operation.

From Pukou near Nanjing, Huimin in 1917 sent laborers to France fourteen times, totaling 18,950 laborers, as reflected in the table on the next page.

Huimin also recruited from Qingdao between August and December 1917. Three cohorts left from Qingdao: the first had 1,411 men, the second 1,002, and the third 2,000.[48] By the end of 1917, the Huimin Company had recruited and sent 32,646 Chinese laborers to France. Besides Huimin, other organizations soon got involved in recruiting laborers. The Société Franco-Chinoise d'Education recruited from Yunnan and Guangxi Provinces.[49] Shanghai Xinye Company, Daoxin Bank, Guangzhou Shamian Zhili Company, and Hong Kong Limin Company, among others, briefly recruited for the French. But Huimin's involvement was the most long-lived. Daoxin Bank drafted skilled workers in the Shanghai area and sent about 700 men. Hong Kong Limin Company recruited about 2,000 laborers.[50] The Shanghai Xinye Company recruited about 600 skilled workers from the Shanghai area who arrived in France in

Date of departure and number of laborers from Pukou, 1917

| Date of departure | Number of laborers |
| --- | --- |
| March 10 | 1,819 |
| March 29 | 2,200 |
| April 12 | 800 |
| May 17 | 660 |
| June 5 | 900 |
| July 20 | 2,000 |
| July 29 | 409 |
| July 30 | 1,200 |
| August 6 | 1,800 |
| September 22 | 1,800 |
| October 1 | 1,437 |
| October 18 | 2,000 |
| October 28 | 600 |
| November 19 | 1,325 |

October 1916. Daoxin Puyi Company recruited more than 1,000 skilled workers from Shanghai.[51] Although these numbers are not absolutely precise, it is safe to say that approximately 40,000 Chinese laborers were recruited for service with the French in the course of the Great War.

The first British contingent of 1,086 Chinese left Weihaiwei on January 18, 1917.[52] The last left Qingdao on March 2, 1918, with 1,899 laborers. A total of 94,458 Chinese men arrived in France under British auspices.[53] On November 30, 1917, the highest war authority, the British Army Council, proposed recruiting a total of 150,000 Chinese laborers for its war effort in France.[54] In early 1918, the British authorities repatriated Egyptian and South African laborers largely due to political consider-ations, and raising 150,000 Chinese had seemed crucial. But this ambi-tious plan was thwarted by the shortage of shipping tonnage.[55] By April 1918, the British Army Council decided that recruitment of Chinese la-borers had to be stopped.[56] On April 30, 1918, "Owing to the impossi-bility of providing transport both now and in the near future, it has been found necessary definitely to close the recruiting of Chinese coolies for labour in France, and to cancel the contracts of those coolies already en-rolled and awaiting embarkation in the depot at Wei Hai Wei."[57]

The majority of Chinese recruited by Britain came from Shandong and Chili (present-day Hebei) Provinces, though a few came from Honan, Ji-angsu, Hubei, Shansi, Anhui, Fujian, Sichuan, Guangdong, Yunnan, and other places.[58] Most were men from the countryside who wanted to make a better living by going to France. Some were soldiers or former soldiers. A large number were skilled workers such as carpenters, blacksmiths, mechanics, and so on. A few even had decent jobs in China as teachers or clerks; these were men eager to see the world, especially the West, to gain new perspectives. Most of the men were illiterate, honest, and hard-working folks, but their numbers also included a few bad apples with major character flaws. According to Shi Yixuan, a Harvard graduate who worked with the Chinese in France for many months, some men came to Europe to satisfy a desire for adventure, some to better their lot, but most came because of economic pressures at home.[59]

W. W. Peter, a Harvard-trained YMCA official, tells of a unique worker who had been a teacher in Shandong Province and even taught some Western subjects. He was quite interested in West and had read widely about it. "Then came your honorable war," he told Peter. "The newspapers said it was a world war. It must have been for even I who lived eight thousand miles away felt its influence." The war truly came close to him, with the British and Japanese forces fighting the Germans in Shandong. "It is impossible for me to tell you how confusing the issues of this war are to me, a Chinese. What is it all about?" He became so interested in the war that he often spent hours discussing the question with friends and neighbors. "Finally we agreed that we did not know why the foreigners were fighting among themselves any more than we knew why they did any one of a thousand things differently from us. We did agree, however, that it was a serious situation." One day he saw a notice put out by the British and French authorities calling for thousands of laborers. It was pasted on the walls of the city gate and had the stamp of the local official. Soon a great crowd gathered. "We concluded the Germans were winning the war as they prophesied. Why else should it be necessary for England and France to appeal to Chinese to help them? Who was winning the war did not interest me. I saw in this notice an opportunity I had not dreamed would be mine. Then and there I resolved to become a coolie myself in order to visit these foreign countries." But those enlisting in the French service had to go to Pukou, which was far from Shandong. So he decided to serve with the British, whose recruitment center was located in nearby Weihaiwei.

This personal story indicates that there was a type of laborer who chose to go to France out of a desire to learn about the world and find out about different civilizations. This man was motivated by both the opportunity to learn and to make money. The same laborer proudly told

Peter that by choosing to become a laborer in France, he had indeed learned a lot:

I had not made a mistake. I was being taught by example the foreign point of view. At the same time they were paying me more money than I received as a teacher. In addition my family was due to get an allotment from the British government direct just as soon as I should leave China for France. There was no squeeze or wine money to pay any of these foreigners. Best of all, within three years I should know more about foreigners than could be found out in any other way. Was it not worth while to sign a contract for three or even five years in order to return to China able to speak with some authority? In my first enthusiasm I forgot even the dangers through which I would have to pass.[60]

Several days before departure, medical reexaminations were carried out, in which about 6 per cent were rejected because of eye troubles. At sunset, they "stood a little apart from their successful mates" and had to return to their villages.[61]

## The Odyssey Begins

The journey from China to France was extremely challenging. Some groups went to France by the Suez Canal and Cape of Good Hope, but most traveled through the Pacific and Canada.[62] Some lost their lives due to German submarine attacks. How many Chinese lost their lives on the sea en route to France? One source suggests that at least 752 Chinese laborers died in German attacks.[63] One official Chinese document indicates that the Chinese laborers killed by German submarines numbered 713.[64] Although these sources do not agree perfectly, we may still safely conclude that at least 700 lost their lives before they reached France.[65] In one incident alone, about 500 Chinese were killed at sea in early 1917.[66] Chinese diplomat Li Jun, whose main job was to look after men working for the French, claimed in a report dated January 18, 1919, that 476 laborers had been lost in a submarine attack on the French vessel *Arthos* (another account suggested the count was 581).[67] But the total figure may never be known because the records are not complete. One woman learned that her husband had died at sea only some years afterward, when returning laborers related how he died in the 1917 attack. Upon learning the nature of her husband's death, she petitioned the Chinese government for state compensation on the argument that her husband had died for the nation *(wei guo juan qu)*.[68]

The laborers also came through rough seas. In the early days of the twentieth century, crossing the Pacific and Atlantic oceans by ship was a challenge for anyone, even military personnel. The Canadian medical captain L. J. Serbert, assigned to the Chinese labor corps, wrote in his diary comments such as "very rough in bay," "rotten day," "rough sea—sick!" "rougher, sicker," "roughest, sickest," "had a rotten sleep, too hot," and "rougher than yesterday, not feeling any too well."[69] And as a captain, his living conditions were much better than those of the Chinese. Moreover, many of the Chinese had never seen the sea or boarded a ship before. One can imagine how hard it was for them. Daryl Klein described their discomfort this way: "I went down into one of the bunk-holds amidships, where an odd-150 of my company are quartered. I could hear their groans before I got down to them. Like a house of mild torture. The majority had collapsed. A few, their strength suddenly gone, lay on the boarded floor, unable to climb into their bunks. It was a spectacle of weakness."[70] Royal Douglas Wood, a British officer who escorted the Chinese from Shandong to France wrote in his war diary that three-quarters of the Chinese had suffered from seasickness in the early stage of their journey.[71]

The already rough journey was made rougher by the long-standing practice in the "coolie trade" of treating the men like cargo.[72] The *New York Times* echoed a long time racial stereotype when it reported that a "Chinese can flourish in a space that would hardly do a white man for his grave."[73] Klein wrote that "the coolies are not passengers capable of finding each his cabin; the coolies are so much cargo, livestock, which has to be packed away, so many head in a hold."[74] An American YMCA chaplain and interpreter who worked with the Chinese in France commented that the transportation provided for the Chinese was "often devoid of even minimum creature comforts."[75] The men were put into a poorly ventilated, cramped hold where each individual occupied a living space the size of a clothes closet, and often even less. One day, proceeding through the Malacca Straits, the Chinese, who were confined sweltering below decks, threatened to storm the deck and stage an uprising against the ship's commanders; violence seemed inevitable. The chaplain enlisted the support of the rest of the Chinese Labor Corps (CLC) team staff to join him in asking the captain to give the Chinese more drinking water and increased time on deck in the open air, as well as authorizing more frequent health checks below decks by the ship's doctor.[76] Sometimes the men did not even have enough to eat. One British NCO in the Army Service Corps remembered that the Chinese laborers were sometimes so hungry that whenever bread was available, they overate so much that they had to lie flat on the deck.[77]

Despite these ordeals and suffering, the Chinese, by and large, held up well. Klein observed, "All things considered, their behaviour is wonderfully good."[78] Their spirit was high when they arrived in France. British officer Manico Gull recalled the arrival at a northern French port of a thousand Chinese laborers. The Chinese, "whose bronzed faces, some as immobile as carved wood, others alight with laughter, in brown felt caps with ear flaps of gray fur . . . bulging canvas knapsacks dyed a dark brick red, and blue cotton jackets and trousers added a touch of color altogether new to a scene stereotyped by nearly three years of war."

Presently somebody raised a cheer. The Chinese responded quickly and in a few moments hundreds of hands were waving and clapping, and the noise of launches and shunting engines was drowned in hurrahs. The skipper of the vessel, a little square-built man with a jolly face, caught the infection of the moment and felt that it called for a speech. "Here you," he said, turning to the group of civilians who stood amidships. "You can talk their funny old jingo; come up, one of you, on to the bridge with me' and tell 'em I wish 'em luck." "Up you go," said a well-known Tientsin man to one of his companions. "Help the skipper to do the polite." "Hold up for a moment," the latter broke in, "let me get a megaphone first. I like people to hear what I've got to say when I make a speech." He soon found a megaphone. "Now then," he said, thrusting it into the hands of his interpreter, "follow me." The two mounted to the bridge, reached the center and faced the bows, the chatter of the coolies below snapping off into silence as they saw what was happening. "Now tell your lads," said the skipper, "that I'm mighty glad to have brought them over, that I hope they'll have a good time in France do a good job of work, and go back to their homes full of money and health and strength. Add any fringes of your own that you like."

After telling this story, Gull commented that for the Chinese laborers,

their emigration from the shores of Shantung will take its place in history certainly as one of the most picturesque and interesting, possibly as one of the most important aspects of the great European War. For never before this war has the East provided the West with manpower on anything approaching the same elaborate scale. It has hurled itself against the West many times, compelled the West to unite more than once and, of course, colored European life and thought in a variety of ways but it has never before, practically the whole of it simultaneously, taken sides in a huge European conflict. And the especially interesting characteristic of China's participation in this unique development is that (at the time of writing at all events) in a conflict waged for the extermination of militarist ideals she is engaged industrially only.[79]

One laborer had never seen a ship before. "I was sharply reminded," he said, "of the beginning of these dangers when one day we were ordered to get everything ready to leave" for France. "I thought of the danger from overcrowding and capsizing. . . . On approaching the big boat, my heart beat fast in fear for I saw with dismay that the boat was already full. Yet we climbed on board and were led down many stairs till I was sure we were near the bottom of the sea. . . . When I climbed back up, the shore was no longer in sight. I had left home." He was both nervous and worried. "My courage almost failed me. What journey into the unknown was I beginning? How unprepared was I for the great adventure!" But he soon became interested in anything Western and his respect for foreign technology increased greatly while he was aboard ship. "The great ship forced its way through the water day and night." "I had seen and heard so many strange and wonderful things that the foreigners were able to do, I believed everything without question. Surely they were superior people. Often I thought to myself, 'What a wonderful blessing to us it would be if without fear, suspicion, or reservation, we could invite them to help us in China.' "[80]

Knowingly or not, these unsophisticated but serious men had set out on a mission, a mission perhaps motivated by their own reasons or even patriotism than to save Western civilization, but a mission nonetheless. Most got their first impressions of the West not from France, but from Canada. The next chapter recounts the Canadian episode of their odyssey, with both helpful mentors and threatening monsters.

# 3

---

## THE HIDDEN HISTORY OF THE
## SECRET CANADIAN PATHWAY

---

Most British-recruited Chinese traveled to France via Canada and re-turned to China by the same route after the war was over. The Canadian transport program was a double success. The first success was to transport Chinese laborers to France via Canada and return them to China by the same route after the war was over. From early March 1917 to late March 1918, 84,244 Chinese laborers crossed Canada on their way to France. The second success, to which we shall return, was to keep the operation secret. But a striking lack of success lay in rewarding the sacrifices and contributions of the Chinese with Canadian recognition, much less gratitude, or in changing general attitudes toward Chinese.

The Canadian transport program would prove significant for several countries in different ways. First, the mass movement of an alien population across the entire extent of its territory was unprecedented in Canadian history, never mind that the Chinese were headed to where so many Canadians had already gone and for the same reason—to join the British war effort. Second, because Canada was the link between China and Europe, many Chinese got their first glimpse of the West through their Canadian experience. Third, the treatment and management of these laborers in Canada provides a unique window into the Canadian national character and attitudes toward the Chinese at the time. In other words, these laborers' experience is an instance where we can study the interaction among the three nations, China, Canada, and Britain. Still, the laborers' experience is a story not known to many people, including Canadians. As one Canadian historian has noted, the Chinese labor corps "finds not a single mention in standard studies of the Canadian war effort, and the political histories of the period equally ignore it."[1] This chapter discusses that hidden history.

## Transportation and the Journey

After the British military began recruiting Chinese laborers to support British expeditionary forces in France, the problem of transportation loomed large. This challenge became even greater once the Germans adopted unlimited submarine attacks. The British soon decided to use Canada as a middle point. In March 1917, the Canadian government, through the British colonial foreign secretary, received an official request from "the mother country" to facilitate transportation of Chinese laborers for the British imperial government; all expenses incurred in connection with the movement were to be borne by the imperial government. The Canadian military authority was to be in charge of the transportation, but many other offices, such as Immigration, soon got involved as well. The Canadian Pacific Railway Company was commissioned to handle the cross-continental stage.[2] Transport of Chinese labor was a top priority for the Canadian government and perhaps the British government as well. There was constant competition for accommodation on ships proceeding to Europe among Canadian troops, U.S. troops, Chinese laborers, and ordinary passengers. On October 29, 1917, the admiralty requested that all arrangements for Canadian troop transport should be made by the Navy Department, and that Canadian troops and Chinese laborers should have precedence over U.S. troops.[3]

The passage of Chinese laborers through Canada began on April 2, 1917 with the arrival of the vessel *Empress of Russia,* and lasted more than three years. On arrival at port and prior to disembarking, the men were once again medically examined under the supervision of the Department of Immigration before being entrained for transit. They would eventually embark for Europe at an eastern port, usually Montreal in the summer months, and St. John or Halifax in the fall and winter.

Canadian medical captain Harry Livingstone witnessed the Chinese laborers' journey firsthand. Livingstone accompanied one group of Chinese across Canada and on to France in 1917 and kept a detailed journal. His unpublished journal gives an intimate and closely observed account of the journey in Canada and on the sea. The account that follows is a compilation of his observations.

Livingstone's journey began at Weihaiwei, where the laborers were to embark on the *Empress of Russia* on October 29, 1917. According to Livingstone, the men were all vaccinated. They were then marched to some tubs, where they were given a rapid disinfectant bath and new underwear, clothes, socks, slippers, hats, and kit bags containing tins, blankets, bed-rolls, and so on. As they emerged again from another door, they were completely different in appearance and according to Livingstone, "looked fine." Most of them had their brown raincoats on by this time, and Livingstone was amused to see the laborers exchanging slippers to find a pair that fit. The laborers were arranged in sections, and a brass number corresponding to their section was pinned onto each chest. Now they marched to the pay department in a small building nearby to receive some money.

This completed, they marched in single file out the gate to the open ground where relatives and friends waited to say goodbye. String after string of firecrackers was set off to ensure a good voyage free from devils, and the travelers then marched down the roadway along the pier to the lighter, where one thousand or more crowded on. As the ship steamed slowly away to sea, the men were allowed up on a restricted area of the deck. They crowded the rail and watched, many with tears in their eyes, as the old familiar hills and mountains of their native land faded from view and a big strange new world lay before them. Many suffered from seasickness.[4]

They arrived in Vancouver on November 14, 1917 and immediately boarded a train bound for Halifax. There were guards stationed at each doorway throughout the train. Each coach had a supply of drinking water and a small stove that the Chinese used to cook their food. The seats were of wood and could be made into berths at night (both upper and lower berths were used). Two laborers slept in the lower and two slept in the upper berth, but sometimes three (or even four) men would huddle together for warmth in one lower berth. Sometimes men slept during the daytime when the upper berths were supposed to be closed. A man might stow away inside an almost closed berth, where he was safe from being caught and sure of getting a good sleep. The cars were cold, so the Chinese would stick their noses well down into their sleeves; because they had no gloves, they shoved one hand into the opposite sleeve.

Each afternoon at around three o'clock, six men with a corporal from each car proceeded to the commissariat and secured food rations sufficient for twenty-four hours. The food would then be cooked in the coaches and served out to the Chinese in small rice bowls and hot water tins. During mealtime, Chinese laborers sat in all kinds of attitudes, scooping large chunks of congealed rice into their mouths with chopsticks and following each mouthful with sips of hot water. They rarely drank cold water; the nearer the boiling point, the more they liked it.

After the evening meal, most Chinese either fell asleep or lounged around listening to stories told by older comrades. Some surely wondered what their friends and relatives way back in their warm country were doing and when would they see them again. Every evening, when Livingstone walked through to see whether they were all comfortable and in good health, they would ask him to sit down and talk. Sometimes he did stop briefly and then the Chinese plied him with all kinds of questions. Often they would ask, "Is this still Canada?" or "How many more days until we get off the train?" Someone might be sitting cross-legged in a dark corner beneath the upper berth, playing a love song on the *erhu,* a small Chinese fiddle. The men around him would lie there listening and dreaming, or someone nearby would sing to the strains of the fiddle. Livingstone sometimes stopped to listen for a few minutes and told them that their music was fine, a comment that delighted the musicians. Sometimes Livingstone would take the instrument and try to play, and all the Chinese in the coach would laugh at his poor efforts. Many men would play chess on boards made out of pasteboard, but a few played on regular boards they had brought from China.

By day, they passed the time by admiring the scenery. In the Rockies they were lost in amazement at the high peaks covered with snow, often exclaiming "Look at that big hill!" At every divisional point where they stopped for twenty minutes or so, the windows would all go up, and as many heads as could fit would stick out, looking at the strange sights. The white officers walked up and down the platform, and the Chinese would hold out money and ask them to buy candies or apples for them. Livingstone and his fellow officers did buy them things such as apples, and the Chinese paid for them. Sometimes Livingstone bought many nut bars at the train stations and then handed them to the Chinese through the windows. At every store Livingstone went into at these divisional points, he picked up small advertisement cards or pictures such as motion picture advertisements and handed them to the Chinese as he walked along the platform. The men always watched for Livingstone coming out of the stores to see whether he had anything under his arm for them. Whenever Livingstone and a fellow officer named Nette had to run and jump onto the moving train, the Chinese would look worried and yell for them to hurry. When Livingstone then walked through, the laborers would all smile and say they were glad he and his friend hadn't been left behind.

Livingstone recorded in his journal that one "good looking, kind-hearted" laborer who had his berth in one corner of a coach used to always smile when Livingstone went through and say "Weihaiwei" in a high-pitched tone. Livingstone guessed the man had heard him saying it that way in fun and would always call it out to him no matter where he and Livingstone crossed paths, whether on the platform at a station or anywhere else. Often on the boats and even at Noyelles, France, Livingstone would pass a gang of laborers and suddenly hear that voice saying those words, and would see the smiling laborer's face among his comrades. Another laborer who was "also good looking" and who had bought an English skullcap of vivid green from a crew member of the *Empress of Russia* knew the words "good morning," and every time he saw Livingstone, no matter what the hour of day or night, he would say these words. When Livingstone responded, he would smile broadly, "showing an elegant set of clean even teeth."

Livingstone relates that two or three times during the trip through Canada a train car had to be changed because of some defect, and all the inmates of the car would pack up their kits and march out. At one place, a first-class coach was given to them, evidently because it was the only spare coach at that divisional point. The seats were all covered in velvet, and the floors were carpeted. The Chinese could be seen jumping up and down on the seats to test the springs and feel the plush upholstered seats. One fellow dropped cigarette ashes on the carpet and at once got down on his knees and carefully swept them up with his hands. The Chinese were not allowed to even visit any other coach, nor were they allowed out at any station. Livingstone wrote in his journal that an officer who had accompanied most of the Chinese labor battalions across the continent said that they were the finest lot of men he had ever seen and the most well behaved. At Halifax, it was not long before the officers had all the Chinese out in line on the platform with their kits and baggage. They shouted with delight at setting foot on the ground again. Officers checked their numbers as they marched past. Half a dozen men were left behind on account of illness; they were transported away in an ambulance that met the train. One or two of them began to cry at being left behind in this big strange place.

On the voyage to Europe, every available space in the hold of the ship was occupied. The second-class cabins and smoking and dining rooms were packed with Chinese. In the evenings, they prepared their beds on top of the tables or on top of steam coils, and some would even swing arm chairs so they faced one another and roll up in their blankets fully clothed. The men sleeping on the chairs struck some very funny attitudes, and Livingstone wondered how they could sleep at all. One night hammocks were given out, and many Chinese fell headlong out the opposite side. Many men did not like them because they had always slept on hard beds at home. Before retiring, they would often have a small theatrical performance down below, where there would be so many gathered that the air grew heavy. When Livingstone and his fellow officers put in an appearance, the Chinese would want them to take a seat up front, which the officers usually did, and then they would listen to the singer who was accompanied by a musician or two, or sometimes a regular Chinese band with drums, cymbals, and flutes. The singer would tell a long story, perhaps, thought Livingstone, about some green-faced robber or pirate who ran away with the king's wife or something like this, singing out words as he went along making all kinds of faces and going through the typical movements with his arms and hands as actors did on the Chinese stage. The audience would listen attentively, and many kept their eyes on the white officers to see how they liked the show. Every little while, Livingstone and his fellow officers would say "Very good, very good!" and the Chinese would all smile.

One twenty-year-old invited Livingstone to visit his hometown Chufu after the war was over. He said he would give Livingstone a horse to ride; and peanuts, candy, crabs, sweet potatoes, and plenty of rice to eat. Another man was painfully cold because he lost his socks and had been going around with only his slippers on. Livingstone bought the man a pair of woolen socks in Halifax, and he almost cracked his skull on the deck bowing in thanks.

Livingstone got several Chinese acts for a concert held for the officers one night after they had entered the War Zone. It opened with a Chinese orchestra selection, and the drums and brass cymbals made such a noise that the officers had to stop them because any submarine in the area would surely have been attracted to the noise. The Chinese laborers all listened attentively when the ladies sang or the piano played.

When the laborers finally arrived in France, Livingstone wrote in his private journal, "I was sorry to leave them as they certainly were to leave us . . . I always found them to be a jolly good-natured easily-managed crowd . . . always appreciating any kindness you would show them, and forever trying to do something for you in one way or another."[5]

## Perilous Journey to France

To expedite the movement of Chinese to France or back to China, the Canadians sometimes lowered their safety standards. For instance, the shipping company wanted its boats to travel without the lifesaving equipment required by law; the excuse was that the Chinese were "recruited for war purposes." But the safety inspector refused to allow it; he was "not prepared to recommend that any exemption should be made in this case unless it is to be looked upon as a war measure, in which case, I think that some other department should take the responsibility of ordering the ships to be moved without having sufficient life saving appliances." Canadian war authorities eventually decided that steamships carrying Chinese laborers could forego the legally required equipment.[6] The Canadian Pacific Railway Company (CPR) also took full advantage of opportunities to cut other corners in the name of military need. On May 4, 1917, CPR's F. L. Wanklyn wrote to the Deputy Minister of Marine and Fisheries, arguing "you are fully aware of all the facts in connection with this special business, and in order to expedite same to the fullest extent we ask authority from the Department to be relieved of the obligation to add additional equipment," which would be necessary in order to comply with existing regulations. In view of "the urgency of the business and the difficulty at the present time in obtaining additional equipment," the CPR asked official inspectors to allow the company to "carry on this business with the equipment already available; better than called for in the regulations just prior to recent change, and providing one life buoy for every soul on board." The request was approved the next day.[7]

British military authorities encouraged the Canadians to waive their safety laws. As early as March 20, 1917, London had sent a secret telegram to Ottawa asking the Canadian government to waive regulations in the case of Canadian liners "in view of importance of using each steamer to the fullest extent possible for the purpose both of reducing tonnage required and of expediting the arrival of coolies in France."[8]

It may have made some sense to lower safety standards in a time of war, but London did the same even after the war's end. Once again the stated reason was to expedite transport of the Chinese, this time returning from Europe. As London informed the Canadians in 1919, "In Europe there are about eighty thousand Chinese coolies waiting transport to China, and the shipping controller hopes that your government will waive regulations . . . as before, as it is very important to complete movement as soon as possible." Boats carrying Chinese did not need full compliance with regulations for adequate numbers of life rafts.[9]

The Chinese were subject to various restrictions. Although they were medically inspected before leaving China and remained under medical supervision on the voyage to Vancouver, they were also required to pass quarantine at William Head, off the port of Victoria. Furthermore, Canada then imposed a $500 head tax on every entering Chinese. Because the Chinese laborers were actually on their way to Europe, the Canadian government agreed to waive their tax. But in exchange, the Chinese were not allowed to leave their trains or have any freedom of movement. As long as they were in Canada, every precaution was taken to prevent escape. Special railway military guards were placed on the trains, and more guards were stationed at the camps—barbed wire–enclosed compounds. Checking these virtually captive workers in and out of Canada was carried out by the Department of Immigration, and the guarding of Chinese returning to China via Canada was performed by a detail called "Special Guard, C.M.P.C.," or the Canadian Military Police Corps.[10]

When there was no ready transportation at Halifax, the Chinese were at first held on board ship at Vancouver, but this proved impractical.[11] In July 1917, the Canadian Minister of the Interior wrote in a memo, "While occasionally these men are taken across Canada and shipped from an Atlantic port without any delay, it sometimes happens that a ship is not available and the coolies are detained in Canada for period which may run up to four weeks. Heretofore these labourers have been kept on board ship but this entails the holding of valuable tonnage and it has been suggested that while waiting they should be accommodated in camps, under guard, and Petawawa [in Ontario] has been considered a suitable locality." The Petawawa camp would be built with a LePage wire fence surrounding the coolie compound; that fence was capped with barbed wire and had four 12-foot gates and two 4-foot gates. The memo went on to suggest that "it might be possible to make use of these coolies during the waiting period, and utilize their labour for harvest or other purposes. It is evident that there are many difficulties in the way of carrying out such a scheme"—such as preventing escapes.[12]

Although the Chinese were not allowed to leave their trains, as soon as they reached the camps, the Canadians were creative about putting them to work. On September 27, 1917, the commanding officer of the

32nd and 38th battalions of the Chinese labor corps reported 2,288 Chinese at the Petawawa camp.

> In regard to detailing further working parties, I regret that I must ask you to inform H.Q. that, owing to the state of the men's shoes, which are flimsy things at best and only intended to last the voyage, it is necessary to withdraw as soon as possible all the men at present on work outside the compound. Tomorrow, Friday, if weather permits, I shall send the men out as before and should be much obliged if you would let me know how soon the work on which they are engaged can be completed. For instance, I understand that a day's work in the quarry would complete the piling of the stone broken. On Saturday, which is a Chinese festival, I am afraid we shall be unable to get the men to work.

The Chinese also did work for the Canadian navy.[13] A military file notes, "At the coolie camp in Canada, some 2,000 were employed for a short period whilst awaiting embarkation and they paid 10 cents per coolie per day."[14]

But the camps had many problems. Captain T. Pugh at the Petawawa Camp stated in early 1918 that the management of the camp "was very unsatisfactory." In the early days, this led to poorly planned and inefficient handling of supplies as different parties of Chinese laborers arrived, resulting in considerable wasted effort and material. Much the same thing happened at the breaking up of camp, and matters were not helped by the commandant's time being fully taken up with managing the laborers.[15]

The military also had problems with the CPR. On September 17, 1917, John Hughes, Inspector General for western Canada, wrote the following in a memo to the adjutant-general at militia headquarters in Ottawa:

> While the responsibility of furnishing railway guards to convoy Chinese coolies across the continent is placed upon me, I receive no official notification from headquarters as to the arrival of steamers at Vancouver, or to what point the guards who are in charge of trains are to proceed. I have endeavoured to cooperate with the CPR officials on every occasion, but the CPR has not done the same with me.[16]

Even given all these problems, the Canadians must be credited for successfully carrying out an unprecedented cross-continental transportation program (in total secrecy).

## Secrecy of the Canadian Transport Program

When the war started in Europe, Canada supported and followed its mother country closely by passing the War Measures Act, which granted the government power to muzzle the press. The act created a brand new office called the Chief Press Censor of Canada. Colonel Ernest Chambers, a former journalist and editor, was appointed as chief censor. When the British asked the Canadians to secretly transport laborers from China to Europe, Canadian Prime Minister Robert Borden agreed.

Chambers's office worked diligently and creatively to make sure nobody knew the Chinese were being brought to Europe through Canada on the British behalf. To that purpose, Chinese communities in Canada were spied on, and many of their communications were reviewed by the censors to make sure that no word of the program got out.[17] In February 1917, Chambers instructed Canadian telegraph companies to "closely watch" the telegraphic correspondence of Chinese who lived in Canada "in view of the suspicion that certain Chinese are being used as a medium of communication by Enemy Agents."[18] Although most offices followed Chambers's orders, some expressed hesitation. For instance, a general manager of the Great North Western Telegraph Company of Canada informed Chambers, "We see considerable difficulty in carrying out the arrangement which you suggest, which you will understand would be a discrimination against the Chinese in Canada. Has this feature of the matter been considered? We shall, however, of course meet your views in every respect."[19] Chambers replied, "In view of the importance of the matter . . . I will be much obliged if you will issue instructions to your branch offices to require Chinamen filing messages in code, cipher, or native tongues to translate the message into plain English, for the benefit of your own staff, before transmission."[20] Soon all post offices, telegraph companies, and other related agencies were working closely with Chambers's office to censor information. Even the Chinese consul in Vancouver was spied on, and his cables and letters were read first by Canadian censors.

On March 14, 1917, Chambers issued an order to all Canadian publications to suppress any mention of the movement of Chinese laborers through Canada. He asked everyone who had information on this to maintain the strictest silence. He wrote, "It is considered highly desirable that the transportation of these men through Canada should occur without any publicity whatever."[21] An official and secret circular was issued on March 17, 1917, for the same purpose. It instructed publishers to totally block any news items related to the Chinese laborers. The circular stipulated that "the press of the Country and the correspondents of outside newspapers are asked to cooperate to prevent the publication of any information relating to this movement."[22]

Chambers seemed not to be clear on why he should impose total silence on the media. He wrote the following to an editor on April 7, 1917:

> I will be much obliged if you will kindly draw the attention of your local staff to the importance of a close observance of the order recently issued regarding the preservation of secrecy as to the movement of Chinese coolies in Canada. It appears that the instructions received from the Home Government that there are important military and international reasons why every effort should be made to preserve absolute secrecy as to the employment of coolies in Europe and as to their transportation from China to France. But the request for secrecy by the Home Government is very specific and they appear to consider the matter of great importance.[23]

And so, when the Ottawa newspaper *Morning Citizen* mentioned briefly the transit of the Chinese laborers on August 7, 1917, Chambers's office immediately notified the newspaper and wrote to the district intelligence office at Kingston where the dispatch originated, possibly through military channels, asking that the attention of the military authorities of this district should be directed to the importance of preserving silence regarding this particular movement of Chinese.[24]

Many Canadians and their newspaper editors eagerly cooperated in the censorship and spying on the Chinese. Here is an example. On April 7, 1917, Chambers's agent in Vancouver reported that

> Mr. J. H. McVety, President of the Trades and Labour Council, whom I interviewed a short time ago in reference to suppressing the news regarding the Chinese proceeding through Vancouver to France, has just returned from Victoria and informs me that a day or two ago he was at a meeting where he saw Mr. David Lou, Lee Mong Kow, and Lin Shin Yuan, the Chinese consul. As the meeting was over David Lou informed McVety in confidence that the Chinese were not going to France, but to England and furthermore they were not coming back. If this sort of thing goes on, it will make trouble here. I further enclose a confidential letter to the Brigade Office.[25]

Chambers's many agents included even church ministers. On April 9, 1917, one agent in the Western section, Rev. J. Somerville, Presbyterian Church of Canada, reported:

> I am afraid we are a little late in trying to suppress information. However, we shall send out confidential letters to all our missionaries who are home on furlough, not to give out any information in any way regarding these men, which may be received from missionaries in China. I can well understand the embarrassment it may cause when information of this kind is scattered abroad through the public press. . . . We shall do what we can on the quiet to put an end to any further information leaking out through returned missionaries, or others who may receive letters from the mission field in China. I am sorry that you have been put to the necessity in the interest of the Imperial Government of making such a request, and we shall do what is possible to aid you in the matter.[26]

The biggest challenge was to make sure the media in the United States did not report on the Chinese labor transit. Chambers was glad to discover that some American journalists would cooperate. For example, on March 20, 1918, the Canadian Bureau editor of the *Christian Science Monitor* wrote the following to Chambers:

> In conformity with your request yesterday, I am herewith forwarding you, for your information, a copy of the story which my Victoria correspondent sent me in regard to Chinese going to the front lines. In justice to the writer of the story, and to show that he is more careful than one might have at first imagined, I quote an extract from a letter which I received from him; he says, "You should have just received a story from me regarding a movement of Chinese troops to France via the Pacific coast. I had intended running it in our paper in the course of a few days but on second thoughts realized that it might conflict with censorship rules. We have decided not to run it so I am letting you know this as it is possible you might like to take the same course as far as the *Monitor* is concerned, or consult the Ottawa censor before doing so.[27]

But not every American editor was so cooperative. The *Seattle Sunday Times* and the *San Francisco Examiner* both published pieces about the movement of Chinese laborers toward France. Chambers was frustrated about how to stop such reports. He wrote to his agent, "I have been trying to have some satisfactory communication with the censorship authorities in the United States for some time and am addressing the United States consul general here, on the subject today."[28]

Because he did not have legal power south of the border, diplomacy was indeed his only tool to plug such leaks. In his April 25 letter to Colonel J. G. Foster, the American Consul General in Ottawa, Chambers asked for assistance in bringing about direct communication with the Americans "in charge of the war censorship of the press, land line telegraphs, telephones, and moving pictures in the United States." Chambers told Foster, "I realize more and more strongly every day that it is necessary that we should arrive at some simple plan of cooperation without delay . . . we have made great efforts to preserve secrecy as to the transportation of these people, but while we have succeeded in preserving silence in Canada, my attention has been drawn to the fact that certain Pacific coast publications, including the *Seattle Times* of April the 8th, and the *San Francisco Examiner* of April 11th, have published illustrated articles dealing with this matter." In exchange for American help with censoring, he promised that his office would do the same for the Americans: "As I have already intimated to you, if the censorship authorities at Washington desire the assistance and cooperation of the Canadian press censorship service, all they have to do is to let us know their requirements."[29]

On April 10, 1917, when one of his agents in Vancouver wired him that a Seattle manager of the Associated Press had dispatches from Vancouver announcing the arrival of the *Empress of Russia* with its load of Chinese laborers bound for France, Chambers agreed that it was "most desirable to stop this story" and ordered the wire dispatches to be held up. In this way, the Associated Press story was killed. To make sure no further problems arose, Chambers decided that he would personally visit Washington to "make arrangement for a satisfactory system of cooperation between our press censorship and that just organized in the United States."[30] What Chambers really hoped was that he would find a counterpart to talk to in the United States, but the United States had no truly comparable office. When the United States joined the war, President Woodrow Wilson had created the Committee on Public Information (CPI) to mobilize and shape public opinion. But the Americans had a different take than the Canadians on press censorship. Walter Lippmann, who apparently had some influence on Wilson, argued that usual military procedures would be dangerous on the question of media censorship and he advised civilian control; the person was in charge of censorship should have "real insight and democratic sympathy."[31] George Creel was appointed head of the committee. For Creel, the word "censorship" should be avoided if possible because it was important for public to have access to a vast amount of information.[32] By and large then, the CPI was created out of a desire to avoid repression and total censorship, while Chambers was focused on censorship.[33] More importantly, Chambers had a certain legal authority that Creel did not have in the United States. Chambers later acknowledged that although he was often in communication with the United States authorities, "Unfortunately the censorship in the United States as yet, is only in an embryonic stage, as they have no actual legal standing yet, but we hope that will be remedied within a short time."[34]

Chambers's censors were so conscientious they sometimes made fools of themselves. For instance, one secret message Chambers received from an agent, Malcolm Reid, reported intercepting a telegram: "I beg to attach hereto copy of a telegram handed to me today by the G. N. W. Telegraph Company sent to one Bourne, Wei Hai Wei, China. Signed by one Cannan, on which no date has been shown, which evidently has reference to the movement of Chinese coolies for your information and files."[35] This agent clearly did not know that "one Bourne" was actually the head of the British recruitment office in China and in charge of the whole operation there, and Cannan was A. M. Cannan, the commanding officer of Battalions 32 and 38, CLC. Reid, based in Vancouver, was sometimes too eager to enforce the censorship. The following example is revealing. He reported, "I beg to enclose herewith three separate sets of snapshots which were taken of the Chinese coolies by person who happened to be standing at the end of the viaduct of Burrard St., when the steamer *Talthybus* carrying these coolies docked here." He reported that in addition to the film confiscated, it was understood that occupants of a car with the license number 569 also took some snaps of the Chinese. He told Chambers that his office was working hard to trace the owner of this car in order to confiscate his films and any copies he had made. Reid acknowledged that people took snapshots unthinkingly and that no great political or military significance should be attached to their confiscation, but he also pointed out "that it does seem that very lax precautions are being taken to prevent these coolies from being seen by the general public at this port."[36] Victoria police later discovered after further investigation that the report was mistaken because the car in question was not in Vancouver that day.[37]

Chambers expressed deep appreciation for Reid's confiscation of film and snapshots, and informed him that he was going to forward the case to the chief of the general staff, who, Chambers said, "I am sure, will appreciate your action in this matter. . . . I feel that I should not conclude this acknowledgement of your letter and enclosures without complimenting you upon the very prompt and effective measure taken by you to prevent the circulation of these pictures."[38]

As if the snapshots incident were not strange enough, the following episode clearly exposes a bizarre example of Canadian censorship. The episode was triggered by the Bourne, the British recruiter in China. On January 10, 1918, a telegram from Bourne to London's War Office was forwarded to the Canadian military authority. It stated: "A Chinese interpreter stationed in hospital at Vancouver has written most damaging and untrue statements to native newspaper here which may seriously affect recruiting. He states that white soldiers in hospital report that Chinese in France are used as soldiers. Please see that no letters are allowed to be sent by post but that all are collected and addressed to me here for censoring."[39] This telegram triggered a chain of reactions from Chambers's censorship office, which immediately sent a coded message to its agent, Malcolm Reid in Vancouver, asking him to identify and locate the interpreter and issued instructions for the censorship of this individual's telegraphic correspondence. Unfortunately, Chambers's message to Reid could not be decoded. Anxiously, Reid wired Chambers, "Your code messages not clear. Repeat using Sherwood's key." Reid further informed Chambers that

in this connection we wish to state the only private code we have belonging to your office is a copy of code B, no. 2, which does not contain all the code words used in your first message, and while we could find some of the uncoded words in the Slater code book we were unable to decode them not having the proper key to go by. However, matters have now been straightened out and we can use the Slater code unless you wish to furnish me with a full copy of your own private code.[40]

Chambers also communicated with the deputy postmaster general, the chief mail censor for Canada, with a view of eventually having the postal correspondence of the same individual intercepted and submitted for examination in country before it was forwarded to China.[41]

On January 18, 1918, Reid reported in a coded message to Chambers that he had discovered the interpreter's identity: Leung Shou Yat (English name Julian Leon), who was employed as the official interpreter for the Chinese laborer patients.[42] With his identity known, Leung's communications were immediately intercepted and censored. It turned out that Leung was well educated, had had a good position in China, and had accepted the interpreter's position only to see Europe.[43] Reid's office also discovered that Leung was quite lonely and had no friends in Vancouver. It also seemed clear that he was unhappy with the payment of his wages but harbored no hidden intentions to sabotage British recruitment. This conclusion was soon confirmed by the War Office. On March 8, 1918, the War Office in London informed Chambers that "it has been found that there is not sufficient evidence readily available on which action can be taken. It is suggested that a strict censorship of this individual's correspondence is the best method of safeguarding further harmful statements reaching China, whilst possibly providing an opportunity for successful prosecution if he offends again." In a handwritten postscript, the War Office official commented, "If any further information should come to hand we will not fail to let you know."[44]

According to Reid's report of April 3, 1918, Leung left Vancouver on March 31, his destination presumably being France.[45] The next day, Reid reported to Chambers that new intercepted and censored letters had arrived at the interpreter's Vancouver address. One was from C. T. Pan, British post office, Hankou, China, postmarked March 1. Pan's letter is quite interesting because it reveals more about British actions in the interpreter's case. Pan acknowledged having received letters sent him by Leung. He then told his interpreter friend that on the morning of March 1, when he arrived at his work at the British-run Hankow post office, the British consul was there waiting for him and gave him a letter to read. Pan discovered that the letter was from the British consulate in Canton and included an article translated from a newspaper published there. The article was entitled "The Hardships of the Chinese Labor Corps." The British consul's letter indicated that "There was a letter published in one of the Canton Chinese newspapers which was received from Vancouver, BC, and after we had read this letter . . . we at once knew what kind of a man this was, and understand his reason for publishing this article against the British government. This man should be dismissed from the service; after he has been relieved of his duties it will then rest with the authorities as to what ultimate action is taken in his case." Pan was then handed another letter from the British emigration bureau, addressed to the British consul at Hankou, China, mentioning the allotments due to his family. In his letter to the interpreter, Pan enclosed a copy of the letter referred to. He explained that he did not enclose the article because it was too long. But Pan wrote that he knew that said article had been written by the interpreter because Leung had expressed the same ideas to him. "I believe therefore that you must be the author of the article, although I have no proof of this."

This whole maneuver was a kind of carrot-and-stick strategy cooked up by the British to scare Leung into making no further negative comments regarding the situation of Chinese laborers. The letter concerning payment to his family served as the carrot. Clearly, every step of this plan was orchestrated by the British, and it seems to have been well thought out because everything was handled through his friend. Pan said that the British consul told him he was certain the article had been written by Leung and had asked Pan to pass along that

> he must remember he is residing in a British possession and is also in the employ of the British government. He has now written this article and had it published in the newspaper in order to slander the British government but this sort of conduct is against the laws of the British. The statements made in the article are all misleading and are not true. . . . You are Liang's friend and are looking after his allotments for his father, have you any knowledge that his father has not been receiving his allotments? . . . I wish you would write to him and ask him to write to the newspaper which published this article stating he was wrong and to refute the statements made in his first letter.

Pan's letter also relayed that the British emigration bureau had sent a letter to Vancouver asking authorities there to investigate the case as well. He further wrote:

> If you think or have heard that your father has not been receiving his allotments you must be misinformed for as you are aware I have been acting for you and have been making the payments to your father. Of course, the payments have been somewhat delayed but this was not due to the fault of the British emigration bureau, but was caused owing to the fact that when you enter the service you are supposed to give your age, name, the district you are from, etc. and owing to this information not being correct there was some misunderstanding when placing your card in the file cabinet. However, your father has been receiving his allotment alright. In view of this I think you should be patient. If you do not want to remain where you are, you can resign and return home. You should not be so excitable, for as

you know the place where your home is located is under the British rule, and if you are not more careful you will get into trouble.

As a British employee, Pan had no choice but to use the strong language and reasoning of his employers.[46]

The Canadian military decided not to take disciplinary measure against Leung, but continued to monitor his correspondence that can be found in the Canadian archives thanks to the continued interception.

Besides spying on Chinese and cajoling Americans into cooperation, Chambers's office sometimes also exerted pressure on diplomats regarding the Chinese laborers. A case in point, Chambers once contacted the Japanese consulate general in Ottawa, saying that he suspected the Japanese steamship *Tamba Maru* might be the source of recent media leakage in the United States about the Chinese laborers.[47] The Japanese consul general took this charge very seriously and did a thorough investigation. He eventually discovered that the Japanese were not source of the leak; rather, it was an American by the name of M. H. Crowford who had conveyed the information to the *Seattle Times* and other publications.[48] Later the Japanese consul general wrote again to Chambers, claiming that he had received an official cablegram from Tokyo that not only pointed toward the exoneration of the Japanese parties referred to but also strengthened his "belief that the Japanese authorities were constantly doing their utmost to assist the cause of our allies, especially the British empire." He continued, "The Japanese government is not only [providing] the coolie transports all the facilities and convenience at their Japanese ports of call, but also has taken necessary measures to prevent the news from being made public in the Japanese press."[49]

Due to Chambers's tireless (if sometimes extreme) efforts, secrecy about the program was so well maintained that few, whether Canadians or people elsewhere, knew anything about it. The success of maintaining total secrecy might also have a lot to do with Canadian attitudes toward Chinese at that time. Of course, other departments' cooperation was important for the success. The Department of Defense in Ottawa, for instance, well aware of the need for secrecy regarding this large-scale operation at the height of hostilities, issued detailed instructions for the formation and operation of a unit designated the "Railway Service Guard," making no reference to the Chinese laborers. According to one Canadian scholar, many of the telegrams sent between the military and the railway were encoded for secrecy measures.[50]

## No Success: Canadians and the Chinese

Canadians, as a whole, treated the Chinese in Canada badly and treated the Chinese laborers on their way to France even worse. This treatment was directly linked to the overall status of Chinese in that country. To keep Chinese out of Canada, the government had for many years imposed a heavy head tax on Chinese immigrants. By the time the laborers were headed to France through Canada, that tax had reached $500 Canadian, an enormous amount of money for anyone, let alone a Chinese immigrant. The tax was main reason behind harsh restrictions imposed on the poor laborers, even though they had no intention to stay in Canada.

As discussed earlier, the Canadian immigration authority had agreed to allow these men to cross Canada without paying on the condition that they were not allowed to leave the trains and had to be guarded everywhere they passed through. The immigration superintendent was explicit about this in a letter to the military chief: "We are interested in the movement because Chinese, upon whom there is a head tax of $500 if entering Canada, have to be very carefully handled and checked in and out. The coolies are carried through Canada virtually in bond."[51] To make sure that the men stayed on the train, Canadian government set up a special railway service guard system. Four guards were assigned to each car on which the Chinese rode, and for each train there were two spare guards, two NCOs, two lieutenants, and one captain. The personnel of the special guard consisted of nineteen officers and 600 troops. Keep in mind that the laborers were also under the command of their section officers and NCOs. The duty of the Canadian special guard was simply to see that no Chinese left the train at any point, except under distinct orders from the medical officer. In cases of absolute necessity, the patient had to be accompanied by a guard or handed to an escort from the district concerned.[52]

To make sure that no Chinese was able to leave, five copies of a list of the laborers, giving their serial numbers, names, and ages, were prepared before the ships arrived in Vancouver. One copy would go to the United States Immigration Department to cover the trains going through the state of Maine to St. John or Halifax when the port of Montreal was closed for the winter. The Americans required that all car doors be locked and a guard posted inside each door during passage.[53] The other lists went to different government agencies such as immigration offices.

Some British officers found this treatment too harsh and reported it to the British government. In a report of August 31, 1917, the medical officer of the 36th battalion wrote, "It is unfortunate in such a long journey, that the coolies have to be kept confined all the time, each to his own coach."[54] Medical supplies were insufficient. "Shortly after leaving Montreal three coolies were found to have Scabies, treatment could not be carried out immediately on account of the delay in getting the necessary drugs and the condition spread somewhat rapidly."[55] These reports eventually reached Bourne, who forwarded them to the minister of militia at Ottawa to draw his attention to the abuse issues.[56] According to British captain Royal Douglas Wood's diary, one day a Canadian NCO of the camp guard struck a Chinese interpreter. The officer in charge considered a simple reprimand adequate, but Wood, who was a British officer escorting the Chinese to France, objected. Largely because of his insistence, the Canadian NCO was punished more seriously.[57]

Despite expressed concerns about their methods of control, the Canadians stood firm. They maintained that on each train, the officer in charge was responsible for the laborers' welfare and general behavior; the guards were to prevent them from absconding and to quell, if need be, collective insubordination. Guards would be warned that they were to hold themselves aloof and not fraternize with the Chinese. The Canadians maintained that although it was desirable for the Chinese to get exercise over the course of the long transit across Canada as opportunities arose, the CO would decide when and where. The form of exercise and its duration would also be decided by the transportation company, not the CO. Such matters would be brought to the notice of officers detailed to take charge of the guards.[58]

However, as we clearly demonstrated, the commanding officer was not the person who could make a decision on the exercise issue. The Canadian Railway Company management actually had the final say. Although the Canadian military thought it a good idea to allow the Chinese some form of exercise,[59] the railway company objected. On October 1, 1917, an assistant general passenger agent in Canadian Pacific Railway Company wrote:

> I do not favor the suggestion of giving the coolies exercise en route, on the Canadian trans-continental journey. We cannot stop our trains between divisional points for the purpose without seriously interfering with other regular passenger and freight train movement. The freight train movements

today are of the utmost importance, and their prompt operation is vital as they are now practically all loaded with food stuffs, munitions, etc. If the coolies are allowed to exercise at divisional points where there are usually a number of tracks, congested yards, etc., I feel that the guards will have some difficulty in preventing the escape of some of their numbers. Therefore, I would think that the immigration department would object to this.[60]

The military authorities seemed unimpressed by the railway's arguments. As one internal memo suggests, "The danger of desertion en route is exaggerated and . . . officers in charge could with safety take advantage of stoppages (if any) in suitable localities."[61] But eventually the military chose to defer to the railway, reasoning that "unless we hear something much more definite, to the effect that the health of the coolies is impaired, we should not call upon the C.P.R to interfere with their train movements; and that it would not be well to run the risk of letting the men out at Divisional points. Perhaps a more effective remedy would be to curtail the diet of the travelers."[62] So the military gave the green light to the railway for whatever it chose to do regarding the exercise issue, "It is not desired to seriously interfere with your train movements but is hoped that any advantage will be taken of safe and otherwise suitable opportunities for exercise, if and when they present themselves."[63] Naturally the railway management chose not to provide any such opportunities, not even at scheduled stops. Faced with a determined railway, the only suggestion the military could make was that "it might be possible that something in the nature of physical exercise might be arranged for in the cars when the train is not in motion."[64]

Another reason the Chinese were not allowed off the trains was the Canadian government's concerns about the laborers' interaction with local Chinese communities. As Chambers wrote to the military authority, "I consider it my duty to transmit these copies to you without a moment's delay, as the letters from Chinamen resident in Canada, translations of which are contained in Reid's letter, seem to indicate the desirability of the military guards in charge of the coolies being moved across Canada en route for France exercising special care to prevent these coolies getting into communication with Chinamen resident in Canada."[65] On April 20, 1917, the military issued the following order: "Special care should be taken to prevent Chinese coolies communicating in any way with Chinese residents in Canada. Evidence obtained that certain

Canadian Chinese are spreading false information to frighten these men from going over so that they will want to escape."[66]

Chinese laborers were treated precisely the same way when they returned to China through Canada after the war was over. Military orders still specified that "no Chinaman is to be allowed to leave the train, unless it is deemed necessary by the medical officer in charge of the train." When a Chinese patient was well enough to be moved from the hospital, he was "immediately sent, under escort, to [the holding encampment at] William Head." The laborers again were under special military police and were watched every minute by their guards, each of whom had been issued a revolver.[67]

Under such tight control, the Chinese were virtually prisoners. Considering the long and challenging return journey between Halifax and Vancouver, and given the many stops en route, it was inhumane and even criminal that the Canadian government did not allow the men to leave the train and stretch their arms and legs periodically. The British again complained about this harsh treatment. In a 1919 cable from the colonial foreign secretary to the governor general of Canada, sent after reports of Canadian treatment of the Chinese had been received by the foreign office from officers who had commanded the labor battalions, the British directly suggested that the Chinese should be given exercise, particularly during the warm summer months, as these men were virtually immobile for more than six weeks.[68] But as happened with the transit to France, the Canadians would not budge.

The Chinese did not always tolerate their mistreatment. On March 11, 1920, a large group of them made a determined attempt to escape from the William Head cantonment. Only at bayonet point were the several hundred men finally rounded up by the guards and herded back into the encampment. More than 8,000 Chinese were stationed there; when the riot occurred, it was estimated that about 2,000 succeeded in breaking through the strongly barricaded enclosure. The exact cause of the riot was not known, but mistreatment or misunderstanding (or both) definitely must have played a role. Canadians subsequently had to use bayonets to maintain order in their camps.[69]

The unique and extended mutual exposure of the Canadians and Chinese did not warm Canadian attitudes. Instead, the laborers' sacrifice was rewarded with the Chinese exclusion laws of 1923. Canadian Prime Minister Mackenzie King even had trouble justifying the measure. "I do not think," he said, "it is possible to talk of excluding the people of any country, or excluding all of the people—regardless altogether of what their standing or standards may be—and not offend the entire nation concerned. I do not think it is in the interest of Canada, or of any part of the British Empire, that any Dominion of the Empire should knowingly pass an Act, which is certain to be regarded as an act of offence to an entire nation by an entire country."[70]

To be fair, not every Canadian was hostile to the Chinese. Some of them were quite friendly. For instance, a group of Nova Scotia ladies from Halifax voluntarily organized a welcoming party for returning Chinese. They found that Canadians warmly welcomed their returned soldiers, but nobody bothered with the Chinese, not even to "give them a word of greeting or wish them God-speed on their long journey" as they passed through Canada. This group decided to raise a sum of money and extend a welcome to the Chinese. For them, the Chinese "were *Our Allies* and had done their part." These women would eventually meet and greet about 20,000 Chinese, giving each man a word of welcome printed in Chinese on a souvenir card and a gift of apples.[71]

When the same Halifax ladies learned that one boatload of the Chinese was traveling to St. John, they decided to extend the same modest welcome there. They obtained official permission for carrying on the welcome committee's work and purchased a supply of apples from a St. John merchant. They were only ones to make any kind gesture to the Chinese that day, because no local committee or individual, man or woman, appeared on the pier at St. John. "The only words of greeting and God-speed were from our committee; and had it not been for the service thus rendered, these three thousand and six Chinese labor-soldiers would have passed thru St. John in the same silence and with same absolute lack of welcome that the first few thousand passed through Halifax."[72] Two interpreters for the Chinese laborers composed a thank-you letter to the key organizer, Clara Archibald Dennis, telling her, "Many thanks for welcoming us with a card and two apples for each of us when we arrived at your precious place. . . . All of us are very grateful for such kindness." The letter was written in Chinese and was immediately published as it was in the *Halifax Herald*.[73]

However, when the word got out about the Halifax ladies' welcome for the Chinese in St. John, some of St. John's citizens took offense. Clara Dennis eventually wrote a long letter to Mrs. E. A. Smith of St. John, explaining that they did not intend to humiliate St. John residents:

It is unnecessary to say that any slight, much less, "insult" to the self-sacrificing workers of St. John was not dreamed of, and I would never have imagined that such an idea could have been harboured by St. John workers. Neither the committee nor myself have the slightest desire to overlap or duplicate any work that you are engaged in or any welcome which you propose to extend to any other portion of the Chinese labour corps who may land in St. John, and, with your assurance that this kindly and simple work will be performed by St. John people, our committee will be only too pleased to be relieved of the labour, the responsibility and the expense.[74]

But the Halifax ladies were still determined that somebody should welcome the Chinese in St. John when they passed through. On January 29, 1920, Clara Dennis again wrote to Mrs. Smith to ask whether St. John women would personally welcome the Chinese expected to arrive the next day. If not, Dennis asked, would they still object to having the Halifax ladies do it? On January 31, Smith informed Dennis that in St. John "a suitable welcome will be accorded Chinese labor-soldiers on arrival"; its committee was composed of ladies and gentlemen. "You can rest satisfied the Chinese will be most cordially greeted."[75]

Offended they might be, but the Halifax ladies' action did in fact motivate people in St. John to organize their own welcoming activities for the Chinese. In early February, residents of St. John indeed welcomed the Chinese and stayed with the men until the last one was safely entrained and speeding toward the land of the celestials. The Chinese received their fruit and cards with expressions of thanks, some endeavoring to speak English; others using the French "Merci," while still more said a Chinese word evidently meaning "thank you." They seemed to appreciate the attention, especially after the tiresome wait at the dock. The Chinese repaid their hospitality by holding an impromptu concert that greatly entertained the members of the reception committee as they whiled away the hours of waiting.[76]

Despite such gestures, by and large the returning Chinese were ignored. One Canadian newspaper article used the title "Great Events Which Pass Unnoticed" to describe the public's general disregard of the Chinese transit. The article noted that such a large number of Chinese passing through "without causing scarcely a ripple of concern is a matter of great wonder."[77] It went on to say:

With the passing of time and the retrospective view of the events that went to create history in the war becoming more and more distant, a truer sense of values is being gradually developed. When all things are seen in their proper perspective the place accorded to the Chinese labor units will be equal to that of the highest and best. Returned soldiers remember the whimsical faces, eternally smiling, the bizarre costumes and the weird songs adding to the long white roads of the Pas de Calais that touch of strangeness which made the traversing of them less of a task. At Hersin Coupigny, Noeux les Mines, Aubigny and Etrun, the largest camps of the Chinese on the Canadian front were subjected daily to long-range shelling and in the moonlight nights they were regularly bombed. The social indifference of the orientals towards this "hunnishness" was indicative of no less courage than that shown by the fighting troops themselves. . . . They were road-builders and were invaluable in maintaining the ration-route; they furnished carrying parties in the sectors where transportation was poor, and in a thousand other ways they carried out work that was in every respect as essential towards winning the war as the barrage, the over-the-top, and the study of red, blue, black, and green objectives.

Yet "after having served gloriously and devotedly on the Western Front," the Chinese were shown neither welcome nor thanks by any citizens' committee. "The organizations that sounded the loud timbrel on the arrival of our own splendid men are not working any more." The article concluded by saying that "Nova Scotia at least has reason to feel proud at the initiative and energy of the small band of devoted ladies who have taken upon themselves the gigantic task of giving these men a welcome to Canada, some small indication that Canada at least recognizes the part they have played and wishes well of them."

But crossing Canada, some 4,000 miles by train, was for the Chinese an absolutely cheerless journey. They were again "herded like so much cattle in cars, forbidden to leave the train and guarded like criminals."[78] Even given their prisoner-like treatment and the near total indifference of locals, however, the Chinese managed to retain a sense of humor. One British captain told a story of how on the rail journey between Vancouver and Halifax the Chinese had exchanged salutes with the police on the train, to the immense surprise of the latter. When arriving at a station, the laborers stuck their heads out of windows and playfully issued nonsense orders to the soldiers patrolling the platform, crying out shrilly and with a gleam of teeth, "Dismiss!"[79]

# 4

---

## WORK

---

Impassive Chu (or should I call thee Chow?),
Say, what hast thou to do with all this fuss,
The ceaseless hurry and the beastly row
The buzzing plane and roaring motor bus.
While far away the sullen Hwang-ho rolls
His lazy waters to the Eastern Sea,
And sleepy mandarins sit on bamboo poles
Imbibing countless cups of China tea?

A year ago thou digged'st in fervent haste
Against the whelming onset of the Hun
A hundred miles of trench across the waste
A year ago—and now the War is won.
But Thou remainest still with pick and spade
Celestial delver, patient son of toil!
To fill the trenches thou thyself hast made
And roll the twisted wire in even coil.

But not for thee, the glory and the praise
The medals or the fat gratuity,
No man shall crown thee with a wreath of bays
Or recommend thee for the O.B.E.
And thou, me thinks, wouldst rather have it so
Provided that, without undue delay,
They let thee take thy scanty wage and go
Back to thy sunny home in old Cathay;

Where never falls a shell nor bursts a bomb
Nor ever blows the slightest whiff of gas
Such as was not infrequent in the Somme.
But on thy breast shall lean some slant-eyed lass
And she shall listen to thy converse ripe
And search for souvenirs among thy kit
Pass thee thy slippers and thy opium pipe
And make thee glad that thou hast done thy bit.

—*"To a Chinese Coolie,"* Punch,
*February 19, 1919*

The preceding poem was published in 1919 in the London humor publication *Punch*. *Punch* tries to find humor in everything, but humor is not what emerges here. Instead, one is struck by a sense of irony and sadness. The Chinese came to Europe to help Britain and France win the war, and many of them would remain to help France with reconstruction after the war. Their work was backbreaking, important, and dangerous. The Great War lasted about 1,500 days. But for many Chinese laborers, their war experience was longer and more horrifying because they stayed behind to clear the battlefields and bury the dead. During and afterward, they witnessed the most frightening and terrible aspects of the brutality of the war.

## The Working Environment and Management

The Chinese working for British Expeditionary Forces (BEF) in France engaged solely in war-related work; they came under the direct control of the military and were supervised in a military style. They were listed as Chinese Labour Corps (CLC). The men usually marched in fours to work and back, and their marching skills sometimes impressed those who saw them. An American officer, Norman W. Pinney of Florida, later recalled, "I often saw these Chinese [under the British] marching along the roads to and from labor details. They were exceptionally neat and clean and their march discipline . . . excellent. At first, I thought they were Chinese troops."[1] According to one report, when the first group of Chinese recruited by the British arrived in France in early April 1917, the French village near their camp "was agog with excitement, the whole po[p]ulation of about 200 old men and women and children turning out to welcome 'les Chinoises.' The Chinese formed up outside the station and the order 'form fours' was given. Stepping out smartly in their new uniforms, their march from the station to the depot along the muddy French roads was really wonderful, and our NCOs gasped with astonishment."[2]

The labor corps was managed in a typical military way. The first officer selected to command the Chinese labor for Britain was Lieutenant Colonel B. C. Fairfax, whose official title was "advisor." The Chinese, and especially those under British command, often worked in or close to military zones. If they broke rules, they would be tried under court martial.[3] According to the regulations, "During the court martial for Chinese, members of a court martial should be familiar with Chinese habits and customs, e.g., 1. Chinamen are very loath to give evidence, as by so doing enmity is incurred. 2. Chinese witness should be 'declared' according to native custom. They can be sworn, but an 'oath' has slight moral weight with the Chinese. 3. Interpreters at a court martial should always be officers of the CLC."[4] In fact, at least ten Chinese laborers under British control were executed under military law during the war. One of them was executed for having murdered his white commanding officer. The other nine were executed because they had killed fellow laborers.[5] But the court martial system for the Chinese was not designed for fairness, since the direct commanding officers usually served as judges. For instance, on October 31, 1917, one officer acted as prosecutor at a court martial of eight Chinese who had been ringleaders in a disturbance at one of the camps.[6] Although this type of court martial might have been typical for enlisted military personnel, the Chinese laborers had been hired as civilians, and the British military authorities promised to treat them as such according to their contracts.

That the Chinese were treated as military men was also reflected in the fact that even their mail service was under military control. One commander of the CLC Company wrote in his diary on September 7, 1917: "Collected 136 letters from the Chinese letter box and sent them off to be censored. Tried three coolies for gambling and fined them four francs each."[7] According to British military rule, the postal arrangements for the labor corps allowed each man to write two letters per month. All these letters had to pass through the corps post office at headquarters, where, after being censored, they were made up into bags and dispatched to the British War Office recruiting agent in China. Similarly, the British recruiting agent made up a bag at Weihaiwei and forwarded it directly to the CLC post office in France from whence the letters were distributed. "All letters written by Chinese personnel must be sent through their commander to a Chinese military post office under BEF and must be closed before leaving the unit."[8] Any letter from a laborer in one unit in France to a laborer in another unit had to bear the registered number of the addressee and the designation of the unit to which the addressee belonged, in English characters. All "reply envelopes" sent to China or elsewhere had to bear the registered number of the sender and the designation of the sender's unit in English lettering.[9] Military censorship rules applied to the Chinese as well: all letters were to avoid conveying any information that might be useful to the enemy. This included references to places, plans of future operations, positions, condition of roads and railways, supplies, effects of hostile fire, and similar information. All communications to the press on the subject of the war, or on matters directly or indirectly connected with military matters, were forbidden. Even photos were not allowed to be sent through the post.[10] Chinese were also forbidden to send picture postcards, photographs, or pictures by post, as well as newspapers and other printed matter.[11]

The Chinese laborers also had to wear uniforms. According to British military rule, they had to wear approved clothing at all times, with the exceptions that civilian underclothing, boots, shoes, or headgear might be worn on or off duty.[12] British-recruited Chinese laborers were organized in companies of 500, and to each was assigned a captain, four lieutenants, and several NCOs—all Westerners. One or more Chinese interpreters were allotted to each company, and foremen or "gangers" were appointed from among the laborers. There was the head ganger who wore "four stripes" *(si dao gang),* and his helpers, the three-, two-, and one-stripe gangers. In his official instructions to British officers who supervised the Chinese laborers, R. L. Purdon, commanding officer of the CLC, informed them that "Supervision should be as unmilitary as is compatible with efficiency. . . . Whenever possible the Chinese should be employed by themselves, and not where they are in a position to judge or criticize the same class of work performed by white men." To achieve this goal, "the Chinese ganger is the most important link between the Officers and the labourers, and his position should be clearly defined and upheld."[13] Chinese labor companies under the British were generally organized into a headquarters and four platoons, each under a subaltern. Each platoon consisted of two sections, each under a sergeant.

The quality of the Chinese laborers' work was directly linked to their management. The British military had serious management problems, however.[14] First of all, the British simply did not have enough officers, let alone qualified ones, to oversee the Chinese. The BEF put whomever it could find in charge. John M. Harrison, who at age 18 had been at Oxford when the war broke out, was recruited as a chemist in July 1915. "I volunteered. We students thought the War Office wanted real chemists, but the Army really wanted plumbers." Having no experience with Chinese and being extremely young, he was nonetheless put in charge of five hundred Chinese laborers because a company did not have a commanding officer. He was later transferred to another Chinese company for the same role of "holding the baby" as an acting commanding officer.[15]

Because of a lack of qualified officers, according to one CLC internal document, "For a long time, C.L.C. companies were sent out from the Depot on formation with but 2 or 3 officers and 7 to 9 NCOs, instead of the 5 and 19 allowed by rule. Chinese Labour was thus handicapped at the very start." This report further indicated, "In addition to the inexperience of the white personnel there was serious mishandling of the Chinese Labour on the work through the failure of the officers of Services and Departments employing the labour to appreciate either the capacity of the Chinaman for work or the necessity of handling the labour through the proper channel of responsibility." When the Chinese finished their assignment for the day, the British forced them to continue working. According to this report, "The Chinese regarded [this] as a direct breach of faith, and their morale was affected accordingly."[16] The report said that "Chinese labour, *properly handled,* was undoubtedly most efficient; the extensive systems of defence organized in the rear at the time of the enemy offensive in 1918 could not have been completed in the time were it not for the excellent work of the C.L.C."[17]

The dearth of interpreters, a problem shared by the French and Americans as well, presented another dilemma for directing and motivating the Chinese. "Owing to the shortage of Chinese-speaking officers, and the difficulty of communicating with the Chinese, compilation of a Chinese Phrase Book was put in hand."[18] The phrase book, prepared by Major R. L. Purdon and approved by the War Council, claimed to include "All the words and sentences that are absolutely necessary to the performance of labor" in simple language. It recommended that the officers "at any rate" learn the first few lessons in "parrot fashion," namely by imitating the sounds uttered by the interpreters attached to each company. The booklet also reminded users that it was written "within the theatre of war, with many interruptions, under trying circumstances, and without any reference books."[19] This was the desperate and fairly irresponsible way the British decided to deal with shortage of interpreters.

The British were selective about complying with contract conditions. So while the standard contract stipulated that Chinese should not be employed inside danger zones, the British rarely paid attention to this crucial term. But as to working hours, one BEF official wrote, "No ruling as to hours for other Labour in France cancels the terms of the [British] Chinese contract to work 10 hours per day, which must be remembered if the Chinese make claims for overtime."[20] According to the BEF, Indian laborers were used for "general service and for one year or for the period of the war," whichever was less.[21] The Indian laborers as a whole "cannot fairly be said to have justified the expense involved in transport and maintenance" as they "did not stand the winter in Northern France well."[22] South African laborers "were unsuitable for work in any dangerous area," and the retention of them in Army areas was "of short duration." Moreover, the military authorities realized that "there would be considerable trouble politically if the South African natives were reported to be near the fighting."[23] This left the Chinese, who were frequently used in or near danger zones.

Many Chinese thus died from bombardment. On September 4 and 5, 1917, the Germans bombed Boulogne and Dunkirk, killing fifteen Chinese laborers and wounding twenty-one.[24] The private diary of a British officer noted, "Chinamen bolted for the country and were all over the place for the next few days. They had evidently been very badly managed."[25] In another case, fifty to sixty Chinese were required in and around the fighting to transport munitions. The Germans soon started to shell or bomb, and their British officer was almost killed by German guns.[26] One officer wrote in his diary that German air raids were frequent at a place where some Chinese camps were located. On the night of May 18, 1918, fifty or more Chinese were killed from such a raid. Survivors fled for their lives by breaking out of their barbed wired camp.[27] Another officer wrote in his diary how "heavy shells very near and from all sides" and "very heavy explosions" took place at one camp where about two hundred fifty to three hundred Chinese worked. "One shell came, every Chinaman straightened his back and then they went. Blue uniforms, tied at waist, otherwise like balloons in breeze." "They did not know where to go—only to get away from shells and put as much distance as possible between themselves and danger. All discipline gone. I lay down on the wet ground and laughed, perhaps the first time for a long time. I stopped on the ground for at that moment German aeroplanes appeared above me, and started dropping bombs." The entry goes on to state that bombing continued until late evening.[28]

Besides bombs, the Chinese also faced deadly threats from gas shells. Captain A. McCormick, an officer for the Chinese, wrote:

> The great fear we had was not so much ordinary shell fire as gas shell fire. Frequently large numbers of gas shells fell in close proximity to our camp and what saved us was simply that the wind was blowing from where our camp was situated to where the shells had fallen. I do not wish to magnify,

but I must not minimize these troubles which were seldom absent. . . . I can convey the best idea to my readers of how it affected me specially who held command of a Labour Company and whose duty it was to look after the safety of my men when I say that for three months after that attack I never dare take my trousers off when going to bed and I had always to have my gas mask in readiness at my side.[29]

Putting the Chinese in the line of danger not only violated their contracts but, more importantly, it also made the Chinese unhappy and negatively influenced their performance. The British Brigadier General W. R. Ludlow wrote in his diary that the Chinese "contend that under their agreement with our Government they were not to be taken into shelled areas so close to the trenches."[30] Naturally, when bombings took place the Chinese became frightened and refused to work. A colonel in the British army once suggested that the Chinese be removed from danger zones, as their contracts stipulated. But the British military authority pointed out that many places where Chinese worked were subject to air raids and that they were not able to regard all those places as danger zones. Moreover, "it would create a precedent if they were removed as it would be open to those at the other places mentioned, to press for removal after an air raid."[31]

The Chinese were obviously not happy about working under enemy fire. When Germans bombed the Chinese camps in Dunkirk and killed a number of them on July 30, 1918, as one British soldier recalled, "For days after they were panic stricken and ran amok, scattering all over the country: nothing seemingly could be done with them, the military authorities had them rounded up, but could not induce them to return on any account to town. I heard that some of them resisted with violence; for several days they were quite out of hand and we would meet them in all sorts of unlikely places. Eventually they were arranged for in a camp some miles out of the town and taken to the docks [to work] in the daytime by lorries or by walking, leaving well before dusk. If a hostile machine [airplane] appeared in the daytime over the district you would see them running for their lives with terror depicted on their faces."[32] Of course, there were also reports that some Chinese were not afraid of the shells. According to one labor corps officer, the Chinese called bombs from German airplanes "German eggs," and sometimes they saw "plenty German eggs." In a daylight raid, Chinese "merely stopped their work in order to gaze better at the altitudinous Germans, and when a bit of shrapnel whizzed to earth the coolies would pounce on it, laughingly crying out, 'plenty souvenir-la.' "[33]

The working environment of the Chinese differed somewhat depending on who they worked for. In the British case, almost all Chinese laborers served at the front, but many of the French-recruited Chinese worked in private factories, such as munitions factories, and some of them were placed directly under French government agencies. These men worked away from the front and did not have to march to work; they certainly enjoyed more freedom than their counterparts under the British.[34] According to one source from the Chinese legation at Paris, a total of 77 stations of French-recruited Chinese with 23,166 men worked in non-army areas. Eleven more stations were located within the military zone, but no number of men was given.[35] But after China officially joined the war in 1917, even French authorities began to assign Chinese workers to military zones more frequently and openly. The Chinese under French supervision were engaged in making explosives, repairing machines, constructing roads, making "cuts and fills," and doing various kinds of manual labor. Compared to the workers under Britain, their deployment was more scattered geographically and diverse. Besides working in French factories, these Chinese dug trenches, loaded and unloaded cargo, transported military supplies, repaired roads, and the like.

## The Work

Despite their chaotic and sometimes dangerous working environment, the Chinese accomplished spectacular feats. A pamphlet called the "Notes on Chinese Labour" issued by the British military in summer 1918 for the British officers in charge of or dealing with the laborers, declared that the Chinese "are very hardy men and properly handled, are among the best labourers in the world. . . . It is astonishing what the coolie is capable of. Careful experiments have been made at the Chinese labour depot with small parties of 6 coolies taken quite at random—one party excavated at the rate of 230 cubic feet of chalk and flint and about 1 foot of surface soil per man per 8 hours. This was on 'time work' and without the incentive of a task." The British liked to give them task work. The "Notes" cautioned, "Faith must be kept with them, and under no circumstances should they be required to do extra work on completion of the day's set task."[36] Captain A. McCormick, a commanding officer of one Chinese labor company, commented, "These sturdy A-class China-men could do much a heavier day's work—especially if kept to task work—and when well officered than the average Labour Corps men could be expected to do."[37]

The Chinese were an important part of the warfare. For the British government, the main objective of the labor organizations was "to re-lease the fighting soldier for his legitimate work" and "to assist the Ser-vices and Departments to carry out their tasks."[38] As one YMCA docu-ment noted, the Chinese laborers' work was as essential as that of the men in the trenches, for in modern warfare physical labor is an integral part of the war machine, which included activities such as building and repairing truck roads, building railroads, clearing and draining camps and flying fields, loading and unloading supplies, and working in muni-tions plants.[39] The London *Times* also wrote: "The coming of the Chi-nese Labour Corps to France relieved our own men from an enormous amount of heavy and miscellaneous work behind the lines, and so helped to release a much larger proportion than otherwise would have been possible for combatant duties. For not only did the Chinese fulfill multi-farious tasks at the various bases, such as loading and unloading ships and trains, building railways, repairing roads, working in petrol facto-ries and at various supply depots throughout the northern region, but they dug hundreds of miles of support trenches in the forward areas, well within shell range."[40] One senior YMCA officer familiar with the Chinese laborers' work put it this way: "They were by far the best work-men that we had in the war zone, for they were all physically fit whereas the best men of the nations actively engaged in the war had been drafted for army service. Not only were they excellent physical specimens but they showed a willingness and eagerness to work that made them spe-cially valuable. They were fearless under fire, and many of them were killed at their work of digging trenches and placing barbed wire entan-glements under fire."[41] Captain McCormick characterized the Chinese as "strong, healthy looking men, capable of enduring great physical ex-ertion, and [they] could work at an extraordinarily high pressure if they thought they could reduce the number of hours to be worked, to free them so that they could sit on their 'hunkers' in little groups gam-bling."[42] One British officer in France wrote in a letter that "I am much impressed with their ability in all directions. . . . [T]he tradesmen, boot-makers, smiths, fitters, engineers etc are as good and in some cases better than English workmen. All this confirms my idea that if China were united, if the Chinese had an idea or an ideal to work or fight for, she could and probably will conquer the world in any sphere. It is an awe-inspiring thought that riches and material and brains are now lying fallow in that great country."[43]

The Chinese engaged in multiple types of work. They repaired roads; dug foundations; worked in powder factories, arsenals, and acid factories; loaded and unloaded trains and boats; and manned paper factories. During wartime, those with the BEF were chiefly engaged in loading and unloading military supplies at the different ports in northern France. But most Chinese soon got involved in digging trenches, and trench digging occupied most of time and labor of the Chinese working under the British. Trench warfare was, of course, a key feature of the Great War. According to Paul Fussell, trenches on Allied side and the Central Powers side added up to 25,000 miles. The total trenches occupied by the British alone reached nearly 6,000 miles. Theoretically, one could walk underground from the coast of Belgium to the Swiss border.[44] The Chinese seemed to be experts at trench digging. One British officer testified that among the 100,000 men under him—English Tommies, Indians, and Chinese—the Chinese dug on an average 200 cubic feet per day, the Indians dug 160, and the Tommies dug 140. This did not go unnoticed by the command. One officer remarked: "In my company, I have found the Chinese laborers accomplish a greater amount of work per day in digging trenches than white laborers."[45] Although no records anywhere indicate how much the Chinese were involved in trench digging, it is safe to say that they were a critically important part of trench warfare.

A fair number of Chinese also repaired roads and constructed railways, while many others near the front handled munitions transportation. The BEF Directorate of Labor's War Diary recorded that the Chinese were allotted to important work, and "indeed, so far as *ammunition* [emphasis original] services are concerned, practically all the labour employed on the Northern L. of C. and a material proportion in the First, Second, and Fifth Army Areas is already Chinese."[46] Chinese with the French and American Expeditionary Forces mainly loaded and unloaded military supplies; but many under the French also worked where skilled mechanical training was required. Some of them became exceptionally skilled. By the end of the war, and for some considerable time thereafter, virtually all the cranes used in Calais, Dieppe, Havre, Rouen, and Zeneghem were operated by Chinese.[47] Fred Sayer, a British officer who worked with the Chinese, was deeply impressed by their skills. He later told the following story: One day, his Chinese laborers were asked by the army engineering depot to lift a huge naval gun from the ground. Sayer thought this job "worthy of the skills of Hannibal and his elephants." To make the situation worse, the Chinese had no means of lifting such a hefty load of naval destruction, "a long barrel weighing tons." Surprising to Sayer, the Chinese figured out a brilliant way to do this job: "wedges put in one end, beams at the point of balance, the other end raised. Slowly and without much effort, . . . the gun was raised, even to having safety beams to prevent rolling." Sayer was so proud of the laborers that he declared that the Chinese had "beaten the army engineers." Sayer even thought all the Chinese laborers were "engineers" to certain extent because they were so skillful in making tools and building things.[48]

The Chinese also did well making duck boards for military purposes. According to Brigadier General W. R. Ludlow's diary, they were contracted to do so many yards of duck boards each day, assuming a twelve-hour day, but they did their work so well that they finished by 4 o'clock and "would not do a stroke of work beyond that hour, but chose to gamble and smoke the rest of the time." An inspector came around and was furious to find them idle, but his protests were absolutely useless. The overseer said they made a contract that they had kept. They produced the required length of duck board each day, and if they chose to work harder and finish earlier, that was their business, and no persuasion or threat would induce them to work overtime, although duck boards were very much in demand.[49]

The British obviously tried to get the most out of its Chinese laborers by finding those who possessed the skills they needed most. The Chinese were tested for their proficiency in various trades. The British certified 4,725 Chinese as highly skilled workers.[50] The BEF Directorate of Labor's war diary noted that skilled Chinese labor was employed at tank shops, in wagon erecting, and at light railway workshops.[51] Three Chinese companies employed in the workshops of the Tank Corps had "become so skilled that they are practically running some of the shops entirely."[52] The No. 51 Chinese Labor Company of the Chinese Labor Corps was the first detachment to arrive, on August 8, 1917, at the central workshops at Erin and Teneur with 200 skilled laborers. On August 26, 1917, an additional 270 skilled laborers arrived. On September 15, 1917, the No. 69 Chinese Labor Company arrived with 476 Chinese. Then on October 10, 1917, the No. 90 Chinese Labor Company arrived, again with 476 laborers. Later, the No. 90 Company went to help them. This company was moved, and No. 173 Company was sent to replace it. The earliest contingent, No. 51 Company, was not released until February 21, 1919, after the stress of work had subsided, but 75 of the most skilled men were transferred to No. 69 Company. No. 69 Company and the greater part of No. 173 Company remained engaged in breaking up tanks after the war.[53]

Although these men were highly skilled, they needed to be trained to handle tanks. After all, tanks were a brand-new type of weapon and machine. But training proved difficult because there were few interpreters and "It was not good policy to allow white tradesmen to coach Chinese at the bench." The Chinese made fascine bundles, tubular radiators, and sledges. The official report indicated that Chinese work on tanks was instrumental for the military to "deliver the goods up in time."[54] One writer concluded that "Chinese labor was able to fill a considerable gap in the skilled-labor market for tank repair in France."[55] The Directorate of Labor declared the work of the skilled Chinese labor in these shops to be quite "satisfactory throughout."[56]

The use of Chinese for highly skilled work was unprecedented, since such roles were otherwise reserved for white workers. As one scholar has pointed out, "Had the skilled-labor situation not been dire enough to demand such a departure from the normal all 'white' workforce, it is difficult to imagine that the Chinese would have been employed in any capacity" at the Central Workshops.[57]

Chinese workers came to France to help the Allies, and they won high marks for their performance and their cheerful nature. According to a London *Times* article, Chinese laborers were always "in blue or terra-cotta blouses and flat hats, hauling logs or loading trucks, always with that inscrutable smile of the Far East upon their smooth yellow faces." The article added that "the Chinaman is more versatile and adaptable. He can handle stores and do other things for which a certain intelligence and initiative are required. But he makes a very good coolie also, and can pile or unload heavy timber all day without feeling the strain. He is a capable worker, and easy to manage if his European supervisors are careful to leave plenty of responsibility to his own headmen and overseers."[58] The French also were pleased with their recruited Chinese laborers because they were "sober, strong, enduring, and peaceful."[59] General Ferdinand Foch called the Chinese "first-class workers who could be made into excellent soldiers, capable of exemplary bearing under modern artillery fire."[60] French officers in charge of them also positively assessed their capabilities. Lieutenant Colonel Gondre reported to his division commander that his laborers were "docile, intelligent, and good workers."[61] Another officer reported that after finishing an inspection of various labor camps he found the Chinese laborers intelligent and much preferred over workers of other nationalities.[62] Because of their good reputation, the French welcomed them with great enthusiasm. According to an article in the *Far Eastern Review*, a French crowd at Le Havre cheered when the Chinese arrived.[63]

Chinese laborers were more welcome than workers from other countries such as India and Egypt. When one French port needed workers, after "examining several categories of foreign workers," it chose to request Chinese. The request report explained that Chinese workers dealt with the ocean climate better than those from Portugal and other countries. For the duration of the war, both the Ministry of Armaments and the Ministry of War continued to press for Chinese workers because they believed them to be more effective.[64]

Chinese workers in France under British control made a good official impression as well. In its evaluation of all kinds of workers, the British War Office pointed out that "a great many of the Chinese workers were skilled or readily became so, and have been used freely in railway, ordnance, and tank workshops."[65] Douglas Haig, the British commander-in-chief of the BEF, came in contact "with the Chinese in France and for the first time learned the splendid material of which a Chinese workman is made." According to Haig, the Chinese worked steadily, were satisfied with small wages, and "can do without the luxuries of the western workman, and that in the great labour competition these Chinese had the great possibility of creating a great army."[66] Another British officer H. R. Wakefield reported that the Chinese laborer was "a splendid and versatile worker, inured to hardship and almost indifferent to the weather. . . . [T]heir speed and endurance are phenomenal."[67] One sergeant said, "I have 1,000 Chinese laborers who have been working under me in mechanical work for the last year. I am absolutely satisfied with them, and, if I can help it, shall have no other."[68] Another officer reported the following story: "During the last big push by the Germans, the Chinese laborers working behind the lines offered their services to help the wounded, who were streaming back from the front in all kinds of conveyances. When official permission was given, they gave their own cigarettes and rations of food to the wounded men they were helping.

The wounded soldiers were greatly touched by such a kindly act, and one of them remarked, 'the Chinese laborers have hearts just as good as ours.' "[69]

The Chinese were not called upon to take active part in the fighting, but there were many instances where they showed courage. One senior YMCA officer wrote, "When the big spring drive of the Germans was in full swing about a year ago, the Chinese were literally indispensable. At that time it was one continuous round of preparing new positions to which our men could fall back in front of the terrible Hun onslaught. These coolies performed work then that I don't believe any other class of labor could have done. It was they, as much as the fighting men, who stopped the gaps and barred the road to Paris and the channel ports."[70] The *New York Times* reported that during the 1918 German offensive on the Western Front, "remarkable incidents connected with the prolonged battle are becoming known. One of the most dramatic was an audacious and successful effort of a scratch battalion in closing a gap in the British line. Major General Sandoman Carey, seeing this gap suddenly open, at once improvised a force to close the breach. It was a miscellaneous body, composed of mechanics, aerial artificers, signalers, machine gunners, and men of the labor corps. For nearly six days this scratch force gallantly held its position on the left of the Fifth Army." Although we do not know how many Chinese were involved in this fighting, we are quite certain that at least some Chinese laborers were there.[71] One officer wrote in his diary in October 1918 that "I hear there is to be a large attack tomorrow and that the Chinese are to take part in the actual fighting. . . . I'm not liking the idea of the slit eyed soldiers but it may be that they will turn out alright." He wrote the next day that the fight went well but did not mention the Chinese.[72] Ogden wrote that when Germans broke through the British defense in March 1918, a group of Chinese "put up a very good fight with spades and pick-axes."[73] One interpreter in another context even reported that some Chinese laborers had been taken prisoner by the Germans.[74]

## Sacrifices and Heroic Action

The Chinese reputation for bravery was an important legacy of the Great War although it has been largely forgotten. After the war, 93,357 Chinese received service medals from the British, with only a few not receiving them due to misconduct.[75] In a speech given at an award ceremony on behalf of the British government, Captain William Bull, an officer stationed in China stated, "By your faithful and loyal service you have upheld the best traditions of China and have formed a closer friendship between the East and the West." In the course of the speech, he mentioned several times how honored the laborers should feel to receive the medals, yet he never expressed gratitude to the men for helping the British win the war.[76]

At least two Chinese laborers received medals for Meritorious Service, and one received the Medal and Scroll of the Royal Humane Society for saving lives. Wang Yushan, who received one of the Meritorious Service medals, was given the following citation: Near Marcoing on June 22, 1919, he observed a fire on an ammunition dump situated close to a collecting station. On his own initiative, he rushed to get two buckets of water, which he threw on the fire and then seized a burning British P Bomb (apparently the cause of the outbreak) and hurled it a safe distance. He then continued to extinguish the fire, which had spread to the surrounding grass in which rifle grenades and German shells were lying.[77] "By his initiative, resource and disregard of personal safety," this laborer averted what might have been a serious explosion.[78] Yen Tengfeng from Jiangsu Province received another Meritorious Service medal. He received the award for his "gallantry in the performance of military duty." His citation related how "On the 23rd, May 1919, at Bailleull during an explosion he worked continuously for hours removing tarpaulins from unexploded stacks of ammunition and drenching them with water."[79] Wu Yongchang, a laborer from Zhejiang Province, received the citation from the Royal Humane Society for saving a man from drowning.[80] According to another source, "In one company two Chinese were awarded the British Distinguished Service Medal for conspicuous bravery. They went through a barrage three times to get food for their company when its supply had been cut off by enemy fire."[81] Wang Zhenbiao from Shandong was one of the men who risked his life to transport food and ammunition for the British. *Chinese Laborers' Weekly* declared that his brave action had won glory for China.[82]

There are many other stories of bravery. One case involved a train incident. One evening a train hauling more than ten cars stopped, and the last car full of munitions suddenly caught fire. The engineer cried for help. Several local bystanders did not dare to go near because the car might explode at any moment. But a Chinese laborer named Sun who was strolling nearby risked his life to unlink the burning car from the rest of the train and thus saved the whole train from destruction. The head of the train station offered him ten francs as a reward for his bravery.[83] During the Battle of Picardy, according to a YMCA source, an officer commanding a group of Chinese laborers was caught in a sudden advance of the Germans. He was gassed and could not move. The Chinese laborers stood around him and fought off the Germans with all sorts of weapons. The officer was finally saved by relief forces, while all but a few of the laborers died around him. They might have run and escaped with few casualties, but they did not. "Thus," he said, "I owe my life to the laborers under my command."[84] According to another source, during the "onrush of the German horde," the Chinese were sometimes swept into the maelstrom of battle. They did not flinch. One company all but refused to leave the field, begging for helmets and a chance to show their allies that the Chinese could fight.[85] Their bravery also was noted by Chinese officials. The London legation diplomat, Pan Lianru, who served as liaison official for the Chinese under the BEF, reported that once, as he was giving a speech to a company of workers, German airplanes arrived. The British commanding officer ordered the men to take cover. But the Chinese laborers insisted that the speaker finish his speech and told Mr. Pan they were not afraid of the German bombs.[86]

Interestingly enough, their appetite for fighting sometimes went too far, or at least their actions did not always follow the ethics of international law. One American officer who worked with the Chinese in France told the following story. One night in Calais, German airplanes dropped a bomb into a Chinese compound, killing several men. Then Australian soldiers quietly went to the aggrieved Chinese and told them, "The German swine killed your friends. See? There are some of the Germans' friends," pointing toward a camp of German prisoners. "You take these hand grenades and get even." So the Chinese took the grenades from the Australians, extracted the pins, and threw them among the German prisoners. Those Chinese got even.[87] This story proves a point the British general Ludow mentioned in his diary: Australian soldiers were "rough riders" who lived "far away from civilization," some of whom he called "scum of the Cities."[88]

This same story was repeated frequently. Captain A. McCormick wrote, "It is said that a Bosche shell landed in a camp of Chinks and they immediately squared accounts by attacking a German prisoner of war camp and killing several of the Bosche."[89] Another witness reported that when German prisoners behind a wire fence shouted derisively at a gang of passing Chinese, the insults were taken without the slightest show of emotion. The following day, however, having purchased some Mills bombs (at 10 francs per bomb) from willing Tommies, the Chinese tried to "mop up" the Germans, forgetting, however, to pull the firing pins that ignited the fuses. The Germans knew how to meet this emergency, and without a moment's delay picked up the bombs, pulled the pins, and hurled them back. The result, the witness recounted, "was disastrous to the Chinese brigade."[90] The story of Chinese using grenades against captured Germans was so widespread that it appeared in "Late Call," a fictional work by Angus Wilson.[91]

Chinese actions against Germans were motivated largely by the traditional idea of "teeth for teeth, blood for blood." The Chinese did not hate Germans as a group. Their capacity for friendship and compassion sometimes led them to fraternize with German prisoners of war who sometimes worked alongside the Chinese. Some of the Chinese were said to go hungry for days to save some portion of their bread rations for their German POW friends. They did this so much that the French authorities found it necessary to issue a special order prohibiting similar acts and setting a fine of two days' wages for any such offense.[92] There was also a story about their helping an old homeless Belgian who begged for food near one of the laborers' camps. The Chinese sympathized with him and gave him food every day. But the French officer in charge eventually drove the Belgian away from the camp area and charged the Chinese with stealing food for someone else. One Chinese laborer argued that they had helped the Belgian from their own rations, and maintained that the French had no right to criticize and intervene. He almost got into a fight with the officer. Sadly, the Belgian was later found to have committed suicide by drowning. The Chinese blamed the French officer for the death and plotted to throw him into the river to avenge the old man. Luckily that officer was transferred elsewhere before they could act on their plan.[93] Their generous behavior also extended to the French. One chilly evening, word got around a Chinese labor company that a large number of French refugees were returning to the shell-shattered town that had once been their home. The refugees had no bedding for the night, so the Chinese laborers immediately donated 500 blankets for them, although that meant they did not have second blankets to keep them warm during the cold nights.[94]

*dangerous work*

Because the Chinese, especially those working under the BEF, usually labored in or near the battlefields, many died on European soil for the Allied cause. After the war, they continued to sustain casualties as they cleared the battlefields because such work involved locating mines and unexploded bombs. As late as October 1919, 50,000 Chinese remained in the British camps.[95] After the Armistice, the French planned to use American troops as labor to rehabilitate France, filling in trenches, removing barbed wire, and doing road and construction work. The American commander-in-chief, John Pershing, strongly opposed the idea. He told the French, "It would be unjust and even criminal . . . to use our soldiers as laborers," he said. "Furthermore, the men would not stand for it."[96]

For most European and American soldiers, the war lasted about fifty months, but for the Chinese, the war lasted sixty months or more. As American doughboys celebrated the end of the war and started to enjoy the fruits of victory, the most challenging job had just started for the Chinese under much harsher circumstances. Never mind the dangerous work, European attitudes changed after the war ended, and the French and Belgians became less grateful and more hostile. The Belgian scholar Dendooven has commented that the general attitude of Belgian civilians toward the Chinese during the war had been moderately favorable. But after the war, their attitude changed and became hostile, and the Chinese in many cases became scapegoats for all sorts of crimes in the lawless postwar environment.[97] Other scholars have made the same observation. They pointed out that "the local population did not like the 'Chinks'; nor did their British commanders. There was a lot of racism."[98] To make the situation worse for the Chinese, the support system that had made their lives bearable in the camps collapsed after the war, with many YMCA secretaries and military officers leaving for home. Some Chinese wanted to go home as well and naturally became discouraged when they learned they could not do so immediately. With the war finally over, the Chinese resented being under military control, and considerable friction grew between the men and their commanding officers. According to a YMCA report:

> If the Chinese laborers in France could have been repatriated immediately after the signing of the armistice, it would have been of great advantage to all concerned. The laborers would have returned with a much higher regard for the West than they hold. The British and French would have had

*[margin note, rotated: YMCA report on reconstruction work]*

*[margin note, rotated: w lack of discipline]*

a much higher regard for the laborers than now is possible. Much misunderstanding would have been avoided. During these long months since the fighting ceased, these men whose efforts in the war had been constructive have been required to stay on and clean up the frightful mess of fields littered with the debris of modern war. The curve of efficiency has gone down rapidly. Gambling and crime have increased, yet we cannot blame the laborers, for their lot has been intolerable. On the other hand, we cannot be critical of their employers, the British and French governments. The work had to be done, and some one must need stay behind to do it. It fell to the lot of the Chinese. . . . The Chinese are seeing a sad side of our Western civilization.[99]

*[margin note: Protests + Strikes]*

Due to hostility, bad management, and mistreatment, the Chinese resorted to petitions or strikes in protest. In one French factory, the officer and interpreter for the laborers abused the men by punishing them baselessly. They could not tolerate any more and collectively petitioned the French Ministry of the Army and the owner of the factory, listing the numerous wrongdoings of the officer and interpreter, and requesting that they be replaced. The military authority investigated and found the complaints of the laborers to be true; subsequently, they arrested both the officer and interpreter and replaced them. An article about the incident in the Chinese journal *Lu Ou Zhoukan* published in France attributed this achievement to the workers' establishment of a "self-rule organization" in the factory.[100] But in its next issue, the same journal reported that all those workers were being repatriated to China by the French military as a sort of punishment.[101] However, after protest and intervention by a Chinese laborers' labor union, the military reversed its decision and reassigned the laborers to different factories.[102]

*[margin note: Salvage Work]*

As soon as the Armistice was signed, the British began to move their laborers from the port towns where they had been handling shipping to the devastated areas, where they were employed in salvage work—picking up shell cases, clearing away barbed-wire entanglements, tearing down huts, and in some cases filling in trenches and moving live munitions. The men under French control at first remained in the industrial plants, but eventually about half of them were moved to areas where they also did salvage and reconstruction work. Those with the American army largely worked in salvage plants processing reusable materials from battlefields and port camps.

Chinese labor helped lay the foundation for the work of French reconstruction. According to a YMCA report, one distinguished Westerner

*[margin note: West good for destruction / East good for construction]*

after having visited the Chinese on the battlefield observed: "It looks as if the Occidentals are good for destruction, while the Orientals are good for construction."[103] But these jobs were awful. The Chinese were often called on to bury dead soldiers' remains. Way out in Alsace, around Verdun, at St. Mihiel, and at several other points, thousands of Chinese did nothing but handle the remains of fallen warriors. Anyone would count this work as gruesome, but it was especially hard on the Chinese, who believed that touching dead bodies is extremely unlucky. The men suffered nightmares and thought they were cursed by the dead. Imagine the psychological toll! T. S. Eliot's lines about the burial of the dead surely convey their distress:

*[margin note: Chinese phobia touching dead]*

> April is the cruelest month, breeding
> Lilacs out of the dead land, mixing
> Memory and desire, stirring
> Dull roots with spring rain.[104]

The most dangerous task was clearing away the still-live ammunition. Nobody bothered to train the Chinese about how to handle these materials. Interpreter John A. Lewis recounted how his laborers, unprepared for handling unspent explosives, sometimes shook them and had "their heads or limbs blown off."[105] Supervisors for this work were in short supply, and the laborers had no clue about the deadly consequences of their curiosity. Some got carried away playing around with grenades and pulled the strings, leading to terrible accidents and loss of life. Another tragic story told by a YMCA secretary concerned a worker in a devastated area becoming weary from toiling in the hot sun. He found a coil of rope, put it under his head, and had a noonday nap. On awakening, he felt like a smoke, so he lit up a cigarette and dropped the lighted match lazily beside the rope, having no clue that the "rope" was cordite![106]

*[margin note: live ammo]*

Lieutenant John M. Harrison related that with munitions located near Chinese labor camps, Mills bombs by the score, eighteen-pound shells left behind by the British, and lots of cordite, accidents were common. One laborer got the idea to bang on the nose of a shell so he could get the cordite out—it blew him to bits.[107] Another officer recalled that "A Chinaman had found a Mills bomb and never having seen one before, he was showing the novelty to two other Chinks when the pin slipped out and they were all blown to pieces."[108]

*[margin note: accidents with live ammo]*

If one can argue that the British were negligent for their failure to provide sufficient training in the handling munitions, the following story indicates that some British could even be sociopathic. Charles Ward, a British private, told the following story: Chinese laborers came to one military camp to clean up, and a soldier put Mills bombs in the dustbins as a joke. Seventeen Chinese were injured.[109]

Many Chinese under British supervision stayed in France until 1920, and most of the Chinese under the French stayed until 1922. The Chinese were the last of the British labor forces to leave France.[110] We still do not know with certainty how many Chinese died in Europe during the war. The lowest estimate is two thousand. Gu Xinqing, who served as an interpreter for the Chinese, recorded this number of Chinese war dead in his memoir.[111] Another count suggests that "between two and three thousand coolies were killed" near Calais alone.[112] Chen Da (also known as Chen Ta) in his report for American Labor Bureau published in 1923 also claimed that about 3,000 Chinese laborers in British employ were killed by German bombs while working in the vicinity of Calais.[113] According to an official Chinese government report of November 1, 1917, nearly 3,000 Chinese laborers died as a result of German submarine attacks on their way to Europe, though this number was perhaps exaggerated.[114] The highest total death figure given is about 20,000.[115] A recent book published in China indicates that death casualties reached about 10,000.[116]

These numbers bear close examination. According to one British War Office report, the exact number of Chinese laborers under the British authority killed by German bombs in France was 147, and 20 by enemy bombardment. This report claims that given the strength of the Anglo-Chinese Labor Corps in France, the mortality from enemy action was "surprisingly light."[117] However, even if this number is correct, it does not reflect the whole picture because it covers only a tiny fraction of the losses documented elsewhere. At a British Parliament debate of December 10, 1919, the number of Chinese workers under British authority who died from wounds and sickness was cited as two thousand.[118] The War Office suggested that 1,834 Chinese died in France and 279 died at sea.[119] This number seems to match the British cemetery evidence. But this figure excludes the deaths of the Chinese who worked on British ships during the war. The Chinese minister to London reported in 1918 that that 448 Chinese who worked aboard British ships died of bombing or submarine attacks.[120] On December 5, 1918, the Chinese consul general in London reported that the total death of Chinese laborers who worked on British ships was 863; among them, 442 died from German fire, and 421 died from other reasons.[121] According to the Chinese minister to Britain, 448 of them died in action.[122] Another Chinese official in late 1918 reported that 1,967 Chinese laborers had worked on British ships during the war period.[123]

If all these numbers on the British side are confusing and difficult to verify, it is even more difficult to get a reliable figure on the French side. We knew at least 700 Chinese died on their way to France due to German submarine attacks, but we have no clue about the Chinese who died in France under the French control. Although it is impossible to arrive at a concrete figure due to lack of authoritative evidence, it is safe to say that around 3,000 Chinese lost their lives in Europe or on their way there due to enemy fire, disease, or injury. The graves of these Chinese can be found in France and Belgium, among other places. According to Dendooven, a Belgian scholar, Chinese graves can be found at fifteen British war cemeteries in West Flanders.[124]

## In the Aftermath of the War

Chinese sacrifices were not meaningfully recognized after the war. According to British official acknowledgement, even though Chinese workers had "borne greater risks than other coloured laborers," they were the last to receive even a few minor war medals.[125] The British government even tried to bargain down the amount of pension money granted on behalf of deceased laborers.[126] At the Paris Peace Conference, Secretary for Foreign Affairs Arthur Balfour claimed that China's contribution during the war had involved neither "the expenditure of a single shilling nor the loss of a single life," completely discounting the considerable sacrifices made by Chinese laborers.[127] One report issued at the war's end even suggested that China had actually harmed the Allies because its laborers had brought the deadly "Spanish flu" that swept through Europe and the world in 1918.[128] Instead of showing appreciation, the Allied countries tried to quickly deny any debt to the Chinese, by claiming that they had disturbed "local stability." From time to time, both the French and Belgian governments expressed the view that the Chinese should be removed from their countries immediately once the war had ended.[129] But at the end of the war, about 3,000 Chinese laborers remained, and many eventually settled down in France, including 1,850 skilled workers who signed new contracts to work in the metallurgical industries. Others found employment in the mechanical or aeronautical sectors. Many of those who remained married French women. Two of them lived long enough to receive the French Legion of Honor in 1989.[130] At the end of 1924, according to the official statistics of Paris, 2,400 Chinese remained in France.[131] But even today, they are rarely credited or remembered for what they had done.

A group of Chinese men wait in line to apply for work in the Labor Corps.
(Courtesy University of Leeds Library special collections: Liddle Collection.)

Those accepted into the Corps were assigned numbers, which were easier for the
Western officials to use than the workers' Chinese names. (Harvard College
Library, Widener Library, Ch2.6.)

Both the French and British required the laborers to cut their queues when they were selected to go to Europe. Despite the efforts of the Chinese republican government to eliminate this visible link to the old Manchu dynasty, some men in the countryside still wore them. (Harvard College Library, Widener Library, H812.533.5.)

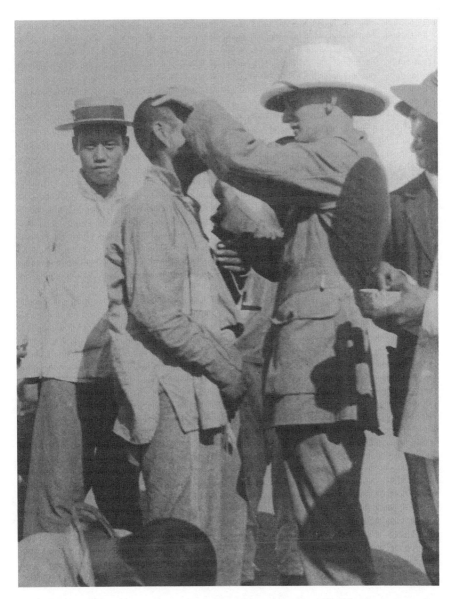

All workers had to pass a physical conducted by a Western official. (Courtesy David Livingstone.)

Men applying for overseas work were confined within an enclosure. (Harvard College Library, Widener Library, Ch2.6.)

Uniforms were provided by the French and British for all overseas workers before they went to Europe. (Courtesy David Livingstone.)

For recreation, the Chinese created their own entertainment, drawing on traditions from home, as in this pantomime. (Andover-Harvard Theological Library, Harvard Divinity School, Harvard University.)

A worker shows off his new uniform before his European journey. (Harvard College Library, Widener Library, Ch2.6.)

Morning exercises were part of a regimented day for the workers even before they arrived in France. (Courtesy David Livingstone.)

Officials held drills designed both to keep the men in good physical condition and to underscore their service to the Allied military. (Courtesy David Livingstone.)

Laborers' relatives in China wait to receive their money from British recruitment centers. (Harvard College Library, Widener Library, Ch2.6.)

British soldiers checked the laborers when they boarded the transport vessels. (Harvard College Library, Widener Library, Ch2.6.)

Workers board the ship at Qingdao for Europe. (Harvard College Library, Widener Library, H812.533.5.)

Laborers prepare for the long and dangerous journey. (Courtesy David Livingstone.)

The Chinese Labor Corps assembled in ranks. (Courtesy University of Leeds Library special collections: Liddle Collection.)

Workers arrived from China on the west coast of Canada and were shipped by train across the country to the debarkation point for the Atlantic voyage. (Courtesy University of Leeds Library special collections: Liddle Collection.)

As they crossed Canada, the Chinese workers were housed in tent camps and kept strictly segregated from the local populations. (Harvard College Library, Widener Library, H812.533.5.)

The Chinese workers provided hard labor for the Allies; this man is hauling dirt. (Courtesy David Livingstone.)

Labor Corps men digging trenches in Europe. (Courtesy University of Leeds Library special collections: Liddle Collection.)

Chief of the Labor Bureau John Price Jackson *(front row, seated fourth from left)* and his staff. (Harvard College Library, Widener Library, H823.616.27.)

The Chinese medical staff with their European colleagues. (Courtesy David Livingstone.)

Four men representing different jobs within the Chinese Labor corps, including guards, skilled workers, and a nonskilled laborer. (Courtesy University of Leeds Library special collections: Liddle Collection.)

A policeman stands outside the workers' hut. (Courtesy University of Leeds Library special collections: Liddle Collection.)

Not free to travel beyond the housing compound after work, workers such as this strongman found various ways to stay occupied. (Courtesy David Livingstone.)

Musical instruments were often fashioned out of available materials or brought from China. (Courtesy David Livingstone.)

A Chinese laborer poses with an Allied airplane crew. (Courtesy University of Leeds Library special collections: Liddle Collection.)

Meals, prepared by Chinese cooks, consisted most often of rice, canned food, and vegetables. The laborers were fed three times a day. (Courtesy David Livingstone.)

This drawing of an original painting shows the burial site of several men in France and the gate erected by the Chinese to mark their sacrifice to the Great War. (Harvard College Library, Widener Library, Ch157.22.)

A victory parade of 10,000 Allied and Chinese troops marks the Armistice in Beijing. (Harvard College Library, Widener Library, Ch157.22.)

Some Chinese laborers remained in France after the war. This is the family of Zhang Changsong, his French wife, and their children. (Courtesy Christian Tchang.)

# 5

---

## TREATMENT AND PERCEPTIONS

---

In the Middle Kingdom he was born,
Frail like, left alone, forlorn;
Among the millet, rape and rice
He seemed unworthy at half price;
Uglier than the dust he seemed:
Love was not his, dead or dreamed.

Among a million little lights
He flickered, hardly shone, at night,
And his lean body manlier grew
All unaware, pale blue to blue,
A godless uneventful span.

Until one day the Great White came
And gave his patterned mind an aim;
And sent him packing overseas
With a hundred thousand more Chinese;
And landed him in warring France
To do his bit and take his chance.

With pick and shovel, pole and spade,
The Happy Labourer, born not made
Bears his burden and does his bit—
With nimble limb and nimble wit,
Side by side with Tommy he toils.
All unaware for immortal spoils.

*—Daryl Klein, "The Happy Labourer"*

The preceding poem comes from the diary of a British officer who supervised Chinese workers. It clearly reflects the common racist attitude held toward Chinese at the time. This type of racism was reflected in British culture, politics, attitudes, and management of the laborers.

## Perceptions

Among nineteenth-century British, the widespread assumption was, "Asians and Africans were children, to be firmly dealt with for their own good."[1] The official code "forbade any hint of sentimental sympathy with colonial or subject peoples. Sternness in dealings with the heathen became a virtue never to be compromised; they were children to be judged, ruled, and directed. And yet mixed with this arrogant belief in racial domination one often finds elements of incredible ignorance concerning, say, Oriental or African customs and cultures."[2] In the course of the war, many laborers were brought to France from South Africa to help the British military forces, and the British imposed a policy of separation for Africans from the white race. This policy, according to an African scholar, was "designed to stifle any signs of incipient class consciousness, and to eliminate, as one officer indicated, possible exposure to 'socialist ideas.' . . . Indeed, a central feature of the contingent's sojourn in France was the extent to which attempts were made to control the socio-political perceptions of members." Upon learning that French women involved in providing refreshments for men engaged in the war effort had also served tea to black dock workers at Rouen, one British officer immediately told the Africans concerned: "When you people get back to South Africa again, don't start thinking that you are whites just because this place has spoiled you. You are black and you will stay black." The same author commented, "It is certainly ironic that German captives, enemies of the British empire, were somewhat better off than South African blacks who, as subjects of the empire, had been sent to France in support of the Allied cause against Germany." The British tried extremely hard to keep blacks from socializing with white women and sequestered them in compounds. British officers declared, "It is absolutely essential that the Kaffir should regard white women as unapproachable; the mischief that can be done by merely good-natured familiarity— apart from anything worse—is incalculable; and the people who will suffer from this . . . are the wives and daughters of our settlers in South Africa." Due to the blacks' resistance to British treatment in France and their likely political awakening there, the British and colonial authorities decided to dissolve the South African Native Labor Contingent in January 1918.[3]

South Africa was a British colony, and the British were deeply worried that politically awakened Africans might present a threat to British interests there. Little matter, given the tenor of the time, that China was no British colony and that the Chinese laborers had come to support the Allied cause. The London *Times* wrote, "The Chink, like the Kaffir, has to be kept under ward when he is not working. He gives little trouble if rightly managed, gambles a good deal, but does not get drunk or commit crimes of violence, and is docile and obedient. But he must be restrained from contact with Europeans, and he has his own little tricks and dodges. As one Chinaman is, to the Western eye, indistinguishable from another, there is always a danger that Ah Lung may try to draw the pay of Weng Chow, who is on the sick list or has gone home. Consequently every coolie has his finger-prints taken and is registered under the supervision of a Scotland Yard expert. He is also taught to conform to British ideas of sanitation, cleanliness, and discipline."[4] With their pervasively ethnocentric attitude, little wonder the British maintained broadly racist views toward the Chinese laborers even though these people had come to help them.

In many British minds, the Chinese laborers were childish, bad, mean, and dirty. Daryl Klein of the CLC believed that he and his follower commanders had been appointed the "new masters" of the Chinese.[5] His diary fully reveals his attitude: "As children we were taught to believe that both Cain and coolies were murderers from the beginning; no coolie was to be trusted; he was a yellow dog."[6] Klein insisted that an ideal officer for a Chinese labor camp was one who did not understand Chinese and did "not laugh or even smile" in front of the Chinese.[7] Klein wrote that "Lieutenant Hitard would not credit the coolie with any sense of gratitude, with any good faith, with any trustworthiness."[8] Jo Carstairs and her friends who went to France to volunteer as drivers during the war claimed that they were afraid of the Chinese laborers.[9] Dolly Shepherd, a British woman who served as a driver with the Women's Army Auxiliary Corps on the Western Front during 1917–1919, was interviewed in 1975 at London's Imperial War Museum. She told the interviewers the Chinese were bloodthirsty and she was scared of them because she did not know them, they were strangers, and they touched everything and wore three hats.[10] John Grainger, a private who served with a Lancashire Fusiliers on Western Front, when interviewed for an oral history project conducted by the Imperial War Museum in 1989, still referred to the Chinese laborers as "Chinks."[11] Major P. H. Pilditch described the Chinese who came to his camp as "queer-looking 'Chinks' belonging to a Labour Corps" in his diary of November 28, 1917. "They were a rum lot, with parchment-coloured faces and rat-tailed wisps of hair, wearing every sort of old hat from toppers to battered straws, all grinning and talking at the tops of their voices. It was, however, not so funny when the officer in charge produced an order giving them the right to the huts used by half our Battery! However, after much protest, out our men had to go and we had to get tents to put them in. Rather typical of the way we do things, to put Chink road-menders in good billets instead of English soldiers!"[12] In a letter to his mother, P. E. Ogley wrote in spring 1917 about the Chinese not far from his camp. "These people were the dirtiest and most horrible people I ever met. The stench from them would stop a clock." They wore many different types of clothes and "one fellow had a khaki English tunic, a little brown pair of trousers, a pair of gaiters, and to top the lot, a woman's hat!"[13] The British army banned the Chinese from using the BEF canteen. One officer wrote in a letter to his wife that the policy "seems rather hard on them," but the canteens "exist for the British Troops."[14] In his letter to his wife on Nov. 1, 1918, he complained that the Chinese singing and playing were very annoyingly strange.[15]

The perception of the Chinese was so negative that one officer of a Chinese labor company complained about it. In his lecture to the British troops, he pointed out that the Chinese laborers were "looked upon as being everything that was bad and treated as such." He asked the British to treat them more as "gentlemen," and noted that the Chinese were more trustworthy than some of his French or English friends. T. O. Wilkins, who heard this lecture, wrote in his diary that he indeed had found some of the Chinese who worked at the airplane area to be "very intelligent."[16]

The good management and treatment of Chinese laborers depended on the general provisions agreed to by national governments, but even more upon local management and the general living conditions at a given place. It would also have been useful for the British and French to develop a decent understanding of the Chinese and their customs, but this seemed to be lacking, especially on the British side. The Great War was fought by trench warfare and the Chinese excelled over all other laborers within the British lines at making and maintaining trenches. But with the many misunderstandings, miscommunications, and especially misperceptions about the Chinese, Britain and France were often not able to foster the great potential of these laborers. Mutual complaints, blame, and finger-pointing happened not infrequently. Many Chinese working for the British were housed in tents, dugouts, or temporary huts; frequently they did not have enough food, warm clothes, and other crucial supplies.

Compared with activities in the base camps, war zone work was carried out on an emergency basis; labor companies were often moved from place to place at short intervals. The need for services and supplies in these areas was the greatest, and the Chinese usually got short shrift.[17]

Captain A. McCormick, the commander of one Chinese labor company, noted that the BEF did not even pay much attention to its British laborers. He wrote that most labor companies were called upon to do dangerous, nerve-wracking work that they were not physically fit for. "We were hard pressed for men to meet this supreme effort of the Hun and the history of how nobly these 'naebody's birnes,' as they were so often justly called, rose to the occasion and did much to help stem the onrush has still to be written." He pointed out that

> indeed without their assistance in trenching in depth, in helping to erect barbed wire entanglements and making machine gun rests, in keeping the columns supplied with ammunition and the roads passable and in 1001 other ways, thereby freeing the fighting troops to do their own proper work, one shudders to think what the result might have been. For several days prior to the launching of the great attack we got hints that the probability was that some of our men who were completing machine gun nests in the region of "Happy Valley" would be captured.

Laborers, even British ones, were the last to be helped. When Germans were coming, the laborers were told to find their own way out. No wonder they sang this song on the way back to camp:

> The Lord made the Bee,
> The Bee makes the Honey
> The Labour Companies do the work
> And the R.E.'s draw the money.[18]

If Britain's own laborers received such treatment, one can just imagine how the Chinese fared. The workers of the Fourth Regiment at Calais worked barefoot and without coats for three months in the winter of 1918.[19] The thinking went that the Chinese would feel better if the British justified the miserable conditions with the excuse that "this was wartime" and asked for their understanding. Overall the British maintained a racist haughtiness. To their minds, it was not the Chinese who had come to help them, but they who were helping the Chinese become civilized; they openly reminded them they were a second-class race.

The British authorities never considered these laborers their mental equals. They maintained the firm colonial attitude that Chinese should not be permitted to associate with either military or civilian Europeans. A. W. Paton served as a corporal gunner during the war and kept a detailed diary of his experience. He wrote that in September 1917, when he visited his friend Claude Betts who had charge of a company of CLC in Reninghelst, Belgium, he noticed on his way through Reninghelst that headquarters had put up a large notice "for the benefit of our troops." "It read: DO NOT SPEAK TO THE CHINESE. Beneath this, in equally large letters, some wag had chalked: WHO THE HELL CAN?"[20] This story, though ironic, clearly reflects the British military authority's perception. One proclamation by Colonel R. I. Purdon, who succeeded Colonel Fairfax as chief of the CLC, declared that because Chinese workers were "separated by distance from their mother-country, parents and kinsmen," he had to look on them as children. Britain wanted the Chinese to "respect and obey."[21] The official policy prescribed that British officers should not become familiar with Chinese because "it caused a loss of prestige and a much decreased efficiency."[22] It "clearly warned" Chinese laborers that "complaints as to quality and quantity of food, errors in pay and allotment, treatment by overseers, work, hours, etc., etc., will receive no consideration if accompanied by unlawful acts." Official notes for the CLC state, "It is essential that discipline should be maintained by the officers and NCOs." To guide officers and NCOs, the notes reminded commanders about a number of points: The Chinese came to France primarily for money, and the Chinese laborer was a rigid adherent to his contract though agreeable to modifications, that is, task work, if it were advantageous to him. The Chinese was unequalled as a judge of human character, so the best procurable class of white overseer was therefore necessary to obtain the best result. Chinese were fond of litigation and lodging complaints, and though they could be "sworn," their evidence must be accepted with considerable reserve. Undue familiarity between any white personnel and Chinese employee was to be deprecated as "subversive of discipline."[23]

## Communication Problems

Besides widespread British racism, cultural ignorance and misunderstandings also explained many management problems. Both France and Britain experienced problems communicating with the laborers. Marius

Moutet, a French politician, wrote that many Chinese were not happy in France due to the ignorance of many of the people who dealt with them.[24] The serious shortage of interpreters made the situation even worse. Chinese college students who could speak foreign languages and foreign missionaries were two major sources for interpreters, and both were in short supply. Many interpreters were poor quality. One British official wrote, "three interpreters were all we could get in time to go with the party as two others who had been sent down were found to be absolutely useless. The majority of the interpreters are a poor lot and I sometimes think that it would be extremely dangerous to allow them to do any interpreting for officers who have no knowledge of Chinese."[25] How could the Chinese workers communicate their complaints?

The lack of effective interlocutors led to misunderstandings on all sides. The quality and quantity of Chinese-speaking officers were such that communication and disciplinary problems were inevitable. On numerous occasions, labor companies had only two or three white officers, none of them able to communicate in Chinese, and no reliable interpreter. Sometimes the commander had to rely on a phrase book with common phrases in English and their equivalents in Chinese, with characters and phonetic pronunciations. The following incident provides a good example of what could happen in the absence of functioning interpreters. A near-riot broke out when one officer started the day's march by shouting to the men, "Let's go!" This command, with its English emphasis on the final word, which sounds like "gou" (dog) in  Chinese, was deemed a serious insult by many of the men, especially northerners. The men assumed they had been basely insulted and refused to move, and the British punished them (a similar situation happened under the Americans as well). As one former labor company commander pointed out, "Gruff commands were misunderstood for insults, and coolies refused to work." But the "phraseology of the 'Tommie' unfortunately is bountifully besprinkled with terms in which 'go' is salient. Interpreters were not only difficult, but almost impossible, to obtain. Much valuable language was wasted on both sides, and more misunderstandings resulted."[26]

Communications between the Chinese and British were strained at best, but even communications between the Directorate of Labor and the persons who ran the CLC were hardly effective. A British officer who knew the whole system extremely well complained in a confidential letter, "Things generally are not going on so well in the Chinese Labour

Corps." The letter went on to point out that management had "reduced the Chinese Labour Corps to an absolutely headless condition." Men who had never seen a Chinese before had been given command; many officers proved quite unsuitable for commanding the companies. "This militates against smooth working and there is no uniform policy being observed." Although the huge CLC had companies all over the British military zone, it had only a lieutenant colonel (B. C. Fairfax) in charge, with his second-in-command only a major (Major Purdon in the beginning). The Chinese labor companies usually worked in places under group commanders who were senior in rank to CLC officers and thus often had the upper hand in deciding how to use the Chinese, although these senior officers might know nothing about effective handling of the laborers. "Mistakes are being made right and left."[27] Although the British recruitment offices and British legation in China seemed to be in close contact, the British military did not bother to maintain effective communication with Britain's legation in China regarding labor issues in France. For instance, the BEF did not notify the legation about the deaths of laborers until 1921. On February 21, 1921, when the British legation finally received a list of the Chinese who had died in France, the legation asked for information about many other deaths; otherwise, it felt it could not explain what was going on to the Chinese government.[28]

Serious problems arose in the field, and when officers could not settle grievances, "drastic measures are taken whereby coolies are shot down, innocent and guilty alike, which all leads to unrest and brings British prestige into danger among them. Practically every week these shooting affrays take place, and in almost every instance they are the outcome of the coolies' inability to make themselves understood to their superior officers." Although Fairfax and Purdon both were "experienced and very competent officers" in their dealings with the CLC, they were "handicapped at every turn." Group commanders "seem afraid of Chinese and restrict them from any liberty outside their barbed wire enclosure" when not at work; others went to the opposite extreme, as in the case of one group commander who officially sanctioned the laborers' access to French prostitutes as happened at Dieppe in November 1917. On one occasion, an officer was sent from general headquarters to try a Chinese laborer by court martial; he brought with him a supply of plates because the British got the idea somewhere that a Chinese way of taking an oath was to break a plate, after which he would speak the truth.

Lack of knowledge about the Chinese and their language prevented officers from being aware of what was going on, and this was reflected in the degree to which gambling was permitted, by which thousands of francs were won and lost, and crimes instigated. Differences of opinion among the Chinese got no guiding hand:

> Quarrels are not quelled, persecutions are permitted and as an instance of this I have in my hospital a coolie who was driven to cut off his own hand from vexation. . . . When troubles arise the only way they can be settled is when help is called for from the Chinese headquarters and a specialist officer is sent out. For an establishment of 150,000 coolies only seven specialists are sanctioned, i.e., officers who can speak Chinese fluently and know the Chinese coolies and can settle an outbreak, when companies have got out of hand. These technical specialists are mostly second lieutenants and are men who have lived for years in China and have their wives and families there. As the Directorate has, as yet, done nothing to encourage or promote or remunerate them, having regard to the mulcting of their pay by exchange in China, it is small wonder that no more are coming forward. The missionary societies are not allowing any more of their men to join the Corps, and they are now the only source of Chinese-speaking help unless you drain the consular service.

This account concludes, "From all I have seen the Chinese will work all right if guided properly but these recurring shootings, beatings and harsh sentences to Field Punishment by people who don't know how to deal with them are only heaping up trouble which will sooner or later assume a serious aspect."[29] Clearly, there were serious problems within the CLC. Lacking a means of effective communication and understanding, the British chose to lock the Chinese up when they were not at work. As one British general wrote in his diary, the Chinese are "very useful for work" but "we have to keep them surrounded by barbed wire in order that they may not break out and make themselves a general nuisance." Along the barbed wire enclosures "there are bells and trip wires everywhere."[30]

The whole management system was chaotic. Direct communications between the CLC in France and the recruitment centers in China were almost nonexistent. John Pratt, a key recruiter in China, wrote a private letter in late 1917 to Colonel Fairfax to complain. Fairfax replied: "I quite agree with you about the absence of coordination. Everything connected with Chinese Labour in France should be centralized in one office. Unfortunately it is not. I am 'Advisor' only, and often not consulted, which caused much difficulty in the administration both in France and in China."[31]

When problems arose, the officers immediately turned to the use of force. But opening fire on their own labor contingent did not really produce the desired results. As one commanding officer of the CLC wrote, "Disturbances among Chinese can, of course, be quelled by drastic measures, i.e., shooting those who are temporarily out of hand, but if this procedure be solely relied on, the recent unfortunate incidents which resulted in possibly innocent Chinese labourers being killed and wounded will seriously endanger our prestige in China and lead to still further unrest amongst Chinese labourers in France." In this same memo, he pointed out the "unsatisfactory state of affairs" in many areas that needed "urgent remedies." These included: (1) nonrecognition of the need for "specialist human machinery" to deal with the Chinese labourers, and the drying up of the main source of such (the missionary societies) because of unwillingness to pay more for competent men; (2) the inexperience and unsuitability of many officers serving in Chinese companies; (3) the inability of the Chinese to make themselves understood to their superiors; (4) the unavoidable drafting of a proportion of professional criminals due to the speed of the recruitment effort; (5) the "bitter feeling created amongst [the Chinese] at the measures taken at Dunkirk for their safety compared to those taken for the safety of the Britishers"; (6) promises made regarding holidays that were not fulfilled due to "the exigencies of the Service." Similarly, "when the system of 'Task Work' is applied, promises have not always been kept." Among twenty major problems, he also listed problems with pay, the "large number of officers and NCOs [who] are afraid of the Chinese" and the "unreliability and inefficiency of a considerable number of Chinese interpreters." Finally, the "the venality of some of the British NCOS serving with Chinese companies" had given rise to difficulties as had the "limited facilities for recreation for the Chinese."[32]

The Chinese did display a certain amount of attitude. Another British officer wrote that a Chinese "will not be driven, nor will he be moved by threats or curses. Quickly responsive to a joke, and with a whimsical humour of his own, he may be led by a jest, and encouraged to 'buck up' by chaff when the sternest admonitions have failed utterly to impress." The same officer commented that the Chinese were "very clannish, too. . . . Damn sight worse than a trade union to deal with." He suggested that "the British officer must be just, sympathetic, well-mannered, firm, and at all cost be possessed of a sense of humour and the ability to turn away evil by a timely jest if he is to succeed in the Chinese Labour Corps."[33]

Due to their ignorance and lack of interpreters, the white officers sometimes did not know how to get the Chinese to do their jobs, and they blamed the Chinese for these problems. One American officer, after struggling all day over difficulties with his laborers once declared in frustration, "I wouldn't give 15 cents for the whole Chinese nation!"[34] A French lieutenant described them as parasites, working when he watched them and stopping when he did not. A British NCO said, "Five hundred of these fellows can't do in a week what one hundred white men can do in a day."[35] It seemed never to occur to these officers that they might not be qualified to lead Chinese labor. One YMCA report mentioned that a certain lieutenant in charge of a group of 1,000 men was of a nervous disposition, disappointed in life, and believed in an "energetic" handling of the Chinese. He himself struck them in the face, kicked them, called them names and they in turn cursed back at him. Finally, a strike occurred. "Immediately the guards opened fire and the laborers were shot," four of whom died.[36]

The Chinese responded to their mistreatment in different ways. They sometimes went on strike or resisted violently. Some resisted passively by committing suicide. According to one YMCA report:

> Suicide was not infrequent. One midnight as the Bosche drove us to our dugout we found suspended in the entrance a dead coolie. This coolie had nursed a grudge against the captain and had decided to show his displeasure in this distasteful manner. Next morning the captain spoke to the company on parade. The coolies expected their captain to be deeply moved over the affair, even remorseful, though the original difference with the coolie had been of the pettiest. But, no. The captain was too astute, he did not even deign to speak directly to the coolies, though he knew their language well. "Tell the coolies," he said to the interpreter, "that last night one of them hung himself in the officers' dugout. Tell them if any more of them must hang themselves to be so good as to do it in their own dugouts. We don't like such a mess in ours."[37]

## Punishment as Discipline

Given the lack of understanding and stereotyped perceptions, the British military recognized that "Many Britishers are bluffed, or frightened, or both, by the Chinese, which the Chinese immediately detect."[38] An official notice to its officers in charge of the Chinese declared:

Chinese are not ignorant. They have brains and intelligence and sum up their supervisors in a very short time. Orders and counter-orders and unintelligent distribution of labour, due often to absence of plans, tools and forethought, have a demoralizing effect on Chinese labourers, and induce them to regard our brains as inferior to their own, and greatly tend to reduced efficiency.[39]

Chinese workers with the British were largely treated like prisoners. Except in already devastated areas, they were kept in barbed wire enclosures and were allowed into French villages only on special passes and "for good conduct." In general, these laborers were worse off than those under the French, and British authorities, far from shy about admitting their tough attitude toward the Chinese, were clearly proud of it. One confidential report from the quartermaster general of British troops in France and Flanders, R. Ford, recognized that "whilst a British Chinese coolie is not allowed to enter cafes or estaminets, the French Chinese coolies are not subject to any such prohibition."[40] The BEF rarely attended to maintaining good relations with its Chinese workforce; all the military was interested in was discipline. Punishment rather than good management was consistently used to control the Chinese. The British boasted that Chinese laborers under their control "are under the strictest discipline and are subject to far greater restrictions than are the coolies working under the French administration."[41] The British military authority even complained that French people were too friendly to the Chinese. The French "civilians, by their actions, have rendered the enforcement of the British orders to the Chinese on this subject most difficult," complained one official from British military headquarters in France.[42]

Of course, there was nothing wrong in stressing discipline, but the root of many problems lay in poor management. The British recognized that the Chinese were "hardy men, and properly handled, are among the best labourers in the world," but "to obtain anything approaching their potential efficiency in France is a difficult matter under army conditions."[43] So in the military setting, inevitably it was coercion not persuasion, and guns not language that were usually used to deal with them. T. O. Wilkins, an air mechanic, wrote in his diary of January 24, 1918, that the Chinese had mutinied and the British took up machine guns against them.[44] On Christmas 1917, the Chinese broke out of their camps and scattered all over the country after their complaints of being brought so close to the trenches and exposed for so many days to bombing and shelling were ignored by the British. The British "got together a scratch picket and machine guns to round up the Chinks who had broken camp." Several Chinese died.[45] On December 28, "a good many of them are still at large and have not yet been rounded up."[46] According to an eyewitness's diary, on December 25, 1917, "All went well until the men's dinner hour, when an urgent message called for two armed parties of 100 men each to deal with an outbreak—'mutiny,' 'insurrection' were words one heard—among the Chinese labourers. By the time our parties reached the Chink camp the Chinks were strolling in by twos, threes, and half-dozens, as quietly satisfied as men coming from a Band of Hope Meeting. They didn't understand what all the pother was about." In this case, the whole mess arose because the Chinese had killed the sergeant-major. They claimed this officer squeezed them too much, had taken 5 francs from each man on the voyage, and punished them too readily.[47] In December 1917, another Chinese labor company rioted at Fonti-nettes, and the men were only subdued after four of them had been shot and a number wounded.[48] According to the official war diary on October 10, 1917, No. 42 Chinese Company in the first army area rioted "due to a lack of appreciation on the part of the officer commanding the company of the standard of discipline to be maintained among his officers and British N.C.Os as regards the treatment of the Chinese labourers. It unfortunately resulted in 5 Chinese being killed and 14 wounded."[49]

Punishment and humiliation were not uncommon methods of discipline. On September 18, 1917, a British soldier named Haigh wrote in his diary that he found six Chinese undergoing field punishment. Their arms and legs were stretched out against a wire fence, where they were tied by wrists and ankles under the broiling sun. This punishment had gone on for hours. One Chinese was made to march around and around the camp with full equipment on.[50] On July 10, 1917, British officer W. A. Dent, who was attached to the CLC, wrote that "about two dozen aeroplanes flew over the camp. . . . One hundred coolies ran away terrified that they were Hun planes! They had experienced the Folkstone raid which had left them very nervous. We had the police out all over the countryside to look for them." The next day he wrote that forty-four of the men had been caught and were tied up to the barbed wire as field punishment. "Each had a card tied round his neck to show the other coolies what the punishment was for." He wrote on July 12 that nearly all the Chinese had returned, many of them only getting as far as Corras.

"One coolie tried to hang himself on the barbed wire but was found in time."[51]

Because of their harsh treatment under the British, Chinese workers occasionally migrated to French camps without authorization. For example, one British document records that "Chinese Coolie 54857 lived in No. 9 French camp for about six weeks from March to May 1919; Coolie 68211, who was absent for over six months, had spent periods of weeks in several French camps. Two coolies from No.149 British Company, when arrested a short time ago, stated that they had been living in a French camp near Litte."[52] In fact, there was a considerable amount of straggling among the Chinese workers. But instead of improving existing management and conditions, the British just adopted stricter measures:

> To facilitate the apprehension and disposal of these stragglers, the following steps will be taken: the registered numbers of all absentees over 5 days will be recorded on the weekly casualty return. The entry on casualty returns will be shown as "absent from company, from date." . . . Whenever Chinese stragglers are apprehended, O.C. CLC, base depot, should be notified by telegram, on receipt of which he will send an escort to conduct the stragglers to C.L.C depot for identification and disposal.[53]

Sometimes even Chinese interpreters working for the British fled without notice. According to Li Jun, the official Chinese inspector of labor affairs in France, interpreters sometimes fled to the Chinese legation in Paris or were caught by police and sent back to the British authorities. Those who chose to flee complained that British treatment was either not fair or the food was too bad, or complained that they were afraid of their exposure to German bombing.[54]

To prevent contact between the Chinese in different camps, British authorities suggested that the French adopt the same strict management. "I would therefore most strongly urge that such steps as you may consider desirable and necessary may be taken to communicate these facts to the inhabitants and that special reference may be made to the extreme importance of their refraining at all times from association or communication with Chinese workers," wrote the British general J. B. Wroughton to his French counterpart in July 1919. At the same time, Wroughton tightened control over his Chinese camps; he justified the tough new regimen by claiming that "numerous cases of complaints as to the behaviour of Chinese workers . . . have recently been brought to notice and it is evident that stricter supervision of these workers is called for."

New rules issued in the middle of 1919 read as follows:

1. Passes should take the form of an entry on the back of the work ticket, dated, stamped and signed. The ganger who was in charge of the party should have a pass giving the regiment number of his party, which should be checked on return. Chinese labor corps are not allowed to leave their camps in the evenings.

2. Surprise roll calls should be frequently held, during which the camp should be searched for possible refugees.

3. Camp police should be held responsible for immediately reporting the arrival of any Chinese laborers visiting the camp.

4. More responsibility should be placed on gangers who are directly responsible for the presence and behavior of all coolies under them, both at work and in camp. Any culpable delay in reporting the absence of any coolies should be severely dealt with.

5. Gangers and coolies should be forbidden to be in possession of civilian clothing [other than headgear] as such was frequently used for the purpose of disguise.

6. Gambling has become one of the chief causes of discipline problems. The proclamation forbidding this crime is being reissued from the Chinese labor corps headquarters and should be maintained prominently posted in each camp.[55]

But the story was not uniformly one of harsh treatment and distrust. Captain A. McCormick wrote that the Chinese "have been of great service to us in this war. I hope we have treated them considerately and wisely, and left no seed likely to breed race hatred with us in future. I have often heard it said if you treated them kindly they just traded on it."[56] Although rare, some British officers did treat the men with kindness and consideration. As much as Chinese laborers hated abusive officers, they did not hesitate to show their appreciation for good ones. F. S. Corke seemed to be one they appreciated. When he left, his laborers wrote a letter expressing their appreciation for his fairness and kindness to them and their regret that he was leaving for the front (he was soon killed).[57] Cormack also wrote that when his labor company had been in Canada, he looked after one man in the hospital, who had undergone a serious operation. This laborer later presented him with a wooden panel he had carved of two animals fighting. In this way, the Chinese showed his appreciation of the attention shown to him.[58]

Besides assigning a few good men to the labor force, the BEF also can be credited with some good deeds. It at least tried to treat the Chinese with respect when they died. If they died in Europe, Chinese wanted their bodies to be sent back to China: "They won't go to Heaven if they are not buried in China."[59] On December 21, 1917, Brigadier General W. R. Ludlow wrote in his diary that he had arranged for burying a dead Chinese laborer in the morning. "The Chinese protested against his being buried here and wanted his body sent to China, but I regretted that I could not make the necessary arrangements."[60] But the British did provide decent graves and funeral rites for the Chinese. Separate graves and coffins were provided for each body. Any boxes or packing cases except those specially ordered to be returned to the bases might be used for this purpose. The British also set up a beautiful cemetery for the Chinese in Noyelles, France.[61] The Chinese were allowed to choose the site of the cemetery. Not far away to the north and west there is a belt of trees and so the "wind and water conditions" (feng shui) were correct. Every funeral was attended by the medical officer for the day. The coffin was covered with the Union Jack and carried to the grave by convalescent patients. A short service in Chinese was conducted at the graveside. A large white cross at the head of the grave bore the name and number of the deceased. On October 29, 1917, one officer wrote in his diary that he "saw three Chinamen being buried at the Chinese cemetery, their coffins covered with the Union Jack."[62]

The British also made real efforts to care for Chinese patients and set up perhaps one of the best hospitals to provide such care. The General Hospital for the Chinese Laborers at Noyelles was well equipped with modern x-ray machines and operation rooms, and staffed with high-grade Chinese-speaking physicians. The medical officers in the hospital, with the exception of two of the three ophthalmic specialists, had all been medical missionaries in China. Twenty-three of these men responded to the call of the government for Chinese-speaking doctors and volunteered for this special service. The facility had sixteen foreign doctors and 300 nurses and attendants. It opened in 1917 and was eventually expanded to a 1,500-bed hospital. Dr. G. Douglas Gray of the British legation in Peking was appointed commanding officer on service in France. "From the very beginning he laid it down as the root principle in the organization of the hospital that the Chinese should have precisely the same equipment as is provided for the British soldier . . . and the ward furniture is precisely that allowed to a British hospital."

The hospital had separate compounds for trachoma patients, and for all other eye diseases and injuries. A very large compound existed for the treatment of mental patients. It included special cells for those who were violent and rooms where occupational training was given to those less affected. It was the most complete facility of its kind under the BEF in France. Another compound was established for the few lepers who had been discovered among the Chinese; these men were necessarily isolated and confined to their own quarters. Another compound was set apart for the various infectious diseases that required isolation. A British ward master was in charge of each of the wards. To help manage the Chinese dressers and the patients, classes were held to teach a little elementary Chinese. A number of them picked up enough to make themselves understood by patients in all the ordinary matters that cropped up in the wards. The actual nursing of the sick was all done by Chinese dressers. Some of them had had several years' training in hospitals in China, but most had had little experience before they arrived in France. When W. W. Peter from the YMCA visited the hospital in 1918, he discovered sixty patients in the isolation ward who were insane. In another ward, there were sixteen lepers.[63]

The commanding officer of the hospital studied the special tastes of the Chinese in every possible way. Knowing how fond the Chinese were of birds, he gradually secured enough canaries to provide each ward with its own little songster. He set the Chinese carpenters to work with odds and ends of timber to erect a small model pagoda near the main entrance of the hospital. It stood about fifteen feet high and gave the place an Oriental touch. The painters spent all their leisure time over several months decorating it with the brilliant colors so dear to the Chinese heart. The pagoda had a useful as well as an ornamental purpose: It housed a clock tower and fire station, and from its eaves hung the gong on which the hours of the day were struck. According to W. W. Peter, a commission of Chinese military officials once paid a visit to the hospital. They went into each of the wards and conversed with the patients. At the close of their tour, the commission leader significantly remarked, "These sick coolies would never have been so well treated by their own people."[64]

## Differences between the British and the French

The camps for British-managed laborers differed markedly from those run by the French. Racism was less pronounced in the French camps. More importantly, the Chinese government had an able diplomat, Li Jun, to watch out for the interests of the men working under the French. When laborers had problems, they sought out Li's help. For instance, one laborer lost his left eye and injured his right leg on the job. When he got into a dispute with his employer about compensation, he immediately decided to contact Li and asked him to seek the compensation on his behalf.[65] Due to their detailed contracts, Chinese working for the French had more legal means by which to protect their interests. On January 15, 1920, representatives of the Chinese laborers in France met with Prime Minister Clemenceau and asked the French government to improve their treatment. They complained about the French military's unfair repatriation policy, and they especially disliked the way the military used a few bad men as an excuse to return a whole company. Clemenceau rather lamely responded that it was difficult for the French to pick out the bad apples from so many Chinese.[66] Besides putting pressure on the French government, the laborers also demanded that the Chinese government do more to seek justice and better treatment for them. On April 6, 1920, some laborers met with Li Jun and other Chinese diplomats in Paris; many of the men criticized Li Jun and the Chinese legation for providing only weak protection of their rights. Li Jun explained limitations of his power and resources. A general meeting passed a resolution to petition the French government for better treatment and to get rid of military rule for laborers. It also passed a resolution asking the Chinese legation to do the same on the laborers' behalf.[67] But the Chinese under the French were already better treated and compensated than their compatriots working for the British. Some French factories even increased Chinese salaries in the face of general inflation.[68]

Where Chinese under the British were quartered in closely packed camps, with the French they were often scattered over a wide territory and enjoyed a certain freedom.[69] "In the British service they are under strict discipline, but under the French are very free, practically having no restrictions placed upon them out of working hours."[70] The French made an effort to become familiar with Chinese culture and treated the foreign laborers on par with their own. Jiang Tingfu, who later became a prominent Chinese educator and historian, worked with the CLC during the war: "From my observation the Chinese laborers with the French were more contented than those with the British. Besides discipline, the difference in the attitude of the officers toward the laborers was also an important factor. Being much less race conscious, they were more democratic in their manner and took a more paternalistic interest in their laborers," while the British officers "stood on their dignity as officers, and perhaps as white men, most of the time."[71] At the government level, the French tried to be fair. One Chinese journal reported the following story in 1920. Two Chinese laborers clashed with a French foreman in a factory. The foreman was badly injured and went to court to sue the Chinese. The French officer in charge of the Chinese got them a lawyer, and the judge eventually ruled that the Chinese had not violated any law; they injured the foreman only by accident. Thus the Chinese walked out free. Another case involved two French women flirting with several Chinese in a bar. A local Frenchman who was also drinking there got jealous and started a fight in which one of the Chinese was hurt. They went to court, and the judge sentenced the jealous Frenchman to several months in jail.[72] Although everyone in France complained about the food at times, the Chinese on the whole were well fed and cared for.

Like the British, however, the French insisted on managing the Chinese by military rule. Punishments were determined in accordance with military law. For serious crimes, laborers were sent to Marseilles, where a special court-martial was convened. A French commandant was at the head of this court, while the administration of local affairs fell to either a lieutenant or a captain. The French had their share of serious management problems. After many tours of inspection, Li Jun concluded that the French did not know how to manage the Chinese and usually put the wrong officers into management jobs.[73] Many Chinese especially disliked the French interpreters, who were generally unfriendly and often abused them.[74] In the French-run companies too, Chinese laborers found occasion to riot and strike. Li Jun listed the following incidents in factories run by the French: On November 8, 1916, all Chinese laborers in one factory rioted. That same November at another site, Chinese laborers went on strike and all had to be removed. On November 13, 1916, Chinese got involved in a fight, and some of them were removed. On January 1917, laborers rioted but the issue was subsequently resolved. On Aril 13, 1917, in one steel factory there was fighting; in July, strikes and major riots took place; in August and September more strikes occurred.[75] According to a YMCA account, "In very many cases the Chinese are in the right."[76]

Of course, the Chinese also must be held to account. As Li Jun pointed out, when they arrived in France, their ignorance of French culture made them suspicious of French rules and policies. They were offended that they had to follow so many rules, with no room for flexibility. Thus suspicion led to misunderstandings. Misunderstandings then led to serious problems, which sometimes proved deadly because the French called in the military to suppress them.[77] Both the British and French set up military prisons for the laborers when they committed crimes:

> When Chinese are committed to military prisons in the Field they will be struck of the strength of their Units from the date of admission to prison, and will be taken on the strength of the 93rd Chinese Labour Coy [company] as from the following day. . . . the military prisons at present in use for Chinese are No. 6 and No. 8. All Chinese on completion of their sentences in these Military Prisons will be discharged to the 93rd Chinese Labour Coy.[78]

Many supplies, such as clothes, shoes, and food items, could not be provided on time. Sometimes the clothes provided were clearly used, and the laborers suspected they came from dead soldiers; this made them extremely angry because they believed it was unlucky to wear dead people's clothes. The French denied this was possible. Sometimes the men got short pants instead of the trousers promised to them. When winter arrived, some laborers went without warm clothes. French promised to make things right, but many times they failed to deliver.[79]

Some Chinese were mistreated by the French on their way home. One case attracted Chinese government attention and intervention. A laborer by the family name of Chao took a French vessel back to China after his service was over. In the course of an argument, a French soldier bayoneted him.[80] Fortunately, he did not die thanks to getting immediate medical attention. The Chinese government demanded an apology and compensation from the French over this incident.[81] The French replied that it had been a case of misunderstanding and the laborer's refusal to follow an order. In other words, they had done nothing wrong but promised to improve their management and policy.[82]

## Armistice and Repatriation

But the worst was yet to come. Chinese laborers who stayed on in France and Belgium after the Armistice inspired fear rather than joy among the returned local population. To the locals, "They were strange guys, conspicuously dressed, with strange eating habits and a strange language. The only thing they were not able to do was work."[83]

The British were eager to get rid of the Chinese they did not need. The first sent back were a group of 365 sick men, who were repatriated on November 1, 1918.[84] Sending sick men on the long journey home was shameful, but it was not a deterrent. In March of 1919, all Chinese in hospitals or recuperating were sent back to China. Their physical and mental state was such that twenty-five died on that voyage and two more committed suicide by jumping overboard.[85] Even Britain's officials in China realized the stupidity of sending the sick men home first. As War Office representative G. S. Moss wrote: "I still think it would have been better, for political reasons, as I have more than once advised the War Office, not to send back many seriously sick and wounded cases until after the bulk of the Chinese Labour Corps had been repatriated. However, it is too late to make any further attempt to prevent this now. I gather that the Authorities are anxious to reduce the number of patients in the Chinese Labour Corps hospital in order to demobilize as many doctors as possible." He further pointed out, in view of impending general repatriation, a hostile protest on the part of the Chinese government, provoked by the return of men wounded by shell fire, "would prove embarrassing."[86] Thirty-two Chinese were never identified and were officially listed as "missing." The rest of workforce started to be repatriated on Feb 14, 1919, with the final contingent arriving in Qingdao on September 13, 1920.[87]

Even CLC head Purdon complained in private about the War Office's rush to send the Chinese back. He called the decision an "unpleasant surprise." "The coolies were rushed down to the Depot and rushed out again—in many cases in a few hours—and my request for more time was over-ruled." He mentioned that in many cases the laborers were not given time to change clothes before they were rushed to sea. "No 18 company arrived in a bad state from the field and the O.C. had to decide whether to let them sail as they were or let them miss the ship and try to get them re-clothed—not an easy matter. He let them go. . . . I have taken disciplinary action against the O.C. I am sorry to say he is a Field Officer and hope it will be the means of coolies arriving at Noyelles decently clothed."[88] This rush perhaps explained why so many laborers arrived at Qingdao in rags. The Qingdao War Office representative reported, "It was unfortunate, but I think unavoidable, that in one point we were open to criticism. I refer to the men's clothes. Tsingtao is a prosperous port. The Japanese see to it that their employees are dressed decently and our men suffered by comparison. They were landed in the kit in which they embarked from France ... the clothes were very dirty and, probably owing to their physical and mental condition, the invalids looked extremely unkempt and apparently took not the slightest pride in their clothes, appearing sometimes on the streets minus buttons, boots and jackets. It was rather humiliating to be requested by the Municipal Authorities to prevent the men selling their clothes in Tsingtao as the Japanese medical authorities considered them, owing to the verminous and dirty condition, to be a menace to the public health."[89]

The BEF's rushed and niggardly repatriation program even triggered complaints from the British. The War Office representative in Qingdao argued the following in an official letter:

> The successful administration of the Chinese Labour Corps will be a potent factor as regards British prestige in China after the war, and I respectfully submit that everything possible should be done by the War Office to ensure that the men return in a contented frame of mind. it would be a grave mistake, which would have a repercussion on British political and commercial interest in China, if the enormous expenditure incurred by the Government and the general fair treatment accorded to the Chinese Labour Corps were to fail in its effect on the Chinese mind for the lack of a certain generosity in official treatment.[90]

A missionary journal based in Britain also noted the following:

> Our correspondent hopes the War Office will see to it that the Chinese go home with no other feelings than those of gratitude and praise for the treatment they have received while in British employ. One hears of some of them going back to their homes in rags. That is a pity. It would cost little, it would accomplish a great deal, if they were each provided with a new suit before leaving for home. One hopes they will not be overlooked in the matter of a medal, or some such token, which they could take home and show to their friends, as a souvenir of the great war in which they laboured and suffered, and of the victory in which they shared.[91]

One can argue that during the war, the treatment of the Chinese laborers reflected more of a general Western cultural blindness, frustration about the ongoing war and with their own society and problems, rather than problems created by the Chinese. To the French and British, the Chinese came to symbolize the war and the West's moral decline. For certain French, the presence of Chinese laborers signaled both French weakness and suffering. By commanding Chinese labor, the French government could send more French to trenches for slaughter while the Chinese enjoyed a comparatively good life and their women. As one scholar commented, "The war represented a crisis of French masculinity, and attacks on nonwhite laborers represented one dimension of that crisis."[92]

By and large, Britain lost a historic opportunity to demonstrate to the Chinese that its people were fair and leave a positive impression. They could have used the opportunity to show the best side of the West and Britain. Instead, as Reverend E. W. Burt commented, "I have met some Chinese in the labour corps who thought they came to see the world. Most of them have been kept within barbed wire. They have not seen much of the world." One scholar has correctly concluded that "Britain's role in the treatment of the Chinese is not one of which anyone can be in the least bit proud," and he contends that the British use of Chinese labor during the Great War was a "regrettable" event.[93]

# 6

---

## STRANGERS IN A STRANGE WORLD

---

### *Chinese Lives in Europe*

The Stranger within my gate,
He may be true or kind,
But he does not talk my talk
I cannot feel his mind.
I see the face and the eyes and the mouth,
But not the soul behind.

The men of my own stock,
They may do ill or well,
But they tell the lies I am wonted to,
They are used to the lies I tell.
We do not need interpreters
When we go to buy and sell.

The Stranger within my gates
He may be evil or good,
But I cannot tell what powers control—
What reasons sway his mood;
Nor when the Gods of his far-off land
Shall repossess his blood.

The men of my own stock,
Bitter bad they may be,
But, as least, they hear the things I hear,
And see the things I see;
And whatever I think of them and their likes
They think of the likes of me.

This was my father's belief
And this is also mine:
Let the corn be all one sheaf—
And the grapes be all one vine,
Ere our children's teeth are set on edge
By bitter bread and wine.

*—Rudyard Kipling, "The Stranger"*

Most of the Chinese who worked in the trenches, factories, and ports of Europe during the Great War rarely ventured far beyond their village borders before they were recruited for France. Now they had come to Europe, the center of so-called Western civilization. But the civilized West was mired in a terrifying war. It was not in position collectively to show off the cultural, intellectual, or political triumphs of peacetime, but in fact could reveal only its ugliest, most barbarous capacities: total mutual destruction and horrendous brutality. Nobody had prepared the Chinese for culture shock or taught them how to adjust to this new life. Everything they saw, everything they were supposed to do, was new and strange to them. The food, the language, the customs, and the management—all were a shock. There was no time or opportunity for them to ponder, digest, and ask questions, since the West needed their labor immediately. This chapter will focus on their experience of the war.

## Clothing, Appearance, and Mood

George E. Cormack, who escorted the Chinese laborers across the Pacific to Canada and then to France, called the Chinese man "a good fellow." "From the time the raw coolie arrived at the depot from his village in the interior of China until we deposited him in France, already half disciplined, I never ceased to admire his philosophic outlook on life; his sense of humour, his natural artistic bent, his generosity and his affection for his parents."[1] Of course, not everyone had the opportunity Cormack did to observe the Chinese so closely. Most Westerners gained only superficial impressions of the laborers from the East. Skimming diaries, personal letters, and memoirs about the Chinese shows how often they were mentioned. Many Westerners were amused by their clothing and style. Captain A. McCormick was amazed at their appearance, "It was a sight to see them tumbling out of the train—a quaint, nondescript, and yet not unpicturesque rabble. About their garb there was no uniformity, which of course arrested the attention when one had grown accustomed to uniformity of dress and action." He pointed out that many of them simply wore pajamas or underclothing. One laborer looked odd with drawers encasing his lower extremities but almost nothing to shield his upper quarters. "Most of them wore straw hats and one Chink had no less than three hats on his head."[2]

It is true that the laborers presented unusual style choices. One British soldier remembered that the Chinese laborers arrived in their traditional padded clothing. "There was a great deal of trouble trying to distribute army issued underclothing etc. and to get them to wear it. I would get hold of a Ganger who gathered 20 or 30 around him: he would have, say, twenty vests and would deal them out as best he could, whatever the size."[3] Another officer remembered differently. A. B. W. Fletcher, a British officer who served with the Royal Artillery at the Rouen and Saigneville ammunitions depots, was deeply impressed by the Chinese attitude toward European clothing. "They would be handed whatever kind of clothes were available at that time. They had very little idea how we used clothes, so they just put everything on in the order in which it was received, so it was no uncommon thing to see a man with his pants on top of his trousers and flannel body-belt on top of his pants, his padded jacket on top of that, and other pullovers and shirts that he had been given on top of that. They made some of the most extraordinary spectacles. Apparently they had a perfect passion for European hats, and whenever they had the opportunity they would buy a hat, and wearing particularly bowler hats seemed to become a status symbol you'd see a man walking about."[4]

Another officer wrote in his personal diary that "the Chinese are very amusing" with strange taste in clothing and kit. "One fellow wears gray pajamas and a top hat and his name is Monkey Joe."[5] Although clothes were provided free of charge, some laborers would purchase worn-out overcoats from British or French soldiers to make their appearance more impressive and local. Some even got in the habit of wearing Swiss watches.[6] One Belgian priest discovered that Chinese laborers liked watches and rings. "Lately I came across a Chinaman who wore a watch on each arm, he was very proud when he saw me looking at his watches."[7] A British officer observed, "These Chinese are extremely interesting to observe in a town. I remember spending an hour or so watching their antics outside a hosiers & outfitters in Rosendahl. They would enter the shop and purchase the most grotesque head-gear you could imagine: they were as 'pleased as Punch' if they obtained a child's sailor hat, it did not make any difference if many sizes too small; others would prefer the trilby shape. You could see some of them clad in velvet suits, others in pajamas or pants only. A walking stick and a cheap watch were apparently the insignia of a gentleman among them; some of them had copied the 'correct London style'—lounge suit and bowler to match, walking stick and gloves. When it is remembered they receive small pay comparatively, it is rather wonderful how they obtain these things. They have the curiosity of children. I had the experience of some of them minutely examining the lining of my sheepskin coat—they were at times a great nuisance in this respect."[8]

Many Westerners were also impressed by Chinese toughness, especially compared with laborers from other quarters, in the face of cold weather. On December 27, 1917, an Indian laborer wrote in a personal letter from France: "You enquire about the cold? I will tell plainly what the cold in France is like when I meet you. At present I can only say that the earth is white, the sky is white, the trees are white, the stones are white, the mud is white, the water is white, one's spittle freezes into a solid white lump."[9] The weather did not seem to greatly bother the Chinese. Captain A. Mc-Cormick mentioned, "One thing surprised me about them. I thought that they would have felt the cold more than we did, but seemingly not, for both when working and walking about, you would see them moving about stripped to the waist."[10] Brigadier General W. R. Ludlow wrote that the weather was "most awfully cold," but the Chinese "are bearing the cold very well, and are wearing thick wadded jackets."[11]

Some observers read political messages in their strange styles. A French reporter noticed that some Chinese wore uniforms decorated with the stripes and badges of all ranks and all armies on their sleeves. They sometimes held umbrellas like British gentlemen, even if the sky were clear and the sun shining. The Chinese in Rouen sometimes seemed to behave as if they lived in a conquered country, like Parisians who visited countryside, making fun of everything, or like Frenchmen in China. When the same reporter visited a Chinese camp, he found the Chinese national flag on display. The reporter observed that the Chinese "were visibly convinced of their superiority over all of the Westerners" and concluded, "They despise us!"[12] Shi Yixuan, the first YMCA secretary to work with the Chinese in France, wrote, "It may be of interest to the reader to know how our men conduct themselves before the public. When our men appear before the French public, they are not as dirty as one is inclined to think. They are, however, conspicuous. Much of this conspicuity may be attributed to their peculiar dress." Most of the men wore uniforms, but some Chinese still preferred to wear Chinese padded gowns and trousers of blue muslin. But Shi pointed out that "the number of men dressed in European style is growing larger and larger each day. It will be only a matter of time before our men will be assimilated entirely by the French as far as outward appearance is concerned."[13]

Of course, not everyone was amused by the strange appearance of the Chinese. Some complained about how dirty the men were. P. E. Ogley joked that these men were so smelly that "the Germans would have bolted for their lives thinking it was some new kind of tear gas" if a half dozen of them had been thrown over into the German trenches.[14] This comment agrees with many sides of the British sensibility and opinion of the Chinese.

Many Westerners were surprised at the laborers' cheerfulness. As matter of fact, given the hostile environment and heavy workloads, the Chinese seemed to enjoy themselves most of time as long as they were not under bad commanding officers. The Chinese laborers by nature were cheerful folks. One observer pointed out that they "do smile most of the time."[15] Another commented that "the most common remark" he heard from Westerners was "the Chinese are always smiling."[16] A. B. W. Fletcher, a British officer with the Royal Artillery at the Rouen and Saigneville ammunitions depots, was deeply impressed by the Chinese interest in European clothing, their reaction to bullying, and a peaceful protest march they held after a dispute with an interpreter. He noted that most of the heavy labour at his depot was performed by the Chinese. "They were very delightful simple people, very strong, extremely good to work with if you treated them properly." He related that they would not stand bullying.[17]

The magazine *Punch* published the following:

O happy Chink! When I behold thy face.
Illumined with the all-embracing smile
Peculiar to thy celestial race
So full of mirth and yet so free from guile,
I stand amazed and let my fancy roam,
And ask myself by what mysterious lure
Thou wert induced to leave the flowery home
For Flanders, where, alas! Flowers are fewer.[18]

Many of the men enjoyed singing, and singing seemed to go with them everywhere. Captain A. McCormick observed the following: "A Chink carrying water—and signing as he jogged along—always struck me as being a very pleasing picture. One day I heard a Chinese lad singing as he jogged along a very quaint though not musical song in a sort of minor key. I think it must have been a love-song for the coolie had a happy yet intent and faraway look in his eyes, and when he observed me a shy smile crept over his face. It must be useful for a Chinese maiden to have little ear for music otherwise that love-song would have fallen on unresponsive ears. It is a wonderfully nicely adjusted thing, human nature."[19] In a letter to his mother, a British officer commented on the roar of song from a nearby Chinese camp.[20] A. Neville J. Whymant, lieutenant of the CLC, recorded and translated many of the songs the Chinese sang while in Europe. Chinese laborers "expressed their mood in songs, thus giving a valuable clue to the secret of his [sic] psychology."[21] They had sung these songs from childhood and learned them from others in their hometowns. One officer commented, "There is never any room for doubt when a coolie is singing. He seems determined that everybody within a pretty wide radius shall be made aware of it."[22]

Still, many aspects of the laborers' lives were not particularly pleasant. Their daily life was also filled with suffering, confusion, misunderstandings, mistreatment, and many other hardships. The Chinese who worked under the British had to deal with more stress and greater challenges for several reasons. Returned behind barbed wire enclosures at the end of each day, the men faced only boredom after their hours of backbreaking work. Harrison's memoir tells of the horror the Chinese endured in the camp at Abancort where one day the Germans bombed the Dump, sending the Chinese fleeing into the woods where they lived from then on. They came in by day to work and scuttled back to the woods to sleep. The bombing got worse and one night the Germans hit the ammunition dump and "blew it for miles into the surrounding country."[23]

James Menzies had been a Canadian missionary in China who volunteered to work for the CLC and was promoted to captain. He had charge of a Chinese contingent. He wrote, "Life among these Chinese is trying because so many misunderstandings arise."[24] Menzies's company usually worked in muddy areas. He wrote, "The mud is deep. Oh so deep that I shudder when I think of the possibility of our moving off into a muddy field with tents and no floorboards."[25] In a letter to his mother, he wrote that "many and many a time I snuggle down in my rough blankets with your quail feather pillow under my head and weep tears of lonesomeness."[26]

If a captain like Menzies had problems dealing with the tough circumstances, how much more must the Chinese who worked under him have suffered? One Chinese laborer described his life in France this way: "All was going well and I was glad I had come, when one night without warning we were suddenly awakened by the sound of a terrific explosion. We ran outside without delay. We heard a faint noise in the air overhead. And nearly every night thereafter our sleep was broken. At the first sound of the gong alarm we were ordered to the cave shelters. One after another fine buildings were destroyed and great holes in the ground could be seen in many places. Many people were killed, even women and children . . . I soon came to dread the clear nights."[27] Another laborer wrote in his diary that on arriving in France, he found he had been cheated because he was sent to the front to dig trenches and transport munitions (although according to his contract, he was not to be working near danger zones). The Chinese often complained about their food and clothes. Sometimes food could not be gotten through, and the laborers worked hungry. When the weather turned cold, they got no heavy clothes, although clothes were promised by contract. Homesickness was widespread.[28]

One of the laborers' greatest frustrations was their inability to express themselves. P. E. Ogley wrote that when the Chinese talked to him, they used a bit of French, English, and Chinese. "We couldn't help but laugh at them."[29] Another observer noticed that "All the coolies picked up a few phrases of English and a word of two of French, always ending a statement with the Chinese termination 'la.' "[30] But they persevered with characteristic good humor. For instance, when they visited French shops to purchase something, the following happened:

> Both sides bursting into occasional fits of laughter over the absurdities of a monosyllabic oriental trying to express himself in French. Or an older man you would see sitting on the corner of some humble village doorstep with one of the little French children in his arms, the fond grandparent looking on with smiling approval at the two children, young and the old, both evidently enjoying themselves; but with conversation mutually unintelligible. Though not an emotional race one could sometimes catch a far off look in the oriental's eye as the dark eyed, dark haired French child reminded him of his own dear babe across the seas. The Chinese love their children and their homes. The two questions I was asked everywhere as soon as they found I could speak their language were, "Which side is winning the war?" and "When are we going back to China?"[31]

Their wish to return home colored the Chinese expressions of solidarity with the Allied fight. British soldier W. A. Dent's diary entry for October 1, 1918, contains the note that when report arrived of Bulgaria's surrender, the Chinese joined the British officers in giving three cheers for the victory, "all to the amazement of the Bosche prisoners."[32] The

188th Chinese Labor Company even sent a note of congratulations to the British king on December 4, 1918. The note was in Chinese, and its translation is as follows: "To his gracious Majesty King George V, hero of the century, and ordained conqueror of the enemies of civilization, May it please your majesty to accept the sincere congratulations of the 188th Company, Chinese Labour Corps, on a great victory; and may we wish you long life and eternal felicity."[33]

Many of the men were homesick and that homesickness was often reflected in their songs. As they would in China, laboring Chinese often made up songs to dispel boredom or reflect their mood on particular occasions. The contents might include their own inventions and references to Confucian ideas and historical stories. They had brought this habit and sensibility with them to Europe. The following song, as recorded by a British officer, seems to be a made-up lyric that reflects the singer's feelings after he received a letter from his brother:

By a stream and a hill is a little town
With narrow streets and small houses.
There are not many shops but I have bought cakes,
And one can buy wine at the New Year.
By a stream and a hill I have a brother.
This little town is my home.[34]

Food was another item that often made them homesick. The laborers, as much as any other Chinese, were obsessed with their home cuisines. So seriously did they take food that they insisted on preparing their own. Brigadier General W. R. Ludlow wrote in his diary that he found the Chinese labor camps he inspected "very interesting": "I never saw cleaner Cook Houses or Kitchens, and the way they cook the rice, which they principally live on, is excellent. They also have little Joss Houses and Temples."[35] Another British commander also noticed that "their camp was spotlessly clean and they were very fond of hot water when they could get it. The cook house hall, made of rough wood, was scraped clean very day."[36] Given the Chinese passion for food, wartime Europe was perhaps the worst place they could have landed. During the war, both France and Britain faced serious food shortages even for the fighting forces. One soldier recorded the following incident in his diary: In spring 1917, he was in a hospital in Estoutre. He "had to sleep on floor—rations almost nil. There was 1 loaf between 14 of us. I soon decided I was well enough to return to duty."[37] Although the Chinese laborers usually had enough to eat, they did not always have the items they wanted and had been promised; they were not shy to complain about the rations and ask for more rice.[38] One YMCA Chinese Secretary observed that the laborers "do always like rice, even in France."[39] The Chinese also complained about the lack of chopsticks, "but after a few days they were quite used to knives and forks."[40]

The Chinese craving for good food made its way into one of their ditties:

> The wild ducks scatter, afraid.
> If only I could fly as my thoughts fly,
> I would have a rich supper to-night![41]

Besides food, the Chinese did not drink cold water and always preferred tea. Fred Sayer, an officer of one Chinese labor company, wrote that the Chinese were absolutely obsessed with tea, "no tea, no workee." For them, the "tea-dixie was the celestial king-kin around which all actions revolved. It was reverenced as a venerable god. One devotedly worshipped the dirty black army Dixie as if it were an idol of gold. From start to finish of a day's work, initiated devotees formed a continuous stream to dip their little tins into the amber colured liquid and quickly swallowed the boiling tea."[42]

## Lived Experience

Sometimes their lives and work seemed so monotonous and dulling that one of them would sing the following:

> Thick mist now hides the sun,
> And gentle dropping of pattering spots
> Urges the dull day on.[43]

But singing could not always kill the time. Occasionally their suffering was so intense that they fell into despair. Anyone who heard the following would understand their frustration and desperation:

> Who says there is no sorrow in this world?
> Alas! Alas!

In the rains the river is not controlled,
Alas! Alas!
Who says there is no sorrow in this world?[44]

Whether they were cheerful, happy, angry, or in despair, overall the lives of the Chinese in France were colorful and enriching. According to one officer of the CLC, "A Chinese is never at a loss to know how to fill in spare time." They smoked, chatted, or studied, or sang.[45] Their songs sometimes gave voice to their attitudes about the future.

What is tomorrow? What will it bring?
One must take thought for this.
He who looks not forth to the morrow
Meet sorrow lurking outside.[46]

They were also curious about the many new things they encountered. That curiosity is reflected in the following wry ditty:

What is it in the big shops?
Soy and pickles, oil and seeds
Are too cheap for these big places.
Do they sell mandarins there?[47]

Because he clearly found the Chinese laborers interesting, a Belgian priest Van Walleghem kept a detailed diary that included his observations of them. He wrote:

They are strange fellows and have very childish manners, not any better than our boys from 10–11 years old. Their favorite occupation is gaping at the shop windows, preferably of the candy and fruit shops and when they see something in their like, they go in with as much as then at the time, asking the price of every item and when it finally pleases them to buy something, they are very suspicious that they will be deceived. However, many shopkeepers are tired of their doings, and that is why the shopkeeper sometimes makes an angry gesture, which makes them fly out of the shop like sparrows. Yellow of color, with a flat nose and oblique eyes, they have nearly constantly a foolish grin on their face and they stare around them, so that it is a mystery that so far none of them has had an accident on our overcrowded roads . . . they are not lazy and work at least as hard as our civilians or as the English soldiers.[48]

On January 8, 1918, he noted that "some shopkeepers have started to learn Chinese, in order to attract these men to their shops."[49]

Curiosity motivated them to learn, to observe, and to understand their new surroundings. Again, they expressed their desire for understanding in the following song, which clearly borrowed Confucian ideas:

Through the senses comes all knowledge;
When you see with your eyes
Do not fail to perceive with your mind.
Where deep waters are, the movement is sluggish
The profound man is slow of speech.[50]

The things they observed frequently made them wonder aloud about the differences between Chinese and Western cultures:

These strange things which barbarians have,
Have devil-bellies which make them go.
But we are a happier people,
Who do not ally ourselves with the devil.[51]

P. E. Ogley wrote that he sometimes ran into Chinese in Belgium who wanted to teach him Chinese to exchange for English lessons.[52] But this was difficult to carry out.

One thing they did learn and enjoy was sports. Fred Sayer observed that outdoor games were played whenever it was light. The favorable game for laborers under Sayer was kicking a paper ball (just paper tied round with string, about the size of a tennis ball). The Chinese formed a ring of any number of players and, using only their feet, kept the ball moving for long periods. Sayer commented that "it was quite fascinating to watch and to the players, good exercise and fun. One came to admire the sportsmanship in this simple game."[53] As a later chapter will explain, the YMCA played an important role in providing entertainments for the Chinese. Klein, a British officer with a Chinese labor company, wrote that the Chinese started to learn about baseball as they waited for their boat in the depot in China. "We would sometimes have a game of baseball, which was always enthusiastically followed by thousands of coolies."[54] The Chinese also practiced boxing, volleyball, soccer and basketball, chess, checkers, puzzle pictures, ping pong, and so on. Captain A. McCormick wrote, "They were fond of wrestling—but their methods seemed more akin to the Scottish than the Japanese style. They were capable of carrying great loads of water by means of Dixies swung on a pole. The load was always heavier than a Tommy cared to tackle and there appeared to be an art in it."[55] In his diary, the soldier Dent wrote on June 23, 1917 that some Chinese played a passing-the-bucket game. "It was great sport to watch them. They got very excited but were very quick."[56]

George E. Cormack wrote that some Chinese passed the time doing artistic projects. "The innate artistic sense of the Chinese came out when they decorated the ground around their tents with elaborate designs picked out on a background of sand, with ground brick, cola, lime, and ochre. Those dragon designs would have made an excellent pattern for a carpet and the pictures of mythological characters seemed to transplant to Canadian soil the traditional art of China stretching back through the centuries."[57] Their artistic taste enriched both their lives and others. When holidays came, they would erect timbers, paint them in red and blue, and make them into a shrine, in front of which they worshiped the spirits of their ancestors who traveled across many oceans to respond to their reverence and remembrance.[58] In a letter to his wife, one laborer related that at Dragon Festival time, the Chinese under the British got the day off. Some Chinese organized themselves into a dance troupe (yang ge) and performed for the different companies. Their show attracted both Chinese and British officers, who seemed to enjoy them very much.[59] A YMCA secretary wrote that one of the labor companies included quite a number of actors, acrobats, musicians, dancers, stilt-walkers, and others, and they gave "repeated and much-appreciated performances" at the different camps.[60]

The French military authority once even asked the Chinese laborers to perform a play written by Prime Minister Clemenceau. The Chinese, the legation diplomat Li Jun, and others performed it on Chinese National Day. Apparently many people, locals and Chinese included, showed up to watch it, but unfortunately the source does not mention what the play was about. On another occasion, Chinese in Roanne took a day off to celebrate their National Day. They set up a beautiful stage decorated with Chinese flags and lanterns. They started the show at 7:00 a.m. with a salute to the national flag. After musical performances, they took a group photo. Then at noon there was a banquet. After the lunch, many games were organized. Fireworks were set off at 7:00 p.m. Dance parties went on until midnight. More than one thousand French locals took part in the celebration. The cost of this event, more than ten thousand francs, was paid by the laborers themselves. The Chinese in Le Havre also celebrated National Day. They used flowers to make huge display characters that read "National Day Celebration." A French factory owner donated holiday lights and more than eighty bottles of champagne for the occasion, and a French officer provided fruit. Chinese laborers held similar events in other places.[61]

Some Chinese were quite skilled at designing and building. One British officer wrote that his company moved to a camp where they found exceedingly comfortable quarters that had been built by a Chinese labor company. The mess hall had been built of bricks made of local clay and dried in the sun. The account went on:

> The interior doors and fittings were unmistakably made by the same hands—the decorative design being remarkable. But more weird still was the Chinese idea of camouflage. The sheds and shelters and the ammunition dumps around were covered with the strangest designs. Chinese Gods abounded, sitting under mysterious orange trees, whose branches extended straight out form the trunks, holding each a golden orange at its end. Dragons and other fearsome beasts were there in every colour. Suns and moons and a perfect constellation of stars met the eye on every side. The whole effect was a perfect riot of Chinese imagination in colour.[62]

As mentioned earlier, the Chinese were master trench diggers. They also produced much of what came to be known as trench art. One scholar has observed, "It was the experience of something new and terrible in human history which produced the greatest flowering of Trench Art." The place of the Great War in our collective historical consciousness "is unique by virtue of the paradoxes and ironies which attended the tragic and hitherto undreamt of scale of death and maiming. . . . It is against this background that every object which can be described as Trench Art tells a story of the momentous experiences of its maker."[63] Trench art pieces from the Chinese thus can tell us a great deal about the Chinese laborers' perceptions of themselves and the war and world. Indeed, the Chinese left many pieces that are both brilliant and thoughtful. More importantly, trench art was the shared art form of all the people involved in the Great War one way or another. The fact that Chinese made their mark in this practice reflects their community with the rest of that world.

After the fighting was finished, the Chinese continued to work, clearing the battlefields and helping to bury the dead. "During this second phase of their activities they continued to make often stunning and elaborate trench art for sale to local civilians, battlefield pilgrims and tourists, the military personnel who supervised them, and those who were engaged in developing the Commonwealth War Graves."[64] As one scholar wrote, "Arguably more secure in their Asian origins were trench-art shell-case vases made by the Chinese Labour Corps. Unlike any other kind of shell-case trench art, these objects tended not only to avoid human figures (generically Oriental or otherwise), but also any reference to the war of which they were a part."[65] According to Saunders, the skills of the Chinese laborers in working metal were "dramatically illustrated in an unusual and beautifully engraved German shell case. Interestingly, the shell case itself was manufactured in a munitions factory at Karlsruhe in 1904 and was presumably fired in the early months of the war in 1914. Almost certainly it lay abandoned in German positions until after November 1918 when the Chinese labourers were clearing the whole battlefield area. The rim of the shell was cleverly flared outward and the body then exquisitely engraved with an elaborate Chinese dragon flanked by a tree adorned with budding flowers in the middle of which a singing bird is perched. Most unusual was the chroming of the finished piece which, by removing the need ever to polish the object, meant that the engraved designs remain as fresh today as they were when made, probably between 1919 and 1922."[66]

The Chinese developed their money-making skills along with their trench arts. Several sources suggest that some laborers made it their business to find out what companies were located in the area and then acquire the appropriate badges and buttons, which they used to decorate trench art items. They sold them as souvenirs to those same companies.[67] In early 1919, a dozen girls from Dublin who volunteered to relieve male drivers in northern France found that Chinese in the Bethune camp, a former aerodrome, used hot tools to beat out patterns on spent shell casings they had found in the fields. These curious jewels became popular among the Irish girls.[68] Joseph M. Woods, an American priest, purchased four brass artillery shells fired on the Western Front, taken from a dump heap, and decorated by a member of the CLC. They were covered with "etched drawings of the most exquisite designs showing dragons and chrysanthemums." He often used these items to illustrate how instruments of destruction could be turned into things of beauty.[69] As one British commanding officer noted, "During leisure hours, they [the Chinese] made souvenirs from scrap materials which had a ready sale."[70]

If life in wartime France was tough for locals, it was even tougher for the Chinese laborers. To survive in this strange and dangerous world, they had to "hang together" and support each other. Because many of them came from the same villages or were related to each other one way or another, these bonds helped many through. The Chinese were also famous for their generosity. G. E. Cormack related the following:

> Just before sailing from China, we handed to each coolie ten Mexican dollars in silver and gave him the option of leaving behind for his parents whatever portion of the ten dollars he cared to allot. In my company [of 500 laborers] the average sum left behind for the parents at home was nine out of every ten dollars, a much greater proportion than would have been left behind for relatives by the privates of any British regiment proceeding overseas under similar circumstances. I can recollect another instance of the coolie's thought for others. Just before embarkation there was a final medical inspection. A small group of very dejected rejects who had failed to pass the doctor passed in front of my company which was on parade. On seeing them coming the Chief Coolie quickly asked my permission to make a collection for the rejects. Soon his hat and the hats of several others were filled with coins, which they handed over to the rejects to cheer them up on their way to their village homes.[71]

When facing common opponents, their bonds became stronger and they invariably chose to present a united front. But this sense of unity had its down side. One YMCA secretary told the following story:

> Yuan comes into our office for money. He hands me his deposit book and asks for five hundred francs. I am struck by the sadness on his face and by the size of the sum he has requested. I inquire what he intends to do with the money. "My brother lost one thousand francs gambling last night. The winners are pressing him for money. The five hundred francs will prevent a fight." "Why don't you and your brother remain separate in your money matters?" I asked. "But he is my brother, of the same father and mother."[72]

The many fraternities might also be attributed to this spirit of community of interest. The fraternities usually consisted of people either from same villages or blood relations or groups based on sworn brotherhood. "They hang together and there are numerous fraternities among them which are very effective in time of strikes."[73] Almost every man had one or two fraternity brothers, and one man had as many as two hundred.[74] A YMCA report pointed out that the Chinese had been found to be good mixers and were popular among the local peasants in spite of much prejudice. They got along well with the people.

The Chinese laborers developed their own codes of behavior. Although they lived under military control, the men did not usually follow military protocol. As one British commanding officer noticed, the Chinese "willingly obeyed their own officers but would ignore any other officer no matter what rank he held." "We should make allowance for the fact that their world and ours are poles apart even if geographically we occupy for the moment common ground."[75] One British officer wrote this about the three Chinese working in his camp:

> The Chinese worry me. They always salute a Corporal or a Sergeant of the British army but never a British officer. I don't know why. They apparently consider a corporal and sergeant superior to an officer and perhaps these children are right. A child whether fully grown or not is usually right, and these Chinks are children. If the Chink did by any chance salute a British officer, he would not be allowed to return the salute—a corporal or sergeant can do as he pleases."[76]

In wartime Europe, many Chinese had daily contact with fellow laborers from other countries. Working side by side with the Chinese were Greeks, Portuguese, Vietnamese, Spaniards, Moroccans, and so on. In spite of the language difficulty, they got on well with their fellow laborers and especially with their French comrades. Their wide grins and good nature, assisted by such familiar phrases as "C'est bon," "bien bon," and "Ça va?," won them many friends. They treated their friends with generosity, and with *vin rouge, vin blanc, café noir,* and cigarettes, all of which were valuable during the war, and their friends were always ready to do them a good turn.[77] Kathleen Charlotte Bottomley served as telephonist with British women's army auxiliary corps in France. She remembered that the Chinese offered her pudding when she was near Chinese labor camps.[78] Although the Chinese were friendly in general, they seemed to be born racists because they did not understand there were different races. To their ignorant minds, only bad people were black. They did not understand why some people had black skins. Nor did the Chinese get along with Arabs; Chinese and Arab laborers frequently got into fights.[79] In one French factory, Chinese laborers worked side by side with Arabs. They did not get on well, and in late May 1917 there was group fighting. Three Arabs were killed and a dozen Chinese wounded. To prevent further trouble, the French government removed the Arabs to other locations.[80] The Chinese especially disliked the Moroccans, whom they called "black devils."[81] Overall they had problems with African laborers simply because of the skin issue.[82] In his reports to the Chinese government, Li Jun mentioned that the black Africans and Chinese often suffered fatal casualties as a result of their fighting. But the Chinese developed close bonds with the Vietnamese, their fellow Asians. Li Jun mentioned that whenever the Chinese got into fights with Africans, the Vietnamese joined in against the Africans. Because Vietnam was then a French colony, the French government did not want the Vietnamese to be influenced by Chinese ideas of patriotism and nationalism and tried hard to keep the Chinese and Vietnamese separate.[83]

Chinese and Westerners sometimes came to blows as well because of misunderstandings and Westerners' discrimination. The Belgian priest Achiel Van Walleghem noted in his diary for Christmas of 1917, "This year's Christmas was particularly noisy. Especially the New Zealanders drink and pour and sway and shout and scream and dispute and look for trouble with the Chinese. The latter become embittered, conspire, and in the afternoon and evening there is fighting in several places. Such wild fellows!" He also wrote that several of the Chinese who fought with the New Zealanders were later executed.[84] This observation is confirmed by the Chinese graves in Belgium and other verified records. On that Christmas day, some Chinese laborers stationed at Reningelst under British supervision got into trouble first with their own fellows. A Chinese foreman and laborer were killed during the quarrel. Then the Chinese began fighting with the New Zealand soldiers. The British immediately sent out soldiers to suppress the so-called "mutiny" or "insurrection" in the "Chink Camp." Nobody knew for sure what really happened then. But according to an official report of IXth Corps, "Three (were) shot, and about nine wounded, by rifle fire." The graves record indicates that five Chinese died that fatal Christmas day: two at their own fellows' hands, three shot dead by the British military. According to an authoritative account, two of these men were buried in Reningelst Chinese cemetery (No. 19665, Su Fengshan and no. 29009, no name registered). They were probably the foreman and the other man who were killed by fellow Chinese. The three who were killed by the British soldiers were buried in Westouter British cemetery (CLC no. 43913, Wu Enlu; CLC no. 43804, Zhang Zhide; and CLC no. 39540, Zhang Hongan).[85]

Although we don't know further details about the Chinese fight with the New Zealanders, we have some detailed information about their fighting with Australian soldiers. British officer T. V. Haigh witnessed group fighting between Chinese and Australians, and his diary preserves a detailed description of what went on. On November 22, 1917, late on a dark afternoon, Haigh saw two Canadians throw a Chinese laborer from the adjoining camp into a ditch, "roll him over and hold his head under the mud and water." After he got free, "The laborer was screaming like a child and some of his pals came up. He told them what happened." Haigh wrote that he knew enough to see that the laborer believed his assailants were Australians, not Canadians. "I could tell this from my knowledge of his Chinese signs." At that point, the Australians occupied Caestre, and the Chinese intended to attack them there that night. Haigh wrote he did not know why, but "the sign of a Chinaman to an Australian is like a red rag to [a] bull," and he presumed that the Chinese knew this and therefore had "jumped to conclusions." Haigh informed his commanding officer of the coming trouble and suggested that he put a notice on the Orderly Notice Board that cancelled all leaves that evening for the British soldiers. Then with permission from his officer, he and some of his friends went to watch the fight. They arrived just as the fighting started. "When we arrived at the village there was an Australian soldier standing in the dimly lit doorway of an estaminet. A rifle shot rang out and he fell dead. Then more shots and Chinese appeared from every quarter, some with picks, shovels, bars of iron, wood handles and, as is usual with them, due to their foot covering, they moved silently about." They ended up watching the fight all night. "When we left in the morning the Australians were massing for an attack on the Chinese camp into which they threw hand grenades and caused a lot of damage and many casualties. They had lost some men in the night. Cavalry were brought into the village to keep order and the Australians were removed from the village and surrounding area."[86] It was still not clear why the Chinese concluded that the Australians were behind the attack. Perhaps they shared the perception of Australian soldiers as "rough riders."[87] It has to be pointed out that certain British soldiers behaved badly toward the Chinese as well and even egged them into violating the rules. P. E. Ogley wrote one day that two English "Tommies" brought a Chinese into "our contaminet and wanted to bet that this fellow could escape out of a chair, no matter how we tied him. They brought no end of ropes and chains with them for the job. Thompson and Ogley would tie him up. Although they tried their best, The fellow escaped alright." The two who brought him over went round with a cap and collected the money.[88]

Although their fighting with the Australians was bizarre, their surprise contact with King George was a remarkable event. In late 1918, George V was inspecting his victorious armies and needed a quiet location for luncheon on a certain Friday. Someone in charge of arrangements decided that "Company 58 Chinese Labour Corps was that quiet place." Word of the king's visit reached the Chinese there only days before. The men got excited. Some asked, "May we receive the emperor?" Others wondered, "How shall we do it?" Somebody suggested, "On parade, with a King's salute, and a cheer." There was not enough time for the Chinese to learn how to pronounce "Hurrah." So a YMCA secretary decided that the Chinese word *hao* or "good" would be used instead. The Chinese thus practiced until three *hao*s sounded something like a British cheer. The Chinese also practiced salutes with sharp turn of hand to the side. They were instructed, "Don't bring it down till the emperor returns your salute." "What? Will the emperor return our salute?" "Yes, of course he will." The cheer was to follow the salute. "Be sure and shout with all your might." "Won't it startle His Majesty?" asked one intelligent laborer. "No, he is used to it," the YMCA secretary answered.

In addition to practicing the cheer, the men took the initiative and added something more after their own style. They quietly pooled their francs and sent into the nearby town (Cambrai) for brightly colored cloth, and from it worked a fantastic yet pretty archway over the door to the royal mess-room. They also erected a real Chinese triumphal arch in his honor. Chinese mottos about the dawn of peace and the virtues of the king and his ministers emblazoned the walls, and flags fluttered everywhere. The best writer of the company wrote a message of welcome in large Chinese characters which meant in English, "All rejoice at the dawn of peace."

On the day the king arrived, the 480 Chinese lined up from the roadway to the mess-hut, and waited with bright faces and eager eyes. The king seemed surprised at the smart appearance of these laborers, all standing at salute, which his majesty smilingly acknowledged. Then the three "haos" rang out, and of course, the king did not know they were shouting "Good, good, good" to him. They shouted a Chinese welcome when his Majesty came, and sent him off with a cheer like "the sound of many waters." The King seemed "highly pleased and the Chinese, of course, were much elated." The king sent out a special message to the men, telling them of his pleasure at their kind welcome and thanking them for the decorations and good wishes. The YMCA secretary who witnessed the whole thing wrote, "Those lads from far Cathay appreciated the king's thoughtfulness, and were delighted that his majesty had acknowledged their salute. You may be sure that incident will be talked of in many a far-off home." After lunch the king paused on his way to the car to ask a few interested questions about the Chinese and shook hands with their captain. The account continues:

> When the cars had sped away, we entered the mess-hut to find that the royal fare had been beef and cheese sandwiches. We took a cheese sandwich to show to the Chinese still standing outside. "Look what his majesty eats!" They peered at the sandwich and scarcely believed what they heard. "It's bread and cheese, just what you eat yourselves. Taste and see." It was an opportunity to show how high and low alike were in the grip of war rations. The sandwich was broken up into a dozen tiny pieces. "It isn't often you will taste royal food," one lad took a morsel and tried to conjure some special flavour into it. "Hm! It has a taste of King," said he.[89]

## Entertainment, Sex, and Romance

Despite all their mistreatment and the challenging environment, the Chinese were relatively well behaved. The official records commented that "generally speaking, the Chinese give little trouble" and "drunkenness is rare." "All British ranks are strictly forbidden to supply any intoxicating liquors to Labourers. All estaminets and cafes are out of bounds for Chinese."[90] According to one source, there was only one case of drunkenness among the whole 100,000 in the British army. But the Chinese did commit wrongdoings. To be fair, some of them were bound to make trouble, no matter what. The worst of them, and their horrifying crimes, gave the Chinese a bad name, which was unfortunate. The following incident is a case in point. A man entered his camp's kitchen one afternoon. He was hungry and demanded food. But the cook was busy and asked him to come back during mealtime. Instead of leaving, the laborer killed the cook and was, of course, soon sentenced to death.[91] In February 1919, a Chinese laborer named Wang Chunchi (no. 44735) killed a fellow Chinese in their camp at De Klijte, Flanders. He escaped, but was later caught by military police in Le Havre. He was tried in Poperinghe on April 19, executed on May 8, and buried in old Poperinghe military cemetery. He might be the last person executed in the Poperinghe area by the military authority. Some records indicate that the execution may have taken place in the courtyard of the town hall. If that was the case, Wang perhaps was only person to be executed there.[92] But such crimes were rare; the chief misdemeanors were gambling and petty theft. In the absence of a trained leader to guide them in other leisure pursuits, they took to the only thing they knew: gambling. Li Jun often mentioned the gambling problem in his reports.[93] Shi Yixuan also noted that the laborers liked to gamble.[94]

By and large, most Chinese were careful with their money. Up to August 1918, the British ran a savings bank for the Chinese. The War Office would collect the deposits and put them into the accounts.[95] Its terms were not friendly, however: Only one deposit could be accepted from each laborer in any month, and no withdrawals were permitted.[96] Despite their lack of access to a flexible banking system, "Eight out of ten of the men are saving up their earnings to take back to their village homes and have already put away in the savings bank no less than 14,000,000 francs. One man recently gave 150 francs (that is to say, 150 days' wages) to send the Gospel to China."[97] Si Zhaoji, Chinese minister to London, reported on May 26, 1919 that Chinese laborers had deposited 51 million francs in French banks. This was a most impressive savings rate.[98]

But in the face of boredom, some of the men could not resist temptation. Gambling, though prohibited by order, was a common pastime. One British officer discovered a laborer with 10,000 francs on his person, the gains of gambling.[99] Gambling became a serious problem, especially for those under British control. Some of them gambled away the fruits of their hard work and got into terrible fights, which sometimes ended tragically in murder or suicide. Lieutenant John M. Harrison, a CLC officer, wrote that the laborers sometimes threw Mills bombs during gambling feuds.[100]

The Chinese, of course, must bear responsibility for such behavior. But as one YMCA official pointed out, the British are also due a portion of the blame. "It was almost criminal to keep five hundred strong, healthy men in an enclosure week after week with nothing to do in leisure time but twiddle their thumbs. Of course they would get into mischief."[101] Some Chinese realized that gambling was bad and they organized antigambling societies. In one camp of 416 men, over 100 were members of the anti-gambling society. An uneducated laborer had initiated this effort. He never gambled himself, and as proof of good faith, he gave his entire savings of two years—some 500 francs—to the Chinese government through the Chinese peace mission.[102]

If gambling was a major problem for the Chinese under the British control, prostitution brought serious trouble for the Chinese under French management; these were the two great evils among the Chinese laborers. Shi Yixuan observed the widespread patronage of prostitutes by the men.[103] The Chinese working under the French enjoyed more freedom and they also had opportunities to work side by side with French women in the factories. They were lonely and bored as this song suggests:

A crow on a far-off bough,
Outlined against the falling snow,
Is such a picture as will find
An echo in my desolate heart.[104]

With ample opportunities to visit prostitutes, some of them yielded to the temptation. A YMCA confidential report noted that at Feisin there was a group of 1,000 of Chinese laborers:

They were quartered in great barracks. On one side were their own quarters, on the other side were the Portuguese laborers, equally as ignorant and ill-kempt as the Chinese. Across street was the compound that sheltered over a hundred women munitions workers who during the day worked in the powder factory side by side with the Chinese. These women were many of them of low, even criminal, class and were forward with Chinese as they worked together, unquestionably seeking their money out of hours.[105]

In China, men and women did not mingle freely during work time. But in France, French women were all around and socially available everywhere—in factories, cafés, and villages. Some French women, as one YMCA secretary pointed out, "are of a questionable character which does not reflect honor upon a great country like France. The Chinese, on the other hand, are just as much a source of shame to China as those women to France, for men, in the face of such temptation, are as spineless as babes." According to official records, 5 percent of the Chinese recruited by France suffered from the consequences of their "immoral life." But this percentage by no means indicated the real situation; according to Shi, who worked with the French-led Chinese as a YMCA secretary, "It overlooks those cases in which the men are doctoring themselves. It would not be an exaggeration to say that twenty percent of the men here are under treatment outside the hospital."[106] According to one YMCA report, the men working under British, due to their treatment as virtual prisoners, had an average of only four out of every thousand afflicted with venereal diseases.[107] One confidential report mentioned that a commander of the British CLC complained of how the white race was being lowered in the estimation of the laborers by their contact with the low white women, and then jokingly remarked that out of this war "there would emerge one chocolate-colored race."[108] In his diary on November 16, 1917, Brigadier General W. R. Ludlow wrote that in the Chinese camps, "There was much chaffing going on, as it was rumoured that there were lady Chinese dressed as men among them."[109] The so-called Chinese lady might have been a French prostitute since it was impossible to have a Chinese woman near the camps.

To be fair, many British and American soldiers also frequented prostitutes in France. Pershing was deeply worried about venereal disease among his soldiers and told Secretary of War Newton D. Baker that he wanted to send the army home "clean physically and clean morally."[110] In wartime, moral values declined with the rising mortality rate. The British, American, and French military all did the same. As one British soldier wrote, "We had tea in a small tea room, officers galore with their women folks, it seems to me soldiers wherever they go manage to pick up women. Our men are no sooner in a place than you see them with girls." "On the Western Front brothers were soon regular appurtenances of base camps and of larger towns serving as rest quarters. Men would queue up, as at the latrines, the only difference being that the military police ensured order."[111] According to one soldier's war memoir, there was a No. 4 Bar in France, which also had many prostitutes working there. The place was always crowded with soldiers:

Along the low wall of the House of God stood a queue of troops stretching two or three deep to where at the end of a sort of cul-de-sac, an estaminet sign could be seen. In the queue were Canadians, Australians, English troops, British West-Indian blacks with rolling eyes and all-embracing smiles, non-combatant corps conscripts, Chinks, out for the evening in clean overalls—taken all round, it was well representative of the allied forces.[112]

It is important to keep in mind that most of the Chinese laborers did not commit crimes or make a habit of visiting prostitutes. It was not fair to jump to the conclusion that the Chinese in France were a debauched people. As Shi Yixuan pointed out, "Our men compare very favorably with other races in their moral fight."[113] Interestingly, these Chinese men were often a popular choice as husbands or boyfriends among French women. During the war and after, with so many men dead from fighting, "many women had to look to the older generation for husbands." In these circumstances, the young hale Chinese laborers were a godsend for many women.[114] The military authorities had run into several love cases, and Shi discovered a poorly written proposal of marriage from an ignorant French girl to one of the Chinese. That may not have been an isolated incident.

The Chinese seemed to be genuinely popular with French women. One Chinese laborer recalled that one old French lady tried hard to get him to marry her daughter. But he had to say no because he was engaged to a girl back in China.[115] Some French women even went to the Chinese legation in Paris to petition that their husbands or fiancées who were laborers be allowed to return. The women complained that their men had been sent off by the officers in charge to Marseilles to be sent back to China; this was a French government measure meant to discourage cross-racial marriages. They wanted the Chinese legation to intervene.[116] Jiang Tingfu, who served as a YMCA secretary for laborers under the French, remembered that one day a French girl dashed into his office and told him she wanted to marry a certain laborer. She asked Jiang for help. Jiang reminded her there were major differences between Chinese and French cultures. She might experience some serious cultural and other challenges after she became a Chinese wife. This lady replied by saying that she had considered everything and was even prepared to go back to China with this man if necessary. Jiang was quite puzzled by her determination and asked the reason. She said that if she did not marry this man (surnamed Yang), she might never find a better husband. She had known Yang for about one year. He did not drink and had never beaten her up. But if she chose to marry a Frenchman, there was a good chance that he, if she was lucky enough to find one, might be alcoholic and spend all their money on wine and beat her up frequently. She thought her marriage with Yang would be a much happier one.[117]

We don't know what happened to this woman and whether she succeeded in marrying her Chinese laborer, but we do know of some successful romances. In one labor camp, three Chinese laborers—Lu Huchen,

Shi Baozheng, and Yang Fushun—all married French women. Lu's wife was his coworker in the factory. Shi's wife was a shopkeeper near his camp. Both Lu and Shi were well off financially, but Yang did not save and was poor when he got married. His French wife did not care at all, however, and told people that she intended to go back to China with Yang in the future.[118]

We know the details of one love story—that of a laborer named Zhang Changsong and his French girl. Zhang, born in 1897 in Jiangsu Province, left for France in June 1917. He worked in a mining factory and stayed behind as a miner after most of his comrades had returned to China. He spoke little French. One day in 1920, the twenty-three-year-old Zhang got into a dispute with a paymaster about an error in a friend's salary and demanded an immediate correction. Largely due to this disagreement and perhaps Zhang's limited language skill, the dispute soon escalated, with Zhang dragging this poor French paymaster to his superior's office. Zhang's action deeply impressed a sixteen-year-old French girl who was cleaning the room when the scene took place. She fell in love with Zhang, they eventually had thirteen children together, and they were happily married for more than sixty years.[119]

Frenchmen obviously disliked the fact their women were marrying Chinese. A police report from Le Havre, dated May 1917, noted that the some local Frenchmen were not happy to see Chinese workers there and even rioted against them. According to the report, the French were disappointed with the high war casualties their country had sustained. "It is frequently said (in the munitions factories), that if this continues, there will not be any men left in France; so why are we fighting? So that Chinese, Arabs, or Spaniards can marry our wives and daughters and share out the France for which we'll all, sooner or later, get ourselves killed at the front."[120] From this anxiety sprang tensions between the Chinese and local people. There appear to have been many cases of this sort, since it attracted the attention of the French government and led the Interior Ministry to issue a notice that discouraged French women from marrying Chinese. The notice claimed that the Chinese laborers were poor fellows, and many of them might have been married before they came to France. The notice also referred to the cultural differences between the two countries. Even the Chinese government got involved and requested that its laborers consider cross-racial marriages carefully. The Chinese diplomat Wellington Koo informed the French government that the Chinese government would make sure that Chinese who were to marry French girls were single. Chinese-French marriage issues sparked serious debate. Li Shizeng, an important Chinese educator, echoing the day's popular thinking on eugenics, argued that cross-racial marriages were a positive for Chinese civilization because mixed marriages would produce a better race for China.[121] Another Chinese thought it was understandable that the French government cautioned women who wanted to marry Chinese laborers. But he thought the French military authority went "too far" and even "violated their human rights" when it sent away laborers who had already married or become engaged to French women.[122]

Unfortunately, we may never know the true picture of Chinese marriages with the French because the French government censored any news that mentioned Chinese-French romances.[123] Although the evidence is sketchy, it seems safe to claim that about three thousand Chinese laborers chose to stay in France, and many of them got married to French women. Sexual relations seemed also to have taken place between Flemish women and the Chinese. The evidence is extremely limited, but cases must have certainly occurred, according to one Belgian scholar.[124]

# 7

## AMERICAN SOLDIERS AND
## CHINESE LABORERS

Most of the major powers quickly became embroiled in the Great War, but the United States was not at first one of them. In 1916 President Woodrow Wilson had run for reelection under the slogan "He kept us out of war." But as soon as he was reelected, Wilson decided to join the war effort. In April 1917 the United States officially declared war on Germany and labeled the American version of the conflict "The War to End All Wars."

### Americans Cried for Support, and the Chinese Arrived

In the fall of 1917, American doughboys began to arrive in France. But the Americans were in no shape to fight—they were poorly trained, and their military was short of everything. They were simply not ready for war. "During 1917, the War Department was only half at war," one scholar pointed out. "Propelled by the exigencies, the United States moved in several directions, all at the same time." During the first six months of the war, few American troops left their camps, and rations of food and other commodities were slow in coming.[1] So bad was the supply situation that a board convened to study troop movement said ominously, "It is a matter for examination and decision whether the flow of troops should not be checked until adequate supply arrangements have been made." The situation was equally bad back home in the United States, where a rising tide of complaints came from all over the country about mix-ups, delays, incompetence, and inadequacies. So great was the uproar that in mid-December the U.S. Congress launched an investigation, summoning camp commanders to testify about conditions. After hearing a recital of horror stories, Senator George E. Chamberlain, the Democratic chairman of the investigating committee, dramatically summarized the findings: "The Military Establishment of America has fallen down," he said. "It has almost stopped functioning . . . because of inefficiency in every bureau and every department."[2]

These systemic problems made the American Expeditionary Forces (AEF) desperate for laborers who could support their war effort; they also explain why the Americans subsequently had so many management problems with the Chinese. As one general pointed out, "At the start two principal problems were revealed. One was labour, the other was tonnage."[3] During the months of December 1917 and January 1918, when the number of AEF personnel was still small, it was clear that the United States lacked the necessary labor for a quick expansion of the war effort. The AEF had to turn to labor from Europe to meet the urgent needs it faced. Charles P. Dawes, general purchasing agent of the AEF, was appointed to fix the labor problem for the military and ordered to create a labor bureau. Specifically, Dawes was charged with procuring civilian manual labor, and he was also designated as the sole agent through whom labor negotiations were to be conducted with the French. He appointed Captain John Price Jackson as chief of the Labor Bureau within the AEF (he was soon promoted to lieutenant colonel) and appointed Captain Jeremiah Smith Jr. as the deputy chief. Jackson had been labor commissioner of Pennsylvania and was supposed to be experienced in labor management. The AEF Labor Bureau was established on February 1, 1918, and by late December it oversaw more than 80,000 civilian or semimilitarized laborers for the American services. But all did not go smoothly. John Jackson acknowledged that "by reason of the lack of knowledge of our American Army personnel of the customs, ways, and manners of the foreign labor procured, which was of a great variety of nationalities, the difficulties of coordinating civilians into the work of an army system, and the need of carrying on the work in full harmony with the French, and the French law, made the project a most complicated one."[4]

With systemic problems in its Labor Bureau, the AEF, under direct order of John Pershing, following a "careful study of the situation in France," went on to create a brand new department, the Army Service Corps, which was charged to coordinate the American military effort. Like the Labor Bureau, the Army Service Corps was created too much in haste. Its functions were not well defined, and it had to develop operations flexible enough to cover any demands made upon it. Still, the Army Service Corps grew from this humble beginning to become a powerful organization. The Labor Bureau would become part of this new unit. The Labor Bureau and administrative labor companies were formally incorporated into the Army Service Corps on August 22, 1918. The total number of men procured by the bureau, including replacements, would reach 82,700 workers by the signing of the Armistice.[5]

On February 5, 1918, the AEF requested an immediate supply of 50,000 laborers from the French "on the grounds that it would result in the release of a proportionate number of our troops now engaged in labor for combative contact with the enemy on the line."[6] On February 15, the AEF again entreated the French minister of war's intervention so that "the American army should receive without delay the labor contingents" the French could dispense. The Americans indicated that they urgently needed at least 30,000 laborers immediately. They justified this urgent request by the following considerations: "The American units now in France and those arriving at the present time are composed of young troops who must continue their intensive training in view of fighting. Whereas the other Allied armies have at their disposal numerous troops of workers of which the total number represents a very important part of the contingents, the American army is only formed of fighting troops." The request further indicated that without labor support, American military value to France would be lessened. "Even now, 26,000 young American soldiers have been withdrawn from military service to perform labor which might be executed by workmen. Different means of obviating that deplorable state of affairs have been considered. The allotted shipping space being limited, asking the U.S. Government to send earth-workers and laborers is not to be thought of, as this would diminish in the same proportions the number of soldiers conveyed to France." To make situation worse, the Americans, who could not bring American laborers to Europe, encountered great difficulties hiring European laborers. The American government had thought of using Italian militarized workers, but that plan did not work out.[7]

Instead, the French government immediately allowed the AEF to borrow about 10,000 Chinese. The Chinese, Indo-Chinese, and North Africans who would work for the Americans were engaged under group contracts, while the European laborers were recruited individually and held individual contracts. According to an official report, as of August 20, 1918, the French had provided 11,539 Chinese laborers for the

Americans.[8] These Chinese worked directly under American supervision and were not returned to the French government until May 1919.[9] Their main job was to transport munitions and dig trenches.[10] When General Johnson Hagood inspected a major American supply base at Gievres, near the city of Tours, he was amazed to find over a thousand Chinese laborers working there.[11]

The Americans' preparation for the war in general suffered from their lack of training, and this also generated many serious problems in their dealings with the Chinese labor force. A quick succession of reorganizations in the Labor Bureau indicated serious management problems. John Price Jackson later acknowledged, "In the early months of the Labor Bureau activities, it was impossible, with the enormous shortage during the winter and spring, of American enlisted and commissioned personnel in France, to obtain the amount of supervisory men required. As a result, the number of commissioned or non-commissioned officers was variable and depended upon the supply. It was found after some experience, however, that two officers and fifteen non-commissioned officers attached to a company of two hundred and fifty civilian laborers formed about the best operating unit." Extra shipments of officers from America began to arrive by early fall of 1918, and this relieved the personnel situation to such an extent that the handling of civilian labor became a comparatively easy matter.[12] John Price Jackson in spring of 1919 declared in a lecture to AEF officers that when labor strikes and lockouts happened, they would usually arise from three causes: wages and working condition disputes; incompetent, harsh, or thoughtless officers (of any rank, from the foreman to the chief executive), who for personal advantage or by reason of inability to see others' point of view, mistreat those under their direction; and selfish agitators for whom there is personal advantage in a strike.[13] This observation pretty well reflects what happened to the Chinese laborers under American control.

In a personal and confidential memo to General Harbord, General Hagood complained, "Labor is not efficiently handled . . . and there is a feeling everywhere that vast quantities of man-power are wasted. The principal cause of this is . . . poor organization. In many cases the men do not live near enough to their work; in other cases they are not properly fed—the Sick Report is too high and in general the labor is not properly officered." To fix the problem, the army transferred labor supervision to the Army Service Corps. Still, the problem was not completely solved, because the key to it, as he pointed out, was "inefficient and inexperienced personnel." The constant shifting of personnel was one of the greatest causes of inefficiency. Many officers thought the labor companies were not a good place to work and secure promotion, and the acute shortage of personnel meant the labor companies usually did not get even reasonably qualified officers.[14]

The French minister of war provided Chinese laborers to Americans on the condition that while the laborers worked, they should be under American officers and enlisted men; when they were in their quarters outside of working hours, they should be charges of the French. Disciplinary measures were to be administered as necessary by the French officers after consultation with the American officers attached to the group. All terms in the French contract with the Chinese should be followed by the Americans, who could not move or transfer the Chinese without prior permission from the French.[15]

American commanding officers in places where Chinese laborers were employed naturally wanted to have entire charge of the Chinese in disciplinary matters, and they requested that an arrangement of this kind be made with the French government. But the French were not in position to give the Americans a free hand, because they had recruited the laborers and employed them under certain obligations. Because of the many unsettled issues regarding how to manage the Chinese, the American authority could not issue definite written instructions to its officers. All they could do was to submit the following suggestions with the knowledge that they constituted the most definite instructions possible at that time:

> The disciplining of Chinese laborers shall be maintained through the Commanding Officers of the Labor Companies, who shall act in accord with, and through the representative of the French Government. The French are under contract with much of this labor, or the countries from which it came, and their representatives should be given full consideration, and the opportunity to have the conditions of such contracts complied with. French officers and enlisted personnel furnished with civilian and semi-militarized labor shall be treated with due courtesy, and assisted in all ways in performing the duties that are required of them by their instructions. They shall also be furnished with comfortable quarters, compatible with their ranks, and shall be given as satisfactory opportunities for mess as is possible.[16]

The AEF's general order stated the commanding general would be guided in his supervision "by letters of instructions, issued from time to time, from these headquarters to meet special requirements in the matter of food, shelter, and general care brought about by reason of different nationalities or required by contract arrangement under which such later was procured." But no such instructions would be issued until much later. The instructions about how to deal with the Chinese laborers were uncertain and unclear to say the least. The same order also stated, "Officers will be assigned by the General Purchasing Agent to care for and otherwise administer the interior economy of these units." No such officers had so far been assigned for this purpose. No wonder the Americans ran into serious problems with both the French and the Chinese!

## Troubles with the French

Miscommunication and misunderstandings between the Americans and French and between Americans and the Chinese were rife. In such cases, the Chinese always came out worse, a point Jackson himself admitted, "There is so much friction between the American and the French officers that the Chinese suffer."[17] The American employment of the Chinese encountered problems from the outset "partly by reason of the lack of understanding on the part of the A.E.F as to the conditions of the contracts, and partly due to the French personnel having a lack of proper knowledge of handling of labor, and the duty which should be expected of it. After sufficient time had elapsed, however, for both sides to become fully acquainted with conditions, these difficulties largely disappeared, and the system worked quite satisfactorily."[18] American officers were not only unfamiliar with the contract terms; most of them were not qualified to command.

With many problems arising regarding the management of the Chinese, the French tried to make the rules clear and frequently reminded the Americans about them. The first major problem was dual control. M. Boschetti, chief of the French Bureau of Colonial Workers, informed the Americans that these laborers were recruited by the French government, which had entered into certain obligations regarding their treatment and discipline. These obligations must be fulfilled by the French government, and French personnel were attached to groups of laborers to make sure they were fulfilled. M. Boschetti told the Americans that he deemed it an "indispensable" right of the French government to control these laborers. The men and their quarters, whenever they were not actually employed in the work of the U.S. Army, should be under the control of the French officer commanding the group; that control would be carried out by him in cooperation with the American authorities. When the American commanding officer wished to administer any discipline, he should request it of the French commandant of the group, who would proceed to take the proper measures. In other words, while the Chinese laborers were actually engaged in labor, they fell under the control of the Americans, but they were under the control of the French from the time they quit work on one day until they began work again the next.

But American officers frequently violated this dual control rule, and the French persistently informed the American command when violations took place. For instance, M. Boschetti informed the command that an American officer at Rimaucourt, claiming to act under the authority of the colonel of the 7th Regiment, U.S. Engineers, demanded that the French officer there turn over control of the Chinese and their quarters.[19] Responding to the many violations, the French told the AEF:

> The French authorities are much disturbed by these incidents. A very large number of Chinese are now employed in France, and it is feared that a serious disturbance among any large group of Chinese may spread to the other groups, causing great damage to the Allied services. The French Bureau of Colonial Workmen therefore requests that the case enclosed be investigated thoroughly, that proper steps be taken to acquaint the Chinese laborers with the fact that these cases are being investigated and persons charged with violence toward the Chinamen will be brought to trial. If [they are] found guilty and punished, that the fact must be communicated to the Chinese through proper channels, so they may understand that justice is being done in the matter.[20]

The subject of discipline was another thorny issue for the French and Americans because the Chinese were provided by the French government and worked on French soil, but under American military supervision.[21] One French officer stationed with a labor company under the Americans complained:

> I am having considerable difficulty in regard to Sunday work with the laborers in this company. I have been ordered to turn out my Chinese for Sunday work on several occasions lately, and it has been necessary to use disciplinary measures to force them to go to work. The other labor companies at this post work for the engineers and they lay off Saturday afternoons as well as Sundays. My Chinese work for the quartermaster and it is sometimes necessary to work them on Sundays. I would like to know how

much authority I have in forcing these laborers to work Sundays as I am having considerable difficulty between the French and the Chinese on one side and the quartermaster on the other. The Chinese do not seem satisfied to take some other day off in place of Sunday.[22]

The French authorities freely offered advice to the American military on how to manage the Chinese. One memo suggested, "There will be no difficulty with Chinese if they understand thoroughly that unfair treatment of them will be investigated by the American authorities and punishment inflicted if it appears that such has taken place."[23]

The French were quite serious about protecting Chinese laborers according to the contract. When it was discovered that Chinese working under the Americans at Mehun did not have their own separate mess (the Chinese had to take their meals seated on their beds), the French protested strongly and argued that this was "against all hygiene requirements and regulations provided for installations of Contomments." The French authority argued that without losing sight of "the difficulties of installation arising from present emergencies, it seems that this State is liable of improvement and I would appreciate greatly if you would kindly urge the American Services to take necessary dispositions to that effect."[24] M. Boschetti contacted the Americans on July 1, 1918, and urged them to take measures that would address the problem. But the American commanding officer replied as follows on July 5 to the American Labor Bureau:

It is true that the Chinese laborers have no mess hall, however conditions here are much better for the Chinese laborers than for many of the American soldiers at this post. We have a large number of soldiers without barracks to sleep in, some of these are sleeping in shelter tents, and they cook and eat in the open, so until we can obtain barracks for men to sleep in I don't see that we are under any obligations to build a mess hall for these laborers.[25]

In another situation, a French officer complained that the detachment of eight hundred Chinese laborers assigned to the American aviation unit at St. Maixent was "installed in defective conditions." Lodgings were bad with insufficient air, the kitchen was too small, and supplies were meager. There were neither lavatories, nor shower-baths, nor basins, nor attendance-room, nor infirmary. The W.C. was installed "in quite rudimentary conditions." He also pointed out the Chinese laborers were subject to search whenever they returned to the cantonment. After a few cases of the mumps occurred, the American authority confined the labor detachment for twelve days, bringing on certain Chinese unrest. To restore peace, about 150 American soldiers armed with revolvers and clubs were stationed inside the cantonment. According to the French, this only increased the exasperation of the French and the Chinese. Complaints continued even after the French had raised all these issues, because the Americans did not improve conditions. The same French officer warned, "This situation cannot be prolonged any longer without giving a blow to discipline and to the rules of hygiene."[26] In the wake of these complaints, an internal American memo responded, "It will be noted that both St. Maixent and Romorantin are air service stations and violations of the contract existing between ourselves and the French are doubtless due to a lack of information as to the requirements of such contract. These incidents emphasize the necessity for promptly publishing, in the form of a general order, instructions governing the treatment of alien labor secured by us from the French."[27] The Americans then rather vaguely promised that they would take "the greatest pains" to "prevent any ill treatment of any kind."[28] Obviously, the AEF was not at this point competent to manage the Chinese.

So the French complained about American violations, and American officers regularly ignored them. In the meantime, the Americans pressed the French to change the rules. In a memo, John Price Jackson wrote:

This dual control has naturally led, in frequent instances, to very unsatisfactory results, as might be expected. This is particularly true for the Chinese, who are averse to accepting several chiefs. The facts, also, that the food, barracks, and bedding must be furnished by the Americans; that certain elements of sanitation (of a high standard) must be maintained in American Camps; and that the numerous duties involved in these matters require Americans to attend the camps more or less frequently, all lead to the desirability of having Americans responsible for the control of the Chinese, with as strict a French inspection as is desired.

He further suggested:

If the French Government will give us any specification of their responsibility for the Chinese to the Chinese Government, in addition to those that they have imposed upon us by contract, we will gladly undertake to carry out these responsibilities in full. If the French personnel are given instructions that their duties are to inspect, with authority to notify both the

Americans if they deviate from the proper procedure, and the French Government in such cases, there is every reason to believe that the entire proposition of working the Chinese will be carried on to better advantage to everybody concerned. We deeply appreciate the very great help the French Government is giving us in letting us have the use of these Chinese which are urgently needed under the urgent circumstances of the enormous American works necessary to handle the American Army, and we make this request for what is, in fact, a slight modification, after mature thought, because we consider it essential to the really effective handling and care of the Chinese at our disposal.[29]

American officers especially complained that the presence of French personnel created difficulties in their management of the Chinese. In July 1918, the Americans suggested that all French personnel be removed except one officer and an orderly to accompany each labor detachment for the purpose of ensuring that contract obligations toward the Chinese laborers were properly met.[30] But the French did not want to do so. The Americans tried many different arguments to persuade the French to accept the idea of sole American control. One of them is especially interesting here. Lieutenant Colonel Frank E. Estes of the AEF asked Jackson to note the following statement the French had made: the effectiveness of the Chinese laborers was increased 30 percent when staff superintended the work and when the work was led by monitors who treated them with kindness. "This, as you know," wrote Estes, "is what we contend and what we are working for," because it seemed to support the American argument that dual control was not effective. Estes pointed out that "As the whole idea is to increase the effectiveness of the forces at the disposal of the Allied governments, it is suggested that, if possible, arrangements be made with the French to let the Americans supervise the Chinese who are working for the American Government."[31]

Dual control created other complications. Regarding the problem of forcing the Chinese to work on Sundays, Estes told the French that it was absolutely necessary for the good of the service that Sunday work should happen sometimes.[32] In article 2 of the rules for Chinese working under the American military, Chinese laborers were entitled to the same rest days given to French laborers employed in the same yard. The French side insisted that if the Chinese had to work on Sundays, they must be given another day's rest in the course of the week.[33] Moreover, the French argued that when Chinese laborers worked on Sunday, the American forces should work, too.[34]

Chinese laborers working for the American expeditionary forces in France were still bound and protected by contracts the French had signed with the Chinese; these men were not to be subject to American punishments. But American officers ignored this rule and frequently punished men with no explanation or repercussions. One reliable French witness testified that at Gievres in May 1918, a Chinese laborer was knocked down and killed with a bludgeon by an American superintendent; another Chinese who was urinating outside the lavatories was shot dead by an American sentry.[35] In still another case in early August 1918, one American officer had a group of forty Chinese in one camp arrested, an incident that was clearly brought about by miscommunication and misunderstanding.

The French were appalled by the violence Americans used against the Chinese, and they made many formal complaints to the AEF, insisting that only the French officers attached to American camps had authority to punish the laborers.[36] As early as July 29, 1918, the AEF, at French insistence, issued the following instruction to officers commanding the Chinese laborers regarding discipline. The order indicated that the Chinese were sometimes wrongly punished, and reminded the officers that these foreign laborers did not fall within American disciplinary jurisdiction, but remained amenable to ordinary French tribunals and penal officers. When a Chinese committed crimes, the order asked the American commanders to turn the culprit over to the nearest French police agent for punishment and to refrain from punishing him directly. The same instruction directed that all Chinese now under imprisonment or facing other punishment by American authorities be forthwith turned over to French officials.[37] But even this instruction was frequently violated. One begins to doubt American sincerity about observing the contract terms. The Americans believed that dual control of the Chinese was not good policy and wanted to secure sole control over this labor force. As late as January 1919, the Americans still wondered whether they should send a new memo to the French about the problems with dual control.[38]

One contract term the Americans violated frequently was the condition that they were not to move Chinese laborers without sending prior notification to the French. M. Boschetti frequently admonished the Americans to abide by this rule. He sent innumerable memos, reminding them that it was essential that the responsible French authority should always be kept closely informed about the movement of Chinese laborers.[39] But the rule was violated so regularly the French had begun to complain with some frequency. On June 2, 1918, Boschetti wrote to the AEF's Labor Bureau that "it has been reported to me that 150 workmen of the Chinese group at Mehun had been placed at the disposal of the Orleans Railway Company by the American services at Mehun."[40]

Jackson at first argued that it was difficult to get advance approval from the French when changes were needed on an urgent basis. In one memo, he suggested that the Americans "be allowed to move Chinese within our military sections without notice to M. Boschetti's representative." But the French reminded him that a rule is a rule, and they could not bend on it. Jackson soon wrote to withdraw his request and promised that his office would "make every endeavor to make no movements of Chinese without first giving the notices we have agreed upon." But in light of the number of ongoing violations, even Jackson felt uneasy, and he frequently made apologies to the French, expressing "my deep regret that these movements had been made without notice to the Labor Bureau, and that, therefore, M. Boschetti had not been given the notice he had agreed to."[41]

But Jackson's apologies and promises did not bring American violations to a halt. Soon after he made the previous promise in early October 1918, more unauthorized redeployments took place. It seems apparent that the Americans and the French were playing a game that cost only the Chinese, so neither side was sincere in observing the contract terms. And the game continued, with the Americans violating the terms and asking the French to reconsider and the French requesting that the American stop the violations.

## Trouble with Qualified Officers and Competent Management

Conflicts with the French over management of the Chinese were only one obstacle the AEF faced; another was the lack of qualified and well-trained officers to take charge of the labor battalions. Some of the labor supervisors were simply bad characters. Peter E. Echo was one of many such examples. Echo was an acting first sergeant overseeing a Chinese labor company. The Chinese under his control reported many wrongdoings against him. Echo once took a ring from a laborer and refused to return it. After the man complained and demanded it back, Echo lied to his commanding officer and claimed that he had already returned it. But he did not return it until after his commanding officer asked about it.

Echo forced some Chinese to give him money and offered them easier jobs as repayment. Given his abuses, Echo could have been court-martialed, but instead his commanding officer recommended only that his commission be cancelled, he be reduced to the rank of private (he was then a sergeant), and that he be transferred out. The commanding officer's reasons were as follows: it was difficult to question the witnesses (Chinese) to ascertain the specifics of his actions; and "the French officer attached to this company, as well as his detachment, are aware of this soldier's actions and hereafter he will be of no use to the company and can command no respect whatsoever from the laborers."[42] In another case, an American soldier tried to sell several used American uniforms to a Chinese laborer. The Chinese paid 38 francs for them. However, when he brought them back to the hut, an American officer claimed it was illegal for laborers to buy military uniforms, so he confiscated them all. But the Chinese did not get his money back. Obviously, it was unfair to punish the Chinese rather than the American soldier who had actually violated the rule.[43]

But the more serious problem was that many of the officers chosen to command the Chinese labor battalions came from the lowest ranks.[44] Many of them were simply incompetent and had no idea how to manage a labor battalion, never mind one composed of men from the other side of the world. In one example, Private Joseph Welgos, attached to the Chinese Company Number One, was eventually transferred, with his commanding officer reporting, "This soldier does not possess the necessary qualification for this work, and in addition is inefficient and indifferent."[45] The challenge for the AEF was finding enough qualified personnel. With shortages and problems on all sides, the agency seemed to just close its eyes and pray that underqualified officers would eventually improve, as in the case of Nicholas A. Fleming. When Fleming's performance drew increasing complaints, his superior, T. S. Chalmers, argued that it was impossible for him to give individual attention to Fleming because he himself was overstretched.[46] Unfortunately, Fleming would continue to create serious problems for both the Chinese and the French.

Thanks to officer incompetence, management errors occurred frequently. For instance, when Chinese laborers arrived at one new depot, their commanding officers had received no data concerning their hours and pay, or the Americans knew nothing about their pay and deductions.[47] Naturally, the Chinese complained. Jackson, the head of the Labor Bureau, had to issue instructions asking commanding officers to make necessary arrangements so the Chinese would "arrive at [a new] destination with a clean slate. If the men cannot be paid up to date of departure, forward with officer or enlisted man in charge such data as will enable the men to be paid by the receiving officer without any considerable trouble."[48] In another case, Chinese laborers arrived at camp with no blankets, shoes, socks, slickers, or canteens; and a good many of them did not even have mess kits.[49] The Chinese cooked their own meals, but sometimes the Americans did not provide them with the right food or crucial ingredients. For instance, the camps at Liffol-le-Grand, Bazoilles, and Rimaucourt lacked cooking oil. After the French intervened, the issue was immediately remedied. But when the Chinese complained about the lack of a variety of fresh vegetables, Jackson only promised that "our best endeavor will be used to remedy this second complaint. However, this is a failing of all stations in the advance section of our army."[50] One time the Americans did not have the right shoes or winter clothes for their Chinese labor force.[51]

Many problems arose because the commanding officers simply did not know what to do with the Chinese for lack of clear instructions. One commander reported to Jackson that the French had demanded that he pay the Chinese who were injured in the line of duty for Sundays. But the American interpretation of payroll instructions was that no laborers received pay for Sundays.[52] The French and Americans even quarreled about who would pay expenses for injured Chinese because there was no agreement regarding the matter of hospitalization. As one American officer reported, "So far as our strictly legal obligations are concerned . . . Chinese by terms of their contracts may be admitted to French hospitals where they will be cared for at the expense of the French government. In case of labor accidents, however, the expense must be borne by the United States."[53]

Besides the lack of general orders regarding how to manage the Chinese, many officers never saw a copy of the contract the United States had signed with the French. William A. Kaufman, who had charge over large numbers of Chinese, was not provided access to the language that set the terms under which the Chinese worked. On March 9, 1918, he finally asked for a copy of the contract. In his letter to John Price Jackson, he wrote:

I wish to ask a few questions that no one here seems able to answer, and that I think are especially necessary if the U.S. is to have records of the same. First: have you an extra copy of the final contract you are going to adopt regarding these laborers? [I w]ould like to have one that I may do the things properly that are required of me. Then: in case this contract does not govern the things that are important, what authority can you give me to dispose of the following subjects: if the French Government are [sic] to pay these Chinese, do you wish me to keep a record of their time for our own use? In case of sickness or injury contracted in line of duty or not, what is considered the dividing point, that is, if a man is sick and confined to quarters is he allowed pay? Or, if he has happened to have an accident, like smashing his finger, is he entitled to full pay so long as this finger keeps him from work? Is this taken from the contract or merely supposition? Also with regard to a man who is absolutely no use, in this special case a man here has a very bad case of gonorrhoea, have you any authority to transfer him to any other place or must he become a dead burden to the U.S.?[54]

From this exchange, we can discern how chaotic the situation was, because commanding officers had no clearly defined guidance regarding management of the Chinese labor force. Given that many officers were incompetent, it is only natural that many of the Chinese companies under the Americans were not smoothly run.

Overall, the Americans had an attitude problem about the contract with the French. Robert J. Bates, a major in the U.S. Army, informed his superiors that he felt the French assigned to the Chinese labor camps were "unnecessary" and argued that American officers should be in charge of the Chinese. He told his superiors that "in fact I believe that I could attain better results from my Chinese laborers" without the French. "As the labor companies are organized and commanded by Americans, and from the fact that we pay these laborers, I feel we should be given the opportunity of exercising full control over them. This cannot be done with the presence of French soldiers, who are continually cross firing with forces, and I respectfully request that all French soldiers and N.C.O's be withdrawn from this station at your earliest convenience." Bates pointed out that "I am aware that the French contract with the Chinese Government provides for these soldiers to be on duty with the Chinese but for the general good this provision should be eliminated."[55] One American officer by name of J. B. Greenwood expressed the same idea. He told his superiors that "I regret that the French won't allow us to work in better harmony. I cannot hold myself responsible for the existing state of affairs." He maintained that if his commanding officer "is not patriotic enough to help us along in this work that is his lookout. I am not here to spend my time studying up all the little niciesies [sic] that the French are used to, but I am here to get results if they are getable."[56]

These feelings were widespread among the Americans. One officer claimed that he could not ensure good discipline among his Chinese laborers if the punishments he inflicted on them were not enforced by the French authorities concerned. Some even suggested that the Chinese France provided for the AEF had been in country for already two years and were accustomed to easy work; they were "spoiled beyond measure." They demanded that they should have power to adopt "stringent" discipline to control the Chinese with all means necessary.[57] Kaufman complained about the way the French provided interpreters: "The French Government has a habit of dropping a man in on us most any time and would like to use the best way of getting rid of them as they seem to break up most everything that we have tried to build with the Chinese."[58]

As with the British, the lack of interpreters made the situation even messier. One camp had 800 laborers but only two interpreters.[59] Many misunderstandings could have been averted had there been a sufficient number of interpreters to help the Americans understand the Chinese. Inexperienced officers lacking a good interpreter had no way of knowing what was really going on with their labor force, and in desperation, they often used whatever came to hand to resolve problems. Additionally, like the French and the British, the Americans had serious problems trying to communicate due to a near total lack of cultural understanding. One Chinese newspaper reported that it was extremely difficult for the Chinese to communicate with the Americans and make them to understand their needs, concerns, and frustrations. The following examples point to the extent of the communication problem: One hardworking Chinese laborer (otherwise in good standing with the Americans) suffered from eye problems. One day, the Americans were going to send him to a dark room because it was supposed to be good for his eyes. But the Americans did not explain their intention clearly enough and this laborer suspected he was being punished for no reason. He resisted and got into a fight.[60] In another case, Chinese workers were not supposed to pay for food, but sometimes "they would come into the shop, lay down a five-franc note and run out with the loaf [of bread], ignoring the cries" of protest from the French bakers at the overpayment. Only when the Americans ordered the Chinese to return the bakery's bread and return to camp for their free supply did the Chinese understand they were supposed to receive food from the Americans free of charge.[61] Even labor camp commander William A. Kaufman, who felt no great affection for the Chinese, wrote, "If I could get hold of one good American soldier who speaks Chinese," he would be able to "keep the men satisfied."[62]

The lack of interpreters and cultural understanding among the Americans naturally created hardships for the Chinese. Missionary Charles A. Leonard, who served for a year with Chinese labor battalions in France, described it this way:

> A great gulf yawned between the 1,400 Chinese secured to drain an aviation camp in France and their English-speaking officers. No one in camp could speak the two languages intelligently or act as an intermediary between the two races. Every few days there was a strike or a riot. . . . The food though good was not suitable. No boiled water was provided—and Chinese drink only hot water or tea. Much sickness and discontent resulted. Doctors could not understand Chinese, so diseases were improperly treated.

Sometimes American orders even became a problem and a source of friction. Like the British, American officers constantly used sentences such as "Come on, let's go!" with special emphasis on the word "go." Again, the laborers thought they were being insulted and refused to work.[63] Others noticed this common problem. One YMCA official observed that this characteristic American command sounded very much like a Chinese curse, *lie sze gou,* meaning "dirty dead dog." These phrases made the Chinese keenly resentful and set the stage for riots and strikes.[64]

Americans are an impatient people. Their impatience during the Great War made them further ill-prepared for dealing with the Chinese. In the early days of Americans using Chinese labor, one YMCA secretary observed, "The work for which [the Chinese] were wanted was being rushed ahead by selected American soldiers who were detailed to oversee the labor. Their inability to speak the Chinese language—and there being no interpreter during the first days—they made use of the universal sign language, with a tendency to make it rather forcible when the slow-going Oriental style of movement irritated the rushing American."[65]

## American Problems with the Chinese Laborers

To the Americans, the Chinese seemed very strange. The perception and image of Chinese in the United States contributed to confusion about and lack of readiness for the "new" Chinese in France. According to one

YMCA report, when five hundred Chinese were sent from Marseilles to an American camp, they arrived at the American camp with a group of French women they had brought along. They naturally became angry when the American commander ordered the women to go away.[66]

Sometimes the American doughboys got into massive fights with the Chinese. According to Chen Baoyu, a Chinese laborer, such fighting broke out frequently. He recalled that once a group of American soldiers insulted some Chinese laborers who were taking a walk near the American camp. They got into a physical fight and a number of Chinese laborers who were nearby came running to support their friends. In the end, about twenty Chinese and ten Americans got injured, among them Chen Baoyu. The Chinese strongly protested that it was the Americans who had started the fight, and when the AEF later sent officers to visit the injured Chinese in the hospital, they promised that it would not happen again. According to Chen, this incident put the Americans on notice that the Chinese were not afraid to fight and could acquit themselves quite well. Afterward, Chen reported, the Americans behaved less aggressively.[67] In another account, a drunken American soldier wandered into a Chinese labor camp and started yelling. One of the Chinese tried to quiet him and move him away, but the American shot at him. Luckily, he missed. The other Chinese laborer decided to grab him and drag him to his superior. That soldier was sentenced to five months in jail.[68]

American problems with the Chinese were more serious than their problems with the French, but problems with the French further aggravated their troubles with the Chinese. Of the three armed forces (British, French, and American), the Chinese seemed least willing to work for the latter. They considered them stingy compared with the French, and believed that the Americans made them work longer hours. According to the report of one American officer, the Chinese began work at 6:30 a.m. and quit at 5:30 p.m., with one hour off for lunch at noon. The reason for quitting at 5:30 was because "at the present time it is so dark at 5:15 pm that it is almost impossible to produce effective work." The commanding officer asked the chief of the Labor Bureau to instruct him as to "whether these laborers are to receive full time for the day, or for the actual time they work."[69]

According to the French contract, the laborers were to receive bonus pay after three months' work. But the Americans had problems with that, and some of the American services declined to pay it. This triggered French complaints on behalf of the Chinese. In a letter dated September

9, 1918, French Commandant Varaigne wrote to Dawes that "upon closely examining your instructions dated July 1 on the subject of payment of wages, I cannot find anything which might amount to an order not to pay this bonus, which is provided for in the existing agreements and has hitherto been paid accordingly, so far as my information goes."[70] On receiving the French complaint at "the failure to pay the 30 francs bonus provided for in our contracts," Jackson wrote back that "our chief paymaster held up these payments for about three days pending a decision as to their validity under the American law. This matter was determined, however, with some promptness, and all bonuses have thereafter been paid, and are now being paid. So far as we have information, no man to whom a bonus is due is now unpaid."[71]

Despite the fact that the Americans did not want to reward the Chinese financially, they were very demanding and treated the men like a disposable tool. One officer recommended the discharge of certain Chinese laborers and interpreters, claiming that neither group was worth its board and the money it took to keep it.[72] Although the AEF desperately needed laborers, its officers and agencies were ill prepared to deal with them. According to the AEF's own investigation, when the Chinese at La Rochelle were sent to work for the Baltimore Car Company, the company was not ready for the men when they arrived, but because it needed their labor, it was unwilling to release them for fear of not getting them back again.[73] Such situations were far from uncommon and generated no end of bad feelings.

The Chinese government knew about the American violations of its terms with the French. According to Li Jun's reports, the Americans managed the Chinese according to their own lights and rarely adhered to the French conditions. They frequently punished Chinese without reason or explanation.[74] Li Jun suggested that the Chinese were unhappy working for the Americans for the following reasons: (1) Chinese in the United States were treated badly, and Americans had the same prejudiced attitude toward Chinese workers in France. (2) Some American soldiers were not well educated or civilized; they behaved with extreme arrogance toward Chinese laborers. (3) Americans were strong and hot-tempered. Whenever they were not satisfied, they became violent and started to abuse the Chinese. (4) Americans treated the Chinese according to their own way in defiance of the contract with the French. (5) Americans stuck to their own rules and never gave the Chinese any rewards. (6) Their rules were too strict. (7) When Americans and Chinese had conflicts, the

French usually supported the Americans.[75] On July 10, 1918, all 160 Chinese laborers under one American company fled for fear of their commanding officer. On July 29, 1918, one American officer struck a Chinese, even in front of Li Jun, when some of the laborers continued smoking after he had asked them not to.[76]

To be fair, the Americans did not lack an intention to learn and improve. In May 1918, Jackson sent his French counterparts with a plea. "I am very anxious to have Mr. L. J. Pigott observe your methods of working and handling Chinese labor. Have you any Chinese working within reasonable distance of Paris at a camp which we could arrange to have Mr. Pigott visit? I shall very greatly appreciate your allowing . . . Mr. Pigott the opportunity of observing your method of work."[77] But the good intentions of high officials was one thing, it is another to change the mind-set of everyone in charge of the Chinese in a timely fashion.

During the Great War, about 200,000 African Americans served with the U.S. Army in France, and many of them were with laborers. One might wonder whether their sometimes hostile attitude toward the Chinese reflected their own suffering in American society and the unjust treatment they received from whites. Black soldiers and black laborers had more chance to work with the Chinese because many of them manned the labor battalions in France. When the Chinese worked under them, how did they treat them? Although the blacks at home were second-class citizens, they were still citizens, while the Chinese were first people in the world not allowed to become American citizens. Did African American soldiers, like their white counterparts, think they could bully the Chinese in France? Although these questions lie beyond the scope of this book, the connection between the treatment of the Chinese and discrimination against the African Americans is important to point out.

Given all the friction, the Chinese under the Americans were generally doing a great job. American evaluations of Chinese laborers ran along the lines of "doing good job," "doing very good job," "doing satisfactory work," "Chinese doing better work than French civilians or Motor Mechanics men," "doing exceptionally good work."[78] In one of his reports, Commander R. E. Woodman wrote that although living conditions were "not good," the Chinese were "cheerful and willing. No complaints are being received." In another report, he wrote they were "willing and easily handled."[79] The attitude of Chinese laborers was "Very Good."[80] The AEF Labor Bureau report acknowledged that the Chinese laborers "were large and strong, and excellent workers on heavy duty."[81]

More importantly, the Chinese generosity also extended to the Americans even given the sometimes atrocious treatment at the hands of the doughboys. Soon after the signing of the Armistice, Chinese Labor Company 23 under the Americans had a holiday. The laborers were greatly excited at seeing American troops march through the town where they were camped, en route to the German frontier. As the long lines continued to wind through the town, one of the laborers suggested that it would be fine if they could do something for the men, since they looked tired and worn by the march. Another man suggested that they carry water to the passing troops. The suggestion took, and they all rushed off to get their buckets and for several hours carried water nearly half a mile, much to the delight of the thirsty travelers. Many a grateful solider offered a franc for his drink, but not one coin was accepted the whole afternoon. When money was offered, the Chinese chattered away in their unintelligible tongue, but one man standing by who could understand heard them say, "We are brothers, and it is our duty to do all we can for you."[82] A YMCA officer from Canada made the following comments regarding this case: "The American doughboy has especial reason to be grateful to the coolie for his kind-heartedness." According to this Canadian, this was not the only time such things had happened. "I remember several occasions last summer, when the Americans were marching into battle, hot, tired and thirsty, that coolies along the line of the march would bring pails of water suspended from poles across their shoulders and pass it among the boys to drink. When the doughboys would attempt to pay for this service, the poor but dignified Chinese would not accept a cent from them."[83] Some Chinese even joined the AEF circus and took part in entertaining the soldiers. According to the organizer of the circus, "These men are very clever and no doubt will be valuable to the show."[84]

More than 2 million Americans fought in World War I, and American casualties reached 116,516. In what is now the Meuse-Argonne American Cemetery alone (26 miles northwest of Verdun), 14,246 Americans died fighting and were buried here, making this the largest American military cemetery in Europe.[85] The record of American sacrifice and contributions is well preserved in forms of monuments, cemeteries, and studies on the United States and the Great War. But where are the memorials for the 10,000 Chinese laborers who worked for the AEF during the war, and even after the war was over? Jackson, the head of the Labor Bureau, wrote in his report that "our Chinese, French, Italians, etc, when they return to their civilian occupations, should go with the knowledge that these who have employed them fully appreciate that they were giving distinct and valuable service to the great cause for which we were fighting."[86] But by and large the Americans seemed not to have really appreciated the Chinese, and both the Americans and the rest of the world soon forgot the Chinese sacrifices and contributions. We may wonder whether the Americans even cared about what was on the minds of those men, never mind asking what they were thinking about.

# 8

## THE ASSOCIATION MEN AND
## CHINESE LABORERS

The presence of these large numbers of Chinese in the Labour Corps in the theatre of War offers to those interested in China a really unique missionary and educational opportunity in the broadest sense of these terms. Taken out of their old conservative environment with their minds awakened by their new surroundings, these men are exceptionally open to new impressions. The danger is that unless a comprehensive program is planned it will be the worst side of Western civilization which will impress itself on them with incalculable injury not only to themselves but to an adequate understanding in their community on their return of what the West really stands for. It is the evident duty of the Christian forces of the West to see to it that they are protected from the evil results of a misinterpreted and incomplete contact with Western civilization upon them. We must be the interpreters to them of the best that we have . . . If our programme is comprehensive and statesman-like enough they will return to their own country to become disseminators of a better understanding between the West and the East among their relatives and friends. Whereas, if we do not undertake this service for them it is almost certain that as a result of their coming to Europe misunderstanding between the East and the West will be increased . . . it is impossible to overstate the urgency and importance of this opportunity, no matter from what aspect it is viewed.

—*Statement in regard to YMCA work for Chinese in France*

The Young Men's Christian Association (YMCA) took a leading role in providing education, social, and entertainment programs for the Allied fighting forces and for the Chinese laborers as well. The national Y organizations in Great Britain, in the United States, and, in particular, the

Chinese National YMCA made the experience of the Chinese workers in Europe less miserable and more fruitful. The Y groups took initiative in setting up effective programs to help and counsel the laborers (over some resistance from the British command), provided key personnel to run the programs, and the Chinese National YMCA provided the bulk of the expenses from subscriptions of Chinese back in China.

In the larger picture, the Y initiative (especially that of the Chinese National YMCA, an independent organization allied with the world movement) was symbolic of the emerging Chinese nation's push to join with global liberal forces in what became known as the "Wilsonian moment."[1] While the picture of the Y's program includes unselfish service and a fighting spirit for global brotherhood, the Y, like the Chinese workers with whom they served, was also met with racism, condescension, and narrow mindedness. There was also a tension between the Y's secular mission of service and the Christian mission of evangelization. One Y "star" declared, "if I were running this shop, I would make every applicant for overseas service take a theological test. And if he passed it, I'd kick him out of the window." Catholics, Jews, Christian Scientists, and those of "no affiliation" wore the Y uniform.[2] The statement at the head of this chapter does not mention the object of converting the Chinese workers to Christianity, yet in the long run globalization of Christianity was assumed by many of the Y men in France. Others found that the experience in France challenged their beliefs. Thus the influences ran in both directions—one part of the "fusion of civilizations" which the Great War engendered.

## The YMCA in China

The introduction of the YMCA to China coincided closely with China's pursuit of a new national identity and early efforts to join the world community as an equal member. In early twentieth century Europe and North America, the Y was part of the social gospel effort to move beyond the evangelical and individual approach and to address the social problems of the city by helping young men avoid the evils of industrialized society. As one recent scholar puts it, "believing that Christian responsibility included community service both by and for young men, the YMCA from the start developed elaborate social service programs."[3]

In China, the Y aimed to move beyond the earlier missionaries who came to proselytize the gospel and set up Chinese churches that would remain under the control of the mission board at home. The Y downplayed theology and emphasized service and education over conversion. Once China had developed into a modern nation led by a middle class, they reasoned, Christianity would naturally find its place. Therefore, the Chinese National YMCA was the first Christian organization to turn control and finances over to Chinese leaders. It was fitting that when the YMCA set up its first branch in Tianjin in 1895, a year of major significance in Chinese history, it introduced the modern Olympic movement and inspired the century-long dream to host the Olympic Games in Beijing.[4]

From the late nineteenth century, the YMCA had devoted enormous attention to China. According to its own assessment in 1918, "The Association work is probably better developed in China than in any foreign country. There are eighty-two foreign secretaries, and also 300 hundred native secretaries. The administrative work of the Association is largely in the hands of able Chinese."[5] The official Association history indicates that "It was to China that the YMCAs of the United States and Canada directed more continuous effort than to any other one country or area." During the Great War, "in the endeavor to encourage and assist Young Men's Christian Associations, more men were maintained in China even than in such regions of major physical dimensions and populations as India, Latin America, and Europe" because of the "importance of China in the world scene, and because the Chinese were accepting Western education and social forms." The Association wanted to help shape the future of a great people who were entering upon a gigantic and sweeping revolution. The history also notes that "it was not until the 1920's that a serious anti-Christian wave swept across the country."[6] When Chinese laborers arrived in France, the YMCA also took a hand in shaping and influencing their lives and thus at least indirectly affecting Chinese history.

The involvement with the Chinese laborers in France was motivated by several interests. Although one might argue that the YMCA, by and large, was not directly interested in proselytizing or saving souls, its involvement with the Chinese laborers in France, however, was quite influenced by its spiritual consideration as well as the Social Gospel. According to an Association-edited volume:

The Chinese laborers form an important part of the fighting forces. To increase and maintain their high morale is, therefore, imperative. They would exert great influence upon China on their return. To help them to imbibe the true Christian spirit is to lay a good foundation for China's future, which means so much to the future of the world. They are also God's children, and we, as Christians, are morally bound to make their brief sojourn in France truly beneficial to their bodies, minds and souls.[7]

Second, it wanted to influence the Chinese future development via these laborers. Third and most importantly, it aimed to support the West by helping the Chinese who were the core of its labor force at the front. But no matter its motivations, the YMCA's involvement in Chinese lives in France to a great extent eased the men's suffering and helped bridge gaps between the Chinese and their Western officers.

The Association wanted to change China by uplifting its young leaders, but work with the CLC posed a question. One official wrote, "We recognize that the Chinese in France do not strictly represent the class among which the Association is called upon to serve, but nevertheless their opportunities and general intelligence make it important for us to attempt a good deal for them, not only on account of the intrinsic value of such service but particularly because of the reflex value of it on China." He added that "We hope that a great interest will be aroused in this work so that it will provide an outlet for the altruistic impulses of socially minded Chinese."[8]

## The YMCA's Offer to Help

As soon as the Great War started, the YMCA made itself available to serve the Allied countries' war efforts by directing the sports activities and other welfare programs at the fronts. When the French- and British-recruited Chinese arrived in France, the British national council of the YMCA offered help to provide social, recreational, and educational services to them as well. At first, the French and British military authorities were not enthusiastic about this prospect. The British authorities were especially suspicious, fearing that the YMCA's Chinese-speaking workers coming into camp and engaging sympathetically with the laborers would bring a prejudice of discipline. Racism perhaps was another reason for its hesitation.[9]

Ironically, it was a serious breakdown in discipline that eventually forced the British military to change its mind. "In our impotence God took a hand in affairs," one YMCA official would later declare. The incident grew from a misunderstanding between the Chinese and their commanding officers into a head-on confrontation; the Chinese thought they had been wrongly blamed and refused to work. When the British had reached their wits' end trying to convince the Chinese to work, a nearby YMCA secretary stepped in to help. After a friendly chat with the Chinese in their own language, he got the laborers to agree to resume work; this avoided what could have been a tragic situation, because the colonel in charge had considered resorting to rifles and bayonets.[10]

After this episode, the British military recognized the YMCA for a useful intermediary and relaxed its resistance to the organization's request to work with the Chinese. Although no immediate formal permission had been granted, by the end of 1917 an unofficial "YMCA experiment" was underway in some Chinese labor camps. The experiment seemed to be a success and the head of the CLC, Colonel Fairfax, soon pressed headquarters to allow the Association to work in all the Chinese camps.[11] On February 12, 1918, the British military authority arranged for the Association to extend its work in the Chinese Labor Corps, and orders were issued for the expeditionary force canteen association to withdraw its personnel and close the canteens. The Y work would include providing entertainment, running canteens, and organizing recreation activities.[12] In March 1918, general headquarters invited the YMCA to set up canteens and recreational programs among all the Chinese companies with the British Expeditionary Force.[13] By the end of 1918, more than eighty centers had been established and manned, and they would provide services for more than 100 of the 194 companies of the Chinese laborers working with the British. Association personnel included thirty-eight Chinese students and a score of missionaries provided by the YMCA's International Committee of North America.[14] The establishment of these programs for British-recruited Chinese laborers can be credited largely to James Wallace, a Canadian who had worked in China as a YMCA secretary, and James Webster, a British missionary who had worked in China for more than thirty years.

The British military, now quite pleased with the YMCA work, considered its value "incalculable" in providing entertainments and amusements "which for the Chinese had not been available in the land of barbarians."[15] Colonel R. I. Purdon, Fairfax's successor, communicated by letter in July 1919 to a YMCA conference, "I have met a number of your workers in different parts of France, and have been greatly impressed by their devotion and self-imposed duty in organizing such high social and refined surroundings for the Chinese. The dreary and monotonous existence in devastated areas and base ports in France has been relieved to a remarkable extent through your efforts, and the material comfort you have provided—often under great difficulties—has been greatly appreciated."[16] The Chinese had seen the terrible side of war and of Europe, but the YMCA tried to show them "a more glorious side than what has fallen to their lot during the war."[17]

Demands for extending the Association's work were persistent. One British commanding officer begged headquarters not to transfer the YMCA secretary from his camp because he could not get along without the programs and the secretary in the administration of discipline. Another officer remarked, "If I had had a man like Mr. so-and-so of the YMCA in my company a year ago, I would have had much less anxiety in dealing with my men."[18] One colonel had requested that a YMCA center be opened in every company in his area, and another raised a protest against removing an Association worker from his district. British authorities eventually requested extensive expansion, but by the end of 1918, the YMCA could only embarrassedly admit that it simply did not have sufficient personnel to satisfy all the military's requests.

Once the war was over, the British YMCA reduced its work among the Chinese and at that point served perhaps one-half of the laborers. In British areas, there was some suggestion that the work have to close due to lack of funds. This raised a general hue and cry from all the commanding officers, who urgently requested that the Association remain because they felt unable to carry on without its assistance. But despite all the urgent calls, Association work with the Chinese was still cut back to much lower levels.

When the war started in 1914, the French military also regarded the YMCA with some skepticism and considered its work to be "possibly religious propaganda."[19] In early 1917, according to a private letter from Emmanuel Sautter, who was responsible for setting up Foyers du Soldat for the French, a general in the French military expressed his desire to have YMCA centers in his district. The French were about to open a large new foyer in a great munitions factory. "In one place we are dealing with a large number of Chinese employed in military munitions factories."[20] An earlier foyer was devoted only to Chinese who were at "the rear," and many Chinese who worked near the front did not have access to the YMCA services until much later.[21] After some trials, it was decided in fall 1917 to invite the YMCA to work with certain Chinese laborers. Shi Yixuan, a Chinese student from Harvard University, started the first YMCA center for Chinese in Feysin, a suburb of Lyons. Shi was actually the first of the YMCA secretaries to work with the Chinese in France.[22] None of the Chinese laborers working under the French received any serious attention until Shi Yixuan arrived in November 1917. Shi traveled on the November 22 from Lyons to Feysin to set up programs for the nearly one thousand Chinese who were stationed there. When he first arrived, the Chinese were suspicious of him. Some thought he was an agent of the French authorities; one laborer asked if he was going to be head of personnel to police them. Others believed he came to sell goods and merchandise; still others thought that he was appointed by the Chinese government to help settle their grievances against the French authorities. All these misgivings and misunderstandings about Shi's mission were soon dispelled in the informal meetings he held with the men at the temporary quarters of the foyer during his first two weeks in Feysin.[23]

Shi also succeeded in winning the confidence of the local officials at Lyons and demonstrated the value and possibilities of the Association work with the labor companies. But it was not until December 1918, that the French military authorities formally granted their consent for the promotion of YMCA work in all Chinese companies under French control.[24] YMCA centers were eventually set up in Marseille, Bordeaux, Le Creusot, Orleans, Le Mans, Brest, and many other places. Eventually, about thirty-eight centers, with twenty-three Chinese secretaries and twelve American secretaries, served more than 70 percent of the Chinese working with the French.[25]

The unavoidable contradictions of circumstances on the ground provided the YMCA with a unique and ongoing opportunity to mediate. Even after the signing of the Armistice, with concentrations of Chinese still working in many areas, its services remained in high demand. In one locality, in which some ten thousand laborers were stationed, the French commandant responsible for salvage and reconstruction there asked the YMCA for one secretary for each thousand laborers; even better (if the Association could manage it), he would like one secretary for every five hundred men. He also asked whether it would be possible to furnish suitable labor directors, to be placed under his control, to take charge of each company. Calls for the Association personnel increased rapidly once the military realized its value. The commandant in charge of all laborers in the French areas personally visited a YMCA official's office and spent considerable time urging him to not only continue the work but also to strengthen it in certain centers where the YMCA had so far done little. He frankly stated that wherever YMCA work was carried on, gambling, opium smoking, and labor disturbances were almost entirely absent, whereas in the few centers where there was little YMCA presence, conditions were bad.

In the spring of 1918, YMCA work was extended to the Chinese under American command.[26] The AEF's turn to the YMCA was natural and easy to understand. The United States joined the war late, but had so many problems with its Chinese labor force that morale among the men was quite low. Most officers could not speak Chinese, and before the YMCA was brought in there had been no adequate and effective intermediary between them. According to one confidential report, from the very beginning the AEF authorities welcomed the Association's efforts on behalf of the 10,000 laborers under their control.[27] The AEF was desperate for help in smoothing out the recurring difficulties and getting the Chinese back to work.[28]

American military authorities, like the French and British, quickly came to appreciate the efforts of the YMCA. One American officer reported that in his company a secretary who spoke fluent Chinese had, over the past eight months, done much to increase the efficiency of the laborers; he was able to explain the ways and customs of the West, the reasons why the Allies were at war, and many other things that were not clear to the average Chinese. This secretary, Charles A. Leonard, had spent seven years as a missionary in North China, where most of the laborers came from. In the eight months he served at that labor camp, the report claimed, he had taken a great interest in Chinese welfare. "It has been found that the Chinese who are not served by the YMCA secretaries who speak their language, have no conception whatever of why we are at war, nor why their own country has entered the war. On the other hand, when they come to know the principles for which we are fighting they immediately see the reasonableness of our cause and enter enthusiastically into it. They need to be reminded of the large part played by the laborer, and the importance and obligation of their doing faithfully their part in the great conflict in which we are engaged." So this officer urged that Leonard be allowed to visit all the large Chinese labor camps as soon as possible, for the purpose of making clear to the Chinese the following:

A. Why the Allies were at war
B. China's part in the war
C. The laborers' share in modern warfare

D. The cordial relationship between China and America

E. Why the Chinese, as laborers, should prove themselves efficient in every respect

F. Something of Western civilization[29]

John Price Jackson immediately responded positively. But he had a problem: Leonard was scheduled to return to the United States and then go to China. Jackson was determined to have him tour the Chinese labor camps and wrote to his superior to request that he be allowed to tour the Chinese labor companies before his return to the United States. Jackson concluded that a favorable consideration from the YMCA "will be greatly appreciated by this Bureau."[30] Some Americans even claimed that the YMCA missionaries such as Charles Leonard "helped to win the war."[31] In the locales where Leonard served as camp interpreter, according to one enthusiastic American officer, "the work of the Chinese labor battalions improved at least twenty-five percent."[32]

The YMCA had only about 109 YMCA staff to work with the 140,000 Chinese laborers and could hardly reach every laborer. About one third of the Chinese had no access to Association programs or any assistance at all. For instance, the fourteen labor companies at Rouen had no Association secretary.[33] Chinese who did not have access to YMCA services were not happy. In one of the military zones, a whole company went on strike because (unlike other companies in the area) it had no YMCA.[34] According to a confidential Association document, just over 140 separate Chinese groups were being served, about 100 of them within the British area. The International Committee had a staff of sixty-one secretaries in the British area, of whom thirty-nine were Chinese and twenty-two American or British, but all of whom spoke Chinese. The British Association had an additional forty secretaries who worked on behalf of the Chinese, but many of them were only part-time. Within the French area, Association staff included twenty-one Chinese and fourteen Chinese-speaking Americans.[35] French areas had fifty-four centers for their labor corps.

Relations among the YMCA branches run by the Americans, British, Chinese, and French were generally cordial. One confidential report claimed that "the Association effort for the Chinese has won the complete confidence of the British, French and American authorities."[36] American, Canadian, Chinese, and Australian YMCAs as well as the Association's International Committee provided personnel, material, and financial support for services for the Chinese laborers. Wherever work had been started, the regional directors cooperated in securing and erecting YMCA huts, some of which were furnished by the American army. In a like manner, the French authorities placed at the YMCA's disposal equipment, facilities, and supplies, and facilitated operations wherever possible. In all its interactions with the French government, the YMCA depended upon a Mr. Tanquerey, who did much to interpret the YMCA movement to French officials.

Problems did crop up in terms of cooperation, personnel, equipment, and budget allocation issues. The Association International Committee's relationship with its British branch, for instance, did not always go smoothly. The British side had never been enthusiastic about close cooperation and had preferred to consider the Chinese work in the British area as a British enterprise, even though it was forced to request financial support from the International Committee when it ran short of funds.[37] The British asked for a loan of 10,000 pounds to help them over a crisis until the end of 1918. Shipments designated to serve the whole Chinese contingent had already been diverted due to the efforts of the British Association.[38] Britain had contributed the bulk of the money for YMCA facilities for the Chinese laborers, but the Americans and Canadians had done considerably more. As one YMCA report claimed in October 1918, "the International Committee of the YMCA of the United States and Canada are doing splendid service in getting us men, and men of good quality."[39] Eventually, the International Committee would spend considerably more than the British Association, so it hesitated to loan money to the British in addition.[40]

Given these financial and management issues, the International Committee's relationship with its British branch would remain troubled, especially in the areas of allocating men and furnishing equipment. In 1919, with 107 secretaries serving in the British area—67 of this number being Chinese—the International Committee also furnished six automobiles together with other equipment including tents, cinema machines, gramophones, and athletic supplies, amounting to 100,000 francs. It even paid the salaries of twenty-five British workers in addition to those of the International Committee representatives. But members of the International Committee privately complained that British YMCA leaders overemphasized nationality in connection with their association service. This was especially irritating to the Chinese staffers.[41]

Despite all the problems, the YMCA created a sort of united front that worked for the Chinese laborers whether they were under the Americans, the British, or the French. The work was financed and controlled by the Association's International Committee and the National Committee of China, in cooperation with its National Council in Britain. G. H. ("Bert") Cole, a former officer of the Canadian YMCA Overseas (from Ottawa), was loaned to the British YMCA for the Chinese laborer programs in Europe. He and the American R. M. Hersey, of the International Committee, directed this work in France; Cole had responsibility for activities and equipment. Both Cole and Hersey had done missionary work in China and spoke Chinese.

## The Association Men and Their Service to the Chinese

The Association staff working with the Chinese included, first (and most numerous), Chinese students who had been studying abroad, especially in the United States; second, missionaries on furlough; and third, church ministers. One of the most interesting and enlightened features of this YMCA work was the international character of its personnel. By 1919, staff working in British areas included forty-five British, forty-five Chinese, one Dutch, one Danish, and thirteen American secretaries; the French area had twenty-three Chinese and twelve American secretaries, and their French assistants.[42] Even within the national YMCAs, there might be many cross-national flavors. For instance, when the British YMCA set to work, it turned to the Canadian YMCA for help. Major J. H. Wallace, then senior officer for the Canadian YMCA in France, with more than ten years' experience in China on the staff of the international YMCA and an adept Chinese linguist, consented to cooperate and was loaned to the British. Major Wallace planned the whole enterprise, on paper and on the ground, and when he returned to the Canadians after a few months, he had created a well-equipped and well-oiled field operation. His place was filled by G. H. Cole, also a Canadian. Besides lending its officers, the Canadian YMCA lent financial support through the British national council, and its contribution for 1918 amounted to $25,000 exclusively committed to the Chinese work.[43]

YMCA offices in China, North America, France, and Britain all got involved in helping the Chinese in France. Because of the increasing need for secretaries, representatives of the national committee in China began recruiting in the spring of 1918. Missionaries (American and British),

Chinese students, and many Christian leaders at once responded to the call. For the first time, China sent Christian workers abroad. More than thirty secretaries came directly from China's YMCA. To succeed in the mission to aid their men laboring in France, said one report, it was "necessary to recruit from China and send men around the globe to help." The Chinese responded "nobly" to this call. This same report also noted that serving the Chinese laborers in France "was a great opportunity" for the YMCA and provided a new way for the Chinese to think about the war and China's relationship to it.[44] The Chinese National Committee also sent hundreds of tons of supplies to the laborers in France and helped recruit personnel.[45]

In addition to the Chinese who went directly from China to France to help their countrymen, in 1918, thirty-eight Chinese students and seventeen American missionaries from America and China went at the invitation of and with support of the International Committee of the YMCA of North America (including both the United States and Canada). At the beginning of 1919, their numbers further increased. The Chinese students who studied in France, Britain, and especially in the United States were recruited by the International Committee. In response to the call to patriotic as well as Christian service in France, these students gave up their familiar surroundings to go work for their fellow countrymen. Besides Shi Yixuan, Chinese Y workers included Yan Yangchu, Jiang Tingfu, Chen Liting, Wang Zhengxu, Quan Shaowu, Gui Zhiting, Lu Shiyin, and many others.[46] At one point, the 160 staffers supported by the International Committee included ninety-two Chinese. Of these, twenty-seven came directly from China, fifty-four from colleges in America, five from Great Britain, and three from among the Chinese students in France.

The presence of this able and dedicated group of young leaders led to the most strategic phase of the YMCA presence. These Chinese staffers developed all the most significant features of the service rendered through the YMCA to Chinese laborers in France. They understood their own people and were able to develop programs along lines most fitted to the laborers' needs. By working with the laborers and by recruiting the best and brightest Chinese students to work for them, the YMCA recognized and embraced the opportunity to attract the future leaders of China to the ideas of the YMCA and Christianity.[47]

Not only did the Chinese secretaries play a crucial role in the Association's work with the laborers, but people back in China and their government also got involved in the YMCA's work. From the beginning of 1919, a large portion of the financial support came from contributions made by private as well as government sources in China. The Chinese back home sent Chinese delicacies, musical instruments, and games to their men in France. Over the long voyage, many of the delicacies spoiled, but the instruments and games were appreciated and put to good use.[48] The YMCA did not transport these things for nothing: the Chinese had raised an enormous amount money for the Association's war fund. There are strong indications that not every penny of those contributions was used for the Chinese. W. W. Lockwood, longtime Y administrator and champion of Chinese autonomy, sent a worried internal YMCA memo. He reported that there had been "immense enthusiasm in connection with the campaign, and results are three times what has ever been secured in China in any previous appeal of similar nature." The sum of US$50,000 came from the central government, and more contributions came from several provincial treasuries. In accepting this fund, Lockwood continued, "the War Work Council has, in the minds of the Chinese at least, become obligated to the highest authorities in China." But Lockwood saw a problem in the fact that the work for the Chinese laborers then going on was disproportionately inadequate to make good use of the money raised. The YMCA should make adequate provision for the Chinese work in France from this donation. He concluded with the warning that it "will end in disappointment and sharpest criticism unless the situation is handled with utmost care." The memo called on the YMCA War Work Council to revise its present budget in connection with the Chinese work in France and increase the part allocated for the Chinese work to provide for it adequately. It also argued that by increasing the money spent for the Chinese in France, it would appeal to the Chinese back home. The memo pointed out that "these men from the orient, 'strangers in a strange land,' without knowledge of language or customs of the West, constitute a peculiar appeal from the standpoint of human welfare." The memo further argued that "to stop sending secretaries from China, to refuse to go forward on an advanced program, is liable to affect payments to the fund." Lockwood called the fund was "virtually a trust fund." The Chinese naturally would feel that the work should be adequately provided because the Chinese had already provided adequately for the work.[49]

The Association had enormous hurdles to overcome. As one secretary complained about his work under the British, "I found myself face to face with difficulties almost incalculable. . . . It was no one's business there to look after the Chinese." First, he had great difficulty setting up a place to work. Then he had no supplies. He complained that without supplies, "We had no way of entertaining these people." He commented that when dealing with the military, "it was the proper attitude to be as harmless as a dove, but I found it was necessary to be as wise as a serpent."

With all the bureaucratic and other challenges, Association men often had the opportunity to go "the second mile," demonstrating a spirit of self-sacrifice and privation to meet the needs of the companies they served. One secretary had the choice of remaining in a well-equipped base hut or following his company into the very heart of a devastated wilderness. He followed his company, living in a small tent surrounded by ankle-deep mud. He spent his days trying to secure enough corrugated iron to put together an Association hut; the laborers volunteered on Sundays and holidays to work under his direction. In another similar case, a YMCA secretary found little being done in preparation for the coming of a Chinese labor company. He at once directed the orderlies to prepare hot water, and when he learned that no plan had been made for their evening meal, he walked two miles to the commissariat and drew rations sufficient for two days. On his return, he found the orderlies intoxicated and was obliged to take matters into his own hands. Later, the colonel in charge of that company testified that this Association secretary was of more value to him than all the officers put together.[50]

## The Content of the Work

The YMCA's work with the Chinese focused on three areas: recreation, education, and moral and religious uplift.[51] The staff's key task was to defuse any misunderstandings between the laborers and the commanding officers to improve morale among the laborers, to promote Western civilization, and (most importantly for the YMCA) to spread God's word to the Chinese.

The YMCA conducted its work from modest centers it established in the Chinese labor camps.[52] A typical YMCA center was a building or tent about 100 feet long with a large central room, a canteen counter, and a smaller adjoining storage room. These were places where the Chinese could come to drink tea after work, buy whatever they needed, play games, hear lectures, enjoy motion pictures, register for educational classes, or attend religious services and Bible classes, among other activities.[53] Some of the facilities were quite impressive, sporting Chinese-style artistic decorations and the national flags of China and other countries. Some also had a large map of the world, a constant source of interest to these "globe-trotters" and a popular subject for the secretaries.[54]

A model program for the YMCA's work week was roughly approximated at each center: Sunday, Bible classes and services; Monday, motion pictures; Tuesday, letter writing; Wednesday, indoor games; Thursday, gramophone entertainment; Friday, amateur theatricals (Chinese); Saturday, voluntarily directed amusements and lantern (slide) lectures. All these activities, except those on Sunday, were usually confined to the hours between 6 p.m. and 8 p.m., between work and bedtime.[55]

These activities show that the YMCA wisely emphasized recreation. It was most successful in promoting sports and entertainment. Soon after the entrance of the YMCA into their lives in France, the Chinese began playing soccer, volleyball, checkers, basketball, ping-pong, quoits, shuttlecock, boxing, chess, and many other types of activities. The laborers took part in these activities with great enthusiasm. A sports program not only kept them fit and active but also taught (many for the first time) the European mode of enjoying outdoor life. The YMCA units attached to the military had a compulsory physical program of its own, and military men were given calisthenic drills, but "the YMCA secretaries made the most of Chinese games and Chinese forms of physical exercise from the start."[56] The result was that kite flying and shuttlecock games, which practically amounted to a "national" sport in some parts of China, spontaneously brought out the native sporting instinct. The Association was in the position to conduct such work successfully because of its contacts with missionaries, Chinese students in America, and agencies in China.[57]

The Association made every effort to find qualified talent to direct physical education activities and recommended Amos N. Hoagland, who had just returned from a term of service in China, to serve as physical director in France. Hoagland was born in January 1884 and graduated from Princeton University. According to the Association's recommendation, Hoagland "is the only man that we know of who is able to do this. We regard it as particularly important that it be put through as rapidly as possible."[58]

Besides sports activities, the YMCA secretaries encouraged the Chinese to use their talents in other ways as well. Probably the most influential and popular activities were drama associations or theatrical groups. The Chinese enjoyed traditional music and opera, and many of the companies had regular theatrical groups organized by the laborers with support of the local YMCA secretaries. The YMCA set up stages so they could put on amateur theatricals. The laborers were passionately fond of these, and many men got involved in their preparation; thus the excitement generated around these efforts effectively offset gambling and other types of temptation. The following example demonstrates the enthusiasm of the Chinese for traditional dramas. In one camp in Calais, the laborers subscribed 2,200 francs, and two tailors worked full time for two weeks to make costumes for their theater troupe. The whole camp was interested and excited. For the first performance, one hundred men from a neighboring camp got up at 4 a.m., walked sixteen miles to see the show, and walked back at 9:30 p.m. They reached their home camp at 3 a.m. and went on duty that same day. During the show, the place was jammed. Windows, doors, and furniture were broken as the eager men tried to gain any vantage point they could to watch. It was reported that four laborers had planned to gamble that night, but called it off and went to the show instead.

The YMCA also organized slide lectures and showed motion pictures. In China, the Y had promoted science and health in local campaigns that used parades, models, lectures, and what were then known as "magic lanterns."[59] Adapting these programs to the work in France was natural. A projector was provided for every hut and used to educate the Chinese about different subjects. For instance, some of the forty-two sets of slides specially selected in London were used to help interpret the West to the Chinese. Sets about Palestine and the life of Christ were also used to promote religious work. Chinese laborers had opportunities to watch movies and soon they came to recognize and look for Charlie Chaplin, just as they did for the "Tommies" and "Yanks." A censorship committee was organized at Dieppe to select films for the Chinese, because many films of the regular circuit were found to be unsuitable from the organization's patronizing or moral perspective. One YMCA secretary promised a show on Chinese New Year's Day in a camp at Dunkirk. On the way, his motorcycle broke down, but to keep from disappointing the men he strapped the six reels on his back and walked the remaining fourteen miles.[60]

The YMCA was instrumental as well in promoting education for the laborers. One confidential report notes, "It is significant that the secretaries, almost without exception, gained conviction regarding the need of mass education in China."[61] The education programs included classes on subjects such as English, French, history, mathematics, Chinese, and geography, among other subjects. YMCA secretaries explained the war and Western civilization to the workers as best they could.[62]

Not every Chinese laborer took advantage of the education programs. Shi Yixuan observed that although some of the men enjoyed the educational opportunities the Association provided in the evenings, others were still to be found gambling in their barracks or loafing on the streets. Of course, there were not sufficient facilities to include everyone. As Shi commented, "We cannot say that with a larger building we can attract all these men . . . or do away with gambling or loafing entirely; we can say, however, that with a larger building we may put up some diversions that will counteract the influence of their present immoral surroundings."[63]

The YMCA, sometimes in cooperation with the military authorities, also arranged for experts to give lectures to the laborers. For instance, Dr. William Wesley Peter was sent to France to present a series of lectures to the Chinese laborers. Peter was educated at Harvard Medical School and went to China as a medical missionary, arriving just in time to tend wounded soldiers in the 1911 revolution. In 1913 he was released from his missionary obligations to work for the YMCA. He and G. H. Cole mounted successful health education campaigns in Tianjin and other cities.[64] According to military rules, everyone who signed up to work with the labor battalions had to remain at least four months from the date of his landing in France. Peter seemed quite happy to have this opportunity to go abroad, especially to render a real service to the Chinese.[65] Over the course of his several-month stay, Peter was able to deliver health lectures in Chinese. During his time in France, he was also able to conduct extended research on how the YMCA was handling the Chinese in Europe, which he reported back to the YMCA and to Chinese leaders after he returned to China to recruit more personnel to work in France.[66] Peter's lectures in France were necessarily "simple, designed rather to stimulate interest and inform about conditions in the West, and to provide an offset to the hard conditions of life which these men necessarily find."[67] From the perspective of the military authorities, the YMCA's value lay in increasing laborer morale and preventing riots. These were key to increased productivity.

Many Chinese secretaries also were involved in the lecture series. For instance, L. T. Chen, a graduate of Yale University and a Chinese Association staffer, gave a number of speeches on the subject of "the relation of the Chinese to the war in Europe." They were interesting lectures, arranged in the camps by permission of the commanding officer and sometimes presided over by him. For many laborers, it was the first time they had listened to lectures by their own country's elites; for some, it was the first time they had ever listened to a public address. And the men listened to and watched the speakers intently. Chen spoke in all sorts of places, on the parade ground with the men sitting in rows, from a theatre stage, standing on barrels, and even from the roof of a YMCA building. At one lecture, the Chinese laborers sat listening near a bomb shelter in the glow of the setting sun. A sudden shower dampened everyone's clothes, but they all remained and listened to the end. Lectures such as Chen's gave the officers a new appreciation of the "D-Chink" as they sometimes called the Chinese. Several later confessed to a YMCA secretary that they did not know the Chinese had such abilities, and with a new spirit of camaraderie, they invited the lecturer to dine with them. It was often the colonel who was thus moved. Many British officers in charge of the Chinese laborers heard about these lectures and were impressed.

The Chinese secretaries played a key role in education programs, especially in teaching basic literacy. Initially more than 80 percent of the laborers were illiterate. Most had to rely on others to read and write letters. This sometimes had lamentable consequences. One illiterate laborer from Shandong by the name of Wang Xiaoshun got a letter from his uncle. His letter reader told him the letter said Wang's mother was dead. On learning this news, Wang cried for several days and was not able to eat because of his grief. Several days later, he got another letter from the same uncle. This time the letter reader told him that the letter said Wang's mother's health was improving and asked him to send money home. Wang realized that something was wrong. He decided to ask another person to read the two letters for him one more time. The new reader told him the first reader had read that letter wrong. Wang was so angry that he tried to beat the man up.[68]

Because only a small percentage of the Chinese could write, one very practical and useful service the YMCA secretaries provided was to help the laborers write letters home. A standard letter was commonly used. In one place, a secretary prepared and printed 2,000 copies of such letters and distributed them among the men. The laborer had to fill in only his name and the date. These letters told of the general good conditions surrounding them.[69] Sometimes the Chinese diplomatic missions also sent officials to help the YMCA secretary in the canteen and assist with the correspondence. YMCA stationery, printed in English and Chinese, was provided free of charge.[70] To make sure that the replies from China would reach the men in France, each laborer was provided with several envelopes with the return address printed in French and Chinese.

Laborers thus had motivation to learn. The most popular class was reading. The great success of the literacy classes can be credited to a single person: Yan Yangchu (whose work is described in more detail in Chapter 9). He invented a revolutionary new teaching method with a selection of foundation characters that proved to be the foundation of widespread literacy programs in China.[71] For those who were illiterate and too old to study regularly, the new phonetic system could be mastered in a few weeks. This enabled them to read and write within a short time. For those who could read and write a little, a select vocabulary of six hundred characters, also easily mastered within a few weeks, enabled the men to read newspapers and other simple literature. For those who were already fairly well educated and really motivated to study, classes in English, French, geography, history, mathematics, and the Chinese classics were offered in many camps. General mass education lectures, accompanied by demonstration apparatus or illustrated by motion pictures and stereopticon slides, tackled questions such as sanitation, forestry, road building, national consciousness, the Great War, citizenship, and so on. These programs were given by special lecturers, so that those who could not or would not take classes could be educated through the eye and the ear. Many laborers reported that YMCA's classes helped them become better citizens and broadened their intellectual horizons. They developed skills for self-governance and independence for their return to China.[72]

The education programs were so popular that an average of 120 men from companies of five hundred regularly attended classes in the twenty-five companies of one area. They were so popular that the classes ran out of material. "It flashed into my mind one day," said Yan to a reporter in 1919,

> that it would be an easy matter, and a tremendous benefit to the Chinese if there could be circulated among them a short newspaper in their own tongue, so that they would know what was going on at Versailles and in London and in Washington and at home. For despite the prevalent belief that the Chinese are as a race incurious, I found that even in that little bulletin a quick answer to the questioning curiosity about the news of the world noticeable in almost all of the Chinese.[73]

The Education Department of the American Expeditionary Force YMCA then asked Yan to come to Paris to edit a paper for all the Chinese in France. Under Edward C. Carter, who had worked with the Student Volunteer Movement in India, the department had done extensive educational work for American soldiers and wanted to give equal treatment to the Chinese. In early February 1919, the department produced 10,000 copies of a four-page paper, the *Ji du jiao qing nian hui Zhu-Fa Huagong zhoubao* (Chinese Laborers' Weekly). Because there was no Chinese type set, Yan wrote out the paper in his own calligraphy, which was then lithographed. Within three weeks, the paid circulation was 2,000, and the total number of copies distributed increased to 15,000. Perhaps because of the Y's moral code, or perhaps because it took too much room, the document contained no fiction. It used colloquial Chinese, which helped the laborers to read and understand both world and Chinese affairs. Graduates from the six-hundred-character class found the paper excellent for practicing their reading. *Chinese Laborers' Weekly* was very popular. "Everywhere the Chinese coolies are eager to possess themselves of copies of this paper, which thus becomes an educational agency."[74]

Many Chinese saved their wages carefully. The YMCA secretaries also helped the Chinese deal with banking issues. With help from the French government, the Banque Industrielle de Chine was set up for handling the Chinese laborers' finances. At the end of June 1921, the Banque Industrielle de Chine closed its doors, and the receipts and drafts it had issued to the laborers suddenly became, as they put it, "dry leaves in their hands." Seriously concerned about getting their money back, some men turned to the YMCA secretaries for help. One camp of 190 Chinese laborers told a YMCA secretary they had "altogether deposited 150,000 francs in that bank. This money is what we have saved during four years of 'sweating blood' in France." With the YMCA secretaries' prodding, the French Ministry of War on August 1, 1921 took up the matter on behalf of those laborers who were then being sent home. It announced in the big repatriation camp at Marseille that all drafts and receipts issued by the bank would be redeemed. When the transport finally steamed out of Marseille on its long voyage back to China with more than 2,500 laborers, the laborers' financial affairs had been happily resolved and they traveled homeward with five years' savings in their pockets. A YMCA report recorded that as the secretaries waved a last farewell to that crowd of happy smiling men, "perhaps this final service was the most satisfying of all."[75]

One missionary summed up the importance of the YMCA's work with the Chinese laborers. He wrote, "I think they will remember. I am sure they appreciated. It made them feel at least that they were men and not mere quarry slaves, driven to their dungeon when the day was done."[76] He was right. The Chinese obviously enjoyed and benefited from the YMCA programs and services; they were "all very grateful for whatever little courtesies were accorded them. Whenever a secretary did some favor for the men they would come back with presents for him as a token of their appreciation."[77] They were not shy about making their appreciation known. For instance, when three Chinese labor companies found out that their beloved YMCA secretary, one H. F. Fan, might be transferred to a different place, the men decided to do something about keeping him. After a long and passionate discussion, they decided the best course of action would be an appeal to the highest official of the labor companies: the *zong ban*. The men most fluent in English of the three companies were summoned to draft a petition. It said:

> Sir: [We], the whole body of the three companies, C.L.C, at . . . Owing to hearing Rev. H. F. Fan will be transferred shortly from here, we beg to respectfully state that he is a nice and gentle and kind man here. As he has been rendering us a great deal of teaching with different kinds of common knowledge. . . . And every one of us applauds for having got such a good man, besides that he quite behaving himself.[78]

The YMCA, of course, was not only interested in helping the Chinese and receiving such appreciation. It also had its own considerations. From its official perspective, by making the Chinese happy, the Association was more effectively helping to save Western civilization and helping the Allies win the Great War. More importantly, its efforts helped to spread the Christian values to the laborers and hence to China. For the YMCA, spreading the values of Christianity and Western civilization was key in its work with the Chinese. The Chinese, like many other foreigner laborers, had been brought from "distant lands in the name of labor and civilization." According to the YMCA, under these circumstances, "the Government can do very little in the way of teaching our civilization to these men"; but the Association could, "if it will, do much." Again the focus on religion was critical. As one official who worked for the French noted, "If we succeed in getting them to understand the first principles of Christian service, God only knows what importance this may have for the future of Christianity when these people return to their own lands."[79]

Within the British and American areas, religious meetings and exercises were carried out freely. Bible classes were established in many camps for laborers who wanted to learn about Christianity. In the French area, by agreement, it was understood that there should be no religious propaganda. In practice, however, the secretaries were able to be of real service to the Christians, and in some centers the men voluntarily requested baptism and church membership.[80] As one YMCA secretary reported, "It is often said that there are no proper religious opportunities among the French. I did not find it so. Whenever we wished to speak on religious topics, no objections were ever raised by the French. During cinema shows, while films were being changed I have often given an earnest, Christian talk. The men were always quiet and attentive."[81] The YMCA obviously hoped that the great mass of the laborers would return to China with a kindly feeling toward the Association. For its officials, their involvement with the laborers was kind of "spiritual engineering." Through its work with the laborers, the YMCA hoped to do some very effective religious work. John Shields, in charge of a YMCA center at Dunkirk, tried to make it a spiritual home as much as a social institute. "Besides the regular Sunday service at 2 pm, we have worship every evening."[82]

The Association was not entirely disappointed. Perhaps due to its influence and by coming to the West, some Chinese did discover a new God and embraced their new religion with enthusiasm. According to the *Missionary Review of the World* (New York), thirteen Chinese workers were converted to Christianity and declared that their purpose was to devote their lives to Christian service on their return to their native land.[83] On another occasion, the Religious Tract Society sent Christian books to Chinese laborers in France. One was titled *The Church's Welcome to Chinese Workmen at the Front* and consisted of a few introductory words of cheer, a selection of scriptural passages, and a number of short prayers. One Chinese worker happened to be Christian, and he was so pleased with the booklet that he sent a donation of 20 francs, two-thirds of a month's pay, to the society.[84]

Largely in consideration of its long-term interests and influence in China, the YMCA was interested in pursuing follow-up work with returned Chinese laborers. According to one YMCA official, "The purpose of the immediate work should conserve what has been done in France. Upon arrival to help the men through temptations, to get them to their homes still possessors of the wealth they have earned, to encourage thrift and good citizenship, and to prepare for them and the Church a relationship that will bring them together." Many Chinese students supported the idea of the YMCA's continued support of the laborers after they returned to China and were enthusiastic about bringing the "hut idea" into China.[85]

To figure out how to help the laborers and the Association itself long term, in April 1919 the YMCA organized an important three-day conference for Chinese YMCA secretaries in the Hotel Suisse, Versailles, to allow the secretaries to get to know each other better, to exchange views, and especially to discuss how to continue their work in China. Sixty-eight secretaries attended the conference: sixty were Chinese, six were American, and two were British. Aside from the rank and file, there were also several distinguished visitors, such as Harry Holmes of the British YMCA; Edward. C. Carter of the American Expeditionary Force–YMCA; D. A. Davis of the Foyers du Soldat; Fletcher S. Brockman of the YMCA International Committee; and Wang Zhengting, a member of the Chinese delegation to the Paris Peace Conference. The participants agreed that the YMCA should "immediately devise ways and means to project the YMCA hut idea in France to China for the uplifting and the education of the masses." They also recommended that the YMCA should "ship as soon as possible the equipment that is now being used in the different centers in France and that later will be of use for the work in China" and "start work first in centers to which most of the laborers return . . . utilize temples and other public buildings when available."

With a clear goal and direction, the YMCA secretaries charged ahead with their postwar plans for the laborers. At the Association's request, the British military provided sailing information to the YMCA secretaries and allowed them to cable the names of the steamers to China so its men there could meet them. This information also allowed the YMCA to set up work for these returning men at Noyelles, where they sometimes waited two weeks for their transport to arrive, and at Le Havre, where they finally boarded a ship for home. Back in China, the general plan consisted of erecting a big mat shed on a back lot recently purchased by the Jinan YMCA chapter in Shandong. In this shed, the YMCA's China officials would organize lectures, socials, movies, and Bible study to keep the laborers busy and happy. But they also tried to focus attention and efforts on meeting the other needs of these men. In addition to their work at Jinan, the capital of Shandong Province, the officials wanted to start a similar center in eastern Shandong where many of these laborers would congregate.[86]

Even given the enthusiasm of the YMCA and the Chinese YMCA sec-retaries, and even with the support of the Chinese government, the idea of bringing the YMCA work to China did not work out well. There were many reasons for its failure. J. A. Mowatt of the YMCA, writing in June of 1919 about his experience at the War Emigration Agency in Jinan, blamed the British military authority. He wrote that "the military ma-chine has control and it has made rather a bad mess of coolie labour. I suppose the military system is the poorest in the world for getting work out of anybody. Someday perhaps the whole coolie scheme will be made public. If the thing is honestly written up then it will be made to appear that the leaven of missionaries in the C.L.C. have saved it from being a ghastly failure."[87]

The rise of Chinese nationalism and the chaotic and unstable political situation in China clearly also played an important role in the disappoint-ing result. The British government, although recognizing the YMCA's plan to help returned laborers as "extremely laudable," decided that it wanted nothing to do with it and would not pay for it. Besides bestow-ing their "goodwill," the British refused to participate in the YMCA plan actively.[88] Still another factor in the long-term effects of the Chinese la-borers' experience was the new attitudes that the Chinese workers in-spired in their Chinese teachers. The Great War precipitated a confron-tation between the Wilsonian model of middle-class revolution and the Leninist model of popular or proletarian revolution.

# 9

## THE FUSION OF TEACHING AND LEARNING

### *Students as Teachers and Vice Versa*

The Chinese workers in France were mostly common villagers who knew little of China or the world when they were selected to go to Europe; still, these men directly and personally contributed to helping China transform its image at home and in the world. Their new transnational roles reshaped national identity and China's internationalization, which then in turn shaped the emerging global system. From their experience of Europe in a time of war and their work with the American, British, and French military, as well as fellow laborers from other countries, they developed a unique perception of China and of world affairs. Further, many future Chinese leaders such as Yan Yangchu, Jiang Tingfu, Cai Yuanpei, and Wang Jingwei, among many others, through their work with the Chinese workers in Europe, became convinced that China could become a better nation through their new understanding of their fellow citizens.

At a time when all concerned agreed that China's future hung in the balance, these young men were China's best talent with the brightest futures. They came to France out of deep belief, not to further their careers or build their fortunes. They came to Europe because they had fallen under the spell of Woodrow Wilson's call for a new world order and the promise of a better world system from which China could benefit. They wanted to use their knowledge, energy, and experience to help bring about the early inception of this new world order. Yet their worldview and understanding of China were very different from those of the laborers. They helped workers to write letters, taught them to read and understand world and Chinese affairs; but, most important, they were determined to make the laborers into better citizens of both China and the world.

This chapter examines how the experience of these elite scholars and students helped them develop a new appreciation for the Chinese working class, spurred them to find solutions to Chinese problems, and changed their perceptions about China and its future. It will explore what the laborers learned from their own experience and from the YMCA workers and other Chinese elites who worked with them, as well as how the laborers eventually became new citizens of China and the world, and developed a new understanding and appreciation of China and its position in the world.

## Students as Teachers

China's decision to send "laborers as soldiers" was based on both expediency and on far-reaching strategic thinking. This unprecedented move was a product of the young Republican China's forward-looking policies. Many political elites and public intellectuals directly linked the "laborers as soldiers" plan to their vision of China's future development and the goal of assuming equal status in the family of nations.

As early as December 28, 1916, Chinese minister to France Hu Weide wrote a memo to his government, suggesting that the Peking government should get involved more actively to help France select the best men, since it was in China's long-term interest to do so. The good reputation of the laborers might even help Chinese manufactured goods become popular and competitive in the world.[1] Li Jun, in his "memorandum on emigration" to the Chinese government, also argued that sending Chinese laborers to France served multiple purposes. First, it would help the men make a living; second, it would expose them to knowledge about industry; third, their experience would make them an important force for change when they returned.[2] Turning Chinese laborers into a new generation of citizens was also the idea of Ye Gongchuo, who was one of the "laborers as soldiers" plan's designers. In autumn 1916, Ye assigned Li Jianshan to negotiate with the French government about including an educational component in the laborers' activities in France. The French military agreed to select a number of younger laborers to learn French and other useful subjects with pay.[3] In late 1918, when Ye visited France, he gave lectures to the laborers and encouraged them to be strong, to love China, and to be good citizens in Europe.[4]

Thus to better understand the intended role of laborers in advancing China's larger national goals, it might be useful to review the origins of the idea of sending them abroad. Social elites such as Li Shizeng and Cai Yuanpei believed that the nation needed citizens who had learned from abroad to propel reform. Li Shizeng was an influential intellectual, entrepreneur, and politician, who had himself studied in France and had translated many French books into Chinese. Li was naturally among those who praised France "as a model republic" from which China should learn.[5] An advocate of reform, he was interested in bringing the Chinese into personal contact with the West, and thus he encouraged them to study and work abroad. As early as 1902, when Li went to France for the first time, he and Wu Zhihui, another key reformer and politician in Republican China, had discussed the possibility of sending ordinary Chinese to Europe.[6] For him, the key to reforming China was education and learning from Western countries. Sending Chinese students to the West as laborers would be a perfect vehicle for gaining that experience. Wu Zhihui described Li's strategy this way: the main point of sending thousands of Chinese to France was the expectation that if a huge number went and returned, they would have an enormous impact on Chinese society.[7] Based on this understanding, Li Shizeng, Wu Zhihui, Wang Jingwei, and Cai Yuanpei organized the Liu-Fa Jianxuehui (Society for Frugal Study in France) in 1912. This organization encouraged young Chinese to go to France: working was the means, and learning was the end. The society aimed to expand educational opportunities, introduce Chinese to world civilization and advanced learning, and develop the Chinese national economy.[8] Under its sponsorship, 120 young Chinese went to France during the period 1912–1913.[9]

Although the society was soon dissolved under political pressure from President Yuan Shikai, leaders of the group such as Li, Cai, Wang, and Wu Yuzhang never gave up on their vision. Li, Cai, and many others continued to vigorously promote the idea of Chinese studying in France. They played an active role in pushing the Chinese government to develop a better organization and system for sending laborer-students abroad. In 1914, these men founded a new work-study program. Cai Yuanpei, its president, explained that its functions included educating Chinese workers in France, promoting Sino-French friendship, and especially learning from the French scientific and intellectual achievements to "help China develop her morality, knowledge, and economy."[10]

So when the Chinese government plan of using laborers as soldiers emerged, Li, Cai, and others supported it immediately and used their influence and prestige to push the Chinese government to organize and systematize the program.[11] They wanted the plan to emphasize the importance of educating the laborers while they were abroad.[12] In their collective memo to the Chinese government, Cai Yuanpei, Wang Jingwei, Li Shizeng, Wu Zhihui, and others strongly suggested that the French recruitment program would have great importance in developing the Chinese national identity and securing the young republic a new position in the world.[13] If China wanted to see its status enhanced, it had to learn from Western civilization, and Chinese laborers in France would be in the vanguard of this trend of learning from the West.[14] These well-connected elites thought that if China devised a sound policy for recruitment, paid attention to laborer education, and made sure the laborers would be treated as legal equals, the plan could benefit China enormously in the long run.[15]

Labor education was a key factor in the Chinese elites' search for ways to internationalize their society and create a new national identity for China. In June 1915 in Paris, Cai, Li, and others organized the Qingong Jianxuehui (Society for Frugal Study by Means of Labor) that was to cooperate in the French recruitment effort. The society would promote "diligence and perseverance in work and frugality (in order to save money) for study, thereby advancing the laborers' knowledge." Li Shizeng claimed that Chinese workers in France would not only contribute to the transmission of industrial skills on their return to China but would also help reform society and eliminate undesirable social customs by having been exposed to European civilization.[16] In March 1916, they became directly involved in the recruitment plan by organizing the Société Franco-Chinoise d'Education, also in Paris.[17] The aim of this association was to "develop relations between China and France and, especially, with the aid of French scientific and spiritual education, to plan for the development of China's moral, intellectual, and economic well being."[18] Its mission was, first, to promote Chinese citizens' education; second, to bring Western civilization to China; third, to explain Chinese traditional virtues and philosophies; and fourth, to improve the Chinese economy and industry.[19] Wu Yuzhang explained that it was to serve as a bridge between Chinese and Western civilizations and create a fusion of these two great civilizations. Furthermore, Wu pointed out at its opening ceremony, the Société would also promote laborer education by participating in the recruitment and so help China take full advantage of the opportunity to train better workers for New China.[20]

The elites were eager to instill in the laborers new knowledge, a new worldview, and new understandings of China and the world. They soon found ways to put their ideas into action. Chinese intellectuals in France "pressed the French government to give the labourers technical education." China needed engineers and skilled laborers, and "factories like those in which the immigrants are employed in France are good fields for training them." The unnamed author of this article was apparently Chinese, and he wrote in conclusion, "On the part of the Chinese I seize the opportunity to say that we are glad to be of use to the Allies, and we hope that the French industrial education will be beneficial for the industrialization of our own land."[21] Many Chinese elites had been active advocates of and a moving force behind the migration scheme.

When he learned that the French government had decided to recruit laborers from China, Cai Yuanpei immediately focused on the problem of how to educate them. In spring 1916, Cai set up a training program to prepare qualified teachers. He personally wrote a short series of textbooks they could use under the general title "Textbooks for Laborers' Schools." In his textbooks, he emphasized the importance of citizenship, personal hygiene, public spirit, personal character, and moral values, among many other topics. He also paid enormous attention to acquiring practical knowledge.[22] Cai himself served as instructor to the field teachers; he also prepared lecture notes and went to teach Chinese workers in France. His textbooks were soon published. Wang Jingwei, a fiery young radical supporter of Sun Yat-sen known for his assassination attempt on a Manchu official in 1905, wrote a foreword to Cai's textbook. He echoed traditional Confucian pedagogics: Cai's purposes were first to instill good traditional virtues and then to help the workers overcome personal shortcomings through education and learning. Cai's ideas would help make the men better people, better workers, and better citizens.[23] For Cai, if China wanted to advance its position in the world it was imperative to understand Western civilization. "China has an opportunity to absorb European civilization. The Chinese in Europe are the first learners," he wrote.[24] In 1917, Cai Yuanpei and others tried to raise funds in China to help support laborer education in France. Cai even pressed the Chinese president to help raise funds. In letters he and his cohort sent to the president, they argued that educating these laborers was crucial to China's future and its international development.[25]

Chinese elites were prime supporters and founders of publications for the laborers in France. For his part, Li Shizeng founded the *Chinese Labor Journal (Huagong zazhi)* in Paris in January 1917 to provide vital information to the Chinese in the field. The journal was edited by Qin-gong Jianxuehui and featured both educational pieces and essays on topics such as science and the arts, news items, and short stories. The editors claimed they wanted it to reflect opinions of the laborers, as well as promote knowledge and improve the laborers' well-being.[26] Cai, Li, and Wang Jingwei all published many pieces in this journal. The journal faced several challenges. It had been planned as a bimonthly publication, but because of lack of funding and censorship, it was sometimes published only once per month. Nevertheless, by July 1918, twenty-four issues had already been published. Its content included news from China and abroad, laborer news, and so on. As Li Jun reported to the Chinese government, despite room for improvement, this journal was crucial *(shi bu ke shao)* for the laborers.[27] *Lu Ou zhoukan* was another journal aimed at the laborers; it was founded on November 15, 1919 near Paris. This publication encouraged Chinese laborers to stand up and take action; it urged them to set a good example for workers back in China.[28] It also translated and published *L'internationale* in Chinese.[29] Among all the journals, the most influential one, however, was the Yan Yangchu's *Chinese Laborers' Weekly*. (This journal is discussed later in the chapter.)

The previous activities indicate how determined the Chinese elites were to prepare their laborers to take part in China's renewal and transformation. They believed that having their own people on the ground in Europe would not only promote exchange between China and the West but also accelerate China's internationalization. The laborers' education had an important role to play.

The French and British governments also recognized the importance of the Chinese laborers for Europe in the future and provided a few education programs as well. As early as the summer of 1917, the British legation in China reminded the British government of the potential implications of the laborers' presence. In one memorandum, legation officials wrote, "The time has come to consider the very important political effect which the sojourn of some hundred thousand Chinese in France will have." It further argued that these laborers would play an important role in China when they returned home, and therefore it was "most important" for the British government to provide educational programs to transform them into "preachers and exponents of British fairness and efficiency."[30] Although neither government took an active role, at least some members of both governments understood the issue and made some effort. The link between sending Chinese laborers abroad and the reformulation of China's national identity must be understood as a direct result of Chinese social elites' involvement in the plan.

Perhaps the organization most successful in shaping the young, inexperienced Chinese was the Young Men's Christian Association.[31] A major mission of the YMCA was to help create for China a new sense of place in world affairs.[32] Association programs for the Chinese laborers were hoped to form "disseminators of a better understanding between the West and the East among their relatives and friends."[33] It was, in fact, largely through the YMCA that Chinese elites were able to realize their goals regarding laborers' education. Under normal circumstances, the life trajectories of Chinese elites would have not crossed those of the laborers. In normal times, there would have been no occasion, no reason, for members of the highest echelons of Chinese society and laborers to interact on a personal basis. But this was not a normal time, and Chinese elites and workers did meet in the West and shared experiences in France during the Great War. Everywhere the laborers were responsive to the services rendered them, and it was a question if their teachers were not inspired and helped as much as the laborers themselves. The work for the laborers enhanced Chinese students' skills of leadership and their understanding of China. They confronted problems with the canteens, the securing and fitting of huts, relationships between westerners and the laborers involving the settlements of strikes and riots, as well as the promotion of programs under war conditions. Their work with the laborers furnished them with a laboratory in which they had ample opportunity for initiative and development in leadership.

Understandably, most Chinese laborers were ignorant of the world and even of their own country in the beginning. One thought that America had entered the war because the crown prince of the United States had become engaged to one of the princesses of France. Many believed that it was personal American friendships with England and France that drew the United States into the carnage of war.[34] Because most of the men were uneducated, their behavior was sometimes embarrassing to the Chinese elites. Shi Yixuan wrote that on tramways he not infrequently found that these men, while traveling first class, talked loudly among themselves, or sometimes ate peanuts or chestnuts and threw the shells on the floor.[35] Chinese elites found the laborers dirty, noisy, and provincial. Yan Yangchu wrote that he noticed they both spit and littered aboard trains. When they saw a foreign couple holding hands, they laughed at them.[36]

The Chinese National YMCA recruited numerous Chinese students to France to help the laborers just after they finished their studies in the United States or other countries. These people were absolutely the top of Chinese society. Most of them came from well-off families in urban areas, and their foreign education guaranteed respected jobs and careers. Gui Zhiting was a native of Hubei Province and an indemnity fund scholar. He graduated from Yale College in 1917 and later became a graduate student in physics at the University of Chicago. He served as editor for a Chinese student monthly in the United States and was chairman of the Tsinghua Alumni Association. He began working for the laborers under the AEF in June 1918. Jiang Tingfu, a native of Hunan Province and graduate of Oberlin College in 1918, had been editor of an Oberlin literary magazine. He was commencement dinner toastmaster and a member of Phi Beta Kappa, the college varsity soccer team, and the Society of Learning and Labor while at Oberlin. After taking a PhD in history at Columbia University, he became an educator and a high-level Chinese diplomat. Shi Yixuan was a native of Shandong and came to the United States as a Boxer indemnity scholar in 1911; he then graduated from Harvard Business School. He was the first YMCA secretary to work with Chinese laborers under the French.[37] Yan Yangchu was recruited fresh out of Yale College in the summer of 1918. Yan had been a star student at Yale. He was a good singer, pianist, and tennis player, and was well liked by fellow students. He was first Chinese student in the Yale men's choir and a member of the Beta Theta Phi fraternity. He worked with the Chinese among the BEF from August 1918 and stayed there for roughly one year. One YMCA official recalled, "Mr. Yen [was] one of the finest men socially that you ever met."[38]

These young men were China's best and brightest. Their worldview and understanding of China were very different from the laborers. The young men helped the laborers write letters, and taught them to read and understand the world and Chinese affairs; most importantly, they were determined to make the laborers into better citizens of both China and the world. They came to Europe because these Western-educated Chinese had fallen under the spell of Woodrow Wilson's call for a new world order and the promise of a better world system from which China could benefit. They wanted to use their knowledge, energy, and experience to help bring about the early inception of this new order. In addition, many recent graduates from fine Chinese universities also went to France to work as interpreters for the French and British military forces and the laborers. Some of these interpreters and later work-study students from China taught evening school for the laborers. In other words, elites from both China and abroad had opportunity to interact with each other, and especially with the laborers, in a situation quite different from any they would have found at home.[39]

One of the most effective tools of laborer education was the *Chinese Laborers' Weekly*, founded on January 15, 1919, in Paris by Yan Yang-chu. At its peak, the journal had a paid circulation of 15,000. Yan was its editor and stayed at this post until June 1919 when he returned to the United States. He was succeeded by Fu Ruoyu, a graduate of the University of Missouri, who served as editor until November 1919, when he returned to the United States to pursue further study at the University of Chicago, whereupon Lu Shiyin became editor. Yan explained the origin of the journal this way: He spent his evenings directing classes and lectures for the Chinese laborers. The men were constantly coming to him—after lecture and at the canteen counter—asking him for news of the day. Yan was so impressed with their longing for some means of keeping in touch with the world, that he used to spend a great deal of time narrating to them the news from the French and English newspapers. It occurred to him that it would be an easy matter, and a tremendous benefit to the men, if a short news bulletin, printed in their own language, could be circulated so that they would know what was going on at Versailles, in London, in Washington, and at home. The journal was thus born.[40]

The aim of the *Chinese Laborers' Weekly* was to promote knowledge, help the men gain moral values and establish good bonds among themselves and with Westerners. It focused on enhancing and broadening their intellectual horizons, enforcing their understanding of nation-state, nationalism, and patriotism. It usually included editorials, news from China, news from the world, and so on. Where it discussed national sovereignty, it urged laborers to defend the national interest.[41] The journal repeatedly asked the laborers not to curse, not to fight with each other, not to gamble, not to steal, and not to visit prostitutes.[42] Yan and his friends worked hard to help the laborers develop self-esteem and patriotism. In one article, Yan wrote how "we Chinese" usually disliked travel and moving beyond the ancestors' land, so he praised the laborers' spirit of adventure in coming to France. He expressed the wish that they would become better people and help China "to become a strong race and nation" when they returned home. He asked them to work hard and "win glory for the motherland." Yan asked the laborers always to put interest of their futures, their families, and China first; he urged them to always try to learn more, to behave well, and to learn thrift and discipline by putting aside bad habits and behavior. He reminded them that their behavior in France was directly linked to foreign perceptions of the Chinese and China. They were "representatives of all Chinese," so in the interests of China and all Chinese, they should think twice before doing anything.[43] In many of his writings, Yan asked the laborers to love China, to help establish a better China. The journal also printed important articles from home. For instance, it carried several articles by Ye Shengtao on women's issues.[44] To get laborer input and active participation, the journal often encouraged the men to submit pieces on topics such as "Chinese laborers in France and their relation to China," "what is the Republic of China?" "Why China is weak?" and "how to improve education in China."

This journal became popular and influential among the laborers. One man wrote to the editor praising the writing as easy to understand and conveying the crucial information the laborers needed. He declared that the journal had helped him understand what was going on in China and the world.[45] But the *Chinese Laborers' Weekly* faced many challenges. Perhaps the biggest was censorship imposed by the British military authority. Wartime censorship was a major problem for everyone. An American YMCA secretary wrote to his family, "It gets harder to write than it was at first, with the censorship forbidding mention of all the real things. Just now it seems to be particularly difficult, so except for saying that our hut is really very near completion (window-glass the main lack now), I won't try to be newsy, but use this letter in catching up with personal matters."[46] In a letter dated November 17, 1917, he wrote, "I hope that when I write again it will be with a new story to tell, of which, however, I may be allowed by the censor to tell you but little. I shall again be 'Somewhere in France.'"[47] The *Chinese Laborers' Weekly* was frequently the victim of strict censorship. Every week, the editor had to submit copy in its entirety to the censor. If the censor had time, he might review it right away, but sometimes he was away and did not return on time, and thus the journal's publication could be irregular.[48]

The British were obviously nervous about rising Chinese nationalism and the laborers' strongly patriotic ideas and many times the editor had no choice but to leave blank space where materials had been taken out. In its eighteenth issue, published on June 18, 1919, the editors complained about the lack of freedom to publish. They wrote that when the Shandong question came up, many laborers submitted letters using rational words or angry sentences to express their strong opposition to giving Shandong to Japan. But due to censorship, the editor explained, many of these pieces could not be published.[49] Then, in its one-year anniversary issue on January 1, 1920, the *Chinese Laborers' Weekly* editor openly complained about the strict censorship. He wrote that many articles from the laborers expressing their patriotic and nationalist ideas often could not be printed. He further pointed out that articles dealing with the Shandong question and the Tibet issue often were censored.[50] In its thirty-first issue, the journal published an article on the origins of the Shandong question, but there were two blank spaces in the article with the editor's note that the censors had made the deletions.

The French authorities did the same for the *Chinese Labor Journal.* Like the *Chinese Laborers' Weekly,* the editors had to send all copy to the French censors for approval before anything could be published. The journal often had blank spaces due to censorship, and was often published late.

## Laborers as Teachers

The laborers were not only good students but also gracious ones. Many laborers themselves chipped in to support the elites' activities. A case in point is the donations in support of journals such as *Chinese Laborers' Weekly* and the *Chinese Labor Journal.* One laborer wrote to Yan Yang-chu that he learned a lot from the *Chinese Laborers' Weekly* and was willing to donate all his savings, 365 francs, to make sure that it would continue to be published.[51] Other laborers made donations, too, including Ma Xinwei and Ma Zuofu, who donated 20 francs to the weekly.[52] Many men made donations to the *Chinese Labor Journal* as well.

The support and understanding that their efforts won from the laborers encouraged the elites and deeply motivated them to continue the work. Many of these highly educated young men became de facto students of the laborers because they learned so much from them, and the experience of working with the laborers forced them to think in new ways about China, the Chinese people, and their future. Jiang Tingfu observed that the laborers had made a careful study of Western society and its successes. Many of them understood that the general success of the West came from the high literacy rate. Jiang was excited about and impressed by the laborers' discovery. He and others developed new confidence in China's future thanks to these men's sharp observations.[53] That working people could come to such conclusions was an eye-opening realization for the Chinese elites in Europe at this critical moment. One Chinese interpreter wrote in 1919 that interpreters like him had "gained an insight into the social conditions of the West, and their ideas have undergone a great change because they came to Europe. . . . It is certain that every one of these labourers will desire to see strong reforms made on his return to China."[54]

The influence of their work on the lives and thinking of the Chinese secretaries was even more striking than the service they rendered to the laborers. They discovered the meaning and joys of serving the common people. One secretary remarked that he had never realized before "that we students have a direct responsibility to the laboring classes. We must go back to China and continue this type of service for the masses."[55] The most famous story of teacher-as-student was that of Yan Yangchu. Yan recalled it this way: "I had never associated with laborers before the war . . . we of the student class felt ourselves altogether apart from them. But there in France I had the privilege of associating with them daily and knowing them intimately. I found that these men were just as good as I, and had just as much to them. The only difference between us was that I had had advantages and they hadn't."[56]

Yan's experience with the laborers in France taught him that they were smart, good-hearted, and eager to learn. What they lacked was education.[57] He, like Jiang Tingfu, developed great confidence in them. In a letter to a friend, Yan wrote that these laborers could think critically about China and the world; they were the hope of China.[58] He thus concluded that although they were only laborers, awakened laborers would have enormous power. Foreigners called these men "coolies" from the Chinese expression that consists of two characters *ku* (suffering) and *li* (power). Yan decided to devote his whole life to easing their suffering and unleashing their power.[59] He realized he had not understood the Chinese working class and life in China before he came to France.[60] It was the laborers who taught him about the real and true China. He explained his awakening this way: "During the war in France, it seemed that I was teacher to the laborers, but actually it was they who educated me." Because his experience was so exciting and rewarding, while still in France, he declared that he was completely transformed and his previous self was gone.[61]

An observer wrote that during the crucial transformation period, "Yen the aristocrat became the democrat. Throwing aside an opportunity of making a brilliant but easy career among his kind, he cast his lot with the toiling, struggling masses of China. Confucian ethics and Christian love covenanted to serve. Something 'clicked' within and his life became his message."[62] It is not surprising that Yan, as a Christian, now concluded that the "three Cs" could save China: Confucius, Christ, and coolies.[63] For Yan, the destiny of China lay with her laborers and peasants. "They represent one-fourth of the nation's population . . . the most strategic group in society. They are impressionable, idealistic, eager to learn, and comparatively free from heavy family responsibility."[64]

Through his work with the Chinese labor corps in France, Yan found a solution for China's problems and identity crisis; more important, he also determined his career for life: mass education. He realized that only through education at the village level, and reform from the bottom up, would China be able to re-create itself and qualify as an equal member of the world community.[65] Eugene Barnett of the YMCA wrote about Yan's transformation this way: "In France, he discovers China. For the first time he comes really to know the Chinese peasant and coolie. . . . Out of this experience is born a Big Idea"[66] That big idea was Yan's rural reconstruction movement, which he started in the early 1920s. Thus Yan brought his experience in France to bear in China. The aim of the movement comes across clearly in its slogan *Chu wenmang, zuo xinmin* ("Eliminate illiteracy and make new citizens").[67]

Yan's movement grew fast and gripped the imagination of the nation. Associations sprang up in every province to promote it. In 1923, the National Association for Mass Education was formed. Yan's dream "dreamed in France, has begun to come true. The possibility of a literate nation does not seem infinitely remote as it did five years ago. This is an epoch-making achievement. And it is the achievement of a man still on the sunny side of thirty years of age."[68] In the 1920s, mass education swept into thousands of villages in every province of China. Classes were even held in Mongolia and on the Tibetan border, and among warlord army troops. It made no difference which warlord the soldiers worked for, as far as Yan was concerned. They were all peasants and in dire need of the help he could give. And in fact, many rival warlords cooperated in the mass education movement by allowing movement workers to hold classes and even by providing funds. Yan became so confident of his movement that he once declared, "Give me adequate financial support, government backing, and peace and I'll educate 100,000 young people between the ages of twelve and twenty-five in five years' time." The 1920s for China was an era of endless fighting among the big and small warlords. But according to one Western commentator, Yan's movement became a sort of "unifying force in the life of the nation. Political rivalries and commercial jealousy or timidity may retard progress, international complications may create ill will, but the program of educating the masses has in a real sense united her peoples."[69] After Yan's mass education movement was launched, officials of all ranks rushed to foster it, and one governor went so far as to issue a proclamation to the effect that after a certain date, anyone who did not know the thousand characters would have to pay an "ignorance tax."[70] The warlord Zhang Zuolin in Manchuria ordered his army of 300,000 men to study Yan's reading system.[71] Yan's experience with the Chinese laborers in France directly led to his education plan in China, a "blossom from Flanders Field." Yan's movement, as one contemporary observer noticed, showed that "a great light begins to shine in Asia."[72] One Western scholar commented that "For the first time in the modern era, Chinese society seemed to be mobilizing its resources to make a fundamental change."[73]

Yan's initial Mass Education Movement (MEM) grew out of his literacy work with the YMCA, and the YMCA claimed that it was "significant for the international involvement of the YMCAs of the USA as well Ys of China."[74] In one of its official publications, Yan's work in the 1920s was credited as "perhaps the most remarkable single YMCA-inspired event among many in public health, education, and athletics."[75] But Yan soon grew beyond the YMCA in China.[76] After he left in 1923, he never allowed his organization to be identified as Christian, and in fact for a time preferred not to be called a Christian, which implied membership in a foreign church, but rather a "follower of Christ," which implied a direct relation with Jesus.[77] And his mass education movement even became a model for many other countries, including the United States. In the 1930s, when the American secretary of education Ray Lyman Wilbur announced that the United States government was embarking on a campaign to wipe out illiteracy in the United States, he added that the plan was not unlike Yan Yangchu's program in China. A *New York Times* article called Yan's method of teaching the masses to read and write could serve as "a striking example for America."[78] Later, the United Nations (UNESCO) would urge Yan to extend his mass education and rural reconstruction work to the world. In its internationalized version, Yan's plan was *Chu tianxia wenmang, zuo shijie xinmin*, or

"Eliminate illiteracy under heaven and make new citizens for the world." In 1943, Yan was chosen as one of the ten most influential men in the world, together with Henry Ford and Albert Einstein.

More importantly, Yan had many like-minded followers among China's elites. As one of Peking's English-language newspapers noted: "It was the most magnificent exodus of the intelligentsia into the country that had taken place in Chinese history to date. Holders of old imperial degrees, professors of national universities, a college president and former member of the National Assembly, and a number of PhD's and MD's from leading American universities left their positions and comfortable homes in the cities to go to the backwoods of Tinghsien to find out ways and means to revitalize the life of an ancient, backward people, and to build a democracy from the bottom up."[79] Yan Yangchu's popular education movement had much to do with the late Qing move to write in a simple literary style and the movement to establish popular education.[80] Hu Shi's *baihua* (vernacular language) movement, which he and others had started in 1917, definitely had played a role in Yan's thinking and approach. The patriotic and populist side of the New Culture Movement gained momentum with the May Fourth Movement of 1919. Yan's literacy campaigns drew the support of Hu, Cai Yuanpei, Liang Qichao, Tao Xingzhi, and dozens of local leaders and scholars. The movement was part of a bigger picture, part of a more general transformation that was occurring in China, namely, the quest of an emerging public to create a new national identity and its absorption and application of ideas and methods from abroad.

One can further argue that Yan's success had something to do with a coming trend in China. Two popular slogans in that day were directly linked to the journey of Chinese laborers to France, namely, "Right over Power" and "The Laborer Is Sacred."[81] After the Great War both laborers and elites realized the importance of labor.

## The Fusion of Teachers and Students in the May Fourth Movement

When Cai Yuanpei returned from France to become president of Peking University, he had gained a new appreciation for the importance of workers. On November 16, 1918, he made an important address in Peking to the general public in which he pointed out that all Chinese elites knew how important the European war was to China and the world.

But among the 400 million Chinese, only the laborers who went to Europe had been directly involved in this important event. "This is not strange," he declared, "the new world belongs to laborers."[82] Interestingly, the laborers Cai referred to in this speech included both elites and regular laborers.[83] In Cai's mind, both were equal now as long as they made their various contributions to society; all of them were laborers. Li Dazhao, a professor at Peking University and later a cofounder of the Chinese Communist Party, agreed with Cai. Li wrote in 1918 that the world after the Great War was a world of laborers. The victory of the Great War was a victory of commoners and of laborism.[84]

On National Day in 1919, students in Peking held a large parade and distributed 170,000 pieces of baked bread impressed with slogans such as "Laborers are sacred!" to local citizens.[85] Even Lu Xun, an influential but often cynical writer, had a high opinion of the men who went to France. He wrote that during the Great War, Chinese intellectuals were very excited and proud of themselves. But did those scholars use the *Analects* to transform German soldiers or the *Book of Changes* to overturn German submarines? No, they did not. According to Lu Xun, all the contributions China made, of which Chinese scholars were so proud, were made by "the illiterate Chinese laborers."[86] Kang Youwei, a great reformer, wrote a letter in 1919 to China's chief delegate to the postwar peace conference, Lu Zhengxiang. He requested that Lu fight for equal treatment for Chinese laborers in Europe and elsewhere. To Kang's thinking, the laborers had earned this because it was they who had truly contributed to the war on behalf of China.[87] Many of the Chinese in France agreed. One laborer argued that Chinese laborers in the world were often discriminated against because China was too weak to protect its citizens. He asked the Chinese delegation to the peace conference to demand that other countries end the discrimination against the Chinese and treat them as equal to everyone else. "This will be good for Chinese laborers and good for China as well."[88] Cai Yuanpei also suggested that because of the Chinese laborers' contribution to the war, China should be awarded an equal place in the postwar world order.[89]

In a lecture given in 1920, Chen Duxiu, one of the most influential thinkers at that time, claimed that laborers were the most important people in the world. He encouraged workers to be rulers rather than ruled.[90] In many of his writings, Chen maintained it was important that China should emphasize popular rather than elite education. Only education focusing on the broader public would produce useful people.[91] In his article revealingly titled "Chinese laborers" *(Huagong)*, Chen Duxiu wrote that "British can boast the British empire exists wherever the sun shines. We Chinese can say with pride that there are Chinese laborers wherever the sun shines." He further commented that although many Chinese politicians argued that China made contributions to the Great War, the real contribution had actually been made by the workers who went to Europe.[92] Chen, like many other elites, believed in the slogan "The Laborer Is Sacred" *(laogong shen sheng)*. In a short article titled "The Laborer Is Sacred and Strikes," he argued that because laborers were sacred, they should be well treated. Otherwise, they had the right to strike for better treatment.[93]

No surprise then that Yan Yangchu declared that whatever China achieved at the peace conference was earned not through her diplomats' eloquence, but instead by the hard work of her laborers.[94] Even into the 1930s, a writer with the pen name Bai Jiao continued to insist that it was the Chinese who went to Europe during the war who "saved face" for China.[95]

In 1919, the widespread and influential May Fourth Movement took place in protest over the issue of Shandong. The movement marked several historic firsts. This student-led movement was the first general cry for political, social, and diplomatic changes. Perhaps because of the phenomenon of teachers and students reversing roles, another new trend emerged: workers and elites joined together in a collective search for a new China. Finally, because it was directly inspired by the independence protests among students in Korea and aimed its own protests to a world audience, it was the first time that a Chinese movement envisioned itself as part of an international movement.

This development was a natural one for many reasons. The May Fourth Movement was triggered by the prospect of the great powers' handing Shandong Province to the Japanese. Because a large number of the laborers sent to France came from Shandong, that province had largely made China's involvement in the Great War possible, and so its fate was a particularly sensitive issue. The betrayal of Shandong was responsible, to a great extent, for China's turn to socialism. China's argument for the return of Shandong at the Paris Peace Conference was based on the role Shandong labor had played in Europe. One influential Chinese asked, "We Chinese feel that we have been loyal to the cause of the Allies, even more loyal than Japan has been and with less selfish motives. Yet we have been criticized and blamed while Japan has been praised. Why? We do not understand."[96] The anguish of the Chinese was not unappreciated. A poem by an American points to the sympathetic understanding of many in the West:

*Shantung*

In the west you free Jerusalem,
But in the east you sell
Tai Shan, the Holy Mountain . . .
I hear a temple bell
Breathing, like a perfume
From it exalted place,
The presence of Confucius,
The wisdom of a race,
The future of a people
The only one of all
Whose conquerors are conquered,
Whose history is tall—
Taller than Fujiyama,
Taller than that red sun
Consuming from Japan . . .
And my face is in the flowers
And my heart is sick with perfume
And I weep because I must,
I weep for you, O masters,

O conquerors, O slavers,
As I hear you stir in China
The quiet of your graves.[97]

This poem by Witter Bynner, an early translator and advocate for Japanese and Chinese poetry, clearly reflects Chinese feelings about Shandong and the impact of the Shandong issue on China. For many Chinese, the Shandong decision made by the Council of Three was more than an injustice; it was a challenge by the old diplomacy to the new international order.[98] Many of the Chinese laborers in France bitterly resented the decision. The special delegates to the peace conference from Shandong during a trip to the United States stated:

The people of our Province are not responsible for any action they may take when their territory is invaded or when they are robbed of their lands, not only because they cannot allow their sacred territory, where Chinese civilization was born, to be dominated by a foreign power, but also because their sense of justice and their self-determination cannot permit them to remain submissive. Shantung has sent tens of thousands of its citizens to Europe to work in the trenches and help win the war. Many sacrificed their lives. Now, as a reward for their service, the economic rights in their own province are to be turned over to Japan. . . . Can we expect these citizens, who have experienced the terror of war on European battle fields and whose national spirit is enlightened, to rest satisfied with the conditions made by the treaty? The Chinese people are known as a peace-loving and law-abiding people. But, under these circumstances, what human beings could endure such outrages and such humiliation?[99]

The political awakening of the laborers and elites made them comrades motivated by the same national bonds. The following letter from a Shandong man in France clearly demonstrates this point:

Many a time have I escaped death by a hair's breadth, but I am thankful to say that I still live and will be ready to render service to my own country. . . . To my great disappointment Japan now claims to be the successor of Germany in Shantung province and moves heaven and earth to enforce the terms of the Twenty-one Demands. . . . The recent European war showed that war was a war of man-power and resources, and in my humble opinion, it would take Japan at least ten years to conquer China, should a war break out with her. For the first three years China would suffer as much as the Belgians and Serbians did in this Great War, but commencing from the fourth year Japan would be hunted down like the Germans and Austrians. Stand firm, my countrymen! . . . Thousands of my fellow-workers are behind the country.[100]

These same ideas were expressed time and time again. One article published in the *Chinese Labor Journal* encouraged the laborers to stand united in the quest for national salvation and urged all Chinese laborers in France to express their opposition to giving Shandong Province to Japan.[101] Interestingly, not only the laborers in Europe started to pay attention to national and international affairs, but their women back in China developed a certain interest as well. Kate Kelsey, a missionary in Shandong, witnessed the worldview changes of Chinese women. She said the women in Shandong were interested in foreign countries and even Christianity because their husbands or sons went to France as the laborers. Chinese women often made comments like "This is the first time I have heard the Christian doctrine . . . but I have a husband who has gone to your country, so I thought I would like to come and hear your teaching." She also was asked the questions such as "you are a foreigner, aren't you? My son has gone to your country. Can you tell me what he will have to do there? Will he have to fight?" Kesley said because of the laborers in France, "It was easy to get into friendly relations with such women."[102]

The phenomenon of students-as-teachers was also a factor in the work-study programs, which would affect China's future development. The Chinese laborers in France would become models in another sense. In January 1919, a new work-study program started to attract widespread attention among the Chinese and eventually would enable future leaders such as Zhou Enlai and Deng Xiaoping to study abroad.[103] Zhou Enlai, the future prime minister of the People's Republic of China, in 1921 openly acknowledged that the laborers in France were the pioneers of the work-study programs. He believed that although some people considered the laborers ignorant and politically short-sighted, they actually played important role in China's reform. If the laborers could do it, Zhou pointed out that Chinese-educated youth could do it by joining a work-study program.[104] In June 1920, when a friend left for Europe to take part in such a program, Zhou wrote a poem to commemorate this important journey. His enthusiasm is palpable:

Go Abroad,
Through the Chinese East Sea
Through the Seas of South and Red
Through the Mediterranean
Through the rapid torrents
And galloping waves,
You will arrive at the coast of France:
The homeland of freedom[105]

By that November, Zhou was on his way to France; he would remain in Europe until July 1924. While in France, Zhou interacted with some of the Chinese laborers who had been part of the Great War. One man, who remained in France as a tea house owner, even provided important support for Zhou's early political activities.[106]

Besides Zhou, Deng Xiaoping, Chen Yi, and many other future top leaders of China sought ideas for national salvation in France. For them,

France represented the best of Western civilization.[107] It was France, not Japan, the United States, Britain, or Germany that was considered by many Chinese to be the most civilized and relevant nation from which China could study and learn. Of course, the friendly immigration policy also explained why so many of them managed to go there as students. France was the center of civilization and the new world order, and young Chinese traveled there in search of personal transformation, national salvation, and a model for China's new national identity. As one scholar wrote, "One of the first lessons for the worker-students was that the 'pioneers' of intercultural experience had really been the Chinese Labor Corps."[108] Even Mao Zedong was tempted to go to France. Xiao Zhisheng, who had traveled with Mao to study Chinese peasant life in their youth, recalled that Mao and many other friends discussed the possibility of going to France and expressed high hopes for the laborers there. They made plans to organize the laborers and encourage them to study French social and political organizations. When those men returned home, they would be a key force for change in China.[109] Xiao and Mao's close friend Cai Hesheng arrived in France in 1919 to take part in the work-study program. Xiao planned to recruit ten thousand Chinese laborers in France to join Mao's political organization, the New People's Society. When Mao received this news, he grew very excited and wrote to Xiao, telling him, "We are setting up the cornerstone for change [in China]. I will work hard to promote revolution in Changsha. But it seems more feasible for you to carry out the plan" among the laborers in France.[110] No wonder the future Chinese leaders such as Mao and Zhou also planned to rely on Chinese laborers in France to support the revolutionary movement in China and the laborers in France contributed to the Chinese revolution.

The work-study program lasted a bit less than three years. The first large group went to France in March 1919, and the last made its journey at the end of 1920. Afterward, due to lack of funds and organization, the program closed. But from 1919 until the end of 1920, a total of nearly 1,600 Chinese students and professionals traveled to France and took part.[111] One might argue that many of the men who later became revolutionary leaders actually followed in the footsteps of the Chinese laborers in the Great War.

The laborers' time in France coincided with activities of this work-study movement. When its members got into serious infighting about the direction and activities of the movement, the laborers became quite upset. One demanded that the work-study students show a spirit of solidarity with the laborers and lectured that they were not ready to "soil themselves with physical labor." That man scolded, "O work-study students! You say that the government is like a pirate. We also see it as a thief. However, if you are seeking government funds, are you not then taking a cut of the pie?"[112] The laborers in France actively took part in debates with the work-study students concerning political issues of the day in China,[113] and European branches of Chinese communist organizations made efforts to recruit them.[114] Interestingly enough, when elites wanted to build a Chinese University of Lyons for the work-study students, Chinese laborers voluntarily provided crucial help.[115]

The presence of Chinese laborers in France served as "an important prelude to the Work-Study Movement." That movement "later provided key issues for agitation within the Chinese community in France during the early twenties. It also operated as a focus for the growth of intercultural relations."[116] The Great War years in France represent the first time such a large number of ordinary Chinese had personal contact with the West. Without a doubt, this experience provided not only an opportunity to observe and experience life in another civilization, but also a chance to reflect on the Chinese way of life and society. When they returned home, they brought with them new ideas, new thoughts, and the inspiration to change. In other words, the laborers who came to the rescue of the Allies were more than hired workers; they were the first wave of a new Chinese participation in world affairs and as such they contributed to the creation of a new national identity.

# 10

## A FUSION OF CIVILIZATIONS

The Chinese laborers in France were representatives of the Chinese people. These common folks had, moreover, witnessed one of the most important events in the history and had taken a part in the historic war. Indeed, as YMCA records report, "The bringing of the Orient into contact with Western civilization was one of the most remarkable phases of the world struggle."[1] During the war and in its immediate aftermath, the Chinese workers found that Europe was no paradise, but rather a waste land. According to one confidential YMCA report, "Certainly, in the eyes of these non-official representatives" of China, "the white race is being stripped of its false glory and supposed Christian civilization, and is standing out in a poor light with little to recommend it."[2]

### Laborers and China's Changing National Identity

The laborers' experience-informed perceptions of the West had an impact on the direction China's cultivation of national identity was to take. It is perhaps no surprise that some Westerners were deeply concerned about Chinese impressions of the West. Kathlene B. Winter wrote in 1919 that what the Chinese "take back to China in the way of intellectual, moral and spiritual currency depends largely on what *we, Western civilization, give them to take back.* [italics original]."[3] She predicted that when they "graduate from these mushroom universities of war-time conditions they will become the articulation of China's masses, shoving toward the day when this newest republic will be a democracy in fact as well as in name."[4] According to Harley F. MacNair, a seasoned China observer in the West, the Chinese laborers once returned to China, "brought back reports, many of which whether accurate or not, did not enhance the reputation of Europe and its civilization. It is the old case of

220

familiarity breeding contempt—a contempt made greater by the renewed discovery that the West is not at unity with itself."[5]

There were certainly grounds for concern. The war, with its titanic expenditure of energy and material display, had made an indelible impression. One Chinese laborer told W. W. Peter, a Harvard-trained YMCA secretary, "When I get back to China, I fear I shall always associate the sight of foreigners with the smell of rotting human flesh in France. I lived in a nightmare. My eyes were opened to new horrors daily. It was no better after the fighting ceased. Then day after day we worked in a region absolutely in ruins. So utterly destroyed were the fields that nothing can possibly be grown on them for many years." Observing what had happened in France, he could not but conclude, "None better than foreigners know how to destroy life and property. They are able to do this by day and by night, by land and by sea, in the air and underneath the sea, by vapor and by flame." This laborer was worried about the new world order the West aimed to establish after the war. He asked: "What do foreigners mean when they use such beautiful words as liberty, justice, democracy, self-determination, permanent peace? . . . Now that your honorable war is over, are the hearts of men at peace? Are you foreigners satisfied with what you have accomplished? Is it all settled? When I go back to my home village, what shall I say to those who eagerly await my words?"[6] Many Chinese went home with a critical view of the West in general and of the officers of their companies in particular: Why all the orders given with no explanation? Why should they be driven by men who knew nothing of their language and who transgressed all the customs of their native land? Their experience of the war only reinforced the dictum that "War is Hell," and these men had lived on the edge of that awful crater. It was to be expected that they would conclude that the war and the West were of a piece.

If national identity emerges when one country compares itself to others, these Chinese saw with their own eyes what a Western country looked like and how people in other countries worked and lived. They obviously shared their fellow countrymen's sense of national crisis and wanted to do their part to resolve it. Laborers returned to China with their intellectual horizons greatly enlarged. Whether they went back to the farm or to larger centers of population, they would always look at their surroundings and circumstances from a new angle. The great steamships and harbors, railroads. and fine highways of the West would remain in their memories long after the unpleasant experiences had faded. When the French, British, and (later) Americans employed the

Chinese in Europe, they actually gave them an opportunity to compare Western civilization in action with their own. To use W. W. Peter's words, the West was creating, in the persons of the laborers, "140,000 moral bombshells, destined to go back to China and there explode the preconceived ideas of their neighbors concerning the virtues of the Western world. For what these men assimilate and carry back with them to China may have a considerable bearing on the attitude which the people of China take on future world problems. Not all world problems are being solved irrevocably in Paris. Our largest concern in the future may yet be to know what the Chinese people think of this or that."[7]

Whether they wanted to or not, the returned laborers would become interpreters of Western civilization as their experiences had shown it to them. As Peter pointed out, "In France they were of value only from the neck down. In China on their return, what they are going to do from the neck up is of infinite concern to the Western world."[8] For Peter and many other Westerners, questions posed by the Chinese were deeply troubling, for example "Is Western civilization only a material civilization? Is Eastern civilization, after all, higher on the moral side than Western? If we adopt Western material civilization, will it destroy our higher moral civilization? Or can it be that, to gain the right to enjoy our moral civilization, we shall have to arm ourselves and fight the West with its own weapons?" Peter warned that the West had to watch carefully what happened after the laborers returned home.[9]

While some Westerners were worried about the impact of the West on Chinese laborers, the Chinese government and elites were excited about their having been awakened. Chinese laborers were to play an important part in the formulation of a new national identity. Both government agencies and members of the social elite wanted to plan ahead for their return and figure out the best ways to use their new skills. Ye Gongchuo visited the laborers in France in 1919 and wrote a memo to the Chinese government on precisely this issue.[10] In 1917, to protect Chinese laborers' interests abroad, the Chinese government had set up the Bureau of Overseas Chinese Workers, an unprecedented move, which fell directly under the State Council. On August 18, 1919, the Chinese president's office asked the bureau to make systematic plans on how to take care of the returned laborers.[11] The bureau came out with a plan called *Anzi huiguo huagong zhangcheng* (Regulations on Employment of Returned Laborers). According to the plan, most returned laborers would be employed in irrigation and railway construction.[12]

To make the most of the men's skills, the regulations required every laborer to have letters from their supervisors in France that reported on their skills. The laborers who wanted to work in a factory after they returned had to register with a local labor bureau. The names of men who had worked in dockyards and munitions factories in France were to be sent to the navy or army and assigned suitable jobs with those organizations.[13] The government also provided registration cards and certification to returned laborers when they arrived in China; this was to assist in arranging employment for them in the future.[14] Peking appointed local labor agents to make sure that nobody became homeless or turned into a bandit.[15] To ensure their safe return to China, the Chinese Consulate General in Paris arranged qualified persons to accompany them home. The individuals best suited for this job were Chinese students who had finished their studies in France, Belgium, and Switzerland; were returning to China; and were interested in public welfare and willing to help the laborers. The Chinese government covered their transportation and provided stipends of 600 francs.[16] In late 1920, the State Council set up a new organization called Society for International Emigration under the Bureau of Overseas Chinese Workers to study how to improve service to overseas Chinese and interact with the similar organizations around the world. Guo Zefang and Li Jun were chosen to represent China in the 1921 International Conference on Emigration.[17] China took an active part in its first conference.

Unfortunately we don't have enough reliable evidence to track what happened to the laborers after they returned to China; most relevant materials were lost either due to China's long war with Japan or the civil war. The little evidence that survives suggests that many of them settled down comfortably as landowners or found decent jobs in the cities. Many of them were excited to use their recently gained perspectives, skills, and knowledge to help China or to test their ideas.[18] As Chen Da (Chen Ta) wrote in a 1927 article:

> Prior to 1918 or 1919, most manual workers unquestioningly submitted to the traditional social hierarchy, which was graded according to the rank and wealth of the old society, and rarely did they raise a voice of protest against the existing social order. But after Chinese students began to lecture to the masses on principles of citizenship and the equality of men, the workers gradually came to realize that they had obvious rights and privileges in society, which slowly became the basis of united demands. Then, too, the literary renaissance has popularized the written language to a certain extent, so that forward-looking workmen can acquire the fundamentals of

popular education by attending evening schools and taking lessons in simplified Chinese.[19]

In September 1919, the returned laborers from France organized their own union in Shanghai and met once a week to discuss how to protect their interests.[20] The union aimed at collective bargaining, increasing common knowledge through frequent association, and promoting a cordial but nonpartisan friendship. Members of the union resolved not to drink alcohol, visit prostitutes, gamble, or smoke opium. The Returned Laborers Union was one of the first modern unions in China[21] and its early membership was 1,600 newly returned men from France.[22] Chinese laborers understood that they must fight for their own cause and work out their own salvation. All these developments grew, more or less, from their experiences in Europe.

As a contemporary Chinese commentator, Diao Minqian (Tyau Min-ch'ien), observed, the returned men brought a new spirit with them. "The returned laborers no doubt find splendid soil for the sowing of their transplanted seeds." These men were indeed a strong force for changing China. In the early 1920s, Chinese workers frequently held strikes and "returned laborers from the scene of recent conflict in Europe may be said to be the stormy petrel of the Chinese labor world." And in some official quarters, the returned laborer was even dreaded as a potential Bolshevik.[23] Chow Tse-tsung, in his authoritative study of the May Fourth Movement, points out that the experiences of these workers helped shape the organization and activities of labor unions in Shanghai during the May Fourth period. They were "instrumental in driving the May Fourth Movement to extremes in both socialism and nationalism early in the twenties."[24] The underpinnings of the new labor movement were more nationalist than Bolshevist.

The returned laborers also brought about positive changes in the countryside. For instance, one returned laborer found that a teacher, newly appointed by the government to establish a free school in his village, illegally charged each pupil three strings of cash. The laborer, to protest this extortion, wrote a notice and hung it outside his door, stating that when he was in France he had been taught to be good and help others. There he had learned to read 600 characters, the phonetic system, geography, and arithmetic. "What I have freely received I will freely give. Any children desiring to study these subjects I will teach without charge."[25] This new awakening was also reflected in the men's love of science and technology. In February 1924, an American named Carrington Goodrich met a returned laborer who was busy working on an invention. Goodrich was deeply impressed by his work. In a letter to Goodrich, this laborer explained that he had become passionate about science because of his experience in France.[26] Another laborer wrote two manuscripts when he returned to his village. One was about his experience in France as a laborer, and the other described what he had observed in wartime Europe.[27]

Despite the high hopes and expectations, not all Chinese laborers played important or even constructive roles in society on their return home. For instance, the 865 laborers from Yongcheng, Henan Province, could not all find jobs after returning to Henan. One of them, Jiang Yao-guang, became a street peddler. He remained so poor he could not even afford to marry until he was thirty-three years old.[28] Another Chinese laborer was to be awarded a medal by the British government for his bravery. But when the British consul-general in Tianjin tried, on May 5, 1921, to locate him so the medal could be presented, he found him in prison in Zhili Province, sentenced to four years for stealing firewood and threatening its owner with a sword. As a result of representations made by the consul-general, the man's sentence was reduced by a higher court to imprisonment for two or three months, and he was released on July 24, 1921. The day after his release, he finally received his medal. Obviously, he had been so destitute he was forced to steal the firewood. The consul-general recommended him to the authorities of the British municipal police in Tianjin, who engaged him on probation as a policeman.[29] Yen Tengfeng, another laborer who received a meritorious medal from Britain, chose to have the medal mailed to him instead of going the nearby consulate in Shanghai,[30] indicating poverty, lack of enthusiasm, or both.

Some returned laborers even ended up as bandits in the 1920s.[31] The Lincheng Incident took place in spring 1923 when about a thousand bandits attacked and derailed a passenger train, the "Blue Express," which was carrying about 300 passengers, including some thirty white foreigners who were kidnapped by the bandits. One Englishman was killed. Returned laborers seem to have been involved in the incident.[32] A letter from a passenger, Lucy Truman Aldrich, daughter of a former U.S. senator and the sister of Mrs. John D. Rockefeller, Jr., to her sister stated that many of the bandits understood and spoke English when they wanted to.[33] Several spoke French. They appeared to be returned laborers from France who had remained unemployed.[34] This observation does suggest the involvement of returned laborers. A Japanese writer, Goto Asataro, suggested that the bandits were originally inspired to carry out the kidnapping by films they had seen in France, and they deliberately sought to create an international incident. Nagano Akira, another Japanese writer, even argued that some of the bandits had political agendas. Phil Billingsley, an expert on the bandit issue, seemed to agree with these suggestions and argued that the bandits had indeed advanced political ideas.[35] According to one insider's information, many returned laborers from France joined bandit gangs and they used their skills to construct military-style trenches which could be used for both cover and shelter.[36]

The returned laborers' experiences overseas significantly broadened their intellectual horizons; more importantly, they also developed a strong sense of national identity. One day, a French family lost 500 francs and suspected that Chinese laborers working nearby had stolen it. The Chinese laborers felt their good names and China's "face" were undermined by this charge, and they decided to donate 500 francs to the family.[37] The men often linked their own fates with that of their nation. One argued, "Chinese laborers not only represent China's contribution to the world, they are also important builders of world civilization."[38] Another Chinese laborer wondered aloud about what he saw in France: "One can go to school unloading ships. How many great ships are there in the world, and how many different things can man make? It seemed as if every great ship at one time or another came from the far corners of the earth to this city in France where I worked, bringing supplies of a thousand kinds. The magnitude of it all simply staggered me. The whole outside world was bringing stores to empty into the lap of France. Thus famine was prevented. We have not yet learned how to do this in China."[39] Another Chinese laborer told a missionary, "I used to write letters to my home village friends telling them of the semi-foreign life I was leading. I told them of each important matter as soon as I learned of it myself. Nor did I hold back from pointing out the contrast between the progressive foreigners and the backwardness of our village customs." He mentioned that in his letters he urged his village friends to join him in France. "Together we could learn many things which might be of great value to the village in the years to come. It was like going to a great school."[40] One Chinese official wrote that during his inspection tours both behind the front lines and in the interior of France, many of the laborers "have come up to narrate their ambitions and their schemes for the industrial development of their fatherland when they return."[41]

In a sense, the Chinese who served in the Great War were not simply hired laborers; they were harbingers of China's progressive internationalization. Many of them started to pay attention to national and international affairs. Chinese laborers working for the British sent about 50,000 letters home each month and received about 15,000 letters in France.[42] Although these letters were largely personal, they conveyed some information about the West and national affairs. One Chinese writer argued that these laborers, with their firsthand knowledge of Western civilization and technology, could apply their new skills to improving Chinese industries and other enterprises. Thus it was important for the nation to take full advantage of them and make plans.[43]

All this suggests that the laborers functioned as a sort of messenger between China and the West. Cai Yuanpei frequently argued that the Chinese should learn about Western civilization to make their nation strong and powerful. These laborers thus were pioneers in Western learning.[44] Many Chinese indeed were thinking about how to learn from the West. The *Chinese Labor Journal* often urged the men to pay close attention to French civilization, to find its advantages and disadvantages. Then they should copy the good parts and try to do better than the weak parts. The men were reminded that it was their "social responsibility" to do so, since among millions and millions of Chinese, only they had the privilege of personally witnessing and observing Western society.[45] The *Chinese Students' Monthly* in the United States declared in 1918 that the laborers served as a bridge between China and the world.[46] The 140,000 laborers thus became 140,000 messengers. Most of them understood and embraced this role.[47]

## Laborers and the New World Order

Although returned laborers did not accomplish all they were expected to, their historic journey did help China achieve its major goal of taking part in the war. This was one of China's most important diplomatic objectives at the time.[48] The major powers, especially Japan, did not want to allow China any role at all. Thus was born the laborers-as-soldiers plan.[49] And it would be the sacrifice of laborers' lives that provided China with a convincing argument for its declaration of war on Germany because several hundred Chinese lost their lives in German submarine attacks. Liang Qichao, a key player in China's war policy, then eloquently argued that as a member of the world community, China had right and responsibility to take action when its citizens had lost their lives due to German violation of China's neutrality.[50] Another important diplomatic objective was gaining a seat at the postwar peace conference. Once again, the sacrifice and hard work of their laborers gave Chinese diplomats an opportunity to appeal to world opinion, especially regarding the Shandong issue, because many of the laborers in Europe came from Shandong Province.

The role of Chinese laborers in establishing the new world order was obviously based on their contributions to the Great War. An address the British king gave to the South African Labour Corps in France applied equally if not more to the Chinese. He said: "I have much pleasure in seeing you who have travelled so far over the sea to help in this Great War. . . . Rest assured that all you have done is of great assistance to my Armies at the front. This work of yours is second only in importance to that of my sailors and soldiers, who are bearing the brunt of the battle. But you also are part of my great Armies which are fighting for the liberty and freedom of my subjects of all races and creeds throughout the Empire."[51]

World War I was a total war; it involved the home front, the military, and the battlefront. According the London *Times*:

> Modern war is modern industry, organized for a single definite purpose. Behind the Army that fights the enemy with bomb, bullet, and shell, and in some cases alongside of it, there is another army whose weapons are the pickaxe, crowbar, spade, and pulley. . . . Little has been heard of the Labour Corps in this country. It does its work unobtrusively, and attracts small notice either from the regular newspaper correspondents, who are, naturally, intent upon more exciting transactions, or from the occasional visitor who is allowed discreet glimpses of the battle-ground. Even the combatants, who pass the toiling, multi-coloured columns on their way to camp and billet, do not know how numerous these workers are, or how important is their share in the general scheme of operations. The Corps is still a novelty, so new that it has hardly as yet asserted its place in the regular military system.[52]

YMCA accounts point out that the military purpose of bringing the Chinese to France was a crucial one to the Allies. It capitalized to the greatest degree possible the manpower available to the Allies by their control of the seas and by the wide sympathy for the fight the Allied nations were carrying forward.[53] The Chinese laborers helped keep the Allies fighting; they were young and strong. British secretary of war and prime minister during the war, Lloyd George, wrote in his *War Memoirs* that they "were immensely powerful fellows, and it was no uncommon spectacle to see one of the Chinese pick up a bulk of timber or a bundle of corrugated iron sheets weighing three or four hundred pounds, and walk off with it as calmly as if it weighed only as many stone."[54] Yale historian Paul Kennedy argues that the main contribution of the United States to World War I was not military: "American intervention in the war could not immediately affect the military balance." The vital contribution of the United States was on the economic front: it kept the Allied side fighting "without embarrassment of bankruptcy."[55] I would argue that China's contribution to the war was its manpower: with 140,000 laborers in the field, China greatly strengthened the Allies' front and support industries.

Because of the laborers' sacrifice, contributions, and then lack of recognition, the Chinese scholar Chen Sanjing has characterized their being sent to Europe as "a great tragedy."[56] However, if we look at the labor scheme as an important part of China's war plan, its results were still significant. Working, if not fighting, side by side with the Allies, China determinedly signaled its desire and ability to play a role in world affairs, and this signal was recognized, if reluctantly, by the rest of the world. The *Far Eastern Review* in 1918 predicted that Chinese laborers' emigration from the shores of Shandong would take its place in history possibly as one of the most important aspects of the European war. "For never before this war has the East provided the West with manpower on anything approaching the same elaborate scale. It has hurled itself against the West many times, compelled the West to unite more than once and, of course, colored European life and thought in a variety of ways, but it has never before, practically the whole of it simultaneously, taken sides in a huge European conflict."[57] But the real contribution to the war was more than moral and political support. One Western China watcher pointed out, "China's declaration of war against Germany has hardly been taken seriously by the Allies as yet, but her help [with laborers] may prove vital before peace is finally restored."[58] Although some scholars continue to suggest that the Chinese laborers in Europe "did not fulfill the expected foreign policy objectives during the First World War,"[59] I argue that they not only made a valuable contribution to the Allied side but more importantly, they also served the Chinese national interest very well by playing a critical role in China's early efforts to take its rightful place on the world stage. This is perhaps why Chinese laborers gathered to welcome President Wilson when he arrived in Port Havre on his way to Paris; they understood that Wilson's new world order would affect China a great deal.[60]

The laborers thought about the war they were taking part in, and some even aspired to be peacemakers. One Chinese drafted a letter to the German Kaiser, asking for world peace. That letter, which was found in a notebook dated August 1918, belonged to Chinese laborer No. 3902, who worked under the British. A translation of the draft reads:

A petition respectfully presented by the writer to the great Monarch, of the Empire of Germany. May it please your Majesty to regard the following: Far be it from me to discuss or inquire into the origin of the European war, for at its inception there were a great many wise men in the world, of surpassing talents, regarding whose opinions your Majesty was well aware. However, the hearts of the rulers of all nations cannot be united by force of arms.

An ancient sage has said, "One who wages war successfully suffers the greatest punishments." Your Majesty is unlike the Ruler in Heaven above, who rejoices in giving life to his creatures, while you dare to regard the life of men as the grass of the field. Is not an insatiable appetite for war an affront to the will of God? And is not a plan to bring about peace of inestimable value at the present juncture?

We Chinese people who have come to Europe are all poor folk in our land; casual laborers whose livelihood is precarious. We have journeyed to Europe in search of food, while you Potentates are insatiably devoting yourselves to strife. Our hearts are sorely troubled and we cannot take our food. Now as I carefully examine the present condition of the world, I am convinced that it is the will of Heaven that all mankind should live as one family. Why does not your noble majesty take this opportunity of abandoning profit and exalting friendship? By so doing you would bring yourself into line with the Will of Heaven and be following the promptings of humanity in bringing all the nations of the world into one League of Brotherhood, for the purpose of putting an end to the evils now rampant in the world, and abolishing the hateful customs which exist among men; thus you would restore the stability of property to mankind and bring to birth the new world.

If your Majesty wishes to establish a reputation for ten thousand generations, why will you not take this opportunity to disarm your soldiers and persuade all the great Powers to select a Lucky spot in which to build a lofty Temple of Peace and five Imperial Palaces. Moreover, having selected an auspicious day, invite all the Rulers of the World in one common League of Brotherhood, and together lay the foundation of peace for all times.

The meaning of Ideal Friendship is unanimity of hearts. . . . Friendship is indeed one of the Five Relationships. It is an aid to right doctrine and

promotes active brotherly kindness; I therefore warn the brethren to reverence and keep the following injunctions:

1. it is forbidden to swear
2. it is forbidden to gamble
3. it is forbidden to fly into temper over trifling matters
4. it is forbidden to utter faultfinding words of the others
5. it is forbidden to speak untruths for the purpose of deceiving a friend.

The foregoing five prohibitions are of the highest value in promoting the
true spirit of friendship and represent the basic principles.[61]

The Chinese laborers in Europe, moreover, served as a kind of rallying
point to mobilize Chinese citizens regarding issues of both national and
international import, and in China's internationalization. An impressive
example of this was the United War Work fund drive in China, which
brilliantly used the laborers in France to make its case. The drive was
launched by the YMCA with the full cooperation of the Chinese government. As the YMCA admitted, "One of the strongest elements in the
whole work was the thorough and cordial cooperation of the Chinese
government." The campaign initially aimed to raise $100,000 in China
for welfare work and reconstruction in Europe.[62] But with a committee
of fifty-two Chinese political and commercial leaders associated with
the YMCA, it secured not $100,000, but more than $1.4 million.[63] In
other words, the Chinese actually oversubscribed the original goal by
1,300 percent, despite the fact that China was then poor and calamity
ridden.

The success of this campaign rested largely on concern for, and interest in, the Chinese laborers in Europe. American minister to Beijing,
Paul Reinsch, made the connection quite early. In a cable to the YMCA
dated November 12, 1918, Reinsch suggested that it would be more
effective to mention the laborers in France in the War Work Fund campaign in China.[64] Campaign organizers brilliantly exploited this opportunity by arguing that Chinese donations were not only part of China's
contribution toward world peace but also showed their support for the
laborers making their own contributions and sacrifices in Europe.[65]
Nearly every high official in China contributed to the drive: the Chinese
president gave $5,000, and Parliament gave $50,000. Most tellingly,
however, the drive took in 7,000,000 coppers in small subscriptions
from Beijing residents. This cash was pegged at 140 to the dollar, and it

nearly broke the campaign staff and caused the banks to go on strike to handle them in such quantity. These subscriptions came from the common citizenry, even school children, and showed that everyone wanted to do his or her part.[66]

Not only the people of Beijing took part; almost every Chinese province was involved. Many people across the nation wanted a chance to help in the war as their laborers were doing in France.[67] In Kirin, the campaign raised 40,000 Mexican silver dollars ($36,000 U.S. gold). The donations "came from every class and organization in the city."[68] The city of Kaifeng donated more than 100,000 coppers.[69] In Shansi, the War Work Fund was oversubscribed by 500 percent. The suggested goal was $2,000 U.S. gold. But as the campaign proceeded, and it became clear that the influential men of the city were behind it, there would clearly be no difficulty exceeding that amount. Most of the subscriptions were made at a very large meeting in the provincial assembly building to which all officials, gentry, and businessmen were invited. The governor was in Peking at the time, but telegraphed instructions that all his staff should cooperate to the limit of their power in the campaign. In addition to the larger meeting, subscriptions were taken at the Young Men's Christian Association and in Christian churches throughout the province. And a total of more than $10,000 U.S. gold was eventually subscribed.[70] This same story was repeated in many other places.

In Tianjin, the whole political and commercial community took part. The military and civil governors, the chairman of the provincial assembly, the chief of the provincial police, the president of the chamber of commerce, and other important officials became honorary officers of the drive's Chinese organization; while several influential businessmen took up administration of the campaign and donated nearly a month of their time to this work. The government subsidized communications, allowing telegrams to be sent for free to all parts of the country. The police board set aside a detail of writers and special police to help with clerical work at headquarters. The most spectacular feature of the whole campaign was a gigantic parade organized entirely by the Chinese committee, which marched 17,000 strong through the foreign concessions and around the native city. The parade involved large contingents of schoolboys and older students; and also good-sized sections of the military and civil police, the chamber of commerce, the Chinese Red Cross, the Young Men's Christian Association, and representatives of the laboring classes.

The governor's band and police bands furnished music, while much interest was added by the ten or so floats interspersed among the marchers, who carried thousands of the Allied nations' flags made locally in Tianjin especially for the occasion. The floats represented all the organizations participating in the drive and the more important nationals. Tianjin eventually donated $358,000, of which $100,000 was a grant from the provincial assembly. Large donations were made by the salt merchants' guild, the native banks, and businessmen's organizations, but most came from individual gifts, ranging from schoolchildren's coppers to the wealthy men's hundreds.[71]

This successful campaign put China far ahead of any country, including the United States, in oversubscription. In November 1917, the YMCA conducted a War Work Fund campaign in the United States and received 50,153,054 pledges, far above its 35 million goal.[72] Compared with the U.S. figure, the Chinese numbers are amazing. Why were the Chinese so interested in the War Work Fund, which was to be used to help Europe rebuild? Several reasons: One, of course, was China's faith in the YMCA organization, which had done good work in China and in France in support of the Chinese laborers. Second, by oversubscription to the War Work Fund, the Chinese demonstrated their interest in world welfare and world peace. But most importantly, many Chinese believed their contributions would benefit the Chinese laborers in France.

## What the Laborers Learned and the Fusion of Civilizations

The Chinese experience in Europe was an education on many levels. Many of the men learned how to read. On their arrival in France, literacy among the laborers was only about 20 percent. But with help from the various Chinese teachers and YMCA secretaries, literacy reached 38 percent by 1921.[73] More importantly, they learned to think in new ways.

One laborer named Fu Shengsan explained the changes well in an article entitled "Chinese Laborers in France and Their Contribution to the Motherland" (Huagong zai Fa yu zu guo de sun yi) that appeared in Chinese Laborers' Weekly. Fu wrote that before their arrival in Europe, most laborers had no clear idea about the relationship between an individual and the nation or between family and the state. But when they saw how the foreigners sacrificed their lives to save France and Britain during the war, they were inspired, their patriotism and nationalism began to take shape, and they started to love their own country, China. He wrote that in China, he thought a woman with bound feet was beautiful. Now he witnessed how Western women with natural feet worked side by side with the men, and realized his old thinking about footbinding was wrong. The laborers should use what they observed, their new knowledge, and their new thinking to educate other Chinese. Fu further commented that before he came to France, he thought foreigners were superior to the Chinese. Now working side by side with them, he discovered that Chinese were at least equal in intelligence and physical strength. He thus became confident about China's future. He said that if the Chinese received a good education, they could build a strong China, equal to any of the Western powers. Fu told his readers that when the big powers treated China like a third-rate nation at the postwar peace conference, the laborers became especially patriotic and indignant. Yan Yangchu was greatly moved by Fu's statements. Yan wrote that many high officials in China did not have such a clear understanding of how things stood, and he later personally visited Fu in his camp.[74]

Like Fu, many other Chinese were changed by their observations and learning. Ma, a laborer from Tianjin, could not read or write Chinese when he arrived in France. He took advantage of the YMCA's education programs and developed a secret desire to be able some day to tell the world that he was a full-fledged citizen of China. One day, in a conversation with a YMCA secretary regarding whether the YMCA hut where he volunteered should admit women, Ma said, "It is all the same to me." With an absolute lack of emotion he said, "I serve whoever you allow here, men or women. When they give me the money, I'll give them the chocolate."[75] He also said, "You may exclude a person because he is bad, but you should not exclude a person because she is a woman." This thinking was surprising at a time when Chinese women still had bound feet and faced many social restrictions such as access to education and office. When asked what he intended to do after he returned to China, Ma answered without hesitation, "I am a Chinese; I ought to do something for China. Perhaps I will be a soldier. I am strong, I can be a good soldier."[76] In another example, Shi, a mechanic from Shanghai, told how impressed he had been once, when there had been floodwater high around a camp, and he saw a French captain going through the cantonment in the mud and water to inspect the buildings. In spite of his rank, he was not above such "disagreeable duties."

In his French factory, the chief engineer was always on time. He also saw a colonel dressed in working clothes, working over a piece of machinery for an entire morning. Comparing his French experience with what he noticed in China, where he rarely even saw the factory manager, he reached the following conclusion: It was true foreigners did not treat the Chinese well, but their own officials in China treated the laborers even worse.[77]

Seeing that even children in France could read the newspaper inspired the Chinese to pursue every educational opportunity. One man surnamed Yang wanted a French teacher for his camp. A YMCA secretary promised that if Yang were willing to take responsibility for attendance, he would come to the camp three times a week to teach. At the first class, the YMCA secretary arrived early, but the men had already assembled. The laborers saluted him when he arrived in the room and were attentive to his lectures, afraid of missing a single word. The teacher commented that "the sight of men trying to work their way through college in America is inspiring enough; the picture of these middle-aged laborers trying to get an elementary education after their heavy day of labor is something which makes me at once humble and proud, and drives me to rebel against the social injustice which denied these men an opportunity for education."[78] Yang told his teacher: "I am too old to get an education myself. Without an education I cannot do much for my country. So I want to help my relatives to prepare themselves for the service of China."[79] Another semiskilled worker in a French factory told a YMCA secretary, "We laborers ought to go back to China, not only with some money, but with new knowledge and new skill."[80] That same secretary noted the following:

This sentiment, voiced by the laborer, is prevalent among the younger and the most ambitious of the Chinese laborers in France. They have seen the efficiency of Western industry, and they desire intensely to carry back to China some part of it. Many of them have spent their leisure hours in study and have saved large part of their wages with the hope of entering French industrial schools after their contracts are fulfilled. . . . Such are the Chinese laborers in France. To me, with my Western education and my inclination to regard them as a national liability, they have taught simple unvaried devotion; they have inspired in me a confidence in the future of my country. With enlightenment they will form the backbone of the nation and will give it an industry surpassing that of any country in the world.[81]

A laborer named Wang once told a YMCA official:

China needs the spirit of mutual helpfulness. Our people must be aroused to see the need of standing together for the good of the country. Patriotism, such as I have seen here in France, must inspire the people of our China to stand and fight for the preservation of our land. . . . That is what the people do over here, and their countries are strong and powerful, while we are not. Every little French boy points a finger at us and says, 'Chinois, pas bon,' simply because our country is weak. We have got to become strong. We are greater than any other country in manpower and our land is rich, but we are all poor and ignorant because we do not know how, like foreign nations, to be strong." He further pointed out, "Our China is in need of JUSTICE, and we must learn how to get it. Every boy must be taught patriotism. Schools must be established everywhere. The things that made foreign nations strong must be adopted by us so that we may become strong.

He was not only thinking of the few hundred fellow Chinese in his own company but also of his nation of 400 million.[82] Yet another laborer wrote that both those who used their minds and those who did physical work were equally laborers. But only with education could manual laborers become truly independent, develop a free personal character *(renge),* and become truly civilized. Thus he encouraged his fellow laborers to become better educated; he encouraged them to seize the moment and take every opportunity to learn.[83]

Their journey to the West made many of the men patriots. One laborer's diary was full of nationalist sentiments, thoughts about how to make China strong, and concerns over China's fate. It also included observations of Western civilization and notes about learning French and English. Most interestingly, it records ideas about setting up an organization he called Lu Ou Tongren Hui (Society for Chinese in Europe) arguing that unity meant strength and power for both individuals and the nation. If such a society were organized, the laborers could do better for themselves and for China. The diary included the organization's charter and rules. Its author even noted ideas on how to set up a labor party. In an entry on the memorial service held for deceased Chinese laborers on October 16, 1919, the diarist wrote: "We laborers worked in European battlefields to win glory for China. We were not afraid of bullets and bombs, nor of submarines and airplanes. We helped the fighting directly . . . now the war is over, our civilizations are restored . . . we over 100,000 Chinese laborers no doubt contributed." This man's writing is full of patriotic feeling, feeling that is forceful and representative of the Chinese who served in Europe. One page is emblazoned with the motto "Everyone high and low has a duty to serve the nation" *(Guojia xingwang, pi fu you ze).*[84]

The idea of China as a nation had once been quite abstract to the laboring poor, but overseas it became directly relevant to them. When Li Jun reported that a damaging flood had struck North China, many workers immediately donated their hard-earned francs to relief efforts. In less than two months, 10,138 francs were collected, and one worker alone donated 200 francs.[85] The total for the relief program reached 14,906 francs in November 1918.[86] When they learned that China had not recovered Shandong Province from Japanese control, many laborers wrote to *Chinese Laborers' Weekly* and other publications to denounce the decision by the great powers; they again donated money toward the national interest. One laborer named Tai Kuiyi donated his entire savings of about 550 francs to the Chinese delegation to the Paris Peace Conference and instructed that the delegates should use this money for the national cause in whatever way they saw fit. Another laborer, Zhen Shutian, gave 30 francs as his share to help China develop industry.[87] These laborers were not the exception. In each issue of *Chinese Laborers' Weekly,* one can find records of donations to programs such as the National Salvation Fund and the Patriot Fund. Upon hearing that Japan might compel China to recognize its control of German interests in Shandong, the laborers sent a petition to Lu Zhengxiang, the head of Chinese delegation to the Paris Peace Conference, urging him not to accept. A pistol was even included with the petition, with the threat that "if [Lu] agrees to Japan's demands, [he] should commit suicide with this pistol. Otherwise we will kill him." On another occasion, when the British army in Belgium organized an international sports event to celebrate the end of the war, Chinese laborers sent 6,000 of their members to attend. When they entered the field to find no Chinese flag among all other countries' flags, they felt China's national dignity had been affronted and immediately left in protest.[88] The workers' new nationalism and patriotism found further expression when they returned to China after the war, with some of them coming back from France via the Pacific. They refused to leave ship when their vessels called at Japanese ports, claiming that Japan "had behaved unfairly to China; being Chinese, they could not land and enjoy themselves."[89]

The Chinese laborers understood their role in the war and in China's new identity in the larger world. In one camp, with help of the YMCA, they set up a stage for concerts. They named the concert stage as *Datong wutai* or "great harmony stage" to reflect their longing for peace. On each side of the stage hung a couplet that conveyed their sentiment as citizens of the world ("Da zhang fu neng qu neng shen, he xian dang ku li zhu lianbang, ping ding huan qiu zhan huo, tong lao zhe nai xiong di, xun ke deng wu tai yan gu shi, sao chu wu dang you chou"). The language is not very stylish, but it reflects their motivations and goals. The laborers donated nearly one thousand francs for opera materials such as costumes and instruments.[90] One Chinese laborer reported how his company celebrated the Allies victory on July 19, 1919. On that day, the men set up a victory gate and decorated it with wildflowers and colored lights. The national flags of the Allied countries were placed on the four corners. At the top of the gate flew the Chinese national flag, and under it was a banner with four great Chinese characters: *ren dao da sheng* (a great victory for humanity). At the beginning of the celebration, they shouted, "Long live the Republic of China!" Then came speeches, music, and the national anthems of France, Britain, and China. At the end of his account, the laborer urged every Chinese to work hard to build a strong China, and said he waited for the day when China would celebrate a great victory.[91]

Chinese laborers in France learned the importance of unity and collective action. The labor union they organized in France, the Liu-Fa Huagong Gonghui (Association des Travailleurs Chinoise en France) was formally registered with Paris police and officially approved in October 1919.[92] Its charter indicates that, like the Shanghai union, its purpose was to "strengthen the laborers' unity, broaden their intellectual horizons, and improve their personal characters and spiritual lives." Union members were to promise not to visit prostitutes, gamble, drink liquor, smoke opium, or disturb social stability.[93] The union published its own journal, *Travailleur Chinois (Huagong xunkan)*. The first issue, published on October 15, 1920, openly stated that its goal was to unite the laborers and help them fight for better treatment and a better livelihood.[94] Standard features included news about the world labor movement and events in China. Some labor companies established their own *zizhi hui* (self-rule organizations). These organizations focused on curbing gambling and other bad habits.[95] Before they returned to China, a number of the men visited one of the Chinese cemeteries to bid farewell to fallen comrades. Between September 4 and 8, 1919, they held three memorials for the deceased. They set up a shrine on top that flew a banner with four Chinese characters: *liu fang qian gu* (to be remembered forever), and to either side hung a couplet that read, "xue sa ou xi zhuang shi yun, hun gui zuguo wan shenzhou" (the blood shed by Chinese laborers in Europe has created a better world; Souls of the deceased return to the motherland to work for China's national salvation).[96]

# CONCLUSION

According to historian James Joll, the Great War era came to stand for "the end of an age and beginning of the new" in the world order.[1] This observation applies to China as well. The broadly defined World War I years coincided with a period of tremendous change within China as the old Confucian civilization began to collapse and China struggled to become a nation and sought to assume equal relations with the West. With the Great War, China embarked on a new journey, namely that of internationalization and national renewal. One Chinese writer noted this in an article published in the late 1918. He wrote, "The Great War was soon to end, it would end with the collapse of nineteenth-century civilization. And twentieth-century civilization started immediately. In other words, the world has entered a new era." He encouraged the Chinese to understand the importance of the transformation of eras and civilizations, and to take advantage of the changes. "China will be discarded" in the new era if the Chinese failed to develop a "great awareness" (*da jue wu*) and prepare themselves well, he warned.[2]

China's new course began with the journey of 140,000 Chinese laborers to Europe during the Great War. More than 21 million men, women, and children died in World War I. The Great War was a total war, fought on both the battlefield and the home front; it consumed fighting forces and other human resources. It was also a great trench war. The Chinese played a crucial part in the trench warfare, but Chinese labor and Chinese sacrifices in the war were brushed aside by the West. Lloyd George wrote in his memoir that China's contribution to the war was "insignificant."[3] The French politician Marius Moutet wrote in the 1930s that the French people should remember the incontestable good will of the Chinese government in providing laborers when the existence of France was at stake, yet few did.[4] As a matter of fact, from the day the laborers were recruited, France and Britain were not honest with them. They were promised by both France and Britain that they would not be sent to the battle zones. But many Chinese died from the hostile bombing, precisely because they worked near the front. Nowhere in their contracts was it suggested that they would be subject to military rule, yet military supervision was exactly what they had to deal with. The Chinese were promised with good money. But when they were repatriated, 1 franc was equal to only 35 cents in Chinese silver dollars due to postwar inflation. And the value of franc had fallen to 7 cents by the time most of the men had returned to China. A common laborer in Qingdao at that time earned 30 to 40 cents daily.[5] It seems that in spite of their good wages, as compared with the wages in China, they were able to make no progress in their savings as the gap between the value of the franc and the silver dollar widened. In other words, these laborers who had risked their lives and went through many an ordeal did not even benefit financially.

Because of the laborers' suffering and lack of recognition, Chinese scholar Chen Sanjing viewed their journey as "a great tragedy."[6] Marilyn A. Levine claimed that the laborers "did not fulfill the expected foreign policy objective,"[7] and Judith Blick has suggested that the whole idea of laborers as soldiers was merely a commercial one. The Chinese had nothing to do with the ongoing Great War.[8] But these points are too narrowly focused and miss the bigger picture. Commercially, the Huimin Company did not really benefit; when the company was dissolved in 1921, it was near bankruptcy, and one source suggested that Liang Shiyi personally lost about 150,000 dollars.[9] The laborers' journey has historic importance if we approach the laborers-as-soldiers idea from the perspective of China's grand quest for a new national identity and internationalization. Or to put it differently, we can argue that the Chinese laborers not only made important contributions to the war; they also contributed enormously in terms of what happened at the postwar peace conference and in China's subsequent development. Instead of being a "tragedy," their journey actually stands as a success story, at least in the sense of their role in China's active participation in national and world affairs and China's powerful demand in the postwar world arena for equal treatment of China and its people. The laborers' success is also reflected in the fact that although nobody has given them this credit, they are an important part of China's own "greatest generation," the generation of the 1910s and 1920s that fundamentally changed China's direction of development during and after the Great War. During the Great War, laborers from many countries served in France. They came to answer the call from their colonial masters (Indians, Vietnamese, and South Africans) or to seek personal material gain (Italians and other Europeans). But none of them had a direct link to their nations' grand strategy and substantially affected national developments as the Chinese laborers did in China, which was then facing a great historical turning point. Unlike China, no country where these laborers came from had attached so much importance to (or had such high expectations for) the Great War. To be sure, Chinese laborers went abroad before to places like California, South Africa, and Cuba. But the Chinese in France during World War I were completely different from previous groups. First, their journey was directly linked to national policies of three countries—China, Britain, and France—that were collectively involved in the laborers' recruitment and treatments in France. Second, their arrival in France represented China's major drive for internationalization and equal status in the world. All these characters were missing in previous groups' journeys.

At a YMCA conference in spring 1919, Wang Zhengting, a member of the Chinese delegation to the Paris Peace Conference, said in his address to the YMCA secretaries (specifically to the Chinese secretaries) that present conditions in China demand the "fighting spirit," including a "spirit of justice and righteousness, a spirit of principle that will make one fearless of death or the loss of selfish interest and ambition."[10] The Chinese laborers in Europe, to a great extent, represented such fighting spirit. Their labor, their sacrifices, and their lives provided Chinese diplomats in Paris with a critical tool in their battle for recognition and inclusion on the world stage.

Furthermore, the laborers' journey to Europe during the Great War has both historical and contemporary resonance with the issues around emigration both within China and internationally. Today, Chinese are a floating population that moves within China and around the globe. China's cooperation with the West in the context of the Great War has strong relevance for the twenty-first century, given China's ongoing modernization, internationalization, and rapid rise toward becoming an economic and cultural superpower. Prominent China historian Philip A. Kuhn, in his recent book *Chinese among Others: Emigration in Modern Times,* wrote that "emigration has been inseparable from China's modern history. . . . At least for the period since the 1500s, I suggest that neither Chinese history lacking emigration nor emigration lacking the history of China is a self-sufficient field of study."[11] The story of the Chinese laborers during World War I sheds important new light on the history of emigration. After all, as Kuhn pointed out, emigration has formed the basis of China's own form of overseas expansion.[12] No country in the world has supported such a long and large-scale emigration process.[13]

Emigration was legalized only in 1893 when the Qing court diplomat Xue Fucheng suggested that adopting a friendly policy on emigration would "have the benefit of bridging the gap between China and the West."[14] From the very beginning of the modern era, Chinese elites have linked emigration with China's internationalization, and nowhere is this point illuminated more clearly than in the case of Chinese laborers during the Great War. In today's fast-growing and changing China, laborers are once again being undermined and marginalized, although it was the laborers who helped the Communist Party come to power and provided the foundation for its fast economic growth and breathtaking transformation, sometimes at enormous sacrifice. The regime gives lip service to their suffering and contributions while elites generally ignore and despise them. They are the new coolies *(kuli),* this time in their own country. Few understand their *ku* (suffering), and fewer realize their *li* (power). In the meantime, the millions of Chinese who live abroad still face stereotyping, misunderstanding, and misperceptions. Both contemporary Chinese and Westerners could learn from the great journey of the laborers during the Great War; their story has clear relevance to the future of China and the world.

In short, internationalization and nationalism were the two sides of the same coin in early twentieth-century China. By studying the Chinese laborers in Europe and their stories, we not only recover a neglected chapter in Chinese and world history but we also improve our understanding of how this seemingly obscure episode affected Chinese and Western societies as well as the modern world order.

# APPENDIX 1:
# HUIMIN CONTRACT WITH THE
# FRENCH GOVERNMENT

The Huimin contract with the French government for unskilled Chinese laborers given here was signed at Beijing on May 14, 1916. The English translation is based on Ta Chen's *Chinese Migrations,* 207–210, with minor revision. Words that appear in the French but not in the Chinese text are given in brackets, and those that appear in the Chinese but not in the French text are given in parentheses.

I, _____, age of _____, an inhabitant of _____ town, _____ county, _____ Province, declare that according to the regulations of labor as laid down by M. Truptil, I agree to be a common laborer for a period of five years, beginning with the date of embarkation. But any time after the three years, Mr. Truptil or his representative has the option of terminating the contract.

This contact is made according the "regulations of labor" and I agree to adhere to them in all respects.

Two copies of this contract are made on _____ day _____ month _____ year, at _____ place.

Signature of laborer, if able to sign.

His      right thumb print, his      left thumb print.

Note.—I hereby declare that because I cannot sign my name, I have made two thumb prints before my witnesses, which will testify my consent to observe all the clauses of this contract.

Signature of witnesses

## Terms of the Contract

1. No Chinese laborer is to be employed in any sort of military operations. He is to be engaged only in industries and agriculture in France, Algeria, or Morocco. [The French minister at Peking shall guarantee the vigorous observance of this clause.]

2. The term of the contract is five years, beginning with the day he embarks, and the date of embarkation shall be mentioned on each individual card, without, however, including the time of his return trip home after the expiration of the contract. Mr. Truptil or his representative, reserves the right to terminate the contract at the end of the third year after the signing. if at the end of five years, a laborer should wish to remain in France, Algeria, or Morocco, he would not thereby forfeit the privilege of a free return passage to China. [This is guaranteed by the French minister in Peking in the name of the French Government.]

3. (a) The wage for a working-day is 5 francs. Laborers receiving board shall get 3.25 francs a day. Those receiving both board and lodging shall get 3 francs a day. On the other hand, the laborer must give from his daily wage 25 centimes for clothing and shoes, and 25 centimes for expenses in case of sickness and insurance against death.

In addition to the regular daily wage, the laborer shall receive bonuses for over-time work, for assiduity, and for economy, as allowed to French laborers doing the same work.

(b) The daily wage of 5 francs, above-mentioned, is only for common laborers. Skilled workers should specify their special professions at the time of enlistment, so that when they arrive in France they will be given a test to show their skill. If proficient, their wage will be paid according to their special work.

(c) In case of sickness or of legal holidays when the laborer shall cease work, he shall receive only board and lodging. [But, at all times, if he quits work without the consent of his employer, he shall receive only his lodging.]

(d) At the request of the laborer, the employer shall arrange a convenient way for remitting his money to his family in China. Furthermore, the employer shall arrange a convenient way for depositing or using his money either in France or in China. The manner in which the laborer may wish to deposit money or send it to China shall be agreed upon between Mr. Truptil or his representative and the Huimin syndicate or its representative. The employer must give a proper receipt to the laborer for deposits or remittances.

4. Each laborer shall receive free transportation from the port of embarkation in China to his destination in France, Algeria, or Morocco. At the expiration of this contract, he shall be sent back to the same port of embarkation free of charge. On the voyage, the laborer is entitled to a bonus of 1 franc a day, and a sum of 40 francs must be advanced at the time of embarkation. This money he can spend at his will. [When he is returning to China he shall get only food.] Imposts, contribu-

tions of all kinds, as well as legal taxes, to which the Chinese laborer in France may now or in the future be subject, shall be assumed by his employer.

5. At the time of leaving China, each laborer shall receive a new outfit comprising the following: 2 blue cotton shirts; 2 blue cotton trousers; 1 pair of cloth shoes; 1 hat; 2 pairs of Chinese socks; I padded garment; 1 pair padded trousers; I padded quilt for traveling, with cooking utensils; I traveling bag; I pair woolen lined trousers; 1 straw mat.[1]

Upon reaching France each laborer shall receive the following: one pair of leather shoes; one hat, according to the season.

Six months after the laborer's arrival in France and in every six months thereafter during the period of this contract, he shall receive clothing as follows: two blue shirts and trousers; one pair of leather shoes; one hat; one padded coat; one pair of padded trousers; two pairs of socks.

In addition, one padded coat and one pair of padded trousers will be given him annually, at the end of September or each year. Thus, for those laborers who want to spend the year 1917–18 in France, these clothes will be given them at the end of September 1917.

6. According to the third article of this contract, laborers shall be given board and lodging and clothing. The minimum ration for each laborer shall be as follows:

|  | Gram [1 gram = 0.03528 ounces] |
| --- | --- |
| Rice[2] | 100 |
| Wheat or Kaffir corn | 1,000 |
| Meat, salt or fresh fish | 180 |
| Salt fish[3] | 100 |
| Dried beans[4] | 60 |
| Fresh vegetables | 230 |
| Tea | 15 |
| Lard or vegetable oil | 15 |
| Salt | 15 |

Besides, the laborer shall receive necessary eating utensils; his lodging house which he shares with other workers shall be as near his working place as possible. He shall be provided with a bed or sleeping boards, with a straw mat and coverlet. Light and fuel shall also be provided for him by his employer.

7. It is agreed that each laborer's family shall be given 30 francs at the time of his embarkation, as a consolation to the family. This sum shall be remitted through a bank decided upon by the Huimin syndicate.

8. The laborer must observe the regulations of the shipyard or factory where he is employed: he shall do his work with celerity, zeal, and in a manner which does not call for reproach on the part of the employer. On the other hand, the employer shall treat him with kindness. The laborer shall have the

same opportunities for rest and vacation as enjoyed by French workers employed in the same establishments. In addition, the Chinese laborers shall have a holiday on October 10, their national holiday. Aside from the above exceptions, the laborer must be punctual in attending to his work. (If at the wish of the employer, the laborer consents to work on holidays for 10 hours a day, he is entitled to the regular wage plus a bonus of 1 franc. Moreover, if at the wish of the employer and the consent of the worker, working hours may be increased from 10 upward and each additional hour is paid at the rate of 50 centimes.)

9. When sick, the laborer shall receive medical care free of charge. If the illness exceeds six weeks, and if the attending doctor advises him to return to China, the employer should inform Mr. Truptil or his representative, who shall notify the Chinese consul in Paris. Not later than eight days after receiving such notices, the Chinese consul may independently engage a physician to examine the case. If both doctors give the same advice, the laborer must be sent back to China, and every clause of the contract shall be terminated without indemnity to either party. If the two physicians do not agree, the case shall be submitted for consideration to a competent court at the place where the worker was taken ill.

The employer shall be responsible for food and travel expenses in sending the laborer home.

10. If the laborer dies within the period of the contract, his family is entitled to compensation as follows:

(a) If the laborer dies a natural non-accidental death within six months after the signing of the contract, the compensation shall be 135 francs [$26.06, par].

(b) If the death occurs six months after the signing of the contract and before the expiration, the compensation shall be 270 francs [$52.11, par]. If a death is caused by an accident when the laborer is returning home, his family is entitled to a compensation of 270 francs. In case of death from a war maritime risk during the voyage to France, the worker's family will be entitled to indemnity (a), or 135 francs. But if the laborer dies a natural non-accidental death at the expiration of the contract, there shall be no compensation.

11. The French law of April 9, 1898, respecting accidents, is applicable to Chinese laborers. But the legal formalities have actually ruled that if a foreign worker dies accidentally no indemnity is paid to his family if they are not residing in France. It is now stipulated that in case of a death caused by an accident during work, the dispositions of article 10 above mentioned shall apply, namely, if the death is within six months from the signing of the contract, the compensation shall be 135 francs [$26.06, par]; and if it is after a period of six months and before the expiration of the contract, the compensation shall be 270 francs [$52.11, par].

12. The dead shall be buried according to local customs of France and at the expense of the employer. Mr. Truptil or his representative shall inform the Chinese consul of the death.

13. During his residence in France the laborer enjoy all the liberties, especially religious liberty, as guaranteed by French laws to its citizens. On his part, the laborer shall conform to the laws of France. The employer shall see to it that the laborer is not subject to maltreatment by his fellow workers.

14. An office shall be established in Paris to have control of all matters pertaining to Chinese laborers in France, Algeria, and Morocco. This office shall assume all responsibility for transmitting the laborer's mail. The laborer's mail to his family and friends shall be received by the Huimin syndicate, sent through this office, and delivered to the addressees. This office shall also receive home mail of the laborer and deliver it to him.

15. During the period of this contract no laborer is permitted to undertake directly any commercial enterprise. If the laborer is employed at a certain establishment or factory, he shall not, before the expiration of that employment, seek another employer. If for some reason his employer can not continue to employ him, Mr. Truptil or his representative shall find him a new employment, according to the terms of this contract.

16. Idleness, in-execution of orders, all deeds which are contrary to discipline and honesty, or persistent disregard of regulations of the shipyard or factory where the laborer is employed shall constitute a cause of immediate repatriation, after due notice is given to the Chinese consul in Paris. The laborer shall then be sent back by the next boat sailing to China.

If the removal occurs at the end of the first year after the signing of this contract, the Huimin syndicate shall be responsible for the repatriation fee to the extent of 300 francs [$57.90, par], but the syndicate may exercise a right of recovery from the laborer if it deems desirable.

17. Workers of the same trade or occupation shall be organized into groups of 25 men each, under a leader. The leader shall receive wages, board, and lodging equal to those of any other laborer, but in addition he gets a bonus of 2½ centimes [0.48 cent, par] a day.

En route to France, each leader who performs his duties satisfactorily shall upon his arrival in France receive a bonus of 10 francs [$1.93, par]. (An interpreter will be assigned to groups in a proportion as large as possible.)

18. At the time of his enlistment the laborer shall have his picture taken, give his name, age, home, etc. Besides, there shall be a record made in the roll book of his number, with his photograph. He must conform to the requirements of physical examination and registration. Before landing he shall be examined by a doctor appointed by Mr. Truptil or his representative and must be recognized as physically efficient. All laborers shall be between the ages of 20 and 35.

19. When a laborer violates the contract before its expiration without a legitimate cause, he must pay to Mr. Truptil or his representative the sum of 600 francs [$115.80, par] of travelling expense. Likewise the laborer forfeits his free

passage home. The Huimin syndicate guarantees the execution of an obligation of 300 francs [$57.90, par] per worker.

20. Mr. Truptil or his representative reserves the right of subletting all or a part of this contract to any responsible factory owner. After the subletting, the sublessee shall receive and be governed by the articles of this contract. Also Mr. Truptil or his representative shall guarantee that the laborer fulfills all the articles of this contract.

21. All difficulties arising between the employer and the laborer which are not amicably settled shall be submitted to French tribunals for examination at the place where the worker is employed.

# APPENDIX 2:
# BRITISH CONTRACT

The following is based on an actual contract signed on August 24, 1917, by laborer Liu Yungxiang.

By the terms of this Contract dated this ＿＿＿ day of ＿＿＿ year, I, the undersigned coolie recruited by the Wei-Hai-Wei Labor Bureau, declare myself to be a willing labourer under the following conditions, which conditions have been explained and made clear to me by the Wei-Hai-Wei Labour Bureau, viz: ＿＿＿＿＿＿＿＿

### Nature of Employment

Work on railways, roads, etc., and in factories, mines, dockyards, fields, forests, etc. Not to be employed in military operations.

### Rates of Pay, etc.

| *Daily Abroad.* | *Monthly in China to family, etc.* |
|---|---|
| Labour: 1 franc | 10 dollars |
| Ganger (60 men) 1½ francs | 15 dollars |

*Bonus (on embarkation)*

20 dollars (additional to pay)

*Compensation to Family in Case of Accident*

| | |
|---|---|
| Death or total disablement | 150 dollars |
| Partial disablement | up to 75 dollars |

*Additional*

Free passage to and from China under all circumstances.
Free food, clothing, housing, fuel, light and medical attendance.

## Duration of Employment

Three years, with liberty for employer to terminate contract at any time after one year on giving six months notice, or at any time for misconduct or inefficiency on the part of the labourer. Free passage to be given back to Wei-Hai-Wei or a Port North of Woosung.

## Deductions

No daily pay abroad during sickness, but food given. Monthly pay in China continues up to six weeks sickness.

After six weeks sickness no monthly pay in China.

No daily pay abroad for time lost owing to misconduct.

In case of offences involving loss of pay for 28 days or more, deductions of monthly pay in China will be made.

## Hours of Work

Obligation to work ten hours daily; but a lesser or longer period may be fixed by the Labour Control on a daily average basis of ten hours.

Liability to seven days work a week, but due consideration will be given to Chinese Festivals, as to which the Labour Control will decide.

# NOTES

## Abbreviations

| | |
|---|---|
| Captain Wood Diary | Captain Royal Douglas Wood, "Official Diary of the 39th and 40th Battalions, Chinese Labour Corps, Party AC," East Surrey Museum, UK, file 3969. |
| China No. 2 Historical Archives | Zhongguo di er li shi dang an guan, Nanjing, China |
| IWM | Imperial War Museum, London |
| LC, Leeds | Liddle Collection (1914–1918), Special Collections, University of Leeds Library |
| NA | National Archives, College Park, Maryland |
| NA, Canada | Library and Archives Canada |
| NA, Kew | National Archives, Kew, United Kingdom |
| *Ouzhan Huagong shiliao* | Chen Sanjing, Lu Fangshang, and Yang Cuihua, eds., *Ouzhan Huagong shiliao*. Taipei: Zhongyang yanjiuyuan jindai shi yanjiusuo, 1997. |
| Quai d'Orsay | Archive of French Foreign Ministry, Quai d'Orsay, Paris |
| Vincennes | Service Historique de l'Armée de Terre, Château de Vincennes |
| YMCA Archives | Kautz Family YMCA Archives, University of Minnesota Libraries, Minneapolis, Minnesota |

## Introduction

1. By comparison, India contributed 50,000 laborers to France to support the British war effort. For details on this subject, see Gordon Corrigan, *Sepoys in the Trenches: The Indian Corps on the Western Front, 1914–1915* (Kent, England: Spellmount, 1999).

2. Dominiek Dendooven and Piet Chielens, eds., *World War I: Five Continents in Flanders* (London: Lanoo, 2008), 8

3. Modris Eksteins, *Rites of Spring: The Great War and the Birth of the Modern Age* (Toronto: Lester & Orpen Dennys, 1989), 116–119.

4. "Letter to Howard Sturgis," August 5, 1914, in Percy Lubbock, ed., *The Letters of Henry James* (New York: Octagon Books, 1970), 2:384.

5. Isaac Frederick Marcosson, *S.O.S. America's Miracle in France* (New York: John Lane Company, 1919), 306.

6. Ta Chen, *Chinese Migrations, with Special Reference to Labor Conditions* (Washington, D.C.: Government Printing Office, 1923), 24.

7. Philip A. Kuhn, a prominent Harvard China historian, has recently published his exhaustive study of Chinese emigration titled *Chinese among Others: Emigration in Modern Times* (Lanham, Md.: Rowman & Littlefield, 2008). However, Kuhn surprisingly did not mention the Chinese laborers in Europe during the Great War at all.

8. YMCA Archives, box 204, folder: Chinese laborers in France.

9. Chen Sanjing seemed to be an exception. He wrote in Chinese a pioneering work on Chinese laborers in Europe during the First World War titled *Hua gong yu ou zhan* (Taipei: Zhong yang yan jiu yuan jin dai shi yan jiu suo zhuan kan, 1986). But his work was not a full study of the topic, and he did not have access to many materials that became available only recently. At the Katholieke Universiteit in 1996 Leuven G. Hagen wrote a licentiate thesis dealing with Chinese laborers on the Western front. It was titled *Eenen dwazen glimlach aan het front: Chinese koelies aan het Westers front in de Eerste Wereldoorlog.* Unfortunately, the thesis has not yet been published in English.

10. Robin D. S. Higham and Dennis E. Showalter, *Researching World War I: A Handbook* (Westport, Conn.: Greenwood Press, 2003).

11. James Hamilton-Paterson, "Chinese Dig Britain's Trenches," *Sunday Times* (London), April 30, 1972.

12. Nicholas Griffin, "The Use of Chinese Labour by the British Army, 1916–1920: The 'Raw Importation,' Its Scope and Problems (PhD dissertation, University of Oklahoma, 1973), 2.

13. Dominiek Dendooven, "The Multicultural War in Flanders," in Serge Jaumain, Michael Amara, Benoit Majerus, and Antoon Vrints, eds., *Une Guerre Totale? La Belgique dans la Première Guerre Mondiale: Nouvelles Tendances de la Recherche Historique* (Brussels: Archives Générales du Royaume, 2005), 380.

14. Ibid., 387.

15. Kate Summerscale, *The Queen of Whale Cay* (New York: Penguin Books, 1999), 53.

16. For details, see Mark Levitch, *Panthéon de la Guerre: Reconfiguring a Panorama of the Great War* (Columbia: University of Missouri Press, 2006), 65.

17. Ibid., 149.

18. The Pershing quote and casualties information can be found in the database of the American Battle Monuments Commission. See also David Laskin, "On Hallowed Ground, a Place of Painful Beauty," *New York Times,* September 30, 2007.

19. In fall 2008, I cosponsored an international conference with Weihai (formally Weihaiwei) Municipal Archives on Chinese laborers in Europe during World War I. The conference and my research generated widespread media and academic attention in China. Under the state archives bureau in its second issue of 2009, the official journal *Zhong guo dangan* [China Archives] highlighted the importance of the topic and published a long interview with me about my research. In May 2009, China Central Television aired a six-episode documentary titled *Huagong Juntuan* [Chinese Labor Corps], showing the Chinese laborers in France during the Great War. The documentary was mainly based on my 2007 book *Wenming de jiaorong: Huagong he diyi ci shijie dazhan* [Chinese Laborers in France and the First World War], published in Beijing by Intercontinental Press, a publishing organ of the State Council. I served as chief academic advisor for the documentary. In 2006 the News Office of the State Council of China first came out with the idea to have a book on the Chinese laborers in Europe during the First World War and then commissioned me to write it.

20. J. M. Winter, *Remembering War: The Great War between Memory and History in the Twentieth Century* (New Haven: Yale University Press, 2006), 4–5.

21. Many private and unpublished sources cited in this book did not have page numbers. Moreover, because this is rather a small book, it cannot discuss many issues in detail. For instance, the social and everyday lives of these laborers should be studied (and are not included in this book). I might devote a whole book to these issues later. Some key issues have to be left unexplored due to lack of evidence. For instance, what happened to the laborers after they returned is a great topic, but despite my great efforts, I discovered that too few reliable sources have been unearthed to develop a good story. Some basic issues about China and the Great War are not discussed in detail, since I devoted a whole volume to topics such as China and the Great War in general, China's international and domestic situations, and the overall Chinese perception of the war and conflict in my previous work, *China and the Great War: China's Pursuit of a New National Identity and Internationalization* (New York: Cambridge University Press, 2005).

## 1. Great War and Great Crisis

1. Charles Dickens, *A Tale of Two Cities* (Oxford: Oxford University Press, 1989), 1.

2. For details on the political, social, and cultural changes in China prior to and during the World War I period, see Xu Guoqi, *China and the Great War,* chapters 1–3.

3. For an excellent argument on the importance of China's international-ization, see William C. Kirby, "The Internationalization of China: Foreign Rela-tions at Home and Abroad in the Republican Era," *China Quarterly* 150, no. 2 (1997).

4. In late imperial China, China was long thought to be the Middle King-dom and the *Tianxia,* the core and heart of the world order. For a detailed ex-planation, see Xu, *China and the Great War,* 20–25.

5. For the best book on the generation of 1914 in Europe, see Robert Wohl, *The Generation of 1914* (Cambridge, Mass.: Harvard University Press, 1979).

6. For such suggestions, see Liu Yan, *Zhong Guo Wai Jiao Shi* [Diplomatic History of China] (Taipei: San min shu ju, 1962), 409.

7. There are no official documents available on this maneuver from Yuan. However, some secondary sources do exist. For example, both George E. Mor-rison and Bertram Lenox Simpson mentioned it in personal letters and official memoranda. Morrison mentioned it several times in his personal letters; see Morrison to Mrs. Moberly Bell, May 8, 1916; Morrison to L. G. Fraser, Beijing, October 12, 1916; Lo Hui-Min, ed., *The Correspondence of G. E. Morrison* (Cambridge: Cambridge University Press, 1976), 2:515–516, 559; and Lai Xinxia, ed., *Beiyang Jun Fa* [Documents on Beiyang Warlords] (Shanghai: Shanghai ren min chubanshe, 1988), 3: 131–136.

8. For a detailed study on Sino-Japanese negotiations regarding the Twenty-one Demands, see Li Yushu, *Zhong ri er shi yi tiao jiao she* [Sino-Japanese Ne-gotiation over Twenty-one Demands] (Taipei: Zhongyang yanjiu yuan ji dais hi yan jiu suo, 1966); and Zhitian Luo, "National Humiliation and National As-sertion: The Chinese Response to the Twenty-one Demands," *Modern Asian Studies* 27, no. 2 (1993): 297–319.

9. Morrison was former reporter for the London *Times* in Beijing.

10. Cyril Pearl, *Morrison of Peking* (Sydney: Angus and Robertson, 1967), 307.

11. De LaPomarede to French Ministry of War, May 10, 1915, Quai d'Orsay, NS, Chine, 189.

12. "Foreign policy public" in this context means groups of the Chinese who paid more than average attention to foreign policy and foreign affairs.

13. Feng Gang and others, eds., *Minguo Liang Yansun xiansheng shiyi nianpu* (Taipei: Commercial Press, 1978), 1:310.

14. Li Jikui, *Liang Shiyi* (Guangzhou: Guangdong renmin chubanshe, 2005), 133.

15. Ibid., 132.

16. Ibid., 142.

17. Zhu Zhuanyu, ed., *Liang Shiyi Zhuanji Ziliao* (Taipei: Tianyi chubanshe, 1979), 14.

18. Chen Fen, ed., *Beiyang zhengfu guowu zongli Liang Shiyi shiliao ji* (Beijing: Zhongguo wenshi chubanshe, 1991), 404.

19. Zhu Zhuanyu, *Liang Shiyi Zhuanji Ziliao*, 7.

20. Between 1913 and 1918, Ye Gongchuo was chief of the Railway Bureau, manager of the Bank of Communications, and vice-minister of the Ministry of Communications.

21. Georges Clemenceau, "The Cause of France," *Saturday Evening Post* 187, no. 17 (1914), 65.

22. For details, see Peter Hart, *The Somme: The Darkest Hour on the Western Front* (New York: Pegasus Books, 2008).

23. J. M. Winter, *The Great War and the British People* (Cambridge, Mass.: Harvard University Press, 1986), 65–99.

24. Le Major General to Monsieur le Ministre de la Guerre, Etat–Major de l'Armée, Vincennes, 7N 398/Chine.

25. Le Ministre de la Guerre to Monsieur le General Commandant en Chef, Paris, October 27, 1915, Vincennes, 7N435/Main–d'oeuvre Indigence.

26. "French Foreign Ministry Report on Chinese Laborers," January 23, 1917, Quai d'Orsay, Ministre des Affaires Etrangères, 1918–1929, Chine, 41.

27. "Ying Fa deng guo gui ding zhao gong ge xiang gong zi an" ("Files on Salaries for Recruited Laborers under Britain and France"), 1917, China No. 2 Archives, 1050–11.

28. Conty to Quai d'Orsay, March 1, 1916, Quai d'Orsay, Ministre des Affaires Etrangères, 1918–1929, Chine, 41.

29. France made similar statements several times. See, for example, "Procés-Verbaux de la Conférénce Interministerielle," Archive Nationale, 14F/11334.

30. G. Charles Hodges, "John Chinaman Breaks Through: How War Needs Are Breaching the Exclusion Walls Erected against Him by the White Races," *Sunset: The Pacific Monthly* 41, no. 3 (September 1918): 25.

31. See "Waijiaobu shou de shi xin ce zhao hui," July 15, 1916, August 3, 1916, August 9, 1916, November 13, 1916; "Waijiaobu fu de shi zhao hui," August 9, 1916; "Waijiaobu fa de shi zhao hui," December 5, 1916, all in Chen Sanjing, Lu Fangshang, and Yang Cuihua, eds., *Ouzhan Huagong shiliao* (Taipei: Zhongyang yanjiuyuan jindai shi yanjiusuo, 1997) (hereafter cited as *Ouzhan Huagong shiliao*), 8–11, 15, 17.

32. "Waijiaobu fa yan jiang yan hai dong san sheng ge dujun sheng zhang mi han," January 30, 1917, in *Ouzhan Huagong shiliao*, 20.

33. "Le Ministre du Travail et de la Prévoyance Sociale à Monsieur le Ministre de la Guerre," October 14, 1916, Vincennes, 6N 149/Fonds Clemenceau/Mission de Recrutement des Ouvriers/Chinois.

34. Note of Quai d'Orsay, Paris, January 17, 1917. Quai d'Orsay, Ministre des Affaires Etrangères, 1918–1929, Chine, 41, 145.

35. Naval Attaché Report, no. 2109, French Embassy, February 6, 1916, Archives de la Marine, SSEB 119/Transport Personnel.

36. "Procés-Verbaux de la Conférénce Interministerielle," February 24, 1917, Archive Nationale, 14F/11334.

37. Archive Nationale, 1917, F14/11331/Chinois/Institution et Affaires General.

38. Quai d'Orsay Report on Chinese Workers, January 23, 1917, Quai d'Orsay, Ministre des Affaires Etrangères, 1918–1929, Chine, 41.

39. Conty to Quai d'Orsay, February 12, 1917, Quai d'Orsay, Ministre des Affaires Etrangères, 1918–1929, Chine, 41, 163.

40. Jean Chesneaux, *The Chinese Labor Movement, 1919–1927,* translated from the French by H. M. Wright (Palo Alto, Calif.: Stanford University Press, 1968), 132–133.

41. *North China Daily News,* November 24, 1916; December 8, 1916.

42. British Foreign Office minutes on the incident, NA, Kew, FO 371/2914/10361.

43. Jordan to Alston, December 21, 1915, NA, Kew, FO 350/13.

44. Jordan to Lord Bryce, February 23, 1916, NA, Kew, FO 350/15.

45. "Guangdong sheng zhang zhi wai jiao bu," February 12, 1917, China No. 2 Archives, 1039–1.

46. For disputes between Conty and Truptil, see "Procés-Verbaux de la Conférénce Interministerielle," March 3, 1917, Archive National, 14F/11334.

47. For the opinion from the Huimin side, see Feng Gang et al., eds., *Sanshui Liang Yansun xiansheng nianpu* (Taipei: Commercial Press, 1978), 448–453.

48. Martel to Quai d'Orsay, February 9, 1918, and February 18, 1918, Quai d'Orsay, Ministre des Affaires Etrangères, 1918–1929, Chine, 42.

49. War Ministry to Quai d'Orsay, July 15, 1918; Quai d'Orsay to War Ministry, July 28, 1918; Quai d'Orsay, Asie, 1918–1929, Chine, 42.

50. For detailed differences between the two sides, please refer to Note pour le Cabinet Militaire/Affaire Truptil (no date), and Secret Telegram from French Minister to China, Boppe, October 22, 1918; both documents are available in Vincennes, 6N149/Fonds Clemenceau/Mission de Recrutement des Ouvriers Chinois. For the best short summary of the differences, see Le Rapport de M. Dubois in Vincennes, 6N 111/Drivers Secret/Fonds Clemenceau. For a detailed view of the French military side, please see Rapport Fait au Sous-Secrétaire d'Etat, Ministre de la Guerre, Analyse au Sujet de la Demande d'indemnité du

Syndicat Wey–min par suite de la Suspension du Recrutement de Main d'Oeuvre Chinoise, Vincennes, 6N 111/Drivers Secret/Fonds Clemenceau.

51. Zhu Zhuanyu, *Liang Shiyi Zhuanji Ziliao,* 26.

52. Quote from Tyler Stovall, "The Color behind the Lines: Racial Violence in France during the Great War," *American Historical Review* 103, no. 3 (June 1998): 749.

53. Ibid., 749–750.

54. Ibid., 754.

55. David Robertson, "Memorandum on employment of Chinese for war purposes," July 23, 1916, NA, Kew, WO 106/35.

56. Jordan to Grey, July 25, 1916, NA, Kew, WO 106/35.

57. "Summary of Information Concerning the Recruiting of the Chinese Labour Corps," January 12, 1917, NA, Kew, WO 106/33.

58. "Great Britain's War Work in 1917," 345.

59. The War Office to Bonard Law, February 25, 1916, NA, Canada, RG 24/1833, 8–34A.

60. Dendooven and Chielens, *World War I,* 17–18

61. Nicholas Griffin, "The Responses of British Labor to the Importation of Chinese Workers, 1916–1917," *Historian* 40, no. 2: 265.

62. "Chinese Labour in Birmingham," *Times* (London), August 6, 1917, 3.

63. Parliamentary Debates, *Commons* (96) (July 16-August 3, 1917): 1147.

64. Jordan to Grey, July 25, 1916, NA, Kew, WO 106/35.

65. Peter T. Scott, "Chinese in France in WW I," *War Monthly* 8(76) (1980): 8–11.

66. Paul Fussell, *The Great War and Modern Memory* (New York: Oxford University Press, 1975), 9.

67. Ibid., 11.

68. Ibid., 14.

69. Ibid., 74.

70. Special order of the day, General Douglas Haig, August 4, 1916, NA, Kew, WO 95/571, 19, Labour BN.

71. Josiah C. Wedgwood, MP to Lloyd George, October 11, 1916, House Lords Records Office: Lloyd George Papers—E/4/2/4.

72. *Times* (London), October 24, 1917, 7a.

73. Parliamentary Debates, *Commons* (93) (April 30-May 25, 1917): 1393.

74. Parliamentary Debates, *Commons* (87) (November 7–23, 1916): 874.

75. Parliamentary Debates, *Commons* (97) (August 6–21, 1917): 1484–1485.

76. Parliamentary Debates, *Commons* (84) (July 10–31): 1379.

77. Minutes of the Proceedings of the Army Council, July 28, 1916, NA, Kew, WO 163/21.

78. War Office memorandum, August 14, 1916, NA, Kew, WO 32/11345.

79. H. R. Wakefield, "Chinese Labour in France," NA, Kew, WO 106/33.

80. War Office document, August 1916, NA, Kew, WO 32/11345.

81. His official title was War Office Representative for the Purpose of Recruiting Labor in North China for the British Expeditionary Force in France.

82. "The Coolie's Place," *Far Eastern Review* 15, no. 4 (April 1918): 159.

83. Parliamentary Debates, *Commons* (87) (November 7–23, 1916): 1626–1727.

84. Parliamentary Debates, *Commons* (88) (November 27–December 22, 1916): 138.

85. The Governor of Hong Kong to the Secretary of State for the Colonies, October 9, 1916, NA, Kew, WO 32/11345.

86. War Office document, January 12, 1917, NA, Kew, WO 106/33.

87. Foreign Office to Jordan, October 15, 1916, NA, Kew, WO 32/11346.

88. Alston to Foreign Office, December 22, 1916, NA, Kew, WO 32/11345.

89. Kathlene B. Winter, "With the Chinese Industrial Army in France," *World Outlook* 5, no. 3 (March 1919): 14.

90. "Zong zhang hui wu ying ai dai ban wen da," December 13, 1916, in *Ouzhan Huagong shiliao*, 456.

91. "Shou guo wu yuan gong han," January 17, 1917, in *Ouzhan Huagong shiliao*, 467.

92. "Fan zhu ying shi gong shi dian," January 25, 1917, "Shou zhu yin Shi gong shi dian," February 6, 1917, in *Ouzhan Huagong shiliao*, 469, 79.

93. "Waijiaobu to Minister Shi Zhaoji," January 25, 1917, Taipei: Zhong yang yan jiu yuan jin dai shi yan jiu suo dang an guan, wai jiao bu dang, British Recruitment, E–1–4–2.

94. Jordan telegram to Foreign Office, November 12, 1916, NA, Kew, WO 32/11345.

95. Alston to Foreign Office, December 3, 1916, NA, Kew, WO 32/11345.

96. La Panouse Report, April 27, 1917, Vincennes, 17N 156/Correspondence; see also "Procés-Verbaux de la Conférénce Interministerielle," Paris: Archive Nationale, 14F/11334.

97. Naval Attaché Naval report, "Au Subjet des Cooliers Tibetains" (1589) (June 1, 1917), Vincennes, Archive de la Marine, SSEB 5/Travailleurs Colonials et Etrangères/Généralités.

98. A. Philip Jones has mentioned the many problems that existed between the two sides; see A. Philip Jones, *Britain's Search for Chinese Cooperation in the First World*, chapters 6 and 8.

99. Foreign Office to Jordan, October 5, 1916, NA, Kew, WO 32/11346.

100. Nicholas Reeves, "Film Propaganda and Its Audience: The Example of Britain's Official Films during the First World War," *Journal of Contemporary History* 18, no. 3 (1983): 476.

101. Ibid., 488–489.

102. For a study on the Chinese overseas, see Wang Gunwu, *China and the Chinese Overseas* (Cambridge, Mass.: Harvard University Press, 2000).

103. Quote from Yen Ching-huang, *Coolies and Mandarins: China's Protection of Overseas Chinese during the Late Ching Period (1851–1911)* (Singapore: Singapore University Press, 1985), 20–22.

104. This policy was not compatible with several treaties the Qing court signed after the Opium War that allowed foreign countries to recruit Chinese to work abroad.

105. See "Waijiaobu shou nong shang bu zi, October 25, 1916," "Waijiaobu fa nong shangbu zhi, November 4, 1916," "Waijiobu shou nong shang bu zi, November 17, 1916," in *Ouzhan Huagong shiliao,* 12–14, 16.

106. For a detailed analysis of the Beijing government's overseas Chinese policy, see Jiang Shunxing and Du Yugen, "Lun Beiyang zhengfu de Qiaowu zhengce," *Minguo dangan* 4 (1993): 68–72.

107. "Ying zhengfu zhaogong zhangcheng," China No. 2 Archives, 1050–11.

108. "Guo wu yuan qiao gong shi wu ju chou ban wei chi qiao gong hui guo sheng ji shi xiang biao," *Xin zhongguo,* 251.

109. Zhun fa gong shi han shang yue shu lu wai hua gong ban fa liu tiao qing zhuan ling ge shang hui shen shen ban li wen, *Zhong Hua Quan Guo Shang Hui Lian He Hui Hui Bao,* no. 3 (March 1, 1917).

110. *Ouzhan Huagong shiliao,* 195.

111. *Ouzhan Huagong shiliao,* 196.

112. *Ouzhan Huagong shiliao,* 8–11, 15, 17.

113. *Ouzhan Huagong shiliao,* 199, 200, 207, 209, 210, 213, 200, 225, 232.

114. *Ouzhan Huagong shiliao,* 246.

115. Secret order addressed to the Magistrate of the Lin Yi district, NA, Kew, FO 228/2893.

116. "Wai jiao bu fa yan jiang yan hai dong san sheng ge dujun sheng zhang mi han," January 10, 1917, in *Ouzhan Huagong shiliao* 20.

117. "Wei she li xie ji yi min you xian gong si chen qing" [Petition for setting up an emigration company], China No. 2 Archives, 1001 (2), file: Ying Fa E wai shang zai yue han wan dian deng di zhao mu chu guo hua gong ke ke nue dai deng qing you guan wen jian (January 1917–May 1918) (Files on mistreatments of Chinese laborers recruited in Guangdong, Hubei, Anhui, and Yunnan provinces by foreign companies from Britain, France, and Russia), 439.

118. "Wai jiao bu fa nong shang bu zi" (Foreign Ministry to Ministry of Agriculture and Commerce) (November 4, 1916); "Wai jiao bu shou nong shang bu zi" (Ministry of Agriculture and Commerce to Foreign Ministry), October 25, 1916, November 17, 1916, in *Ouzhan Huagong shiliao,* 12–14, 16.

119. *Ouzhan Huagong shiliao,* 16.

120. For details on Beijing's policy on emigration issue, see Jiang Shunxing and Du Yugen, "Lun Beiyang zhengfu de qiaowu zhengce," *Minguo Dang'an* 4 (1993): 68–72.

121. *Ouzhan Huagong shiliao*, 29.
122. *Ouzhan Huagong shiliao*, 228.
123. *Ouzhan Huagong shiliao*, 285.
124. *Ouzhan Huagong shiliao*, 286.
125. *Ouzhan Huagong shiliao*, 514.
126. Pan's reports can be found in *Ouzhan Huagong shiliao*, 519–520, 34–37, 42–47, 57–59, 63–64.
127. "Zhu Fa qiao gong wei yuan yu fa guo gong bu ju wang fan wen jian" [Communications between Li Jun and French Authorities], *Xin zhongguo*: 267–268.
128. Boppe to Quai d'Orsay, Beijing, Nov. 24, 1919, Quai d'Orsay, Ministère des Affaires Etrangères, 1918–1929, Chine, 42, 170.
129. YMCA, *Young Men's Christian Association with the Chinese Labor Corps in France*, YMCA Archives, box 204, folder: Chinese laborers in France.

## 2. The Recruitment and European Odyssey of the Men for Britain and France

1. There are records of several orders given with regard to this treatment from the military authorities. See, for example, Vincennes, 17N 156/Correspondence.
2. Chinese laborers contract, NA, RG 120, entry 1760, box 107, folder: Misc., class A.
3. See "Instruction Relative to Employment of Chinese Laborers," September 26, 1916, issued by Commander of Colonial Troops, Vincennes, 17N 156/Correspondence.
4. For details, see "Procés-Verbaux de la Conférence Interministerielle," 14F/11334.
5. Michael Summerskill, *China on the Western Front: Britain's Chinese Work Force in the First World War* (London: Author, 1982), 94–95.
6. Alston telegram, August 13, 1917, NA, Kew, WO 106/33/T11610.
7. Nicholas Griffin, "Britain's Chinese Labor Corps in World War I," *Military Affairs* 40, no. 3 (October 1976): 103.
8. G. S. Moss to War Office, November 27, 1918, NA, Kew, FO 228/2894.
9. Foreign Office to John Jordan, February 11, 1919, NA, Kew, FO 228/2894.
10. For details, see Secretary of Treasury to War Office, June 20, 1919, NA, Kew, T1/12343.
11. War Office representative G. S. Moss, report on the demobilization of the Chinese Labor Corps, October 31, 1920, NA, Kew, FO 228/2895.
12. For details, see Secretary of Treasury to War Office, June 20, 1919, NA, Kew, T1/12343.

13. YMCA, *Young Men's Christian Association with the Chinese Labor Corps in France,* YMCA Archives, box 204, folder: Chinese laborers in France.

14. "China's Man Power Aids France in War," *New York Times,* February 25, 1917, 3.

15. "Procés-Verbaux de la Conférénce Interministerielle," 14F/11334.

16. French Ambassador Paul Combon to Quai d'Orsay, October 9, 1917, Quai d'Orsay, NS, Chine, 137.

17. Foreign Office to Alston, February 22, 1917, NA, Kew, FO 371/2905/28360.

18. Internal exchange paper of Foreign Office, February 21, 1917, NA, Kew, FO 371/2905/28360.

19. Foreign Office document, May 25, 1917, NA, Kew, FO 371/2906/40.

20. British Foreign Office to Quai d'Orsay, October 5, 1917, Quai d'Orsay, NS, Chine, 137.

21. Alston to Foreign Office, October 5, 1917, NA, Kew, FO 371/2906/296–297.

22. Balfour to Combon, October 11, 1917, NA, Kew, FO 371/2906.

23. For a detailed explanation of the Allied shipping issue, see J. A. Salter, *Allied Shipping Control: An Experiment in International Administration* (Oxford: Clarendon Press, 1921).

24. Ibid., 138–139.

25. David Kennedy, *Over Here: The First World War and American Society* (New York: Oxford University Press, 1980), 333.

26. British Foreign Office to Quai d'Orsay, October 5, 1917, Quai d'Orsay, NS, Chine, 137.

27. "Secret Note sur la Question du Transport de Contingents Chinois," January 25, 1918, Vincennes, 16N 3246.

28. Quai d'Orsay to War Ministry, July 28, 1918, Quai d'Orsay, Asie, 1918–1929, 42.

29. Parliamentary Debates, *Commons* (97) (August 6–21, 1917): 1479.

30. Michael Summerskill has given an excellent description of the British suspension of recruiting Chinese labor corps; see his *China on the Western Front,* 179–194.

31. Maclay to the War Cabinet, January 17, 1918, NA, Kew, War Cabinet minutes, CAB 23/5/324.

32. Foreign Office to Jordan, April 14, 1918, NA, Kew, WO 106/33.

33. Bourne to James Stewart Lookhart, August 9, 1918, NA, Kew, CO 873/538.

34. K. Winter, "With the Chinese Industrial Army in France," 14.

35. Captain L. J. Sebert Diary.

36. E. J. Stuckey, "Trachoma among the Chinese in France," *British Journal of Ophthalmology,* no. 4 (January 1920): 1–12.

37. Manico Gull, "The Story of the Chinese Labor Corps," *Far Eastern Review* 15, no. 4 (April 1918): 130.

38. He told his personal story to W. W. Peter in France; see YMCA, "Yellow Spectacles," YMCA Archives, box 204, folder: Chinese laborers in France.

39. Daryl Klein, *With the Chinks* (London: John Lane Company, 1919), 2, 7.

40. "The C.L.C.: With the Coolie from China to France," *Times* (London), April 23, 1919, 14.

41. Harry B. Wilmer, "Chinese Coolies in France," *North China Herald,* September 21, 1918.

42. Sir Alwyne Ogden files, Chinese Labor Corps handwriting materials, LC Leeds, chap. 3, 2–3.

43. Sir Alwyne Ogden files, Chinese Labor Corps oral interview, LC Leeds, transcript 13.

44. Gull, "Story of the Chinese Labor Corps," 130.

45. YMCA, "Yellow Spectacles," YMCA Archives, box 204, folder: Chinese laborers in France.

46. Klein, *With the Chinks,* 3, 6.

47. Ibid., 10.

48. "Guo wu yuan qiao gong shi wu ju chou ban wei chi qiao gong hui guo sheng ji shi xiang biao," *Xin zhongguo:* 251–253.

49. "Di yi ci da zhan shi qi fu ou huagong," in Chen Hansheng, *Huagong chu guo shi liao hui bian* (Beijing: Zhonghua shu ju, 1984) (10): 293–327.

50. "Zhao lu zhu fa Hu gong shi lai han," China No. 2 Archives, 1001 (2)-400, folder: Diao cha huagong Fu jian chu hou ji zai fa huagong yu hui guo zi qian qing xing bao gao ji you guan wen jian, October 1917–July 1920.

51. "Guo wu yuan qiao gong shi wu ju chou ban wei chi qiao gong hui guo sheng ji shi xiang biao," *Xin zhongguo:* 251–253.

52. Gull, "Story of the Chinese Labor Corps," 127.

53. Statement showing movement of vessels conveying Chinese coolies to France and numbers reported on each vessel, NA, Kew, WO 32/11345.

54. Directorate of Labour/War Diary, entry November 30, 1917, NA, Kew, WO 95/83.

55. Controller of Labour to the Quartermaster General, Report of labour with the BEF during the war, November 14, 1919, WO 107/37, 114.

56. Foreign Office to John Jordan, April 14, 1918, NA, Kew, FO 371/3178.

57. Secretary of Treasury Cubitt's letter, April 30, 1918, NA, Kew, T1/12178.

58. G. S. Moss report to the War Office, "Report on the Working of the War Office Emigration Agency in Cooperation with the Chinese Post Service," September 3, 1919, NA, Kew, CO 873/578.

59. I. H. Shi, "With the Chinese Laborers 'Somewhere in France,'" *Chinese Students' Monthly* 13, no. 8 (June 1918): 447–452.

60. YMCA, "Yellow Spectacles," YMCA Archives, box 204, folder: Chinese laborers in France.

61. Klein, *With the Chinks,* 62.

62. YMCA, *Young Men's Christian Association with the Chinese Labor Corps in France,* YMCA Archives, box 204, folder: Chinese laborers in France, 4.

63. Chen Sanjing, *Hua gong yu ou zhan,* 72.

64. See "Waijiaobu fa guo wu yuan han, January 8, 1919," in *Ouzhan Huagong shiliao,* 38.

65. China No. 2 Archives has approximately twenty volumes of materials on Chinese laborer casualties, including those who worked in British vessels. The volumes listed the names of those who died from German submarine attacks or airplane bombing. For details, see China No. 2 Archives, 1050–18–34.

66. For details, see China No. 2 Archives, 1050–18, vol. 2, 4, 5, 6.

67. "Fa chuan ya die shi hao huagong bei hai an," China No. 2 Archives, 1050–3.

68. "Huagong Sun Chengzhi bei hai an, 1919," China No. 2 Archives, 1050–6.

69. Captain L. J. Sebert Diary.

70. Klein, *With the Chinks,* 114–115.

71. Captain Wood Diary, entry of September 25, 1917.

72. For details on "coolie trade," see Lisa Yun, *The Coolie Speaks: Chinese Indentured Laborers and African Slaves in Cuba* (Philadelphia: Temple University Press, 2008).

73. "China's Man Power Aids France," 3.

74. Klein, *With the Chinks,* 197.

75. John F. Lewis, *China's Great Convulsion, 1894–1924: A Dynasty Overthrown, Chaos and Warlords, and How the Chinese Helped the Western Allies Win World War I* (Heathsville, Va.: Sun on Earth Books, 2005), 79.

76. Ibid., 111.

77. Walter Edward Williams interviews, IWM, 9754.

78. Klein, *With the Chinks,* 29.

79. Gull, "Story of the Chinese Labor Corps," 125–135.

80. YMCA, "Yellow Spectacles," YMCA Archives, box 204, folder: Chinese laborers in France.

### 3. The Hidden History of the Secret Canadian Pathway

1. Peter M. Mitchell, "Canada and the Chinese Labour Corps, 1917–1920: The Official Connection," in Min-Sun Chen and Lawrence N. Shyu, eds., *China Insight: Selected Papers from the Canadian Asian Studies Annual Conference Proceedings, 1982–1984* (Ottawa: Canadian Asian Studies Association, 1985), 7.

2. Major-General C. G. S memo, July 24, 1917, NA, Canada, RG 24/3767, 1048–45–1 vol. 1: The transportation department memo to director or naval service, March 24, 1917; Memo from W. D. Scott, Superintendent of Immigration to General Sir Eugene Fiset, Department of Militia and Defense, July 24, 1917, NA, Canada, RG 24/2553, HQC 2115.

3. Chief of staff memo to director of the navy service, November 6, 1917, NA, Canada, RG 24/3767, 1048–45–1, 1.

4. Harry D. Livingstone Journal.

5. Ibid.

6. Memo from T. R. Ferguson to W. J. Cullum, Steamship Inspector, April 17, 1917, NA, Canada, RG 42/255, 37467.

7. Johnston to Wanklyn, May 5, 1917, NA, Canada, RG 42/255, 37467.

8. Ibid.

9. Memo from the Secretary of State for the Colonies to the Governor General, London, September 9, 1919. See also memo from the Deputy Minister regarding transportation of returned Chinese coolies from British Columbia to China, September 18, 1919, NA, Canada, RG 42/255, 37467.

10. "Chinese Coolies—Great War," NA, Canada, RG 24/1833/G.A .Q 8–36, HQ 968.24, 23.

11. Memo from Department of Militia and Defense to the High Commissioner for Canada of Britain, July 8, 1918, NA, Canada, RG 25, A-2/229, M60/23-M61/23.

12. Memo to W. J. Roche, Minister of the Interior, Ottawa, July 23, 1917, NA, Canada, RG 24/3767, 1048–45–2, 3.

13. Petawawa Camp, A. M. Cannan, Commanding Officer 32 and 38 battalions, CLC to Lieutenant Colonel W. C. Bryan, September 27, 1917, NA, Canada, RG 24/2553, HQC 2115.

14. "Chinese Coolies—Great War," NA, Canada, RG 24/1833/G.A .Q 8–36, HQ 968.24, 23.

15. Captain T. Pugh report, NA, Canada, RG 24/2553, HQC 2115.

16. John Hughes, Inspector General of Western Canada, memo to adjutant-general, militia headquarters, Ottawa, September 17, 1917, NA, Canada, RG 24/2553, HQC 2115.

17. Dominion Immigration Inspector for B.C. to Chambers, May 1, 1917, NA, Canada, RG 6-E, T 101.

18. Chief Press Censor for Canada to Hulatt, Confidential, February 28, 1917, NA, Canada, RG 6-E, 168, part 2.

19. Perry to Chambers, March 3, 1917, NA, Canada, RG 6-E, 168, part 2.

20. Chambers to Perry, March 4, 1917, NA, Canada, RG 6-E, 168, part 2.

21. Chambers's instruction to media, March 14, 1917, NA, Canada, RG 6-E, T/101.

22. Circular no. C.P.C 48, officially issued on March 17, 1917, NA, Canada, RG 6-E T/101.

23. Chambers to W. Banks, global editorial office, Toronto, Confidential, NA, Canada, RG 6-E T/101.

24. Chambers to Colonel A. W. Richardson, August 8, 1917; Chambers to W. D. Scott, August 8, 1917, NA, Canada, RG 6-E/620, folder 331, part 1.

25. Reid report to Chambers, April 7, 1917, NA, Canada, RG 6-E T/101.

26. Rev. J. Somerville, Presbyterian Church in Canada, reported to Chambers, April 9, 1917, NA, Canada, RG 6-E T/101.

27. NA, Canada, RG 6-E/620, folder 331, part 2.

28. Chambers to Livesay, April 25, 1917, NA, Canada, RG 6-E/620, folder 331, part 1.

29. Chambers to General Gwatkin, April 19, 1917, NA, Canada, RG 6-E/ 620, folder 331, part 1.

30. Chambers to J. F. Liversay, April 11, 1917, NA, Canada, RG 6-E T/ 101.

31. Stephen Vaughn, *Holding Fast the Inner Lines: Democracy, Nationalism, and the Committee on Public Information* (Chapel Hill: University of North Carolina Press, 1980), 5.

32. Ibid., 17–18.

33. Ibid., 22.

34. Chambers to C. F. Grandall, April 28, 1918, NA, Canada, RG 6-E T/101.

35. Malcolm Reid, Dominion Immigration Inspector for B. C. to Chambers, September 19, 1917, NA, Canada, RG 6-E/620, folder 331, part 2.

36. Reid to Chambers, July 6, 1917, NA, Canada, RG 6-E/620, folder 331, part 1.

37. Reid to Chambers, July 17, 1917, NA, Canada, RG 6-E/620, folder 331, part 1.

38. Chambers to Reid, July 12, 1917, NA, Canada, RG 6-E/620, folder 331, part 1.

39. Bourne to War Office, January 10, 1918, NA, Kew, WO 106/33.

40. Reid to Chambers, January 16, 1918, NA, Canada, RG 6-E/620, folder 331, part 2.

41. Chambers to the chief of the general staff, January 16, 1918, NA, Canada, RG 6-E/620, folder 331, part 2.

42. Reid to Chambers, January 18, 1918, NA, Canada, RG 6-E/620, folder 331, part 2.

43. Reid to Chambers, confidential and rush, January 18, 1918, NA, Canada, RG 6-E/620, folder 331, part 2.

44. War Office to Chambers, March 8, 1918, NA, Canada, RG 6-E/620, folder 331, part 2.

45. Reid to Chambers, April 3, 1918, NA, Canada, RG 6-E/620, folder 331, part 2.

46. Reid report, April 3, 1918, NA, Canada, RG 6-E/620, folder 331, part 2.

47. Chambers to Imperial Consul General for Japan in Ottawa, May 1917, NA, Canada, RG 6-E T/101.

48. Imperial Consul General for Japan in Ottawa to Chambers, June 2, 1917, NA, Canada, RG 6-E T/101.

49. Imperial Consul General for Japan in Ottawa to Chambers, June 5, 1917, NA, Canada, RG 6-E/620, folder 331, part 1.

50. Elizabeth A. Tancock, "Secret Trains across Canada, 1917–1918," 39–43.

51. Memo from W. D. Scott, Superintendent Of Immigration to General Sir Eugene Fiset, Department of Militia and Defense, Ottawa, July 24, 1917, NA, Canada, RG 24/2553, HQC 2115.

52. Instructions concerning special guards, CMPC for Chinese laborers, NA, Canada, RG 24/3771, 1048–45–11, 1.

53. Elizabeth Tancock, "Secret Trains across Canada, 1917–1918," 39–43.

54. Bourne to the Minister of Militia, December 17, 1917, NA, Canada, RG 3768/1048–45–2, 10.

55. Medical officer's report, September 15, 1917, NA, Canada, RG 3768, 1048–45–2/10.

56. Bourne to the Minister of Militia, December 17, 1917, NA, Canada, RG 3768, 1048–45–2/10.

57. Captain Wood Diary, entry of November 2, 1917.

58. Surgeon General, Deputy Minister of Milita Eugene Fiset, Ottawa, to E. J. Bourne, Weihaiwei, April 22, 1918, NA, Canada, RG 24/3769, 1048–45–2/12.

59. W. D. Scott, Superintendent of Immigration, to Colonel MacInnes of the Canadian military, September 27, 1917, NA, Canada, RG 24/2553, HQC 2115.

60. Assistant General Passenger Agent, Canadian Pacific Railway Company, to Lt. Colonel C. S. MacInnes, October 1, 1917, NA, Canada, RG 24/2553, HQC 2115.

61. Major General, internal memo, October 2, 1917, NA, Canada, RG 24/2553, HQC 2115.

62. C. S. MacInnes, internal military memo, October 2, 1917, NA, Canada, RG 24/2553, HQC 2115.

63. C. S. MacInnes to Maughan, Assistant CPR General Passenger Agent, October 5, 1917, NA, Canada, RG 24/2553, HQC 2115.

64. C. S. MacInnes to Inspector General of Western Canada, October 1917, NA, Canada, RG 24/2553, HQC 2115.

65. Chambers to General Gwatkin, April 19, 1917, NA, Canada, RG 6-E/620, folder 331, part 1.

66. Gwatkin to Chambers, April 20, 1917, NA, Canada, RG 6-E/620, folder 331, part 1.

67. Military memo on transportation of coolies, September 15, 1919, NA, Canada, RG 24/4324, 34–1–171.

68. Memo from Department Of Militia and Defense to the High Commissioner for Canada of Britain, July 8, 1918, NA, Canada, RG 25 A-2/229, M60/23-M61/23.

69. "Chinese Coolies Riot at Victoria," 17.

70. "Chinese Labour in Canada," *Times* (London), June 7, 1923, 13.

71. "Chinese Welcomed by Men and Women of St. John," *Halifax Herald,* February 11, 1920, 2.

72. Ibid.

73. Ibid., 5.

74. Ibid., 2.

75. Ibid.

76. Ibid.

77. "Great Events Which Pass Unnoticed," *Halifax Herald,* February 17, 1920, 15.

78. "The Chinese Troops Heard the Strange, Mellow Songs of Their Homeland as They Disembarked from the *Bohemian,*" *Halifax Herald,* February 16, 1920, 11.

79. Klein, *With the Chinks,* 29.

## 4. Work

1. Lewis, *China's Great Convulsion,* 146.

2. Ibid.

3. "Le Ministre de Guerre Messiurs les Commandants de Groupements de Travailleurs Coloniaux," Paris, December 22, 1916, Vincennes, 16N 2450/6h/98/9.

4. Controller of Labour to the Quartermaster General, Report of Labour with the BEF during the war, November 14, 1919, Appendix C: Notes for Guidance of Officers of Labour Corps in France, September 1918, NA, Kew, WO 107/37, 68.

5. Compared with other troops, the Chinese committed far fewer crimes. During World War I, among British and Commonwealth military forces, 3,080 men were sentenced to death. Twenty-eight soldiers of the New Zealand Expeditionary Forces were among the number sentenced to death. Some 2009 New Zealanders were convicted by courts martial; this is in the context of 100,444 men and women who served overseas in New Zealand forces, roughly the same number of Chinese under Britain. But the New Zealanders were not worse compared with others. The percentage of New Zealand courts martial to troops in theatre was less than one-third that of the Australian rate and half that of the Canadian rate. For details, see Christopher Pugsley, *On the Fringe of Hell,* 7, 300.

6. W. A. Dent Diary, October 31, 1917, LC, Leeds, GS 0453.

7. Ibid., September 17, 1917.

8. General routine orders, no. 285, December 11, 1918, NA, Canada, RG 24/1833/G. A .Q, 8–36.

9. Ibid., February 11, 1918.

10. Directorate of Labour: Notes for Officers of Labour Companies, issued by General Headquarters, April 2, 1917, IWM Misc 214 Item 3104: Report on the Administration of labour in XVII Corps, February 1917–February 1918.

11. Controller of Labour to the Quartermaster General, Report of Labour with the BEF during the war, November 14, 1919, Appendix C: Notes for Guidance of Officers of Labour Corps in France, September 1918, NA, Kew, WO 107/37, 72.

12. General routine orders, February 11, 1918, NA, Canada, RG 24/ 1833/G. A .Q, 8–36.

13. General routine orders, the handbook, 6–7, February 11, 1918, NA, Canada, RG 24/1833/G. A .Q, 8–36.

14. Controller of Labour to the Quartermaster General, Report of Labour with the BEF during the war, November 14, 1919, NA, Kew, WO 107/37, 47.

15. Second Lieutenant John M. Harrison, "The Great War: Private Harrison and the Chinese," typed memoir, IWM, 06/92/1.

16. Controller of Labour to the Quartermaster General, Report of Labour with the BEF during the war, November 14, 1919, NA, Kew, WO 107/37, 52.

17. Ibid., 55.

18. Directorate of Labour War Diary, October 1917, NA, Kew, WO 95/83.

19. The handbook can be found in the Major W. A. Dent file, LC, Leeds, GS 0453, box 1. For the quote, see the handbook preface, 4–5.

20. Controller of Labour to the Quartermaster General, Report of Labour with the BEF during the war, November 14, 1919, Appendix C: Notes for Guidance of Officers of Labour Corps in France, September 1918, NA, Kew, WO 107/37, 60–61.

21. Ibid., 50.

22. Ibid., 45.

23. Ibid., 25.

24. Directorate of Labour War Diary, October 1917, NA, Kew, WO 95/83.

25. S. F. Hopwood Diary, entry September 5, 1917, 91, LC, Leeds GS 0796; W. A. Dent Diary, October 31, 1917. LC, Leeds, GS 0453.

26. W. J. Shaw Diary, LC, Leeds.

27. Douglas Wilson, "Flanders Fling, a 1918 episode" [memoir based on his letters and diary, in typed format], LC, Leeds, GS 1761, 24A.

28. T. V. Haigh Diary, entry of September 1, 1917, LC, Leeds, GS 0684.

29. Captain A. McCormick files: typed draft memoir, IWM 02/6/1, 131–132.

30. Brigadier General W. R. Ludlow Diary, entry of August 30, 1917, LC, Leeds, GS0984.

31. "Aircraft attack on Dunkerque on the night of 4th and 5th September 1917," NA, Kew, WO 95/83.

32. H. E. Cornwall files, IWM 06/70/1, 18–19.

33. Laurence Salisbury, "Chinese Coolies and the War," *Saturday Evening Post*, October 25, 1919, 130.

34. Li Jun, "First Report on the Chinese Laborers under the French," December 4, 1917, and "Second Report on the Chinese Laborers under the French," June 10, 1918, in *Ouzhan Huagong shiliao*, 352–59, 379–392.

35. "The Chinese Laborers in France in Relation to the Work of the Young Men's Christian Association: Report to the International Committee of Young Men's Christian Association of North America of Special Mission of Dwight W. Edwards in France April 13–May 11, 1918," YMCA Archives, box 204, folder: report 1919.

36. Controller of Labour, Notes on Chinese Labour, August 2, 1918, NA, Kew, WO 95/83.

37. Captain A. McCormick files: typed draft memoir, IWM 02/6/1, 209.

38. Controller of Labour to the Quartermaster General, Report of Labour with the BEF during the war, November 14, 1919, Appendix C: Notes for Guidance of Officers of Labour Corps in France, September 1918, NA, Kew, WO 107/37, 4.

39. G. H. Cole, "With the Chinese in France," YMCA Archives, box 204, folder: Chinese laborers in France reports, 1918–1919.

40. "The C.L.C.: With the Coolie from China to France," *Times* (London), April 23, 1919, 14.

41. G. H. Cole, "With the Chinese in France," YMCA Archives, box 204, folder: Chinese laborers in France reports, 1918–1919.

42. Captain A. McCormick files: typed draft memoir, IWM 02/6/1, 206.

43. Letter extract from an officer with the Chinese coolies in France, NA, Kew, FO 228/2894.

44. Fussell, *Great War and Modern Memory*, 37.

45. YMCA, *Young Men's Christian Association with the Chinese Labor Corps in France*, YMCA Archives, box 204, folder: Chinese laborers in France, 14.

46. Directorate of Labour War Diary, October 18, 1917 [document signed by Brigadier General E. Gibb, Director of Labour], NA, Kew, WO 95/83.

47. Scott, "Chinese in France in WW I," 8–11.

48. Fred Sayer, "No Tea—No Workee!" Western Front Association *Bulletin* 25 (1989): 15.

49. Brigadier General W. R. Ludlow Diary, entry of September 29, 1917, LC, Leeds, GS 0984.

50. Controller of Labour to the Quartermaster General, Report of Labour with the BEF during the war, November 14, 1919, NA, Kew, WO 107/37, 51.

51. Directorate of Labour War Diary, October 1917, NA, Kew, WO 95/83.

52. Controller of Labour War Diary, July 1918, NA, Kew, WO 95/83.

53. Controller of Labour to the Quartermaster General, Report of Labour with the BEF during the war, November 14, 1919, Appendix K: Memorandum Showing the Steps Taken to Apply the Skilled Chinese Tradesmen to Suitable Work, NA, Kew, WO 107/37.

54. Anonymous, "Central Stores & Workshops" (believed to be written by Lieutenant Colonel John Brockbank), Tank Museum, UK, E 2006. 1703.

55. David J. Childs, *A Peripheral Weapon? The Production and Employment of British Tanks in the First World War* (Westport, Conn.: Greenwood Press, 1999), 67.

56. Controller of Labour to the Quartermaster General, Report of Labour with the BEF during the war, November 14, 1919, Appendix K: Memorandum Showing the Steps Taken to Apply the Skilled Chinese Tradesmen to Suitable Work, NA, Kew, WO 107/37.

57. Childs, *A Peripheral Weapon?*, 65

58. "An Army of Labour," *Times* (London), December 27, 1917, 8.

59. De Lapomarede to Commander-in-Chief of the French Army, Beijing, April, 1916, Vincennes, 16N 2912/Chine.

60. General Foch's secret report to the Prime Minister, August 11, 1917, Vincennes, 16N 2450/GQG/6498.

61. Gondre report, May 26, 1918, Vincennes, 18N 107.

62. General Taufflieb report, June 27, 1918, Vincennes, 18N 207.

63. "Story of the Chinese Labor Corps," *Far Eastern Review* (Shanghai) 15, no. 4 (April 1918): 126.

64. "Au Sujet de l'Emploi de la Main–d'Oeuvre Chinoise dans les Ports," July 18, 1917, Paris, Archive Nationale, 14F/11331, 12/E/Sous–Secretary des Transports.

65. War Office report, December 31, 1918, NA, Kew, WO 106/33.

66. YMCA, *Young Men's Christian Association with the Chinese Labor Corps in France,* YMCA Archives, box 204, folder: Chinese laborers in France; Conference of Workers Reports, Report of Conference of Workers Held at Peronne on July 23–24, 1919.

67. Wakefield report, NA, Kew, WO 106/33.

68. YMCA, *Young Men's Christian Association with the Chinese Labor Corps in France,* YMCA Archives, box 204, folder: Chinese laborers in France, 14–15.

69. Ibid., 15.

70. Ibid.

71. "London Is Learning Who Held Back Foe," *New York Times,* April 3, 1918, 3.

72. T. Tarlson Diary, entry of October 16, 1918. LC, Leeds, GS 1569.

73. Sir Alwyne Ogden files: Chinese Labor Corps (handwriting materials), LC, Leeds, chap. 3, 5.

74. "Fa guo huagong jin kuang," *Qinghua Zhoukan* 168 (May 3, 1919): 29.

75. A total of 9,796 medals were returned by the postal service because the men no longer lived at the addresses they had listed when they signed up for work in France. William Bull to Alston, October 15, 1921, NA, Kew, FO 228/2896.

76. Vice-Consul Archer to Sir Beilby Alston, enclosure, P. G. no. 31 of June 13th 1921, NA, Kew, FO 228/2896.

77. Consul-General in Tianjin, W. P. Ker to Alston, July 25, 1921, NA, Kew, FO 228/2896.

78. William Bull to consul-general in Tianjin, April 2, 1921, NA, Kew, FO 228/2896.

79. William Bull to J. T. Pratt, February 28, 1921, NA, Kew, FO 228/2895.

80. William Bull to the post commissioner, Hangzhou, March 10, 1921, NA, Kew, FO 228/2896.

81. *Current History Magazine,* October 1919–March 1920, 525.

82. "Huagong Jin kuang," *Huagong Zhoubao,* no. 5 (February 19, 1919).

83. "Fen yong ke jia," *Huagong zazhi,* no. 24 (July 25, 1918), 20.

84. YMCA, *Young Men's Christian Association with the Chinese Labor Corps in France,* YMCA Archives, box 204, folder: Chinese laborers in France, 16.

85. *Current History Magazine,* October 1919–March 1920, 525.

86. "Guo wu yuan qiao gong shi wu ju diao cha zai fa huagong qing xing shu: di yi ci pi lu," *Xin Zhongguo* (November 1918), 202.

87. Laurence Salisbury, "Chinese Coolies and the War," *Saturday Evening Post,* October 25, 1919, 130.

88. Brigadier General W. R Ludlow Diary, entry of November 22, 1917, LC, Leeds, GS 0984.

89. Captain A. McCormick files: typed draft memoir, IWM 02/6/1, 209.

90. *Current History Magazine,* October 1919–March 1920, 525.

91. Angus Wilson, *Late Call,* 261.

92. I. H. Shi, "With the Chinese Laborers," 447–452.

93. "Huagong zhi ce yin xin," *Huagong Zazhi,* no. 24 (July 25, 1918): 24.

94. R. M. Hersey to the International committee of the YMCA, Annual report letter, 1919, Yale University Divinity School Library Special Collections, John Hersey Papers, RG 145; G. H. Cole, "With the Chinese in France," YMCA Archives, box 204, folder: Chinese laborers in France reports, 1918–1919.

95. Vincennes, 7N 1297/Chinois Evacuation.

96. Donald Smythe, *Pershing, General of the Armies* (Bloomington: Indiana University Press, 2007), 246.

97. Dominiek Dendooven, "Living Apart Together: Belgian Witness Accounts of the Chinese Labour Corps," paper presented to international conference on Chinese labor corps during the Great War, Weihai, Shandong, China, September 2008, Author's collection, 1–11.

98. Piet Chielens and Julian Putkowski, *Unquiet Graves: Execution Sites of the First World War in Flanders* (London: Francis Boutle, 2000), 42.

99. W. W. Peter, Occasional report, YMCA Archives, box 204, folder: Chinese laborers in France, 1918–1919.

100. *Lu Ou Zhoukan,* December 20, 1919, 4.

101. Ibid., December 27, 1919, 3.

102. Ibid., March 12, 1920, 3.

103. YMCA, *Young Men's Christian Association with the Chinese Labor Corps in France,* YMCA Archives, box 204, folder: Chinese laborers in France, 6.

104. T. S. Eliot, *The Waste Land and Other Poems* (New York: Harvest Books, 1962), 29.

105. Lewis, *China's Great Convulsion,* 113.

106. G. H. Cole, "With the Chinese in France," YMCA Archives, box 204, folder: Chinese laborers in France reports, 1918–1919.

107. Second Lieutenant John M. Harrison, "The Great War: Private Harrison and the Chinese," typed memoir, IWM 06/92/1.

108. Captain A. McCormick files: typed draft memoir, IWM 02/6/1, 209.

109. Charles Ward interview files, IWM catalogue 12026, 14897.

110. "General Statement Regarding the YMCA Work for the Chinese in France," March 1919, YMCA Archives, box 204, folder: Chinese laborers in France reports, 1918–1919.

111. Gu Xingqing, *Ouzhan gongzuo huiyi lu* [Recollections on My Experiences with Chinese Laborers in World War I] (Shanghai: Shangwu Yinshuguan, 1937), 45. See also Wou Pen-chung, *Travailleurs Chinois et La Grande Guerre* (Paris: Editions A. Pedone, 1939), 13.

112. Judith Blick, "The Chinese Labor Corps in World War I," *Papers on China* (from Harvard East Asia Regional Studies Seminar) 9 (1955): 123.

113. Ta Chen, *Chinese Migrations,* 152.

114. Feng Gang et al., *Sanshui Liang Yansun xiansheng nianpu,* 1:446.

115. Li Huang, *Xue Dunshi huiyilu* (Taipei: Zhuanji wenxue chubanshe, 1973), 58.

116. Yuan Li and Chen Dazhang, *Haiwai Huaren ji qi juzhu di gaikuang* (Beijing: Zhongguo Huaqiao chuban gongsi, 1991), 273.

117. Emigration Agency, October 9, 1919, NA, Kew, FO 371/3682, 125.

118. British Parliamentary meeting minutes, December 10, 1919, NA, Kew, FO371/3682, 154.

119. War Office Representative G. S. Moss, Report on the Demobilization of the Chinese Labor Corps, October 31, 1920, NA, Kew, FO 228/2895.

120. "1918 nian shou zhu ying Shi gong shi dian," China No. 2 Archives, 1050–1: "Diao cha ou zhan hou hua ren bei hai zong an."

121. "Lun dun zong ling shi Cao Yunxiang bao gao, December 5, 1918," China No. 2 Archives, 1050–1: "Diao cha ou zhan hou hua ren bei hai zong an."

122. Waijiaobu, "Shou zhu ying gong shi dian," December 7, 1918, China No. 2 Archives, 03–36/4-(5).

123. "Wei yuan Guo Zefan bao gao, December 22, 1918," China No. 2 Archives, 1050–1: "Diao cha ou zhan hou hua ren bei hai zong an."

124. Dendooven, "Multicultural War in Flanders," 377–389. 380.

125. British Parliamentary meeting minutes, December 10, 1919, NA, Kew, FO 371/3682, 154.

126. *Ouzhan Huagong shiliao,* 50.

127. Balfour to Curzon, May 8 1919, in E. L. Woodward, ed., *Documents on British Foreign Policy, 1919–1939* (London: H. M. Stationery Office, 1946), Series 1, 6:565–66.

128. Ellen N. La Motte, *Peking Dust* (New York: Century Co., 1919), 240. So far, there is no scientific evidence to suggest that the Chinese brought the virus to Europe. As a matter of fact, although from 20 million to 100 million died from the 1918 flu, to the present day, nobody really knows for sure how it started and where it came from. For details, see Gina B. Kolata, *Flu: The Story of the Great Influenza Pandemic of 1918 and the Search for the Virus That Caused It* (New York: Farrar, Straus and Giroux, 1999); and Alfred W. Crosby Jr., *Epidemic and Peace, 1918* (Westport, Conn.: Greenwood Press, 1976). This book was later published by Cambridge University Press in 1989 under a different name). For other studies, see Mark J. Gibbs, "Recombination in the Hemagglutinin Gene of 1918 'Spanish Flu,'" *Science* 293, no. 5536 (2001): 1842–1845; and John Pickrell, "The 1918 Pandemic: Killer Flu with a Human-Pig Pedigree?" *Science* 292, no. 5519 (2001): 1041.

129. Ta Chen, *Chinese Migrations,* 156.

130. Lynn Pan, *Sons of the Yellow Emperor: The Story of the Overseas Chinese* (Boson: Little, Brown, 1990), 82. See also Lynn Pan, ed., *The Encyclopedia of the Chinese Overseas* (Cambridge, Mass.: Harvard University Press, 1999), 311.

131. Tyler Stovall, "National Identity and Shifting Imperial Frontiers: Whiteness and the Exclusion of Colonial Labor after World War I," *Representations* 84 (Autumn 2003): 59–60.

## 5. Treatment and Perceptions

1. V. G. Kiernan, *The Lords of Human Kind: Black Man, Yellow Man, and White Man in an Age of Empire* (New York: Columbia University Press, 1986), 153.

2. Griffin, *Use of Chinese Labour,* 14.

3. Albert Grundlingh, *Fighting Their Own War: South African Blacks and the First World War* (Johannesburg: Raven Press, 1987), 100–114.

4. "An Army of Labour," *Times* (London), December 27, 1917, 8.

5. Klein, *With the Chinks,* vii.

6. Ibid., viii.

7. Ibid., 14–15.

8. Ibid., 97.

9. Summerscale, *Queen of Whale Cay,* 51.

10. Dolly Shepherd interviews, IWM Sound Archives Catalogue, 579–610.

11. John Grainger interviews, IWM Sound Archives Catalogue, 10768.

12. Major P. H. Pilditch served at Royal Field Artillery during the war. Major P. H. Pilditch Diary, entry November 28, 1917, 490, LC, Leeds, GS 1268.

13. P. E. Ogley was a private serving with the Yorkshire and Lancashire Regiment. P. E. Ogley handwritten memoirs (including letters), LC, Leeds, GS 1200, book 2, 26.

14. Percival Gardner-Smith's letter to his wife, November 5, 1918, LC, Leeds, Air 130.

15. Percival Gardner-Smith's letter to his wife, November 1, 1918, LC, Leeds, Air 130.

16. T. O. Wilkins Diary, entry of November 19, 1917, LC, Leeds, Air 351.

17. "General Statement Regarding the YMCA Work for the Chinese in France," March 1919, YMCA Archives, box 204, folder: Chinese laborers in France reports, 1918–1919.Archives,

18. Captain A. McCormick files: typed draft memoir, 126–130, IWM 02/6/1.

19. James Hamilton-Paterson, "Chinese Dig Britain's Trenches," *Sunday Times* (London), April 30, 1972.

20. A. W. Paton, *Occasional Gunfire: Private War Diary of a Siege Gunner* (London: Bishop-Laggett, 1998), 121.

21. "Proclamation by Purdon to All Chinese Labourers under British Armies in France," June 16, 1919, Vincennes, 7N 1297.

22. Notes on Chinese Labour, August 2, 1918, NA, Kew, WO 107/37.

23. Controller of Labour to the Quartermaster General, Report of Labour with the BEF during the War, November 14, 1919, Appendix C: Notes for Guidance of Officers of Labour Corps in France, September 1918, NA, Kew, WO 107/37, 4.

24. Marius Moutet, "Preface," in P. Wou, *Les Travailleurs Chinois et la Grande Guerre* (Paris: Editions A. Pedone, 1939), 7.

25. Cornabe Eckford letter to Bourne, December 29, 1917, Chinese Labour Corps, NA, Kew, FO 288/2892.

26. *Current History Magazine,* October 1919–March 1920, 523.

27. Colonel C. D. Gray confidential letter, January 1, 1918, NA, Kew, FO 371/3178.

28. Draft telegram from British legation to Foreign Office, May 23, 1921, NA, Kew, FO 228/2896.

29. Colonel C. D. Gray confidential letter, January 1, 1918, NA, Kew, FO 371/3178.

30. Brigadier General W. R. Ludlow Diary, entries of November 19, 1917, and December 12, 1917, LC, Leeds, GS 0984.

31. J. T. Pratt to John Jordan, April 28, 1918, NA, Kew, FO 228/2893.

32. Commanding Officer of the Chinese Labour Corps to Director of Labour in General Headquarters, December 25, 1917, NA, Kew, WO 106/33.

33. J. C., "With the 'Chinks' in France," *The War Illustrated,* November 9, 1918, 205.

34. "The Chinese Laborers in France in Relation to the Work of the Young Men's Christian Association: Report to the International Committee of Young Men's Christian Association of North America of Special Mission of Dwight W. Edwards in France April 13–May 11, 1918," YMCA Archives, box 204, folder: report 1919.

35. Ibid.

36. Ibid.

37. Laurence Salisbury, "Chinese Coolies and the War," *Saturday Evening Post,* October 25, 1919, 130.

38. Notes on Chinese Labour, August 2, 1918, NA, Kew, WO 107/37, 2.

39. Ibid., 4.

40. "General R. Ford Report," September 18, 1919, NA, Kew, PRO, FO 371/3682, 144.

41. War Office document, May 25, 1917, NA, Kew, FO 370/2906.

42. Note from J. B. Wroughton, Headquarters of British Troops in France and Flanders, July 17, 1919, Vincennes, 7N 1297/Chinese Evacuation.

43. Notes on Chinese Labour, August 2, 1918, NA, Kew, WO 107/37.

44. T. O. Wilkins Diary, entry of January 24, 1918, LC, Leeds, Air 351; see also David H. Doe file, IWM, catalogue 12171, 326.

45. Brigadier General W. R. Ludlow Diary, entry of December 26, 1917, LC, Leeds, GS 0984.

46. Ibid., December 28, 1917.

47. J. C. Dunn, *The War the Infantry Knew, 1914–1919: A Chronicle of Service in France and Belgium with the Second Battalion* (London: P. S. King & Son, 1938), 425–426.

48. Scott, "Chinese in France in WW I," 8–11.

49. Directorate of Labour War Diary, October 1917, NA, Kew, WO 95/83.

50. T. V. Haigh Diary, entry of September 18, 1917, LC, Leeds, GS 0684.

51. W. A. Dent joined the CLC on June 5, 1917, and stayed there until August 14, 1920. W. A. Dent Diary, entries of July 10–12, 1917, LC, Leeds, GS 0453.

52. From the British Troops Headquarters in France and Flanders, October 23, 1919, signed by Burrowes, Vincennes, 7N 2289/Affairs Britanniques/Travailleurs Chinois.

53. General routine orders, no. 209, September 8, 1918, NA, Canada, RG 24/1833, G.A .Q, 8–36.

54. "Guo wu yuan qiao gong shi wu ju diao cha zai fa huagong qing xing shu," second part, *Xin Zhongguo,* 282.

55. Headquarters of British Troops in France and Flanders, July 4, 1919, Vincennes, 7N 2289/Affairs Britanniques/Travailleurs Chinois.

56. Captain A. McCormick files: typed draft memoir, IWM 02/6/1, 210.

57. F. W. Corke was the commanding officer of the No. 41 Chinese labor company. F. W. Corke file: Chinese labor corps, LC, Leeds, GS 0366.

58. G. E. Cormack files: "War Times in Russia," typed memoir, IWM 92/21/1, 19.

59. Brigadier General W. R. Ludlow Diary, entry of September 29, 1917, LC, Leeds, GS 0984.

60. Ibid., December 21, 1917.

61. General routine orders, no. 200, General Headquarters, August 28, 1918, NA, Canada, RG 24/1833, G.A Q, 8–36.

62. W. A. Dent Diary, entry of October 29, 1917, LC, Leeds, GS 0453.

63. W. W. Peter, Occasional report, Chinese YMCA France, YMCA Archives, box 204 folder: Chinese laborers in France reports, 1918–1919.

64. The Chinese general hospital BEF, France, February 25, 1919 report, YMCA Archives, box 204, folder: Chinese laborers in France reports, 1918–1919.

65. Ting Fu-Tsiang, "Chinese Philosophy in France," *Asia* 19, no. 7 (July 1919): 648.

66. *Lu Ou Zhoukan,* February 7, 1920, 3.

67. *Lu Ou Zhoukan,* April 17, 1920, 3–4.

68. "Fa ren you dai huagong zhi yi duan," *Huagong Zazhi,* no. 25 (August 25, 1918): 18.

69. Report of conference of workers held at Peronne on 23/24 July 1919, YMCA Archives, box 204, folder: Chinese laborers in France: conference of workers reports.

70. "The Chinese Laborers in France in Relation to the Work of the Young Men's Christian Association: Report to the International Committee of Young Men's Christian Association of North America of Special Mission of Dwight W. Edwards in France April 13–May 11, 1918," YMCA Archives, box 204, folder: report 1919.

71. Jiang Tingfu (1895–1965), who received a Ph.D. in history from Columbia University, was a professor of history at Nankai and Tsinghua Universities before becoming ambassador to the Soviet Union and later to the United States. The quote is from his "Letter to the United States Bureau of Labor Statistics," October 16, 1922, quoted from Ta Chen, *Chinese Migrations,* 147.

72. *Shi Shi Xin Bao,* December 26, 1920.

73. *Ouzhan Huagong shiliao,* 410.

74. Ibid., 381.

75. "Guo wu yuan qiao gong shi wu ju diao cha zai fa huagong qing xing shu," second part, *Xin Zhongguo,* 283–284.

76. "The Chinese Laborers in France in Relation to the Work of the Young Men's Christian Association: Report to the International Committee of Young Men's Christian Association of North America of Special Mission of Dwight W. Edwards in France April 13–May 11, 1918," YMCA Archives, box 204, folder: report 1919.

77. *Ouzhan Huagong shiliao,* 380–381.

78. General routine orders, no. 166, July 21, 1918, NA, Canada, RG 24/1833, G.A .Q 8–36.

79. "Guo wu yuan qiao gong shi wu ju diao cha zai fa huagong qing xing shu," second part, *Xin Zhongguo,* 288–289.

80. *Ouzhan Huagong shiliao,* 147.

81. Ibid., 155, 171, 177.

82. Ibid., 173–174.

83. Dendooven, "Multicultural War in Flanders," 377–389.

84. Moss to War Office, List of repatriated labourers, March 20, 1020, NA, Kew, FO 228/2895.

85. James Hamilton-Paterson, "Chinese Dig Britain's Trenches," *Sunday Times* (London), April 30, 1972.

86. G. S. Moss to John Jordan, March 13, 1919 NA, Kew, FO 228/2895.

87. G. S. Moss, Report on the Demobilization of the Chinese Labor Corps, October 31, 1920, NA, Kew, FO 228/2895.

88. R. I. Purdon to Moss, private letter, September 24, 1919, NA, Kew, FO 228/2895.

89. G. S. Moss to War Office, May 29, 1919, NA, Kew, FO 228/2895.

90. G. S. Moss to War Office, November 27, 1918, NA, Kew, FO 228/2894.

91. "Returning Chinese," *British Weekly,* January 2, 1919, 225.

92. For details on this point, see Stovall, "Color behind the Lines," 758.

93. Griffin, *Use of Chinese Labour,* 4, 256.

## 6. Strangers in a Strange World

1. G. E. Cormack files, "War Times in Russia" (typed memoir), IWM 92/21/1, 18.

2. Captain A. McCormick files, IWM 02/6/1, 205.

3. Second Lieutenant John M. Harrison, "The Great War: Private Harrison and the Chinese" (typed memoir), IWM, 06/92/1.

4. A. B. W. Fletcher was a British officer serving with the Royal Artillery on the Western Front. A. B. W. Fletcher, BBC Great War Series, IWM Sound Archives Catalogue 4102.

5. G. A. Willis Diary, entry of June 25, 1918, LC, Leeds, GS 1751.

6. Cheng Sih-Gung, *Modern China, a Political Study* (Oxford: Clarendon Press, 1919), 273.

7. Dendooven and Chielens, *World War I,* 142.

8. H. E. Cornwall files, typed memoir, IWM 06/70/1, 19.

9. Letter 628, in David Omissi, *Indian Voices of the Great War,* 342.

10. Captain A. McCormick files, IWM 02/6/1, 207–208.

11. Brigadier General W. R. Ludlow Diary, entries of November 19 and December 6, 1917, LC, Leeds, GS 0984.

12. Auguste Dupouy, "Un Camp de Chinois," *La Revue de Paris,* no. 21 (November 1919): 147–162.

13. I. H. Shi, "With the Chinese Laborers," 447–452.

14. P. E. Ogley memoirs, LC, Leeds, GS 1200, 36–37.

15. Ting Fu-Tsiang, "Chinese Philosophy in France," 645.

16. G. H. Cole, "With the Chinese in France," YMCA Archives, box 204, folder: Chinese laborers in France reports, 1918–1919.

17. A. B. W. Fletcher, BBC Great War Series, IWM Sound Archives Catalogue 4102.

18. "To a Chinese Coolie," *Punch* 156, no. 4050 (February 19, 1919): 150.

19. Captain A. McCormick files, IWM 02/6/1, 207–208.

20. H. S. Innes was a private serving in the 14th Battalion, Royal Fusiliers on the Western Front. H. S. Innes to his mother, September 14, 1917, H. S. Innes letters, LC, Leeds, GS 0833.

21. A. Neville and J. Whymant, "Chinese Coolie Songs," *Bulletin of the School of Oriental Studies* (University of London) 1, no. 4 (1920): 148.

22. Ibid., 145.

23. Second Lieutenant John M. Harrison, "The Great War: Private Harrison and the Chinese" (typed memoir), IWM, 06/92/1.

24. JMM to ABM June 1, 1917, Arthur Menzies family papers.

25. Ibid., December 10, 1917.

26. JMM to mother, December 25, 1918, Arthur Menzies family papers.

27. YMCA, "Yellow Spectacles," YMCA Archives, box 204, folder: Chinese laborers in France report.

28. Mu Lei, "Huagong shi er yue ge," Mu Lei Diary.

29. P. E. Ogley memoirs, LC, Leeds, GS 1200, 36–37.

30. Salisbury, "Chinese Coolies and the War," 130.

31. G. H. Cole, "With the Chinese in France," YMCA Archives, box 204, folder: Chinese laborers in France reports, 1918–1919.

32. W. A. Dent Diary, entry of October 1, 1918, LC, Leeds, GS 0453.

33. War Diary, December, 1918, NA, Kew, WO 95/83.

34. Neville and Whymant, "Chinese Coolie Songs," 146–147.

35. Brigadier General W. R. Ludlow Diary, entry of November 27, 1917, LC, Leeds, GS0984.

36. Major R. D. Oliver, memoirs, IWM Catalogue 11235.

37. David H. Doe files, diary entry of April 16, 1917, IWM Catalogue 12171, 326.

38. War Diary, June 15, 1917, NA, Kew, WO 95/83.

39. Ting Fu-Tsiang, "Chinese Philosophy in France," 645.

40. S. G. C., "Chinese Labour in France," *The Statesman,* January 13, 1917, 343.

41. 9.

42. Fred Sayer, "No Tea—No Workee!" 15.

43. Neville and Whymant, "Chinese Coolie Songs," 151.

44. Ibid., 152.

45. Ibid., 145.

46. Ibid., 158.

47. Ibid., 153.

48. Quote from Dendooven, "Multicultural War in Flanders," 377–389.

49. Dominiek Dendooven, "Living Apart Together: Belgian Witness Accounts of the Chinese Labour Corps," presented to an international conference of Chinese laborers, 2008 (author's collection).

50. Neville and Whymant, "Chinese Coolie Songs," 164.

51. Ibid., 149.

52. P. E. Ogley memoirs, LC, Leeds, GS 1200, 35.

53. Sayer, "No Tea—No Workee!" 21.

54. Klein, *With the Chinks,* 42–43.

55. Captain A. McCormick files, IWM 02/6/1, 207.

56. W. A. Dent Diary, entry of June 18, 1917, LC, Leeds, GS 0453.

57. G. E. Cormack files, "War Times in Russia," IWM 92/21/1, 19–20.

58. Cheng Shih-Gung, *Modern China,* 273.

59. A laborer's letter to his wife, June 24, 1918, IWM, Misc 130 (1999).

60. E. W. Burt, "With the Chinese at Havre," *Missionary Herald* 101, no. 4 (April 1919): 42–43.

61. "Guo qing ri lu fa huagong zhi re nao," *Huagong Zazhi,* no. 27 (October 25, 1917): 23–25.

62. Captain T. C. Thomas, *With a Labour Company in France; Being the War Diary of the 58th Labour Company* (London: Hudson & Son, n.d.), 51.

63. Nicholas J. Saunders, *Trench Art: A Brief History and Guide, 1914–1939* (London: Leo Cooper, 2001), 15.

64. Ibid., 44.

65. Ibid., 66.

66. Ibid.

67. Ibid., 30.

68. Summerscale, *Queen of Whale Cay,* 49.

69. Lewis, *China's Great Convulsion,* 150.

70. Major R. D. Oliver, memoirs, IWM Catalogue 11235.

71. G. E. Cormack files, "War Times in Russia," IWM 92/21/1, 19.

72. Ting Fu-Tsiang, "Chinese Philosophy in France," 647.

73. "The Chinese Laborers in France in Relation to the Work of the Young Men's Christian Association: Report to the International Committee of Young Men's Christian Association of North America of Special Mission of Dwight W. Edwards in France April 13–May 11, 1918," YMCA Archives, box 204, folder: report 1919.

74. I. H. Shi, "With the Chinese Laborers," 449–450.

75. Major R. D. Oliver, memoirs, IWM Catalogue 11235.

76. T. V. Haigh Diary, entry of September 4, 1917, LC, Leeds, GS 0684.

77. I. H. Shi, "With Chinese Laborers," 447–452.

78. Kathleen Charlotte Bottomley, interview, IWM Sound Archives Catalogue 172.

79. *Huagong Zazhi,* no. 24 (July 25, 1918): 23.

80. *Huagong Zazhi,* no. 23 (June 25, 1917): 19.

81. I. H. Shi, "With the Chinese Laborers," 449–450.

82. Ma Chonggan, "Huagong zai fa zhi qing xing," *Yue Han Sheng,* 29, no. 8 (November 1918): 13.

83. *Ouzhan Huagong shiliao,* 380–381.

84. Dominiek Dendooven, "Living Apart Together," 4–5.

85. Chielens and Putkowski, *Unquiet Graves,* 27–28.

86. T. V. Haigh Diary, entry of November 22, 1917, LC, Leeds, GS 0684.

87. Brigadier General W. R Ludlow Diary, entry of November 22, 1917, LC, Leeds, GS 0984.

88. P. E. Ogley, memoirs, LC, Leeds, GS 1200, book 2, 38.

89. Henry Payne [with the Chinese labour corps], "John Chinaman in France: How He Saw and Greeted King George," *Missionary Herald* 101, no. 3 (March 1919): 29–30; V. G. Liernan, "The King and the Chinese Labour Corps," 225.

90. Controller of Labour to the Quartermaster General, Report of Labour with the BEF During the War, November 14, 1919, Appendix C: Notes for Guidance of Officers of Labour Corps in France, September 1918, NA, Kew, WO 107/37, 67.

91. Salisbury, "Chinese Coolies and the War," 130.

92. Chielens and Putkowski, *Unquiet Graves,* 42, 45.

93. For instances, see Li Jun, "The Third Report," in *Ouzhan Huagong shiliao,* 410.

94. I. H. Shi, "With the Chinese Laborers," 449–450.

95. B. B. Cubitt, memo, August 3, 1918, NA, Kew, NSC 9/850.

96. Rules and Regulations: Chinese Labour Corps Savings Bank, NA, Kew: WO 95/83.

97. Burt, "With the Chinese at Havre," 42–43.

98. Ta Chen, *Chinese Migrations,* 154.

99. "The Chinese Laborers in France in Relation to the Work of the Young Men's Christian Association: Report to the International Committee of Young Men's Christian Association of North America of Special Mission of Dwight W. Edwards in France April 13–May 11, 1918," YMCA Archives, box 204, folder: report 1919.

100. Second Lieutenant John M. Harrison, "The Great War: Private Harrison and the Chinese" (typed memoir), IWM, 06/92/1.

101. Letter to C. W. Harvey, April 25, 1918, China Correspondence and Reports, September 1917 to October 1918, YMCA Archives, box 204.

102. Conference of Workers Reports, Report of Conference of Workers Held at Peronne on July 23–24, 1919.

103. I. H. Shi, "With the Chinese Laborers," 447–452.

104. Neville and Whymant, "Chinese Coolie Songs," 165.

105. "The Chinese Laborers in France in Relation to the Work of the Young Men's Christian Association: Report to the International Committee of Young Men's Christian Association of North America of Special Mission of Dwight W. Edwards in France April 13–May 11, 1918," YMCA Archives, box 204, folder: report 1919.

106. I. H. Shi, "With the Chinese Laborers," 449–450.

107. Report, possibly from Mark Wheeler in November 1919, YMCA Archives, box 154, folder China correspondence and reports, November–December 1919, Chinese correspondence and reports, November 1919-July 1920.

108. "The Chinese Laborers in France in Relation to the Work of the Young Men's Christian Association: Report to the International Committee of Young Men's Christian Association of North America of Special Mission of Dwight W. Edwards in France April 13–May 11, 1918," YMCA Archives, box 204, folder: report 1919.

109. Brigadier General W. R. Ludlow Diary, entry of November 16, 1917, LC, Leeds, GS 0984.

110. Smythe, *Pershing, General of the Armies,* 250.

111. Eksteins, *Rites of Spring,* 224.

112. Aubrey Wade, *Gunner on the Western Front* (London: B. T. Batsford, 1959), 101.

113. I. H. Shi, "With the Chinese Laborers," 447–452.

114. Summerscale, *Queen of Whale Cay,* 37.

115. Zhao Shanlin, "Yi zhan qi jian wo zai fa guo ren huagong ji cha de hui yi," in Zhong guo ren min zheng zhi xie shang hui yi tianjin shi wei yuan hui wen shi zi liao wei yuan hui, ed., *Tianjin wen shi zi liao xuan ji,* vol. 69 (Tianjin: Tianjin renmin chubanshe, 1996), 149.

116. *Lu Ou Zhoukan,* November 22, 1919, 3.

117. Jiang Tingfu, *Jiang Tingfu hui yi lu* (Taipei: Zhuanji wenxue chubanshe, 1979), 70–71.

118. *Huagong Zazhi,* no. 31 (February 25, 1919): 23.

119. For details on Zhang's story, see Christian Tchang, "Papa Etait Chinois, Maman Berrichonne," unpublished family stories and photo collections (private collection).

120. John Horne, "Immigrant Workers in France during World War I," *French Historical Studies* 14, no. 1 (1985): 85.

121. Wu Xiangxiang, *Yan Yangchu zhuan: wei quan qiu xiang cun gai zao fen dou liu shi nian* (Taipei: Shi bao wen hua chu ban shi ye you xian gong si, 1981), 243.

122. *Lu Ou Zhoukan,* December 6, 1919, 3.

123. "Bao zai lu fa huagong zhuang kuang zhi shi shi," *Huagong Zazhi,* no. 29 (December 25, 1918): 15–16.

124. Dominiek Dendooven, "Living Apart Together." 8.

## 7. American Soldiers and Chinese Laborers

1. Peter Liddle, J. M. Bourne, and Ian R. Whitehead, *The Great World War, 1914–45,* 156–157.

2. Smythe, *Pershing,* 65.

3. Marcosson, *S.O.S.,* 22.

4. John Price Jackson to officers of the Labor Bureau, Army Service Corps, December 10, 1918, NA, RG 120, entry 1764, box 318.

5. General Headquarters Commander-in-Chief Reports, NA, RG 120, entry 1748, box 31, folder 312: Historical report of the Labor Bureau.

6. Charles G. Dawes, *A Journal of the Great War,* 72.

7. Correspondence of the Labor Bureau, folder 31: Memo from American headquarters to Minister of War, France, February 15, 1918, NA, RG 120, entry 1758, box 110.

8. NA, RG 120, entry 1767, box 117.

9. Chief of Labor Bureau to Section Representative, May 1, 1919, NA, RG 120, entry 1748, box 53, folder 230.14.

10. William H. Taft and Frederick M. Harris, *Service with Fighting Men: An Account of the Work of the American Young Men's Christian Associations in the World War* (New York: Association Press, 1922), 2:364.

11. James J. Cooke, *Pershing and His Generals: Command and Staff in the AEF* (Westport, Conn.: Praeger, 1997), 54.

12. General Headquarters Commander-in-Chief Reports, NA, RG 120, entry 1748, box 31, folder 312: Historical report of the Labor Bureau.

13. John P. Jackson, *Some Industrial Problems* (Dijon: Imp. R. de Thorey, 1919), 7.

14. Johnson Hagood, *The Services of Supply: A Memoir of the Great War* (Boston: Houghton Mifflin, 1927), 275–276.

15. John Price Jackson to C. O. Rimaucourt (through chief engineer section), June 14, 1918. NA, RG 120, entry 1760, box 107, folder Miss., class A.

16. John Price Jackson to C. O. Rimaucourt (through chief engineer section), June 14, 1918. NA, RG 120, entry 1760, box 107, folder Miss., class A.

17. "The Chinese Laborers in France in Relation to the Work of the Young Men's Christian Association: Report to the International Committee of Young Men's Christian Association of North America of Special Mission of Dwight W. Edwards in France April 13–May 11, 1918," YMCA Archives, box 204, folder: report 1919.

18. General Headquarters Commander-in-Chief Reports, NA, RG 120, entry 1748, box 31, folder 312: Historical report of the Labor Bureau.

19. Charles G. Dawes to general purchasing agent, Commanding general, S.O.S, Subject: Control of Chinese workmen by French Government, May 29, 1918, NA, RG 120, entry 1748, box 53, folder 230.14.

20. Charles G. Dawes to Commanding general, Subject: treatment of Chinese workers, May 29, 1918, NA, RG 120, entry 1748, box 53, folder 230.14.

21. Letter from adjutant general, L. H. Bash, dated March 22, 1918, NA, RG 120, entry 1759, box 124, folder 250.

22. James T. Isbister, 2nd Lieut. A. S. C, to chief, Labor bureau, Army Service Corps, A.P.S.#717, March 17, 1919, Subject: Working days of North Chinese Laborers, NA, RG 120, entry 1748, box 60.

23. Charles G. Dawes memo on treatment of Chinese, May 31, 1918, NA, RG 120, entry 1748, box 53, folder 230.14.

24. Le Sous Secrétaire d'État de l'Administration Général to Monsieur le Chef de la Section Française de l'Office Central des Relations Franco-Americaine, Paris, June 26, 1918. NA, RG 120, entry 1759, box 125, folder 331.4.

25. From G.P.A. Labor Bureau to C.O. Mehun, Subject: Separate mess for Chinese at Mehun, NA, RG 120, entry 1759, box 125, folder 331.4.

26. Lieutenant Colonel Mouries to commanding general, 9th region, Tours, May 15, 1918, NA, RG 120, entry 1758, box 112, correspondence of the Labor Bureau, folder 97.

27. H. C. Smither, Assistant chief of staff, G-4, to general purchasing agent, Subject: Complaints against treatment afforded Chinese labor, May 16, 1918, NA, RG 120, entry 1758, box 112, correspondence of the Labor Bureau, folder 97.

28. Commanding General, S.O.S., to general purchasing agent, Paris, July 25, 1918, RG 120, entry 1758, box 112, correspondence of the Labor Bureau, folder 97.

29. Jackson to Commandant Varaigne, Chief, Franco-American Mission, October 11, 1918, NA, RG 120, entry 1748, box 53, folder 230.14.

30. John P. Jackson to C. O. Camp Montoir, July 6, 1918, NA, RG 120, entry 1748, box 53, folder 230.14.

31. Frank E. Estes to Major Jackson, May 7, 1918. NA, RG 120, entry 1748, box 53, folder 230.14.

32. From chief, Labor Bureau, A.S.O. A.P.O.#717 to Commandant Varsigne, Franco-American Mission, April 1, 1919, NA, RG 120, entry 1748, box 60.

33. Memo from Service de L'Organisation des Travailleurs coloniaux, Ministre de la Guerre to Monsieur le Chef de la Mission Francaise du Commissariat general pres les Services Americains de Paris, April 10, 1919, NA, RG 120, entry 1748, box 60.

34. Frank E. Estes to section representative, A.S.C, April 24, 1919, NA, RG 120, entry 1748, box 60.

35. Correspondence of the Labor Bureau, NA, RG 120, entry 1758, box 114, folder 150.

36. Correspondence of John Price Jackson, May 31, 1918, NA, RG 120, entry 1760, box 108, folder: daily reading files, letters.

37. G. T. Perkins to C. O. 482nd Aero construction Squadron, Trampot, Vosges, Subject: Discipline of foreign laborers loaned by the French government to the American army, NA, RG 120, entry 1758, box 115, folder: Royce Hancock. See also memo from Adjutant General G. T. Perkins, July 29, 1918 on discipline of Chinese loaned by the French to American army, NA, RG 120, entry 1759, box 124, folder 250.1.

38. S. H. Wellman to Major Estes, January 17, 1919, NA, RG 120, entry 1748, box 54, folder 230.3.

39. Commandant Varaigne to Colonel Dawes, June 5, 1918, NA, RG 120 entry 1748, box 56, folder 230.36.

40. Boschetti to American Labor Bureau, June 2, 1918, NA, RG 120, entry 1748, box 56, folder 230.36.

41. John Price Jackson to Commandant Varaigne, October 3, 1918, Subject: Movement of Chinese laborers, NA, RG 120, entry 1748, box 55, folder 230.36.

42. Memo to the general purchasing agent, July 15, 1918, NA, RG 120, entry 1758, box 114, Correspondence of the Labor Bureau, folder 174.

43. "Wu tan bian yi," *Huagong Zazhi,* no. 25 (August 25, 1918): 21.

44. "General Statement Regarding the YMCA Work for the Chinese in France," March 1919, YMCA Archives, box 204, folder: Chinese laborers in France reports, 1918–1919.

45. Memo from CO Chinese labor CO. 1 and 3, June 6, 1918, Correspondence of the Labor Bureau, NA, RG 120, entry 1758, box 114, folder 174.

46. Correspondence of the Labor Bureau, NA, RG 120, entry 1758, box 114, folder 175.

47. Correspondence of the Labor Bureau, memo from Capt. Ashley Herron to Labor Bureau, Subject: Pay for Chinese laborers, May 4, 1918, NA, RG 120, entry 1758, box 114, folder 177.

48. Memo from John Price Jackson to Capt. J. O. J. Shellenberger, Subject: Forwarding of laborers, July 22, 1918, NA, RG 120, entry 1748, box 57, folder 230.36.

49. Memo from William C. Anderson to Labor Bureau, Subject: Clothing drawn for Chinese laborers, records of AEF–WW I organization records, Army Service Corps, NA, RG 120, entry 1748, box 29, file 132.3–160.

50. Jackson to Commandant Variaigne, chief Franco-American mission, Subject: Chinese rations, date July 19, 1918, Correspondence of John Price Jackson, NA, RG 120, entry 1760, box 108.

51. William A. Kaufman to Labor Bureau, April 27, 1918, NA, RG 120, entry 1758, box 111, folder 68.

52. Memo from Sergeant S. M. Semple to chief of Labor Bureau, September 9, 1918, Subject: Pay for Chinese laborers, NA, RG 120, entry 1759, box 124, folder 248.45.

53. J. Smith, Jr. memo for Captain Honor, May 16, 1918, Records of AEF–WW I Correspondence of Labor Bureau, February-August, 1918, NA, RG 120, entry 1758, box 115, folder: hospital charges.

54. William Kaufman to John Price Jackson, March 9, 1918, NA, RG 120, entry 1758, box 111, folder 68.

55. Robert Bates to Labor Bureau, April 19, 1918, NA, RG 120, entry 1758, box 112, folder: 113 Major Bates.

56. Letter from Sgt. J. B. Greenwood, NA, RG 120, entry 1759, box 122, folder 230.43.

57. Officer interpreter Bernard Desouches to Major Bates, Post commander, April 18, 1918, NA, RG 120, entry 1758, box 112, folder: 113 Major Bates.

58. Kaufman to Frank E. Estes, April 4, 1918, NA, RG 120, entry 1758, box 111, folder 68.

59. Captain Ashley M. Herron to Major Jackson, chief of Labor Bureau, April 10, 1918, NA, RG 120, entry 1758, box 110, folder 32.

60. "Qiao fa huagong yu mei guo ren zhi hu zhu," *Nu Duo Bao* (no date and issue number available), 46; Bai Jiao, "Shi jie da zhan zhong zhi huagong," part 2, *Ren Wen Yue Kan* 8, no. 3 (April 15, 1937): 30.

61. John F. Lewis, *China's Great Convulsion*, 145–146.

62. William Kaufman to John Price Jackson, March 27, 1918, NA, RG 120, entry 1758, box 110, folder 32.

63. "A Cup of Tea and a Riot," *Association Men* 44, no. 5 (January 1919): 375; see also Taft and Harris, *Service with Fighting Men*, 2:365.

64. Walter Scott Elliott, "Wang Gin-Guay," *Association Men* 47 (12) (August 1922): 537.

65. Ibid.

66. "The Chinese Laborers in France in Relation to the Work of the Young Men's Christian Association: Report to the International Committee of Young Men's Christian Association of North America of Special Mission of Dwight

W. Edwards in France April 13–May 11, 1918," YMCA Archives, box 204, folder: report 1919.

67. Chen Baoyu, "Wo ceng zai ou zhou dang huagong," in Zhong guo ren min zheng zhi xie shang hui yi tianjin shi wei yuan hui wen shi zi liao wei yuan hui, ed., *Tianjin wenshi ziliao xuanji,* 69 (Tianjin: Tianjin Renmin chubanshe, 1996), 159.

68. *Huagong Zazhi,* no. 31 (February 25, 1919): 25.

69. R. E. King, commanding officer of company No. 7 to chief, Labor Bureau, ASC, October 29, 1918, NA, RG 120, entry 1748, box 60.

70. Le Commandant Varaigne, to Colonel Dawes, September 9, 1918, Correspondence of the Labor Bureau, Subject: Foreign labor bonus, NA, RG 120, entry 1759, box 124, folder 242.1.

71. Jackson to Varaigne, September 13, 1918, Correspondence of the Labor Bureau, NA, RG 120, entry 1759, box 124, folder 242.1.

72. William Kaufman to John Price Jackson, March 27, 1918, NA, RG 120, entry 1758, box 110, folder 32.

73. From Major T. S. Chalmers, director civilian labor, base section 1 to headquarters, Labor Bureau, Subject: Chinese labor at La Rochelle, August 31, 1918. NA, RG 120, entry 1759, box 125, folder 333.

74. Li Jun, "Di san ci bao gao," November 30, 1918, in *Ouzhan huagong shiliao,* 398.

75. Ibid.

76. "Qiao gong shi wu ju da fu zhan hou jing ji diao cha hui guan yu qiao gong diao cha shi xiang," *Xin Zhongguo,* 238; see also *Ouzhan huagong shiliao,* 398.

77. John Price Jackson to Boschetti, May 13, 1918, NA, RG 120, entry 1760, box 108.

78. Inspection of Chinese Labor, A.P.O. 713, NA, RG 120, entry 1759, box 125, folder 333.

79. Daily report of field officers for Chinese labor Co. # 3, March 25, 1918, March 21, 1918, NA, RG 120, entry 1758, box 110, folder 32.

80. W. C. Anderson daily report for Chinese labor Co. #2, March 14, 1918, NA, RG 120, entry 1758, box 110, folder 32.

81. General Headquarters Commander-in-Chief Reports, NA, RG 120, entry 1748, box 31, folder 312: Historical report of the Labor Bureau.

82. R. M. Hersey to the International committee of the YMCA, Annual report letter, 1919, Yale University Divinity School Library Special Collections, John Hersey Papers, RG 145.

83. Misc. YMCA Archives, box 204, folder: Chinese laborers in France.

84. J. F. Johnson, Section representative to headquarters Labor Bureau, April 29, 1919, NA, RG 120, entry 1748, box 53, folder 230.14.

85. The Pershing quote and casualties information can be found in the database of the American Battle Monuments Commission. See also David Laskin,

"On Hallowed Ground, a Place of Painful Beauty," *New York Times,* September 30, 2007.

86. John Price Jackson to officers of the Labor Bureau, Army Service Corps, December 10, 1918, NA, RG 120, entry 1764, box 318.

## 8. The Association Men and Chinese Laborers

1. For the best study on this topic, see Erez Manela, *Wilsonian Moment: Self-Determination and the International Origins of Anticolonial Nationalism* (New York: Oxford University Press, 2007).

2. Katherine Mayo, *"That Damn Y": A Record of Overseas Service* (Boston: Houghton Mifflin, 1920), 363, 396.

3. Jun Xing, *Baptized in the Fire of Revolution: The American Social Gospel and the YMCA in China, 1919–1937* (Bethlehem, Pa.: Lehigh University Press 1996), 33.

4. For details, see Xu Guoqi, *Olympic Dreams,* 25–34.

5. Elijah W. Halford, "A World Brotherhood," *Association Men* 43, no. 6 (February 1918): 427.

6. Kenneth S. Latourette, *World Service* (New York: Association Press, 1957), 245, 252.

7. YMCA, *Young Men's Christian Association with the Chinese Labor Corps in France,* YMCA Archives, box 204, folder: Chinese laborers in France, 6–7.

8. Letter to C. W. Harvey, April 25, 1918, YMCA Archives, folder: China Correspondence and Reports, September 1917 to October 1918, YMCA Archives, box 204.

9. The following story clearly suggests British racist attitudes toward the Chinese, even in the case of the YMCA's work. When Yan Yangchu went with G. H. Cole, a Canadian YMCA official, to have a conference with a British general, the officer refused to speak with a Chinese. Cole was indignant and wanted to leave at once, but Yan insisted that the work go on, saying, "No, you go ahead, and I'll just sit in the car and *pray.*" See Hayford, *To the People,* 25.

10. YMCA, *Young Men's Christian Association with the Chinese Labor Corps in France,* YMCA Archives, box 204, folder: Chinese laborers in France, 6–7.

11. Young Men's Christian Association International Committee, *For the Millions of Men Now under Arms,* no. 13, 12.

12. J. S. Cameron to First Army, Third Army, Fourth Army, Fifth Army, February 12, 1918, Statement in regard to YMCA work for Chinese in France, NA, Kew, FO 228/2894.

13. YMCA, *Young Men's Christian Association with the Chinese Labor Corps in France,* YMCA Archives, box 204, folder: Chinese laborers in France.

14. Taft and Harris, *Service with Fighting Men,* 2:365.

15. Controller of Labour to the Quartermaster General, Report of Labour with the BEF During the War, November 14, 1919, Appendix C: Notes for Guidance of Officers of Labour Corps in France, September 1918, NA, Kew, WO 107/37, 54.

16. Conference of Workers Reports, Report of Conference of Workers Held at Peronne on July 23–24, 1919.

17. Ibid.

18. YMCA, *Young Men's Christian Association with the Chinese Labor Corps in France,* YMCA Archives, box 204, folder: Chinese laborers in France.

19. Young Men's Christian Association International Committee, *For the Millions of Men Now under Arms,* no. 13, 4.

20. Ibid., no. 10, 27.

21. Ibid., no. 12, 28.

22. Shi was born in 1886 in Shandong. He received a boxing scholarship in 1911 to study in the United States, and was educated at Harvard University (among other schools) and received a master's degree in business management from Harvard Business School. He was the first YMCA secretary chosen by the British War Office to accompany Chinese laborers back to China after the war. He returned to China with a group of laborers on April 19, 1919. He attended the Washington Conference in 1921–1922 as a staff member of the Chinese delegation and later served as an official in the ministries of transportations and foreign affairs. In 1923, as a representative of the ministry of transportation, he became involved in investigating the Lincheng Incident. Besides his government service, he also taught at Nankai University and Shanghai Jiaotong University.

23. Young Men's Christian Association International Committee. *For the Millions of Men Now under Arms,* no. 13, 10–12.

24. "General Statement Regarding the YMCA Work for the Chinese in France," March 1919, YMCA Archives, box 204, folder: Chinese laborers in France reports, 1918–1919.

25. Taft and Harris, *Service with Fighting Men,* 2:365–366.

26. Ibid.

27. "General Statement Regarding the YMCA Work for the Chinese in France," March 1919, YMCA Archives, box 204, folder: Chinese laborers in France reports, 1918–1919.

28. Taft and Harris, *Service with Fighting Men,* 2:365.

29. Jackson to D. A. Davis, September 12, 1918, NA, RG 120, entry 1759, box 125, folder 250 old file.

30. Ibid.

31. "A Cup of Tea and a Riot," *Association Men* 44, no. 5 (January 1919): 375.

32. Ibid.

33. Conference of Workers Reports, Report of Conference of Workers Held at Peronne on July 23–24, 1919, YMCA Archives, box 204.

34. YMCA Report, February 25, 1919, YMCA Archives, box 204, folder: Chinese laborers in France reports, 1918–1919.

35. "General Statement Regarding the YMCA Work for the Chinese in France," March 1919, YMCA Archives, box 204, folder: Chinese laborers in France reports, 1918–1919.

36. Ibid.

37. Ibid.

38. Ibid.

39. G. H. Cole to Rev. W. E. Soothill, October 1918, YMCA Archives, folder: China Correspondence and Reports, September 1917 to October 1918, YMCA Archives, box 204.

40. R. M. Hersey to the International committee of the YMCA, Annual report letter, 1919, Yale University Divinity School Library Special Collections, John Hersey Papers, RG 145.

41. Ibid.

42. YMCA, *Young Men's Christian Association with the Chinese Labor Corps in France,* YMCA Archives, box 204, folder: Chinese laborers in France.

43. "The 'Y' Suits the Chinese: The Oriental under the Wind of the Canadian 'Y,'" *Canadian Manhood,* April 1919, YMCA Archives, box 24, Chinese Labor Corps.

44. Annual report letter of D. W. Edwards, Secretary of Princeton's work in Peking, China, for the year ending September 30, 1919, YMCA Archives, Annual and quarterly reports, 1919–1920, box 128.

45. Latourette, *World Service,* 271.

46. YMCA, "Zhu fa huagong dui qing nian hui shi ye lu shui," YMCA Archives, box 204, folder: Chinese laborers in France.

47. Annual and quarterly reports, 1919–1920, YMCA Archives, box 128.

48. G. H. Cole, "With the Chinese in France," YMCA Archives, box 204, folder: Chinese laborers in France reports, 1918–1919.

49. Memo from W. W. Lockwood to John R. Mott, general secretary War Work Council, December 6, 1918, YMCA Archives, box 204, folder: Chinese laborers in France reports, 1918–1919.

50. R. M. Hersey to the International committee of the YMCA, Annual report letter, 1919, Yale University Divinity School Library Special Collections, John Hersey Papers, RG 145.

51. G. H. Cole to Rev. W. E. Soothill, October 1918, YMCA Archives, folder: China Correspondence and Reports, September 1917 to October 1918, YMCA Archives, box 204.

52. Charles Howard Hopkins, *History of the YMCA in North America* (New York: Association Press, 1951), 491.

53. The China press, August 9, 1918, Shanghai, YMCA Archives, box 171, folder: Robertson newspaper articles, 1909–1927.

54. G. H. Cole, "With the Chinese in France," YMCA Archives, box 204, folder: Chinese laborers in France reports, 1918–1919.

55. Paul P. Faris, "Preparing the Red Triangle for China," *The Continent* (New York), May 8, 1919, 13.

56. Taft and Harris, *Service with Fighting Men,* 2:367.

57. Ibid., 2:368.

58. Memo for the War Personnel Board, July 2, 1918, YMCA Archives, folder: China Correspondence and Reports, September 1917 to October 1918.

59. Shirley S. Garrett, *Social Reformers in Urban China: The Chinese YMCA, 1895–1926* (Cambridge, Mass.: Harvard University Press, 1970), 91–113.

60. G. H. Cole, "With the Chinese in France," YMCA Archives, box 204, folder: Chinese laborers in France reports, 1918–1919.

61. "General Statement Regarding the YMCA Work for the Chinese in France," March 1919, YMCA Archives, box 204, folder: Chinese laborers in France reports, 1918–1919.

62. Elliott, "Wang Gin-Guay," 537.

63. Young Men's Christian Association International Committee. *For the Millions of Men Now under Arms,* no. 13, 10–12.

64. Garrett, *Social Reformers in Urban China,* 141–145.

65. David Yui to William Wesley Peter, September 7, 1918, YMCA Archives, box 204: folder: China Correspondence and Reports, September 1917 to October 1918.

66. W. W. Peter to R. C. Beebe, December 6, 1918, information concerning Dr. W. W. Peter. YMCA Archives, Chinese labor battalions, Chinese Correspondence and Reports, November 1918 to October 1919, box 153, folder: China Correspondence and Reports, November to December 1918.

67. Letter sent to C. W. Harvey, April 25, 1918, YMCA Archives, box 204, folder: China Correspondence and Reports, September 1917 to October 1918.

68. "Bao zai lu fa huagong zhuang kuang zhi shi shi," *Huagong Zazhi* 29 (December 25, 1918): 18.

69. Taft and Harris, *Service with Fighting Men,* 2:364.

70. Ibid., 2:366–367.

71. Hopkins, *History of the Y.M.C.A.,* 491.

72. "Zai fa huagong zhi hao yin," *Hua Duo Bao* 1, no. 9 (October 14, 1918).

73. *Red Triangle Overseas* 1, no. 29 (February 22, 1919): 1, 4.

74. Conference of Workers Reports, Report of Conference of Workers Held at Peronne on July 23–24, 1919, YMCA Archives.

75. Chinese Labor Corps, YMCA Archives, box 204, folder: Chinese laborers in France reports, 1918–1919.

76. Quote from Nicholas Griffin, "Chinese Labor and British Christian Missionaries in France, 1917–1919," *Journal of Church and State* 20 (1978): 302.

77. I. H. Shi, "Upon Their Return to China," *Association Men* 62, no. 12 (August 1922): 538.

78. Paul P. Faris, "Consternation in China Camp," *World Outlook* 5, no. 3 (March 1919): 15.

79. Young Men's Christian Association International Committee, *For the Millions of Men Now under Arms,* no. 13, 4–7.

80. "General Statement Regarding the YMCA Work for the Chinese in France," March 1919, YMCA Archives, box 204, folder: Chinese laborers in France reports, 1918–1919.

81. Conference of Workers Reports, Report of Conference of Workers Held at Peronne on July 23–24, 1919, YMCA Archives, box 204.

82. John Shields, "With the Chinese in France," *Missionary Herald* 100, no. 7 (July 1918): 88.

83. "What the Chinese Learned in the War," *Literary Digest* 62, no. 11 (September 13, 1919): 33–34.

84. John Darroch, "The China Labourer's Reading," *North China Herald,* August 3, 1918.

85. Lawrence Todnem to David Yui, October 6, 1919, YMCA Archives, Chinese Correspondence and Reports, November 1918 to October 1919, box 153, folder: China Correspondence and Reports August to October 1919.

86. David Yui to W. W. Lockwood, March 28, 1919, YMCA Archives, Chinese Correspondence and Reports, Nov. 1918 to October 1919, box 153, folder: China Correspondence and Reports, March 1919.

87. Quote from Margo S. Gewurtz, "For God or for King: Canadian missionaries and the Chinese labour corps in World War I," in Min-Sun Chen and Lawrence Shyu, eds., *China Insight,* 49.

88. G. S. Moss to Archer, March 14, 1919, NA, Kew, FO 228/2895.

## 9. The Fusion of Teaching and Learning

1. *Ouzhan Huagong shiliao,* 238, 242–243; see also "Zhun zhu fa gong shi han shang yue shu lu wai huagong ban fa liu tiao qing zhuan ling ge shang hui shen shen ban li wen," *Zhong hua quan guo shang hui lian he hui hui bao,* no. 3 (March 1, 1917): 10–11.

2. Li Jun, "Yi min yi jian shu yi lan," in *Ouzhan Huagong shiliao,* 293.

3. Xia an nian pu hui gao bian yin hui, ed., *Ye Xiaan xian sheng nian pu* (Beijing: Beijing tu shu guan chubanshe, 1999), 50.

4. Ibid., 69.

5. Paul Bailey, "The Sino-French Connection: The Chinese Worker-Student Movement in France, 1902–1928," in David S. G. Goodman, *China and the West: Ideas and Activists* (Manchester, England: Manchester University Press, 1990), 78.

6. Yang Kailing, ed., *Min guo Li Shizeng xian sheng Yuying nian pu* (Taipei: Taiwan shang wu yin shu guan 1980), 15.

7. Quote from Chen Sanjing, *Hua gong yu ou zhan,* 13.

8. Beijing Liu-Fa Jiangxuehui, "Beijing Liu-Fa Jiangxuehui jiangzhang," *Xin qingnian* 3, no. 2 (1917); Yang Kailing, *Min guo Li Shizeng,* 32.

9. Yang Kailing, *Min guo Li Shizeng,* 28–29.

10. Gao Pingshu, ed., *Cai Yuanpei quan ji* (Beijing: Zhonghua shu ju, 1984), 3:219.

11. See Li's "Yimin yi jian shu" (Proposal for Allowing Emigration), in Li Shizeng, *Li Shizeng xian sheng wenji* (Taipei, 1980), 1:220–225.

12. Ibid.; see also Paul Bailey, "The Chinese Work-Study Movement in France," *China Quarterly* 11, no. 5 (1988): 448.

13. "Wai jiao bu shou nei wu bu zi," November 11, 1916, in *Ouzhan Huagong shiliao,* 14.

14. Gao Pingshu, *Cai Yuanpei quan ji,* 3:219.

15. *Ouzhan Huagong shiliao,* 799.

16. Bailey, "Chinese Work-Study Movement in France," 448.

17. The Society was officially founded in June 1916.

18. Bailey, "Chinese Work-Study Movement in France," 449.

19. Gao Pingshu, *Cai Yuanpei nian pu chang bian* (Beijing: Renmin jiaoyu chubanshe, 1996), 2:28.

20. Qinghua daxue Zhonggong dangshi jiaoyanzu, ed., *Fu Fa qingong jianxue yundong shiliao* (Beijing: Beijing chubanshe, 1979), 1:181–183.

21. S. G. C, "Chinese Labour in France," *The Statesman* (January 13, 1917), 343.

22. Xinchaoshe, ed., *Cai Jiemin xian sheng yan xing Lu* (Beijing: Xinchaoshe, 1920), 2:485–569.

23. Ibid., 2:483–484.

24. Gao Pingshu, *Cai Yuanpei quan ji,* 3:219.

25. "Hua fa jiao yu hui zhong guo dai biao Cai Yuan Pei deng fa qi wei hua gong jiao yu jing fei mu juan," 1917, China No. 2 Archives, 1003 (2)-85.

26. "Ying zhao hua gong zai fa zhi gong zuo," *Huagong Zazhi,* no. 24 (July 25, 1918): 17.

27. *Ouzhan Huagong shiliao,* 406.

28. "Huagong ying gai you de sixiang," *Huagong Xunkan* (October 25, 1920): 1.

29. *Huagong Xunkan* (November 5, 1920): 4.

30. Jordan to Balfour, August 14, 1917, NA, Kew, WO 106/33.

31. For details on the laborers' misunderstanding of world affairs, see Captain Harry L. Gilchriese, "Managing 200,000 Coolies in France," *Current History* (December 1919): 324; I. H. Shi, "With the Chinese Laborers" 452; and "What the Chinese Learned in the War," *Literary Digest* 62, no. 11 (1919).

32. For a detailed study on YMCA and Chinese workers in Europe, see Chen Sanjing, "Jidu qingnianhui yu ou zhan huagong," *Zhongyang yanjiuyuan jindai shi yanjiusuo j kan* 1, no. 17 (1988).

33. The statement was dated around April 1918, PRO, NA, Kew, FO 371/3179.

34. "The Chinese Laborers in France in Relation to the Work of the Young Men's Christian Association: Report to the International Committee of Young Men's Christian Association of North America of Special Mission of Dwight W. Edwards in France April 13–May 11, 1918," YMCA Archives, box 204, folder: report 1919.

35. Young Men's Christian Association International Committee, *For the Millions of Men Now under Arms,* no. 13, 10–12.

36. Yan Yangchu, "Ping min jiao yu," in Ma Qiufan and Xiong Mingan, eds., *Yan Yangchu jiaoyu lunzhu xuan* (Beijing: Renmin jiaoyu chubanshe, 1993), 3.

37. *Chinese Students' Monthly* 13, no. 6 (April 1918): 327.

38. W. W. Lockwood to J. M. Manley regarding Chinese at Silver Bay, Summer 1919, dated July 24, 1919, YMCA Archives, Chinese Correspondence and Reports, November 1918 to October 1919, box 153, folder: China Correspondence and Reports, July 1919.

39. "Lu ou xin wen," *Lu Ou Zhoukan* (December 30, 1919): 3.

40. "Red Triangle Overseas," Paris, February 2, 1919, YMCA Archives, Biographical records, James Yen, box 233.

41. "Zhong guo de zhu quan," *Huagong Zhoubao* (February 12, 1919): 1.

42. "Huagong dang gu guoti," *Huagong Zhoubao* (February 5, 1919): 1.

43. "Gong he xin nian, san xi san si," *Huagong Zhoubao* (January 19, 1919): 1.

44. Ye Shengtao, "Nü zi de ren ge wen ti (1)," *Huagong Zhoubao,* no. 17 (June 11, 1919): 4; Ye Shengtao, "Nü zi de ren ge wen ti (2)," *Huagong Zhoubao,* no. 18 (June 18, 1919): 3; Ye Shengtao, "Nü zi de ren ge wen ti (3)," *Huagong Zhoubao,* no. 19 (June 25, 1919): 3.

45. Lu Shiqing, "Quan huagong yue du huagong zhoubao," *Huagong Zhoubao,* no. 31 (September 17, 1919): 7–8.

46. The letter was dated September 15, 1917. Shepherd Knapp, *On the Edge of the Storm: The Story of a Year in France* (Worcester, Mass.: Commonwealth Press, 1921), 6.

47. Ibid., 21.

48. Conference of Workers Reports, Report of Conference of Workers Held at Peronne on July 23–24, 1919, YMCA Archives, box 204.

49. "Huagong jinkuan," *Huagong Zhoubao,* no. 18 (June 18, 1919).

50. "Ben bao zhou nian zhi hui gu," *Huagong Zhoubao,* no. 45 (January 1, 1920): 1.

51. Song Enrong, ed., *Yan Yangchu quan ji* (Changsha: Hunan jiao yu chu-banshe, 1989), 2:256.

52. *Huagong Zhoubao,* no. 38 (November 12, 1919); *Huagong Zhoubao,* no. 15 (May 28, 1919).

53. Wu Xiangxiang, *Yan Yangchu zhuan,* 46.

54. C. F. Summers, "The Chinese Labour Corps: What They Learned in France," *North China Herald* 132 (1919).

55. YMCA report, February 25, 1919, YMCA Archives, box 204, folder: Chinese laborers in France reports, 1918–1919.

56. Grace Overmyer, "Jimmy Yen," *Century* (April 1929): 719.

57. Yan Hongguo, *Yan Yangchu zhuan lue* (Chengdu: Tiandi chubanshe, 2005), 45.

58. Ibid., 55–56.

59. Ibid., 59.

60. Pearl S. Buck, *Tell the People: Talks with James Yen about the Mass Education Movement* (New York: John Day Company, 1945), 8–9; Song Enrong, *Yan Yangchu quan ji,* 1:526; Yan Hongguo, *Yan Yangchu zhuan lue,* 59.

61. Song Enrong, *Yan Yangchu quan ji,* 2:178.

62. Frank B. Lenz, "'Jimmy' Yen of China," *Association Men* (July 1929): 493.

63. Wu Xiangxiang, *Yan Yangchu zhuan,* 32.

64. Lenz, "'Jimmy' Yen of China," 531.

65. The best book on this subject is Charles Hayford's *To the People: James Yen and Village China* (New York: Columbia University Press, 1990).

66. "The thousand characters invented by Yen," YMCA Archives, Biographical records: James Yen, box 233.

67. The slogan can be found on the Chinese national association of the mass education movement letter to Ray Lyman Wilbur, November 14, 1927, Rare Book and Manuscript Library, Columbia University, IIRR Collection, box one, Yen's letter report, November 14, 1927.

68. Eugene E. Barnett, "A Crusade in China's Renaissance: Brief Glimpse of a Romantic Career," YMCA Archives, Biographical records: James Yen, box 233.

69. Lenz, "'Jimmy' Yen of China," 494, 531.

70. Clark Brockman, "The Greatest Volunteer Educational Movement in History," 1924, Yale University Divinity School Library Special Collections, Dwight W. Edwards papers, record group 12, box 12, folder 135: Chinese laborers in France, 1918.

71. Eugene E. Barnett, "A Crusade in China's Renaissance: Brief Glimpse of a Romantic Career," YMCA Archives, Biographical records: James Yen, box 233.

72. Quote from Hayford, *To the People,* 46.

73. Garrett, *Social Reformers in Urban China,* 162.

74. Hopkins, *History of the Y.M.C.A. in North America,* 491.

75. Ibid., 695.

76. Frank Ritchie to A. W. Hanson, July 17, 1929, YMCA Archives, Biographical records: James Yen, box 233.

77. Hayford, *To the People,* xii, 52.

78. Nathaniel Peffer, "Yale's Yen Charts a Course for China," *New York Times Magazine* (February 1, 1931), 7.

79. "The Chinese Mass Education Movement—an Outline" (typed document with no author and date, page 2), Columbia University, Rare Book and Manuscript Library, IIRR Collection, box 1, articles on the program.

80. Paul Bailey, "Popular Education Developments, 1904–11," and "Popular Education Developments in the Early Republic," in his *Reform the People: Changing Attitudes towards Popular Education in Early 20th Century China* (Edinburgh: Edinburgh University Press, 1990).

81. "Gong li zhan sheng qiang quan" and "Lao gong shen sheng" were the two most popular slogans in China immediately after World War I. According to Li Yongchang, these two slogans had direct links to China's declaration of war and its laborers in Europe. Li Yongchang, "Jue xing qian de kuang re: lun 'gong li zhan sheng' he 'lao gong shen sheng' liang ge kou hao," *Jin dai shi yan jiu,* no. 4 (1996).

82. Zhongguo Cai Yuanpei yan jiu hui, ed., *Cai Yuanpei quan ji* (Hangzhou: Zhejiang jiaoyu chubanshe, 1997), 3:464.

83. Ibid.

84. Li Dazhao, "Shu min de sheng li," in *Beijing daxue ri kan* (December 6, 1918), 4–5.

85. "Guo nei xinwen," *Lu Ou Zhoukan* (December 30, 1919), 2.

86. Lu Xun, *Lu Xun quan ji* (Beijing: Renmin wenxue chubanshe, 2005), 3:136.

87. Kang Youwei, "Zhi Lu Zixin shu," *Chen Bao* (January 9, 1919), 3.

88. Yi hua gong (One Chinese Laborer), "Huagong yu heping hui yi," *Huagong Zazhi,* no. 30 (January 25, 1919): 5.

89. Zhongguo Cai Yuanpei yan jiu hui, *Cai Yuanpei quan ji,* 3:488.

90. Chen Duxiu, *Duxiu Wen cun,* 1:449–452.

91. Ibid., 2:657.

92. Ibid., 2:103.

93. Ibid., 2:104–105.

94. Song Enrong, *Yan Yangchu quan ji,* 2:257.

95. Bai Jiao, "Di yi ci shi jie da zhan zhi zhong guo can zhan," *Ren Wen Yue Kan* 7, no. 1 (February 15, 1936): 31.

96. J. S. Tow, "China's Service to the Allied Cause," *Economic World* 17, no. 6 (February 8, 1919): 185.

97. Witter Bynner, *A Canticle of Pan: And Other Poems* (New York: Knopf, 1920), 196–197.

98. J. S. Tow, "Both Sides of the Shantung Issue: The Chinese Side," *Economic World* 5, no. 11 (November 1919): 5.

99. Ibid., 65.

100. Min-ch'ien Tyau, *China Awakened* (New York: Macmillan, 1922), 166.

101. Shou Shi, "Tong bao su xing," *Huagong Zazhi,* no. 31 (February 25, 1919): 3–4.

102. Kate Kelsey, "The Women Left Behind by the Men of the Chinese Labour Corps," *Missionary Herald* 101, no. 11 (November 1919): 135–137.

103. For an excellent collection of original thoughts on this, see Lu-Ou Zazhi she and Chen Sanjing, eds., *Liu-Ou jiaoyu yundong* (Taipei: Zhongyang yanjiuyuan jindai shi yanjiusuo, 1996).

104. Zhou Enlai, "Liu fa qin gong jian xue zhi da bo lan," in Qinghua daxue Zhonggong dangshi jiaoyanzu, *Fu Fa qingong jianxue yundong shiliao,* 1:5.

105. Zhou Enlai wrote this poem in 1920. The original poem can be found in Nankai daxue Zhou Enlai yanjiushi, ed., "Zhou Enlai qing shaoning shidai ji shi," in *Tianjin wen shi zi liao xuanji* (Tianjin, Tianjin Renmin chubanshe, 1981), 15:44.

106. Wei Fang shi di fang shi zhi bian zuan wei yuan hui, ed., *Wei Fang shi zhi* (Beijing: Zhong yang wen xian chubanshe, 1995), 2:1236.

107. Chen Duxiu, *Duxiu Wen cun,* 1:11–15.

108. Marilyn A. Levine, *The Found Generation: Chinese Communists in Europe during the Twenties* (Seattle: University of Washington Press, 1993), 65.

109. Xiao Yu, *Mao Zedong qian zhuan ji Mao Zedong xingqi mixin* (Taipei: Li Bai chubanshe, 1989), 244.

110. Ibid., 262.

111. For details, see Qiu Shi, "Liu fa qin gong jian xue de lishi zuoyong," *Xue xi yu yanjiu,* no. 1 (1982): 42–46.

112. Wuming huagong (Unnamed Laborer), "Qingong jianxue gai qiu zizhu ya!" ("Work-Study Students Must Help Themselves!"), *Lu Ou zhoukan* 70 (March 12, 1921): 3–4.

113. Levine, *Found Generation,* 113.

114. Ibid., 205.

115. "Lu ou xinwen," *Lu Ou zhoukan* (May 15, 1920): 3.

116. Levine, *Found Generation,* 71.

## 10. A Fusion of Civilizations

1. Young Men's Christian Association, *Summary of World War Work of the American YMCA,* 59.

2. "The Chinese Laborers in France in Relation to the Work of the Young Men's Christian Association: Report to the International Committee of Young

Men's Christian Association of North America of Special Mission of Dwight W. Edwards in France April 13–May 11, 1918," YMCA Archives, box 204, folder: report 1919.

3. Kathlene Winter, "With the Chinese Industrial Army," 15.

4. Ibid., 31.

5. Harley F. MacNair, *China's New Nationalism and Other Essays* (Shanghai: Commercial Press, 1932), 220.

6. YMCA, "Yellow Spectacles," YMCA Archives, box 204, folder: Chinese laborers in France.

7. W. W. Peter, "Mr. Chang Goes to War," *World's Work,* July 1919, 274.

8. Ibid., 275.

9. Ibid.

10. *Ouzhan Huagong shiliao,* 128.

11. Ibid.

12. *Lu Ou Zhoukan,* November 15, 1919, 3.

13. Ibid., November 22, 1919, 4.

14. Ibid., November 22, 1919, 2.

15. *Ouzhan Huagong shiliao,* 139.

16. Chinese consulate general, "Zhao pin hu song huagong hui guo yan tu zhao liao yuan zhang cheng," *Lu Ou Zhoukan,* February 28, 1920, 4.

17. Guo wu yuan qiao gong shi wu ju, ed., *Guo wu yuan qiao gong shi wu ju guo ji yi min yan jiu hui bao gao shu* (N.p., n.d.), 27.

18. Min-ch'ien Tyau, *China Awakened,* 239–243.

19. Ta Chen, "The Labour Movement in China," *International Labour Review* 15, no. 3 (March 1927): 340.

20. *Lu Ou Zhoukan* (May 1, 1920): 3.

21. Blick, "Chinese Labor Corps in World War I," 132.

22. Min-ch'ien Tyau, *China Awakened,* 231.

23. Ibid., 240.

24. See Chow Tse-Tsung, *The May Fourth Movement: Intellectual Revolution in Modern China,* Harvard East Asian Studies (Cambridge, Mass.: Harvard University Press, 1960), 40.

25. Young Men's Christian Association, *The Year Book of the YMCA of North America for the Year May 1920 to April 30,* 68–69.

26. Wu Xiangxiang, *Yan Yangchu zhuan,* 35.

27. Zibo shi zhi bian zuan wei yuan hui, *Zibo shi zhi,* 1:652.

28. "Yi ci d an zhan henan yong cheng lao hua gong de hui yi, in *Hua qiao li shi xue hui tong xun* (March 1985), 24.

29. Consul-general in Tianjin to Captain William Bull, July 25, 1921, NA, Kew, FO 228/2896.

30. William Bull to Consul-general in Shanghai, April 2, 1921, NA, Kew, FO 228/2896.

31. MacNair, *China's New Nationalism*, 220.

32. Qinghua daxue Zhonggong dangshi jiaoyanzu, ed., *Fu Fa qingong jianxue yundong shiliao* 2, part 2: 790; See also "Bandit Rule in China," *Literary Digest* (May 19, 1923): 8–9.

33. Lucy T. Aldrich, "A Week-end with Chinese Bandits," *Atlantic Monthly* (November 1923): 677.

34. Chen Wuwo, *Lincheng jie che an ji shi* (Changsha: Yuelu shu she, 1987), 6.

35. For more details, see Phil Billingsley, *Bandits in Republican China* (Stanford: Stanford University Press, 1988), 73.

36. Chen Wuwo, *Lincheng jie che an ji shi*, 232.

37. "Lu fa huagong zhi ai xi ming yu," *Yi Shi Zhu Ri Bao* (335): 9.

38. Ji Zhe, "Kan xing zhe ben za zhi de yi si," *Huagong Zazhi*, no. 46 (May 25, 1920): 1.

39. YMCA, "Yellow Spectacles," YMCA Archives, box 204, folder: Chinese laborers in France.

40. Ibid.

41. Cheng Shih-gung, *Modern China*, 272.

42. Summerskill, *China on the Western Front*, 101.

43. Zhang Yizhi, "Ying Fa huagong gui guo hou zhi chu zhi," *Min Xin Zhoukan* 3 (n.d.): 36–37.

44. Gao Pingshu, *Cai Yuanpei quan ji*, 3:219.

45. Liu Hou, "Sui Chu Liu Xin," *Huagong Zazhi* 9 (July 10, 1917): 5–8.

46. *Chinese Students' Monthly* 13, no. 6 (April 1918): 301.

47. Jun Yuan, "Huagong gui guo hou gai zen yang," *Huagong Zazhi*, no. 43 (February 25, 1920): 1–6.

48. For details, see Xu Guoqi, *China and the Great War*.

49. Bai Jiao, "Shi jie da zhan zhong zhi huagong," *Ren Wen Yue Kan* 8, no. 1 (February 15, 1937): 2.

50. Xia Xiaohong, ed., *Yin bing shi heji ji wai wen* (Beijing: Beijing daxue chubanshe, 2005), 2:696–698

51. "The King's Day with the Tanks," *Times* (London), July 17, 1917, 5.

52. "An Army of Labour: Behind the Lines in France," *Times* (London), December 26, 1917, 8.

53. Young Men's Christian Association, *Summary of World War Work of the American YMCA*, 59.

54. David Lloyd George, *War Memoirs of David Lloyd George* (London: Odhams Press, 1942), 2:800.

55. Paul Kennedy, "The First World War and the International Power System," *International Security* 9, no. 1 (Summer 1984): 24.

56. Chen Sanjing, *Huagong yu ou zhan*, Preface, 1.

57. *Far Eastern Review* 15, no. 4 (1918): 126–127.

58. "China's Strong Arm to Be Felt in War," *New York Times,* October 14, 1917.

59. Levine, *Found Generation,* 71.

60. J. S. Tow, "Both Sides of the Shantung Issue," 39.

61. Translation of rough draft of letter, found in the pocket book of coolie No. 3902, B. Coy, Chinese Labour Corps, August 1918; the translation can be found in "The Laborer's Attitude," YMCA Archives, box 204, folder: Chinese laborers in France reports; the original pocket book can be found in London IWM, box: Chinese labour corps notebook, 1917–19, misc 92 (1372).

62. Tianjin shi di fang zhi bian xiu wei yuan hui, ed., *Tianjin tong zhi: da shi ji,* 195.

63. Taft and Harris, *Service with Fighting Men,* 2:366.

64. Reinsch to C. V. Hibbard, YMCA Archives, Chinese Correspondence and Reports, November 1918 to October 1919, box 153, folder: China Correspondence and Reports, November to December 1918.

65. Warren I. Cohen, *The Chinese Connection: Roger S. Greene, Thomas W. Lamont, George E. Sololsky and American–East Asian Relations* (New York: Columbia University Press, 1978); "Ben xiao ji shi," *Beijing daxue ri kan* (November 20, 1918): 2–3.

66. Report from Peking YMCA, 1919: Annual report letter of D. W. Edwards, Secretary of Princeton's work in Peking, China, for the year ending September 30, 1919, YMCA Archives, Annual and quarterly reports, 1919–1920, box 128.

67. Ibid.

68. Annual report letter of O. R. Magill, general secretary, YMCA, Kirin, Manchuria for the year ending September 30, 1919, YMCA Archives, Annual and quarterly reports, 1919–1920, box 128.

69. C. S. Bishop, "In the Crisis Hour for China," *Association Men* 45, no. 1 (September 1919): 12.

70. Roger D. Arnold in Shansi Annual letter for the year ending September 30th, 1919, YMCA Archives, Reports of foreign secretaries, vol. 3, 1919, box 41.

71. A. G. Robinson, Sixth annual letter, 1919, Tientsin, September 1, 1919, YMCA Archives, Reports of foreign secretaries, vol. 3, 1919, box 41.

72. *Association Men* 43, no. 4 (December 1917): 257–259.

73. Blick, "Chinese Labor Corps in World War I," 128.

74. Fu Shengsan, "Huagong zai fa yu zhouguo de sunyi," *Huagong Zhoubao,* no. 7 (March 12, 1919); Yan Hongguo, *Yan Yangchu zhuan lue,* 56; Wu Xiangxiang, *Yan Yangchu zhuan,* 30–31.

75. Ting Fu-Tsiang, "Chinese Philosophy in France," 645–646.

76. Ibid., 646.

77. Ibid., 646–647.

78. Ibid., 647.

79. Ibid., 648.

80. Ibid.

81. Ibid.

82. Elliott, "Wang Gin-Guay," 537.

83. Li Jinhua, "Hao jihui," *Huagong Zazhi,* no. 43 (February 25, 1920): 50–53.

84. Mu Lei, "Huagong riji," Diary of Mu Lei [Laborer in France].

85. Li Jing's fourth notice to Chinese workers in France, December, 1917 and Li Jing's second report, in *Ouzhan Huagong shiliao,* 288, 391.

86. Li Jing's fourth report, in *Ouzhan Huagong shiliao,* 418.

87. Gu Xingqing, *Ouzhan gongzuo huiyi lu,* 50; see also "Huagong jin kuang," *Huagong Zhoubao,* no. 14 (May 21, 1919).

88. Gu Xingqing, *Ouzhan gongzuo huiyi lu,* 50–51.

89. See Min-ch'ien Tuk Zung Tyau, *China Awakened,* 240.

90. "Deng ke er ke Huagong qing nian hui jin kuang," *Huagong Zhoubao,* no. 36 (October 22, 1919).

91. "Ai ba huagong qing zhu lian jun de sheng li," *Huagong Zhoubao* (August 27, 1919).

92. *Lu Ou Zhoukan* (November 29, 1919): 3; *Lu Ou Zhoukan* (December 6, 1919): 3; *Lu Ou Zhoukan* (November 15, 1919): 4.

93. Guo wu yuan qiao gong shi wu ju, ed., *Qiao gong shi wu ju di qi ci diao cha zai fa huagong qingxing shu,* 17–25.

94. "Fa kan ci," *Huagong Xunkan* (October 15, 1920): 1.

95. *Lu Ou Zhoukan* (November 15, 1919): 4.

96. "Huagong jin kuang," *Huagong Zhoubao,* no. 33 (September 31, 1919).

## Conclusion

1. James Joll, *The Origins of the First World War* (New York: Pearson Longman, 1984), 1.

2. Yi Feng, "Ou zhan za gan," (6), *Chen Bao* (December 23, 1918), 2.

3. Lloyd George, *Memoirs of the Peace Conference* (New Haven, Conn.: Yale University Press, 1939), 1:134

4. Marius Moutet, "Preface," in P. Wou, *Les Travailleurs Chinois et la Grande Guerre* (Paris: Editions A. Pedone, 1939), 7.

5. War Office representative G. S. Moss, Report on the demobilization of the Chinese labor corps, October 31, 1920, NA, Kew, FO 228/2895.

6. Chen Sanjing, *Hua gong yu ou zhan,* 1.

7. Levine, *Found Generation,* 71.

8. Blick, "Chinese Labor Corps in World War I," 112.

9. Li Jikui, *Liang Shiyi,* 227.

10. S. J. Chuan, "A Brief Report of the Versailles Conference for the Chinese Secretaries of the Chinese Department of the YMCA in France," YMCA Archives, box 204, folder: Chinese laborers in France reports.

11. Kuhn, *Chinese among Others*, 5.

12. Ibid., 12.

13. Ibid., 16. It is strange that Kuhn did not mention the Chinese journey to Europe during the Great War at all, although this episode could have substantially strengthened his thesis.

14. Quote from Kuhn, *Chinese among Others*, 243.

## Appendix 1

1. The last three items are omitted in some contracts.

2. In the French contract, rice and wheat or kaffir corn are combined.

3. Not in the French contract.

4. Not in the French contract.

# SELECTED GLOSSARY

*Bao gong wei yuan* 保工委员

Cai Yuanpei 蔡元培

Chen Liting 陈立廷

*Chu tianxia wenmang, zuo shijie xinmin* 除天下文盲, 做世界新民

*Chu wenmang zuo xinmin* 除文盲, 做新民

*Da ji* 大計

*Da jue wu* 大觉悟

*Da tong wu tai* 大同舞台

Da zhang fu neng qu neng shen, he xian dang ku li zhu lianbang, ping ding huan qiu zhan huo, tong lao zhe nai xiong di, xun ke deng wu tai yan gu shi, sao chu wu dang you chou 大丈夫能屈能伸, 何嫌当苦力助联邦, 平定环球战祸, 同劳者乃兄乃弟, 洵可登舞台演故事, 扫除吾党忧愁

*Er zong tong* 二总统

Fu Ruoyu 傅若愚

Fu Shengsan 傅省三

Gui Zhiting 桂直廷

"Guo jia xing wang, pi fu you ze" 国家兴亡, 匹夫有责

Guo Zefang 郭则范

Gu Xingqing 顾杏卿

*Huagong zai Fa yu zu guo de sun yi* 华工在法与祖国的损益

Huimin 惠民

Hu Weide 胡惟德

Jiang Tingfu 蒋廷黻

*Lao gong shen sheng* 劳工神圣

Laoxikai 老西开

Liang Shiyi 梁士诒

Li Jianshan 李兼善

Li Jun 李骏

Lin Yutang 林语堂

Li Shizeng 李石曾

*Liu fang qian gu* 流芳千古

Lu Huchen 吕虎臣

Lu Ou Tongren Hui 旅欧同人会 (Society for Chinese in Europe)

Lu Shiyin 陆士寅

Ma Xinwei 马心维

Ma Zuofu 马作夫

Pan Lianru 潘连茹

Qiao gong shi wu ju 侨工事务局

Quan Shaowu 全绍武

*Ren dao da sheng* 人道大胜

Shi Baozheng 史宝贞

"Shi bu ke shao"    实不可少

Shi Yixuan    史译宣

*Si dao gang*    四道杠

Tai Kuiyi    邰魁义

Wang Chunchi    王春池

Wang Jingwei    汪精卫

Wang Xiaoshun    王小顺

Wang Yushan    王玉山

Wang Zhenbiao    王振彪

Wang Zhengxu    王正序

"Wei guo juan qu"    为国捐躯

Weihaiwei    威海卫

*Weiji*    危机

*Wei qu qiu quan zhi ku xin*    委屈
    求全之苦心

Wu Tingfang    伍廷芳

Wu Yongchang    邬永昌

Xue sa ou xi zhuang shi yun, hun gui
    zu guo wan shenzhou    血洒欧
    西壮世运, 魂桂归国挽神州

Yang Fushun    杨福顺

Yan Yangchu    晏阳初

Ye Gongchuo    叶恭绰

Ye Shengtao    叶圣陶

*Yigong daibing*    以工代兵

Zhang Hu    张弧

Zhan Yougu    詹幼谷

Zhen Shutian    郑书田

Zhou Laichang    周来昌

"*Zi dang an zhong jin li, bu bian
    ming zhu ye*"    自当暗中尽力,
    不便明助也

# SELECTED BIBLIOGRAPHY

## Archives

*Canada*

LIBRARY AND ARCHIVES CANADA, OTTAWA

RG 6-E/168, part 2
RG 6-E/620, folder 331, part 1
RG 6-E/620, folder 331, part 2
RG 6-E T/101
RG 24/1833
RG 24/2553
RG 24/3767
RG 24/3769
RG 24/3771
RG 24/4324
RG 25 A-2/229
RG 42/255
RG 3768/1048–45–2/10

OTHER DOCUMENTS

Livingstone, Harry D. Journal, Diary, and Photos. David Livingstone Family Collection.
Menzies, Arthur. Family Papers. Arthur Menzies Family Collection.
Sebert, L. J. Diary of Captain L. J. Sebert, 1917: Mission to China, 1917. John Sebert Family Collection.

*China*

ZHONGGUO DI ER LI SHI DANG AN GUAN
(CHINA NO. 2 HISTORICAL ARCHIVES), NANJING

03–36/4-(5)
1001 (2)-400
1003 (2)-85
1039-1
1050-1
1050–3
1050–6
1050-11
1050–18
1050–18–34

ZHONG YANG YAN JIU YUAN JIN DAI SHI YAN
JIU SUO DANG AN GUAN, TAIPEI

Wai jiao bu dang: British Recruitment, E-1-4-2

OTHER DOCUMENTS

Jiang Jinghai. "Lu Ou Wen Ji." Writings of My Time in Europe. Personal
    collection. (The author was a laborer in Europe.)
Mu Lei. "Mu Lei Ri Ji." Diary of Mu Lei. Personal collection. (The author was
    a laborer in France.)
Sun Gan. "Ou Zhan Hua Gong Ji." Records of Chinese laborers in the War in
    Europe. Private collection. (The author was a laborer in France.)

*France*

ARCHIVE NATIONALE, PARIS

14F/11331/Chinois/Institution et Affaires General
14F/11334

ARCHIVE OF FRENCH FOREIGN MINISTRY, QUAI D'ORSAY, PARIS

Asie, 1918–1929, Chine
Ministre des Affaires Etrangères, 1918–1929, Chine
NS, Chine

SERVICE HISTORIQUE DE L'ARMÉE DE TERRE,
CHÂTEAU DE VINCENNES

6N 111/Drivers Secret/Fonds Clemenceau
6N 149/Fonds Clemenceau/Mission de Recrutement des Ouvriers/Chinois
7N 398/Chine

7N 435/Main–d'Ouvriers Indigence
7N 1297/Chinese Evacuation
7N 2289/Affairs Britanniques/Travailleurs Chinois
16N 2450/6h/98/9
16N 2450/GQG/6498
16N 2912/Chine
16N 3246
17N 156/Correspondence
18N 107
18N 207

ARCHIVES DE LA MARINE, CHÂTEAU DE VINCENNES

SSEB 5/Travailleurs Colonials et Etrangères/Généralités
SSEB 119/Transport Personnel

OTHER DOCUMENTS

Tchang, Christian. "Papa Etait Chinois, Maman Berrichonne." Unpublished family memoir with photos. Private and Unpublished Collections.


*United Kingdom*

EAST SURREY MUSEUM, SURREY

Wood, Captain Royal Douglas. "Official Diary of the 39th and 40th Battalions, Chinese Labour Corps, Party AC," file 3969.

IMPERIAL WAR MUSEUM, LONDON

Bottomley, Kathleen C. Interview Files.
"Chinese Labour Corps Notebook, 1917–1919"
Cormack, G. E. Files.
Cornwall, H. E. Files.
Doe, David H. Files (including diary).
Fletcher, A. B. W. Interview Files.
Harrison, Second Lieutenant John M. Files.
McCormick, Captain A. Files.
Oliver, Major R. D. Memoirs.
"Report on the Administration of Labour in XVII Corps," February 1917–February 1918.
Ward, Charles. Interview Files.

LIDDLE COLLECTION (1914–1918), SPECIAL COLLECTIONS, UNIVERSITY OF LEEDS LIBRARY

Corke, F. W. Files.
Dent, W. A. Diary.

Gardner-Smith, Percival. Files.
Haigh, T. V. Diary.
Hopwood, S. F. Diary.
Innes, H. S. Files (including letters).
Ludlow, Brigadier General W. R. Diary.
Ogden, Sir Alwyne. Files.
Ogley, P. E. Memoirs (including letters).
Pilditch, Major P. H. Diary.
Shaw, W. J. Diary.
Tarlson, G. S. Files.
Wilkins, T. O. Diary.
Willis, G. A. Diary.
Wilson, Douglas. Files.

NATIONAL ARCHIVES, KEW

CAB 23/5
CO 873/538
CO 873/578FO 288/2892
FO 228/2893
FO 228/2894
FO 228/2895
FO 228/2896
FO 350/13
FO 350/15
FO 371/2905
FO 371/2906
FO 371/2914
FO 371/3178
FO 371/3179
FO 371/3682
NSC 9/850
T1/12178
T1/12343
WO 32/11345
WO 32/11346
WO 95/83
WO 95/571
WO 106/33
WO 106/35
WO 107/37
WO 163/21

THE TANK MUSEUM, BOVINGTON

Anonymous. "Central Stores and Workshops" (believed to have been written by Lieutenant Colonel John Brockbank). E2006.1703.


*United States*

NATIONAL ARCHIVES, COLLEGE PARK, MARYLAND

RG 120, entry 1748 box 29
RG 120, entry 1748, box 31
RG 120, entry 1748, box 53
RG 120, entry 1748, box 54
RG 120, entry 1748, box 55
RG 120, entry 1748, box 56
RG 120, entry 1748, box 57
RG 120, entry 1748, box 60
RG 120, entry 1758, box 110
RG 120, entry 1758, box 111
RG 120, entry 1758, box 112
RG 120, entry 1758, box 114
RG 120, entry 1758, box 115
RG 120, entry 1759, box 122
RG 120, entry 1759, box 124
RG 120, entry 1759, box 125
RG 120, entry 1760, box 107
RG 120, entry 1760, box 108
RG 120, entry 1764, box 318
RG 120, entry 1767, box 117

DIVINITY SCHOOL LIBRARY SPECIAL COLLECTIONS,
YALE UNIVERSITY

Edwards, Dwight W. Papers.
Hersey, John. Papers.

KAUTZ FAMILY YMCA ARCHIVES, UNIVERSITY OF
MINNESOTA LIBRARIES, MINNEAPOLIS

Annual and Quarterly Reports, 1919–1920
China Correspondence and Reports, September 1917–1918
China Correspondence and Reports, November–December 1919
Chinese Labor Corps in France
Reports of Foreign Secretaries
Robertson, Clarence Hovey. Biographical Records.
Yen, James. Biographical Records.

RARE BOOK AND MANUSCRIPT LIBRARY, COLUMBIA UNIVERSITY

International Institute of Rural Reconstruction (IIRR) Collection

## Newspapers and Journals

*Asia*
*Association Men*
*The Beaver*
*Beijing daxue ri kan*
*British Journal of Ophthalmology*
*British Weekly*
*Century*
*Chen Bao*
*Chinese Students' Monthly*
*The Continent*
*Current History Magazine*
*The Economic World*
*Far Eastern Review*
*Halifax Herald*
*Hua Duo Bao*
*Hua qiao li shi xue hui tong xun*
*Huagong Xunkan*
*Huagong Zazhi*
*Huagong Zhoubao*
*Journal of Church and State*
*Literary Digest*
*Lu Ou Zhoukan*
*Military Affairs*
*Minguo dangan*
*Missionary Herald*
*New York Times*
*North China Daily News*
*Nu Duo Bao*
*Punch*
*Qinghua Zhoukan*
*Ren Wen Yue Kan*
*Saturday Evening Post*
*Shi Shi Xin Bao*
*The Statesman*
*Times* (London)
*The War Illustrated*

*War Monthly*
*World Outlook*
*Xin Zhongguo*
*Yi Shi Zhu Ri Bao*
*Yue Han Sheng*
*Zhong Hua Quan Guo Shang Hui Lian He Hui Hui Bao*


## Secondary Sources

Atwood, J. Howell, Arthur W. Hardy, and Owen E. Pence. *The Racial Factor in Y.M.C.A.'s: A Report on Negro-White Relationships in Twenty-four Cities.* New York: Association Press, 1946.

Audoin-Rouzeau, Stephane, and Annette Becker. *14–18: Understanding the Great War.* New York: Hill and Wang, 2002.

Bai Jiao. "Diyici shijie dazhan zhi Zhongguo canzhan." *Renwen Yuekan* 7 (1936).

———. "Shijie dazhan zhong zhi huagong." *Renwen Yuekan* 8 (1937).

Bailey, Paul. "The Chinese Work-Study Movement in France." *China Quarterly* 11, no. 5 (1988).

———. "From Shandong to Somme: Chinese Indentured Labour in France during World War I." In A. J. Kershen, ed., *Language, Labour, and Migration.* Farnham, England: Ashgate, 2000.

Billingsley, Phil. *Bandits in Republican China.* Stanford, Calif.: Stanford University Press, 1988.

Blick, Judith. "The Chinese Labor Corps in World War I." *Papers on China* (from Harvard East Asia Regional Studies Seminar) 9 (1955).

Bryson, A. G. "China in France." In London Missionary Society, ed., *In the Whirlpool of Races: Missionaries at the Battle Fronts.* London: London Missionary Society, 1920.

Buck, Pearl S. *Tell the People: Talks with James Yen about the Mass Education Movement.* New York: John Day Company, 1945.

Burt, E. W. "With the Chinese at Havre." *Missionary Herald* 101, no. 4 (April 1919).

Chen, Min-sun, and Lawrence N. Shyu. *China Insight: Selected Papers from the Canadian Asian Studies Association Annual Conference Proceedings, 1982–1984.* Ottawa: Canadian Asian Studies Association, 1985.

Chen, Ta. *Chinese Migrations, with Special Reference to Labor Conditions.* Washington, D.C.: Government Printing Office, 1923.

———. "The Labour Movement in China." *International Labour Review* 15, no. 3 (March 1927).

Chen Baoyu. "Wo ceng zai Ouzhou dang Huagong" ["I Was a Laborer in Europe"]. In Zhongguo renmin zhengzhi xie shang hui yi Tianjin shi weiyuan hui wen shi ziliao yan jiu wei yuan hui, ed., *Tianjin wenshi ziliao xuanji*. Tianjin: Tianjin Renmin chubanshe, 1996.

Chen Duxiu. *Duxiu wen cun*. Hong Kong: Yuandong tushu gongsi, 1965.

Chen Fen, ed. *Beiyang zhengfu guowu zongli Liang Shiyi shiliao ji*. Beijing: Zhongguo wenshi chubanshe, 1991.

Chen Sanjing. *Hua gong yu ou zhan*. Taipei: Zhong yang yan jiu yuan jin dai shi yan jiu suo zhuan kan, 1986.

———. "Jidu qingnianhui yu ou zhan Huagong." *Zhongyang yanjiuyuan jindai shi yanjiusuo ji kan* 1, no. 17 (1988).

———. *Lü Ou jiao yu yun dong*. Taipei: Zhong yang yan jiu yuan jin dai shi yan jiu suo, 1996.

Chen Sanjing, Lu Fangshang, and Yang Cuihua, eds. *Ouzhan Huagong shiliao*. Taipei: Zhongyang yanjiuyuan jindai shi yanjiusuo, 1997.

Chen Wuwo. *Lincheng jie che an ji shi*. Changsha: Yuelu shu she, 1987.

Cheng, Sih-Gung. *Modern China, a Political Study*. Oxford: Clarendon Press, 1919.

Chesneaux, Jean. *The Chinese Labor Movement, 1919–1927*. Translated from the French by H. M. Wright. Palo Alto, Calif.: Stanford University Press, 1968.

Chielens, Piet, and Julian Putkowski. *Unquiet Graves: Execution Sites of the First World War in Flanders*. London: Francis Boutle, 2000.

Childs, David J. *A Peripheral Weapon? The Production and Employment of British Tanks in the First World War*. Westport, Conn.: Greenwood Press, 1999.

"China's Man Power Aids France in War." *New York Times*, February 25, 1917, 3.

"Chinese Coolies Riot at Victoria." *Halifax Herald*, March 13, 1920, 17.

Chow Tse-Tsung. *The May Fourth Movement: Intellectual Revolution in Modern China*. Harvard East Asian Studies. Cambridge, Mass.: Harvard University Press, 1960.

Clemenceau, Georges. "The Cause of France." *Saturday Evening Post* 187, no. 17 (1914).

Cohen, Warren I. *The Chinese Connection: Roger S. Greene, Thomas W. Lamont, George E. Sokolsky and American–East Asian Relations*. New York: Columbia University Press, 1978.

Cooke, James J. *Pershing and His Generals: Command and Staff in the AEF*. Westport, Conn.: Praeger, 1997.

"The Coolie's Place." *Far Eastern Review* 15, no. 4 (April 1918).

Crosby, Alfred W., Jr. *Epidemic and Peace, 1918*. Westport, Conn.: Greenwood Press, 1976.

Cross, Gary. "Toward Social Peace and Prosperity: The Politics of Immigration in France during the Era of World War I." *French Historical Studies* 11, no. 4 (1980).

Culp, Robert J. *Articulating Citizenship: Civic Education and Student Politics in Southeastern China, 1912–1940.* Cambridge, Mass.: Harvard University Press, 2007.

Dawes, Charles G. *A Journal of the Great War.* Boston: Houghton Mifflin, 1921.

Dendooven, Dominiek. "The Multicultural War in Flanders." In Serge Jaumain, Michael Amara, Benoit Majerus, and Antoon Vrints, eds., *Une Guerre Totale? La Belgique dans la Première Guerre Mondiale: Nouvelles Tendances de la Recherche Historique.* Brussels: Archives Générales du Royaume, 2005.

Dendooven, Dominiek, and Piet Chielens, eds. *World War I: Five Continents in Flanders.* London: Lanoo, 2008.

Dong Linfu. *Cross Culture and Faith: The Life and Work of James Mellon Menzies.* Toronto: University of Toronto Press, 2005.

Drage, Charles. *Two-Gun Cohen.* London: J. Cape, 1954.

Dreyer, Edward L. *China at War, 1901–1949.* Modern Wars in Perspective. London: Longman, 1995.

Dunn, J. C. *The War the Infantry Knew, 1914–1919: A Chronicle of Service in France and Belgium with the Second Battalion.* London: P. S. King & Son, 1938.

Dupouy, Auguste. "Un Camp de Chinois." *La Revue de Paris,* no. 21 (November 1919).

Edgar, Adgey. "The Chinese Labour Corps." *Journal of Chinese Philately* 11, no. 1 (1963).

Eksteins, Modris. *Rites of Spring: The Great War and the Birth of the Modern Age.* Toronto: Lester & Orpen Dennys, 1989.

Elliott, Walter S. "Wang Gin-Guay," *Association Men* 47, no. 12 (1922).

Faguo huagong jinkuang. *Qinghua Zhoukan* 168:29.

Faris, Paul P. "Consternation in China Camp." *World Outlook* 5, no. 3 (1919).

Fawcett, Brian. "The Chinese Labour Corps 1917–1921—Sources of Oral History." *Stand To!* (Western Front Association), no. 84 (December 2008–January 2009).

Feng Gang et al., eds. *Sanshui Liang Yansun xiansheng nianpu.* Taipei: Commercial Press, 1978.

Fisher, Wendy. *Dr. E. J. Stuckey and the Chinese Hospital at Noyelle-sur-Mer: A Biographical Fragment of World War I.* Honors thesis, University of Melbourne, 1985.

Fu Shengshan. "Huagong zai Fa yu zuguo de sun yi." *Huagong Zhoubao* no. 7 (1919).

Fussell, Paul. *The Great War and Modern Memory.* New York: Oxford University Press, 1975.

Gao Pingshu. *Cai Yuanpei nian pu chang bian.* Beijing: Renmin jiaoyu chubanshe, 1996.

———, ed. *Cai Yuanpei quan ji.* Beijing: Zhonghua shu ju, 1984.

Garrett, Shirley S. *Social Reformers in Urban China: The Chinese YMCA, 1895–1926*. Cambridge, Mass.: Harvard University Press, 1970.

Gewurtz, Margo S. "For God or for King: Canadian Missionaries and the Chinese Labour Corps in World War I." In Min-Sun Chen and Lawrence N. Shyu, eds., *China Insight: Selected Papers from the Canadian Asian Studies Association Annual Conference Proceedings, 1982–1984*. Ottawa: Canadian Asian Studies Association, 1985.

Gibbs, Mark J. "Recombination in the Hemagglutinin Gene of 1918 'Spanish Flu.'" *Science* 293, no. 5536 (2001).

Goodman, David S. G. *China and the West: Ideas and Activists*. Manchester, England: Manchester University Press, 1990.

"Great Britain's War Work in 1917." *Current History Magazine* 8, Part 1 (May 1918).

Griffin, Nicholas. "Britain's Chinese Labor Corps in World War I." *Military Affairs* 40, no. 3 (October 1976).

———. "Chinese Labor and British Christian Missionaries in France, 1917–1919." *Journal of Church and State* 20 (1978): 287–304.

———. "The Responses of British Labor to the Importation of Chinese Workers, 1916–1917." *Historian* 40, no. 2 (1978): 252–270.

———. "The Use of Chinese Labour by the British Army, 1916–1920: The 'Raw Importation,' Its Scope and Problems." PhD diss., University of Oklahoma, 1973.

Grundlingh, Albert M. *Fighting Their Own War: South African Blacks and the First World War*. Johannesburg: Ravan Press, 1987.

Gull, Manico. "The Story of the Chinese Labor Corps." *Far Eastern Review* 15, no. 4 (1918).

Guo wu yuan qiao gong shi wu ju, ed. *Qiao gong shi wu ju di qi ci diao cha zai fa huagong qingxing shu*. Beijing, 1920.

Gu Xingqing. *Ouzhan gongzuo huiyi lu* [Recollections of My Experiences with Chinese Laborers in World War I]. Shanghai: Shangwu Yinshuguan, 1937.

Hagood, Johnson. *The Services of Supply: A Memoir of the Great War*. Boston: Houghton Mifflin, 1927.

Hao Xianyu. *Liu Fa qin gong jian xue yun dong shi gao*. Chengdu: Ba Shu shu she, 1994.

Harding, Gardner L. "China's Part in the War: Her Contributions of Labor, Raw Materials, Munitions and Food to the Allies." *Asia* 17, no. 8 (October 1917).

Hart, Peter. *The Somme: The Darkest Hour on the Western Front*. New York: Pegasus Books, 2008.

Hayford, Charles W. *To the People: James Yen and Village China*. New York: Columbia University Press, 1990.

Higham, Robin D. S., and Dennis E. Showalter. *Researching World War I: A Handbook*. Westport, Conn.: Greenwood Press, 2003.

Hodges, G. Charles. "John Chinaman Breaks Through: How War Needs Are Breaching the Exclusion Walls Erected against Him by the White Races." *Sunset: The Pacific Monthly* 41, no. 3 (September 1918).

Hopkins, Charles H. *History of the Y.M.C.A. in North America*. New York: Association Press, 1951.

Horne, John. "Immigrant Workers in France during World War I." *French Historical Studies* 14, no. 1 (1985): 57–88.

———. *State, Society, and Mobilization in Europe during the First World War.* Cambridge: Cambridge University Press, 1997.

Howard, Michael E., and Stephen Badsey. *A Part of History: Aspects of the British Experience of the First World War.* London: Continuum, 2008.

Jackson, John P. *Some Industrial Problems*. Dijon: Imp. R. de Thorey, 1919.

Jiang Shunxing and Du Yugen. "Lun Beiyang zhengfu de qiaowu zhengce," *Minguo Dang'an* 4 (1993).

Jiang Tingfu. *Jiang Tingfu hui yi lu*. Taipei: Zhuanji wenxue chubanshe, 1979.

Joll, James. *The Origins of the First World War.* New York: Pearson Longman, 2006.

Jones, A. Philip. *Britain's Search for Chinese Cooperation in the First World War.* London: Garland Publishing, 1986.

Kennedy, David M. *Over Here: The First World War and American Society.* New York: Oxford University Press, 1980.

Kennedy, Paul. "The First World War and the International Power System." *International Security* 9, no. 1 (1984).

Kershen, Anne J. *Language, Labour and Migration.* Farnham, England: Ashgate, 2000.

Kiernan, V. G. *The Lords of Human Kind: Black Man, Yellow Man, and White Man in an Age of Empire.* New York: Columbia University Press, 1986.

"The King and the Chinese Labour Corps." *British Weekly,* January 2, 1919.

Kirby, William C. "The Internationalization of China: Foreign Relations at Home and Abroad in the Republican Era." *China Quarterly* 150, no. 2 (1997).

Klein, Daryl. *With the Chinks*. London: John Lane Company, 1919.

Knapp, Shepherd. *On the Edge of the Storm: The Story of a Year in France.* Worcester, Mass.: Commonwealth Press, 1921.

Kolata, Gina B. *Flu: The Story of the Great Influenza Pandemic of 1918 and the Search for the Virus That Caused It.* New York: Farrar, Straus and Giroux, 1999.

Kuhn, Philip A. *Chinese among Others: Emigration in Modern Times,* Lanham, Md.: Rowman & Littlefield, 2008.

Lai Xinxia. *Beiyang Jun Fa* [Documents on Beiyang Warlords]. Shanghai: Shanghai ren min chubanshe, 1988.

La Motte, Ellen N. *Peking Dust.* New York: Century Co., 1919.

Latourette, Kenneth S. *World Service.* New York: Association Press, 1957.

Levine, Marilyn A. *The Found Generation: Chinese Communists in Europe during the Twenties.* Seattle: University of Washington Press, 1933.

Levitch, Mark. *Panthéon de la Guerre: Reconfiguring a Panorama of the Great War.* Columbia: University of Missouri Press, 2006.

Levy, Daniel S. *Two-Gun Cohen: A Biography.* New York: St. Martin's Press, 1997.

Lewis, John F. *China's Great Convulsion, 1894–1924: A Dynasty Overthrown, Chaos and Warlords, and How the Chinese Helped the Western Allies Win World War I.* Heathsville, Va.: Sun on Earth Books, 2005.

Liddle, Peter, J. M. Bourne, and Ian R. Whitehead. 2000. *The Great World War, 1914–45.* London: HarperCollins, 2000.

Li Huang. *Xue Dunshi huiyilu.* Taipei: Zhuanji wenxue chubanshe, 1973.

Li Jikui. *Liang Shiyi.* Guangzhou: Guangdong renmin chubanshe, 2005.

Liu Yan. *Zhong Guo Wai Jiao Shi* [Diplomatic History of China]. Taipei: San min shu ju, 1962.

Li Yongchang. "Juexing qian de kuangre: lun 'gongli zhansheng' he 'laogong shensheng' liangge kouhao." *Jindaishi Yanjiu* 4 (1996).

Lloyd George, David. *Memoirs of the Peace Conference.* New Haven, Conn.: Yale University Press, 1939.

———. *War Memoirs of David Lloyd George.* London: Odhams Press, 1942.

Lo, Hui-Min, ed. *The Correspondence of G. E. Morrison.* Cambridge: Cambridge University Press, 1976.

Lubbock, Percy, ed. *The Letters of Henry James.* New York: Octagon Books, 1970.

Luo, Zhitian. "National Humiliation and National Assertion: The Chinese Response to the Twenty-one Demands." *Modern Asian Studies* 27, no. 2 (1993).

Lu Xun. *Lu Xun quan ji.* Beijing: Renmin wenxue chubanshe, 2005.

MacNair, Harley F. *China's New Nationalism and Other Essays.* Shanghai: Commercial Press, 1932.

Ma Qiufan and Xiong Ming'an. *Yan Yangchu jiaoyu lunzhu xuan.* Beijing: Renmin jiaoyu chubanshe, 1993.

Manela, Erez. *Wilsonian Moment: Self-Determination and the International Origins of Anticolonial Nationalism.* New York: Oxford University Press, 2007.

Marcosson, Isaac F. *S.O.S.: America's Miracle in France.* New York: John Lane Company, 1919.

Mayo, Katherine, *"That Damn Y": A Record of Overseas Service.* Boston: Houghton Mifflin, 1920.

Mitchell, Peter M. "Canada and the Chinese Labour Corps, 1917–1920: The Official Connection." In Min-sun Chen and Lawrence N. Shyu, eds., *China Insight: Selected Papers from the Canadian Asian Studies Association Annual Conference Proceedings, 1982–1984*. Ottawa: Canadian Asian Studies Association, 1985.

Neville, A., and J. Whymant. "Chinese Coolie Songs." *Bulletin of the School of Oriental Studies* (University of London) 1, no. 4 (1920).

Omissi, David. *Indian Voices of the Great War: Soldiers' Letters, 1914–18*. New York: St. Martin's Press, 1999.

Pan, Lynn. *The Encyclopedia of the Chinese Overseas*. Cambridge, Mass.: Harvard University Press, 1999.

———. *Sons of the Yellow Emperor: The Story of the Overseas Chinese*. Boston: Little, Brown, 1990.

Paton, A. W. *Occasional Gunfire: Private War Diary of a Siege Gunner*. London: Bishop-Laggett, 1998.

Payne, Henry. "John Chinaman in France: How He Saw and Greeted King George." *Missionary Herald* 101 no. 3 (March 1919).

Pearl, Cyril. *Morrison of Peking*. Sydney: Angus and Robertson, 1967.

Peter, W. W. "Mr. Chang Goes to War." *World's Work,* 1919.

———. "With the Chinese Coolies in France." *China Medical Journal* 33, no. 3 (1919).

Pickrell, John. "The 1918 Pandemic: Killer Flu with a Human-Pig Pedigree?" *Science* 292, no. 5519 (2001).

Pugsley, Christopher. *On the Fringe of Hell: New Zealanders and Military Discipline in the First World War*. Auckland: Hodder & Stoughton, 1991.

Putkowski, Julian. *British Army Mutineers, 1914–1922*. London: Boutle, 1998.

Qinghua daxue Zhonggong dangshi jiaoyanzu, ed. *Fu Fa qingong jianxue yundong shiliao*. Vol. 1. Beijing: Beijing chubanshe, 1979.

Reeves, Nicholas. "Film Propaganda and Its Audience: The Example of Britain's Official Films during the First World War." *Journal of Contemporary History* 18, no. 3 (1983).

———. *The Power of Film Propaganda: Myth or Reality?* London: Cassell, 1999.

Salisbury, Laurence. "Chinese Coolies and the War." *Saturday Evening Post,* October 25, 1919

Salter, J. A. *Allied Shipping Control: An Experiment in International Administration*. Oxford: Clarendon Press, 1921.

Saunders, Nicholas J. *Trench Art: A Brief History and Guide, 1914–1939*. London: Leo Cooper, 2001.

———. *Trench Art: Materialities and Memories of War*. New York: Berg, 2003.

Sayer, Fred. "No Tea—No Workee!" Western Front Association *Bulletin* 25 (1989).

Scott, Peter T. "Chinese in France in WW I." *War Monthly* 8 (1980).

Shi, I. H. "With the Chinese Laborers 'Somewhere in France.'" *Chinese Students' Monthly* 13, no. 8 (1918.)

Shi Yixuan. "Faguo Li'ang shi fu jin zhi Huagong qingnian hui baogao." *Qingnian Jinbu* 15 (1918).

"Shipping and Shipbuilding in China." *Economic World* 17, no. 2 (1919).

Smythe, Donald. *Pershing, General of the Armies.* Bloomington: Indiana University Press, 2007.

Song Enrong. "Story of the Chinese Labor Corps." *Far Eastern Review* 15, no. 4 (1918).

———. *Yan Yangchu quan ji.* Changsha: Hunan jiao yu chubanshe, 1989.

Stovall, Tyler. "The Color behind the Lines: Racial Violence in France during the Great War." *American Historical Review* 103, no. 3 (June 1998).

———. "National Identity and Shifting Imperial Frontiers: Whiteness and the Exclusion of Colonial Labor after World War I." *Representations* 84 (Autumn 2003): 59–60.

Stuckey, E. J. "The Chinese General Hospital in France." *China Medical Journal* 33, no. 4 (1920).

Stuckey, E. J., H. Tomlin, and C. A. Hughes. "Trachoma among the Chinese in France." *British Journal of Ophthalmology,* no. 4 (January 1920).

Summerscale, Kate. *The Queen of Whale Cay.* New York: Penguin Books, 1999.

Summerskill, Michael. *China on the Western Front: Britain's Chinese Work Force in the First World War.* London: Author, 1982.

Taft, William H., and Frederick M. Harris. *Service with Fighting Men: An Account of the Work of the American Young Men's Christian Associations in the World War.* New York: Association Press, 1922.

Tancock, Elizabeth A. "Secret Trains across Canada, 1917–1918." *The Beaver* (October–November 1991).

Thomas, T. C. *With a Labour Company in France; Being the War Diary of the 58th Labour Company.* London: Hudson & Son, n.d.

Ting, Fu-tsiang. "Chinese Philosophy in France." *Asia* 19, no. 7 (July 1919).

"To a Chinese Coolie." *Punch* 156, no. 4050 (February 19, 1919).

Tow, J. S. "Both Sides of the Shantung Issue: The Chinese Side." *World Outlook* 5, no. 11 (1919).

———. "China's Service to the Allied Cause." *Economic World* 17, no. 6 (1919).

Tyau, Min-chien. *China Awakened.* New York: Macmillan, 1922.

Vaughn, Stephen. *Holding Fast the Inner Lines: Democracy, Nationalism, and the Committee on Public Information.* Chapel Hill: University of North Carolina Press, 1980.

Verhey, Jeffrey. *The Spirit of 1914: Militarism, Myth and Mobilization in Germany.* Studies in the Social and Cultural History of Modern Warfare. Cambridge: Cambridge University Press, 2000.

Wade, Aubrey. *Gunner on the Western Front,* London: B. T. Batsford, 1959.

Wang Gunwu. *China and the Chinese Overseas.* Cambridge, Mass.: Harvard University Press, 2000.

———. *The Chinese Overseas: From Earthbound China to the Quest for Autonomy.* Cambridge, Mass.: Harvard University Press, 2000.

Watson, Alexander. *Enduring the Great War: Combat, Morale and Collapse in the German and British Armies, 1914–1918.* Cambridge: Cambridge University Press, 2008.

Weifang Shi di fang shi zhi bian zuan wei yuan hui. *Weifang Shi zhi.* Beijing: Zhong yang wen xian chubanshe, 1995.

"What the Chinese Learned in the War." *Literary Digest* 62, no. 11 (1919).

Willcocks, James. *With the Indians in France.* London: Constable and Co., 1920.

Wilson, Angus. *Late Call.* London: The Viking Press, 1965.

Winter, J. M. *The Great War and the British People.* Cambridge, Mass.: Harvard University Press, 1986.

———. *Remembering War: The Great War between Memory and History in the Twentieth Century.* New Haven: Yale University Press, 2006.

———. *Sites of Memory, Sites of Mourning: The Great War in European Cultural History.* Cambridge: Cambridge University Press, 1995.

Winter, J. M., Geoffrey Parker, and Mary R. Habeck. *The Great War and the Twentieth Century.* New Haven, Conn.: Yale University, 2000.

Winter, Kathlene B. "With the Chinese Industrial Army in France." *World Outlook* 5, no. 3 (March 1919).

Wohl, Robert. *The Generation of 1914.* Cambridge, Mass.: Harvard University Press, 1979.

Woodward, E. L. *Documents on British Foreign Policy, 1919–1939.* London: H. M. Stationery Office, 1946.

Wu, Pén-chung. *Les Travailleurs Chinois et la Grande Guerre.* Paris: A. Pedone, 1939.

Wu Xiangxiang. *Yan Yangchu zhuan: wei quan qiu xiang cun gai zao fen dou liu shi nian.* Taipei: Shi bao wen hua chu ban shi ye you xian gong si, 1981.

Xiao Yu. *Mao Zedong qian zhuan ji Mao Zedong xingqi mixin.* Taipei: Li Bai chubanshe, 1989.

Xia Xiaohong, ed. *Yin bing shi heji ji wai wen.* Beijing: Beijing daxue chubanshe, 2005.

Xinchaoshe, ed. *Cai Jiemin xian sheng yan xing Lu.* Beijing: Xinchaoshe, 1920.

Xing, Jun. *Baptized in the Fire of Revolution: The American Social Gospel and the YMCA in China, 1919–1937.* Bethlehem, Pa.: Lehigh University Press, 1996.

Xu Guoqi. *China and the Great War: China's Pursuit of a New National Identity and Internationalization.* New York: Cambridge University Press, 2005.

———. "China's Great War: An Unwritten Chapter of World History." *Chinese Historical Review* 12, no. 1 (2005).

———. *Olympic Dreams: China and Sports, 1895–2008.* Cambridge, Mass.: Harvard University Press, 2008.

———. *Wenming de jiaorong: Huagong he diyi ci shijie dazhan* [Chinese Laborers in France and the First World War]. Beijing: Intercontinental Press, 2007.

———. "Yizhan qijian Zhongguo de 'yi gong dai bing' can zhan yanjiu" ["Chinese Laborers and the First World War"]. *The Twenty-First Century* 10, no. 62 (2000).

Xu Xiaoya. *Bai nian Zhong Fa guan xi.* Beijing: Shi jie zhi shi chubanshe, 2006.

Yan Hongguo. *Yan Yangchu zhuan lue.* Chengdu: Tiandi chubanshe. 2005.

Yang Kailing, ed. *Min guo Li Shizeng xian sheng Yuying nian pu.* Taipei: Taiwan shang wu yin shu guan, 1980.

Yen, Ching-huang. *Coolies and Mandarins: China's Protection of Overseas Chinese during the Late Ching Period (1851–1911).* Singapore: Singapore University Press, 1985.

Young Men's Christian Association. *Service with Fighting Men: In the Service of Youth.* Vol. 2. New York: Association Press, 1922.

———. *Summary of World War Work of the American YMCA.* New York: Association Press, 1920.

———. *The Year Book of the YMCA of North America for the Year May 1920 to April 30, 1921.* New York: Association Press, 1921.

———. *Young Men's Christian Association with the Chinese Labor Corps in France.* Paris: Association Press, 1919.

Young Men's Christian Association International Committee. *For the Millions of Men Now under Arms.* New York: Printed by the Methodist Book Concern, 1918.

Young Men's Christian Association National War Work Council. *Summary of World War Work of the American Y.M.C.A.; with Soldiers and Sailors of America at Home, on the Sea, and Overseas; with the Men of the Allied Armies and with the Prisoners of War in All Parts of the World.* New York: Association Press, 1920.

Young Men's Christian Associations of North America International Committee. *Report on a Survey of the International Committee of Young Men's Christian Associations of North America.* New York: Association Press, 1923.

Yuan Li and Chen Dazhang. *Haiwai Huaren ji qi juzhu di gaikuan.* Beijing: Zhongguo Huaqiao chuban gongshi, 1991.

Yun, Lisa, 2008. *The Coolie Speaks: Chinese Indentured Laborers and African Slaves in Cuba.* Philadelphia: Temple University Press, 2008.

Zhao Shanlin. "Yi zhan qi jian wo zai fa guo ren huagong ji cha de hui yi." In Zhong guo ren min zheng zhi xie shang hui yi tianjin shi wei yuan hui wen shi zi liao wei yuan hui, ed., *Tianjin wen shi zi liao xuan ji,* vol. 69. Tianjin: Tianjin renmin chubanshe, 1996.

Zheng Mingzhen. *Liu Fa qin gong jian xue yun dong.* Taiyuan: Shanxi gao xiao chubanshe, 1994.

Zhongguo Cai Yuanpei yan jiu hui. *Cai Yuanpei quan ji.* Hangzhou: Zhejiang jiaoyu chubanshe, 1997.

Zhongguo guo min dang dang shi wei yuan hui. *Li Shizeng xian sheng wen ji.* Taipei: Jing xiao chu Zhong yang wen wu gong ying she, 1980.

Zhonghua Renmin Gongheguo guo wu yuan xin wen ban gong shi jian zhi. *Liu Fa qin gong jian xue yun dong shi lu.* Beijing: Wuzhou chuanbo chubanshe, 2005.

Zhu Zhuanyu, ed. *Liang Shiyi zhuanji ziliao.* Taipei: Tianyi chubanshe, 1979.

Zibo shi zhi bian zuan wei yuan hui, ed. *Zibo shi zhi.* Beijing: Zhonghua shu ju, 1995.

# ACKNOWLEDGMENTS

The idea of this book grew out of my previous work on China and the Great War. I have been working on this project on and off for more than a decade. It might have taken me longer to finish it if the Inter-continental Press in Beijing had not been so persistent in inviting me to write a short volume on the same topic for general public. In preparing that short book for Chinese and French readers, my ideas for this book became crystallized and I was motivated enough to bring this book to completion. I had the good fortune to finish this book as a fellow at Radcliffe Institute for Advanced Study at Harvard University. This is the best place and community in the world for research and writing such a book. To everyone at the Institute, especially its director of fellows program, Judy E. Vichniac, I am forever in your debt.

Many archives and libraries provided enormous assistance for this book. Among them, the following were especially helpful: the French Foreign Ministry Archives in Paris and the Archives of the French Army and Navy at Chateau de Vincennes; the Second Historical Archives in Nanjing, China; the Qingdao Archives and the Weihai Archives in Shandong Province; the Shanghai Municipal Library; the National Library in Beijing; and the Institute of Modern History Archives, Academia Sinica, in Taipei. Also the German Foreign Ministry Archives in Berlin; the Kautz Family YMCA Archives in Minnesota; the James Yen Personal Archives now at Columbia University; the Library and Archives of Canada in Ottawa; the National Archives in College Park, Maryland; the National Archives in Kew Gardens, UK; the Imperial War Museum in London; the Widener Library and Yenching Library, both at Harvard University; Yale Divinity School Library; and Columbia University's rare book and manuscript library. I am very grateful to all the librarians and archivists in those places.

The following people deserve to be especially thanked for their kind assistance: Tara C. Craig of Columbia University; Joan R. Duffy of Yale's Divinity School Library's special collections; everyone at Widener Library's interlibrary loan office for unfailing support for finding too many requested rare materials with good spirit and speed; Raymond Lum of Harvard's Yenching Library and Widener Library, who went out of his way to find many valuable materials through his worldwide connections and who even initiated the purchase of several rare sets of publications for my immediate use through the Harvard University libraries; Richard Davies and the staff members of special collections at the University of Leeds, UK, who provided wonderful research assistance when I visited them; David Fletcher of the Tank Museum, Bovington, UK, who was very kind and located some great materials for me; Katy Newton of the East Surrey Museum, UK, who went out of her way to help me have access to Captain Wood's collections at the museum; Dominiek Dendooven of In Flanders Museum in Belgium, who provided many relevant materials; and staff members of the Imperial War Museum, especially John Delaney and Alan Jeffreys, who were very helpful in addressing my questions and many access requests; Zhang Jianguo and Zhang Junyong of the Weihai Municipal Archives, and Zhang Guilin of China Central Television, who used their influence to help me unearth some previously unknown diaries and memoirs.

I have had the privilege of consulting private collections from the following people: David Livingstone and John Sebert (both live in Canada, and their fathers were Canadian officers who were involved with Chinese laborers); Ambassador Arthur Menzies, also from Canada, who opened his door and allowed me to examine his father James Menzies's personal files related to his work with Chinese laborers; Christian Tchang and Gerand Tchang in France, whose father was a Chinese laborer, who kindly sent me their family materials; and Sun Guanglong in Shandong Province, who kindly allowed me to examine his grandfather Sun Gan's handwritten record of his life in France as a laborer. I also have had the good fortune to talk with several descendants of the former laborers in Shandong and savor their stories.

My four research assistants in the Radcliffe Institute—Sophie Legros, Lily Zhu, Michael Song, and Yichen Chen—all brilliant Harvard students, provided valuable assistance when I was working on this book. Sophie was especially instrumental in helping me to deal with French materials. The following people assisted me in collecting research materials or other ways for this book: Chang Li, Chen Sanjing, Gregory James, Jing Guangyao, Ma Jianbiao, Judy Maxwell, Mu Tao, Wang Lixin, Jay Winter, Wu Lin-Chun, and Xia Lei, among many others.

Vicki Caron, Judy Coffin, Chuck Hayford, and Akira Iriye read all or portions of the manuscripts and gave me valuable feedback and great suggestions. Terre Fisher, as always, served as my quality control person and read the whole manuscript several times to check the flow of my ideas and to make sure my style was appropriate. I should express my special gratitude to Akira Iriye, my formal mentor at Harvard. He has taken a keen interest in this project and gone out of his way to help whenever I need support. The two anonymous readers provided excellent suggestions and advice. Thanks to Kathleen McDermott, my editor at Harvard University Press, for her faith in this book and her unfailing guidance; and to Matthew Hills, also at Harvard University Press, for his efficient handling of my questions and requests. I would like to express my gratitude to my production editor, Barbara Goodhouse, and my copyeditor, Nancy Sixsmith. Their sharp eyes and editing skills saved me from many embarrassing errors and typos. Kam Louie, dean of the faculty of arts at the University of Hong Kong and a great colleague and administrator, was very supportive of my work and kindly allowed me to have access to the faculty's China-West Studies Initiative Fund when needed. They all helped make this book better, but I alone am responsible for all errors or other shortcomings in this book.

My kids—Margaret, Julia, and Tom—have all grown into great children when I was working on this book, and they understood and supported their father's strange devotion to Chinese laborers. As always, it is to my wife, Ann, that I owe the most. Without her support, sacrifice, and encouragement, this book could not have been written. This book is dedicated to her as a small token of my gratitude.

# INDEX

African Americans, 171
Alcohol, laborers and, 145
Aldrich, Lucy T., 225
Alston, Beilby, 28, 30, 39–40, 43
American Expeditionary Forces (AEF), 4–5, 152–173; support needs of, 152–157; Labor Bureau of, 153–155, 171; treatment of laborers by, 155, 158–160, 162, 170–171; management problems of, 155–156, 163–168; conflict with French and, 157–163, 169–170; problems with Chinese laborers and, 168–173; YMCA and, 181–182
Artistic projects, 137–139
Association men. See YMCA (Young Men's Christian Association)

*Baihua* (vernacular language) movement (Hu), 211
Bai Jiao, 214
Balfour, Arthur, 43, 101
Banditry, returning laborers and, 225–226
Banking, laborers and, 146, 193
Barnett, Eugene, 210
Bates, Robert J., 166
Blick, Judith, 241
Bombardments of laborers, 85–88, 100
Boredom of laborers, 146
Boschetti, M., 157–159, 162–163
Bottomley, Kathleen Charlotte, 141

Bourne, Thomas J., 27, 30, 68–69, 74, 260n81
Bravery of laborers, 93–96
Britain: Laoxikai Incident and, 20–21, 30; laborers as soldiers strategy and, 23–31; labor unions in, 24–25; laborer contracts of, 39–42; recruitment and, 42–48, 49–51
British Army Council: recruitment and, 27; on contracts, 41–42; recruitment and, 43, 49
British Expeditionary Forces (BEF): recruitment by, 40, 48; CLC work environment and, 81–85, 89–90; Directorate of Labor of, 89–91, 109–111; treatment of laborers by, 107, 110, 114–121, 124
British Foreign Office, 28, 30, 42
British War Office, 41, 70, 92, 146; recruitment by, 24–25, 27–28, 30, 44–45; repatriation and, 123–124
Brockman, Fletcher S., 196
Building designs of laborers, 138
Bull, William, 94
Bureau of Overseas Chinese Workers, 32, 35, 222–223
Burials, laborers and, 118, 248
Burt, E. W., 125
Bynner, Witter, "Shantung," 215

Cai Hesheng, 218
Cai Yuanpei, 198, 200–203, 212–213, 227

329